HITLER'S
ROCKETS

The Story of the V-2s

HITLER'S ROCKETS

The Story of the V-2s

Norman Longmate

Skyhorse Publishing

Frontline Books, London

Skyhorse Publishing books may be purchased in bulk at special discounts for sales promotion, corporate gifts, fund-raising, or educational purposes. Special editions can also be created to specifications. For details, contact the Special Sales Department, Skyhorse Publishing, 555 Eighth Avenue, Suite 903, New York, NY 10018 or info@skyhorsepublishing.com.

www.skyhorsepublishing.com

Library of Congress Cataloging-in-Publication Data

Longmate, Norman, 1925–
   Hitler's rockets : the story of the V-2s / Norman Longmate.
      p. cm.
   Previously published: London : Hutchinson, 1985.
   Includes bibliographical references and index.
   ISBN 978-1-60239-705-7
   1. World War, 1939–1945—Aerial operations, German. 2. V-2 rocket. 3. Great Britain—History—Bombardment, 1940–1945. I. Title.

D787.L653 2009
940.54′4943—dc22
                                    2009006535

10 9 8 7 6 5 4 3 2 1

Printed in the United States of America

Hitler's Rockets: The Story of the V-2s

This edition published in 2009 by Frontline Books, an imprint of Pen and Sword Books Ltd, 47 Church Street, Barnsley, S. Yorkshire, S70 2AS.
For more information on our books, please visit www.frontline-books.com, email info@frontline-books.com or write to us at the above address.

Hitler's Rockets by Norman Longmate
First published in 1985
by Hutchinson & Co. (London)
World copyright © Norman Longmate, 1985
This edition © Pen & Sword Books Ltd., 2009

UK edition: ISBN 978-1-84832-546-3

A CIP data record for this title is available from the British Library

To B. H. AND M. H.

ACKNOWLEDGEMENTS

Grateful acknowledgement is made for the use of copyright material, as follows: to the Public Record Office for quotations from Crown Copyright documents; to A. D. Peters Ltd for Constance Babington Smith, *Evidence in Camera*; to the London Borough of Croydon for W. C. Berwick Sayers, *Croydon and the Second World War*; to Lewis Blake for *Bromley in the Front Line*; to the *National Geographic Magazine* for Marquis W. Childs, *London Wins the Battle*; to British Railways Board for Norman Crump, *By Rail to Victory*; to Walter Dornberger for *V-2*, published by Hurst and Blackett Ltd, now an imprint of the Hutchinson Publishing Group Ltd; to Julian Friedmann Ltd for Jozef Garlinski, *Hitler's Last Weapons*; to Macmillan Publishing Co., New York, for A. B. Hartley, *Unexploded Bomb* and Helen Walters, *Werner von Braun, Rocket Engineer*; to David and Charles Ltd for Jeremy Howard-Williams, *Night Intruder*; to John Farquharson Ltd for R. V. Jones, *Most Secret War*, published by Hamish Hamilton Ltd and Coronet Books; to Chatto and Windus Ltd for James Lees-Milne, *Prophesying Peace*; to the estate of the late Sonia Brownell Orwell and Martin Secker and Warburg Ltd for *Collected Essays, Journalism and Letters of George Orwell*; to Harrap Ltd for Frederick Pile, *Ack Ack*; to Faber and Faber Ltd for William Sansom, *Westminster at War*; to Weidenfeld and Nicolson Ltd for Albert Speer, *Inside the Third Reich*; to Chubb Fire Security Ltd for Les Staples, *Somewhere in Southern England*; to Purnell Publishers Ltd for George P. Thompson, *Blue Pencil Admiral*; to the London Borough of Waltham Forest for Ross Wyld, *War over Walthamstow*; to William Collins and Sons Ltd for R. Wright and C. F. Rawnsley, *Night Fighter*.

Owing to the lapse of time and to the ephemeral nature of many wartime publications, some copyright holders have proved untraceable. Apologies are offered for any inadvertent breach of copyright and appropriate amends will gladly be made in any future edition.

CONTENTS

ILLUSTRATIONS

Acknowledgements for Illustrations

Associated Newspapers: 36
BBC Hulton Picture Library: 15, 33, 34
Bildarchiv Preussischer Kulturbesitz, Berlin: 20, 21
Bilderdienst Süddeutscher Verlag, Munich: 5, 22, 23
Deutsches Museum: 4
Major-General Walter Dornberger: 2
Fox Photos: 18
Illustrated London News: 7
Imperial War Museum: 6, 19, 32
Professor R. V. Jones: 17
Keystone: 14
Lewisham Library Services: 29
London Fire Brigade: 35
Press Association: 16
Colonel T. R. B. Sanders: 8, 9
Syndication International: 25, 26, 27, 28, 31
Ullstein Bilderdienst, Berlin: 1, 3, 10, 11, 12, 24
Colonel Max Wachtel: 13
Westminster City Libraries: 30

FOREWORD

Hitler's Rockets is the sequel to *The Doodlebugs*, published in 1981 and just reissued in paperback, of which it was originally intended to form part. The decision to treat the two subjects separately has enabled me to deal independently with the two weapons, which are in fact totally distinct, although almost all previous authors, British and American, have written about them together. Although they enjoyed a common name as 'revenge' or 'wonder' weapons – the latter being entirely justified in the case of the V-2 – and were both indiscriminate, they were the product of different research teams, working for different services, were (though the two bombardments overlapped) fired at different periods and, above all, produced very different reactions on the part of the civilians at the 'receiving end'. More fundamental still, while the flying bomb was a development of existing technology, and was eventually beaten by conventional military means, against the rocket there was never any defence and it was a totally unexpected and, for a long time, unsuspected, innovation which pointed the way forward to a totally new type of warfare, under whose shadow we have lived ever since.

The V-2s, for reasons I have described in the pages that follow, presented the British government with an embarrassing and, indeed, insoluble problem, dealt with at first by simply concealing its existence. Even after the war in Europe was over, details of rocket incidents were still being suppressed – a policy which made it more difficult to present a comprehensive picture of their effects, but which has meant that very few of

11

the details given here of the location and consequences of the thousand rockets that landed have ever appeared in print before. Because so much of the story is unfamiliar, I have tried to include at least the number of rockets and the casualty figures for every borough in the rocket-affected area and, also for the first time, to give fuller details of all the major incidents, especially those whose seriousness was concealed. A minor but constant problem has been the changes in local government boundaries that have occurred since 1945 and the popular practice of referring to locations by the name of a district rather than of the local authority responsible for it. I have followed the Ministry of Home Security records in trying to identify every incident by the name of the borough or urban district council concerned, referring for example, to Deptford, rather than New Cross, Southgate, not Bounds Green, and Waltham Holy Cross not Waltham Abbey, though I have occasionally included the district where (as in the case of the New Cross Woolworths) it has become identified with a particular incident. Repeatedly in writing the book I have been amazed at the success of the censorship in force at the time. Although stationed in the army in central London for the whole of the V-2 period, I had no conception at all of how serious and widespread were the sufferings of other parts of the capital, or that a brief journey by bus or train could have taken me to areas where 'incidents' were sometimes a more than daily occurrence. For those in the provinces, out of sight or earshot of even the most distant rocket, ignorance was even more total. I hope the present book may help to give those who lived elsewhere in the country, or belong to later generations, some conception of what a small proportion of their fellow citizens had to endure for seven months in 1944–45.

The wartime documents from which I have quoted were often written under pressure and are rarely consistent, even internally, over matters like punctuation and abbreviations. I have tried to introduce consistency in these matters, while giving full details of the source so that the original document can readily be consulted. I have, similarly, felt justified in making comparable minor changes in the contributions from private citizens which form my other principal source.

I am grateful to Miss Idina Le Geyt for her indefatigable

research in the Public Record Office, Imperial War Museum and other libraries, and to Miss Eve Cottingham who, at short notice, filled in for me from a number of local authority libraries gaps in my knowledge which became apparent when the manuscript was nearly complete. I am much in the debt of Professor R. V. Jones, who answered several questions for me and supplied exceptionally helpful documents. Lord Boothby generously allowed me to quote his characteristically forthright (and, I have no doubt, accurate) opinion of Lord Cherwell. Mr G. L. Dennington kindly supplied me with a copy of a local history which he had published under a pseudonym. Miss Barbara Bagnall of Hutchinson admirably undertook the picture research. I also met unfailing courtesy and helpfulness from all the archivists and librarians I approached for information, and they were certainly guiltless when, as sometimes happened, a local authority apparently failed to regard the events of forty years ago as 'history' and had not troubled to preserve even such basic documents as a list of local incidents and casualty figures. It is sad to reflect that there are places where facts of this kind may now be lost for ever.

I must particularly acknowledge the assistance of the following: Mr D. M. Laverick, Borough Librarian, London Borough of Bromley; Mr Richard Knight, Local History Library, London Borough of Camden; Mr. L. J. Reilly, Local History Library, London Borough of Greenwich; Mr David Mander, Archives Department, London Borough of Hackney; Mrs Carolyn Hammond, Local History Library, Chiswick, London Borough of Hounslow; Mr John Hart, Central Reference Library, London Borough of Redbridge; the staff of the Inquiry Desk, Central Library, London Borough of Richmond upon Thames; the staff of the Local History Collection, London Borough of Tower Hamlets; the Reference Librarian, Battersea, London Borough of Wandsworth; Mr J. A. S. Green, County Archivist, Berkshire County Record Office; Mr P. R. Gifford, Librarian, Local Studies, Colchester, Mr S. M. Jarvis, Area Team Librarian, and Mr D. Waugh, Chelmsford, Mr Denys Bishop, Area Team Librarian, Grays, Miss Sheila Sullivan, Area Team Librarian, and Miss Barbara Pratt, Loughton, all of Essex; Mr Victor Gray and Miss K. Watson of the Essex County Record Office; Mr Colin Crook, Group

Librarian, Gravesend, Kent; Miss Jean Kennedy, County Archivist, Norfolk Record Office; Mr C. Wilkins-Jones, County Local Studies Librarian, Norfolk; Miss Amanda Arrowsmith, County Archivist, and Mr D. Jones, of the Suffolk County Record Office.

Among the printed sources I owe a particular debt to David Irving's *The Mare's Nest*, which deals in detail with the scientific background to the V-2. I hope my book, which concentrates on the subsequent campaign, may to some extent complement his.

Hitler's Rockets rounds off the series of studies of the British civilian experience between 1939 and 1945 which I began with *How We Lived Then*, published in 1971. This is a fitting moment, therefore, to thank the several thousand people whose recollections have made them possible and have, I believe, provided an element of first-hand experience which future generations too may find of interest and historical value. I am also grateful to the hundreds of people, many from overseas, who have written to me about already-published works. I am particularly appreciative of those who (invariably with the utmost courtesy and desire to help) have pointed out minor errors of fact which I have subsequently been able to correct.

In writing *Hitler's Rockets* I have once again been made aware how uneven were the sacrifices, so far as enemy action was concerned, required from different parts of the country. I feel all the more grateful that by birth, by upbringing and subsequently by choice I belong to that vaguely defined but, during the war, constantly battered area 'southern England'.

N.R.L.

1

THE BEGINNING

We had made a beginning.

Major-General Walter Dornberger, recalling December 1934

When in the early evening of Friday, 8 September 1944, two loud explosions echoed across London they caused no particular alarm. The population had become accustomed during five years of war to unexplained noises in the distance, even when, as on this occasion, no warning had sounded. In Whitehall, however, these sudden detonations were not misinterpreted. In many an office ministers, civil servants, government scientists and intelligence officers looked pointedly at each other, aware not merely that a new phase in the bombardment of London, but that a new era in the whole history of warfare, had begun. To the enemy armoury of manned bomber and pilotless aircraft had been added a new and even more formidable weapon, the long-range rocket.

The history of the rocket as a short-range, tactical weapon was in fact longer than that of ordinary firearms. Rockets had been employed by the Chinese in defence of a town besieged by the Mongols in AD 1232, and had been used by a rebellious Indian ruler against the British around 1780. In 1807 the British themselves had employed 'Congreve's Rockets', named after the Colonel Congreve who had developed them, against Boulogne. They made their appearance in the United States during the attack on Fort McHenry, Baltimore, in 1814 and became immortalized in a famous poem later adopted, under a different name, as the United States national anthem:

> And the rocket's red glare;
> The bombs bursting in air,

15

Hitler's Rockets

Gave proof through the night
That our flag was still there.

So popular did rockets become during the nineteenth century
that they seemed for a time likely to replace conventional
artillery, but the development of rifled barrels and more
powerful explosives had by 1900 restored the pre-eminence of
the field-gun and mortar. Rockets had invariably up to now
been battlefield weapons, not used for long-range bombardment, and by far the longest flight of a projectile achieved in
the First World War was that of the 25 lb (11.5 kg) shell
fired by the 'Paris Gun' which between March and July 1918
bombarded the French capital from a range of 75 miles. (To
the fury of artillerymen, it was often wrongly described as 'Big
Bertha', a conventional heavy mortar used on the western
front.)

The Treaty of Versailles, by limiting the calibre of weapons
with which the future German army, also severely restricted
in size, could be equipped, encouraged the Army Weapons
Department in Berlin to search for new types of armament
which would not violate its provisions while providing the
maximum fire power. Numerous articles in technical and
popular magazines drew attention to the progress, usually
vastly exaggerated, supposedly being made in rocket development. 'Each individual inventor', observed one young scientist
with a special interest in ballistics, Walter Dornberger, 'maintained a feud with everyone else who took an interest in
rockets', and to boost their claims to public money the
researchers 'were forced to resort to the inflated language of
publicity propaganda'. All this was now to change, for in 1930
the Ballistic Council of the Army Weapons Department
selected Dornberger to run its rocket research programme, a
post for which he was ideally suited by both background and
temperament.

The son of a pharmacist, Walter Dornberger had joined the
artillery in August 1914, at the age of nineteen, and served
throughout the war, later attending the Berlin Technical Institute before rejoining the army. In 1930 he was a thirty-five-
year-old captain, intensely interested in rockets but with his
feet firmly on the ground. 'We wanted', he wrote later,

16

recalling his first two years of struggling with impractical visionaries, 'to have done once for all with theory, unproven claims and boastful fantasy and to arrive at conclusions based on a sound scientific foundation.' During his visits to the airfield in Berlin where the Amateur German Rocket Society carried out its experiments, he was, he later admitted, 'struck . . . by the energy and shrewdness with which' one 'tall, fair young student, with a broad, massive chin, went to work and by his astonishing theoretic knowledge'. When General Becker, in charge of the Army Weapons Office, authorized the creation of an expanded research unit, this young man, Werner von Braun, headed Dornberger's 'list of proposals for technical assistants'.

Thus began what was to prove one of the classic scientific partnerships of all time. Von Braun's family were Prussian aristocrats – his father was a former government minister – and his 'scientific bent', Dornberger learned, had at first aroused their disgust. Born in March 1912, von Braun developed while at boarding school on the Friesian Islands in the Baltic a passionate interest in astronomy, went on to become a student at the Berlin Technical College, and in 1927 joined the newly formed German Society for Space Travel. By the time he was recruited to Dornberger's team one important conclusion, which was to have a decisive influence on the whole rocket story, had already been reached. 'It is not even possible to say with certainty', wrote Dornberger later, 'who first gave expression to the idea of using liquids of high energy content instead of powder for propulsion in airless space' – but this was the first of the giant leaps forward which were to lead to those explosions in London in 1944 and ultimately to the conquest of space.

Hitherto rocket technology had barely progressed since the Chinese had first invented fireworks. The basic principle remained unchanged: the continuous combustion of chemicals in a confined space generated hot gases which, unable to escape except at the rear, forced the rocket forward until they burned out, after which it continued its flight for a time under the thrust already developed. Up to now, however, the weight of fuel needed to achieve the sort of range and payload – i.e. high-explosive warhead – already achieved by ordinary artillery

17

had made the rocket impractical. By using liquid fuel Dornberger hoped to prolong the combustion period and to provide a continuous thrust powerful enough to carry a militarily significant weight far further than any shell so far fired. What, Dornberger rightly saw, was needed was not a single short-lived explosion but an actual motor able to sustain a flight of several minutes at a speed which would carry the missile upwards into space until it curved back to earth at a distance so far unattained by any man-made projectile. Dornberger set his sights initially on a liquid-fuelled engine able to provide a thrust of 650 lb. 'We meant', he wrote, 'to bring this motor to a high level of performance, to gather experience, tabulate laws and principles and so create a basis for further construction.'

Even for established scientists this was totally new territory, and to explore it Dornberger needed men who, like von Braun, combined soaring imagination with a firm grasp of basic scientific principles, accompanied, if possible, by experience in this thinly populated field of technology. Remarkably, he rapidly discovered the ideal person to serve as his test designer and chief engineer, Walter Riedel, then working for the Heylandt company near Berlin, a firm which had actually handled liquid-propelled rockets until a fatal accident had stopped development of their pet project, a rocket-powered racing car. Temperamentally, too, he seemed just what was needed:

Riedel was a short, sedate man, with a permanently dignified and serious expression and a somewhat phlegmatic temperament. He was a most versatile practical engineer. He seemed to me to provide the right counterpoise to the rather temperamental, self-taught technician von Braun. With his calm, deliberate mind, his deep knowledge and his experience in the handling of liquid oxygen he repeatedly managed to guide the bubbling stream of von Braun's ideas into steadier channels.

The little team began work at the Kummersdorf West Experimental Station, close to an existing firing range in the pine woods seventeen miles south of Berlin. Their accommodation was modest: wooden huts, now converted into 'improvised offices, a designing room, measurement rooms, darkrooms and a tiny workshop', where for the first few months 'everyone was bent over drawing-boards or busy at a lathe'.

The Beginning

Meanwhile, as the pleasant autumn of 1932 gave way to a wintry December and frost flecked the branches of the surrounding pine trees and the raw earth of the scientists' new home, half an hour's drive away in Berlin ordinary citizens had more to worry about than either rocket design or the weather. A general election, on 6 November 1932, left the Nazis the largest party in the Reichstag, with 196 seats, well ahead of the Social Democrats' 121 and the Communists' 100. Already the brown-shirted stormtroopers swaggered the streets, elbowing Jews into the gutter, and beating up their political rivals. At Kummersdorf, however, the scientists were indifferent to everything except their work. On 21 December 1932, while other German citizens were thinking of Christmas presents and singing 'Silent Night', the little group in the clearing amid the Christmas trees were eagerly awaiting the results of the first combustion test of a liquid-powered rocket motor, as Dornberger later described:

The cold bit through the thick soles of my riding boots. It crept up my body until I felt miserably frozen in my short fur jacket. I had snuggled up close to a fir tree. Whenever I showed any sign of abandoning my position I was brought up short by a shout of 'Keep under cover! Ignition any moment now!'. . . . In the control room the engineer, Riedel, stood on a narrow wooden grating, grasping two big steering wheels. When pressure was right in the spherical containers a turn of the wheels would open the two main valves and let the fuel into the combustion chamber. At the main door of the test stand, von Braun, very cold, was standing first on one leg and then on the other. He was holding a rod twelve feet long with a mug of petrol fastened to the end. Riedel called out from behind the wall that pressure was now correct and von Braun lit his gigantic match and held the flame under the exhaust. . . .

There was a swoosh, a hiss, and – crash!

Clouds of smoke rose. . . . Cables, boards, metal sheeting, fragments of steel and aluminium flew whistling through the air. . . . In the suddenly darkened pit of the testing room a milky, slimy mixture of alcohol and oxygen burned spasmodically with flames of different shapes and sizes, occasionally crackling and detonating like fireworks. Steam hissed. Cables were on fire in a hundred places. Thick, black, stinking fumes of burning rubber filled the air. Von Braun and I stared at each other. We were uninjured. The test stand had been wrecked.

19

Hitler's Rockets

One month later, on 30 January 1933, Hitler became Chancellor of Germany and the Nazi takeover of the state, and its steady preparation for aggressive war, began. On 12 November, in Hitler's words, 'the German people restored its honour to itself', fifteen years after its defeat in 1918, and endorsed Germany's withdrawal from the League of Nations by a massive 95 per cent vote. A general election on the same day left Nazi-supported candidates forming 92 per cent of the new Reichstag. These events passed the scientists at Kummersdorf by. *They* were solely exercised, as Dornberger acknowledged, by such problems as how 'to avoid burning out the chamber and setting the injection nozzles on fire' when starting up the rocket motor, as had happened during the first test, and by 'the difficulties of stabilization . . . as the propellant was consumed'. Their dedication to the task in hand was total. In March 1934 three men were killed while testing a premixed solution of hydrogen peroxide and alcohol though well aware this was highly dangerous, but their leader insisted on going ahead and simply 'telephoned the Mess . . . and asked that help should be sent if there were an explosion. . . . When help came a few minutes later, nothing was left of the test stand except the lead piping of the water supply'. Thereafter such hazardous experiments were discouraged, and these men, wrote Dornberger, conveniently forgetting the thousands of *Untermenschen* (i.e. non-Germans) who were to perish before his project finally succeeded, 'were the first and last to give their lives for rocket development under the Army Weapons Department'.

Every advance brought some new problem in its train. A promising plan to use the exhaust gases to steer the rocket's rudders, for example, came up against the existing limits of metallurgical knowledge. There was, it seemed, no 'material which . . . would not melt, like butter in the sun, at a gas velocity of almost 6500 feet per second'. But, looking back, Dornberger had no doubt that this was the happiest period of the whole vast and protracted enterprise:

The early years of our activity shine in my memory with imperishable lustre. They were years of groping towards creation, of the delight of success, of progressive work in common among inseparable

20

companions. . . . Luckily the difficulties were for the most part still entirely unknown to us. We attacked our problems with the courage of inexperience and had no thought of the time it might take us to solve them.

Although money for military research was now plentiful, and the Army Weapons Department could order without difficulty any scientific equipment needed, the full implications of the new regime had not yet sunk in among the bureaucrats in Berlin. The supply of office machinery, for example, still required Treasury approval, and to avoid intolerable delays the Kummersdorf scientists were forced to resort to such devices as describing a pencil sharpener as an 'appliance for cutting wood rods up to 10 mm in diameter' and a typewriter as an 'instrument for recording test data with recording roller'. There was an epic battle over an order for two boxes of children's sparklers, which were being tried as a means of igniting the rocket's fuel mixture. In the hope of saving time they were said to be needed for the office Christmas tree, but a whole year later some vigilant official observed that they had been ordered in midsummer, the correspondence being terminated only when he was told bluntly they were for 'secret experiments' and no further questions could be answered.

With the problems of fuel and combustion in process of being solved, at least experimentally, those of guiding the rocket once it had taken off became equally pressing, until von Braun discovered in the Gyroscope Company at Brietz near Berlin a former Austrian naval officer 'full of ideas and far ahead of his time in all questions relating to gyroscopes'. The development of this system of keeping the rocket stable and on course was another major breakthrough, for, Dornberger learned, 'according to the standard *Textbook of Ballistics* experiments had proved it impossible to impart a steady flight to bodies with arrow-stability at supersonic speed, but supersonic speed was needed to obtain access to space'. Eventually it became clear that no single gyroscope would suffice, but one working simultaneously 'on three axes'.

Gradually the Kummersdorf experimenters discovered that most of the existing data about the behaviour of projectiles in flight was invalid when applied to rockets and that the evidence of small-scale experiments was no guide to what happened when the quantities were scaled up. In October 1934 Dornberger was briefly posted away to take command of the first ever German artillery battery armed with rockets – of the conventional, solid-fuel variety – but the work continued in his absence and he kept in touch with it.

By now the main outlines of the first rocket had been agreed. the A-1 – the 'A' stood for 'aggregate' or 'prototype – marked a tremendous advanced on any missile so far constructed. It was to be 4ft 6½ in (1.395 metres) long, 11⅞ in (0.3 m) wide, and was to weigh 329 lb (149 kg). The propellant, a mixture of liquid oxygen and alcohol, would produce a thrust of 660 lb (300 kg) for 16 seconds, and the missile was to be steered by self-contained gyroscopes and held steady by tail fins, after being 'fired vertically from a slipway several yards high'. In fact, although its motor worked perfectly during a static test on the ground, it was never built, for the designers had moved on to a more ambitious model, the A-2, and early in December 1934 the first two A-2s were successfully launched over the North Sea from a test range on the island of Borkum. They behaved perfectly, reaching a height of one and a half miles (8100 ft, or 2500 m), a remarkable achievement for a totally new piece of technology, developed from scratch in a mere two years. Dornberger himself was more conscious of the distance still to be travelled, before the rocket became the supersonic, stratospheric, heavy-load-bearing projectile surpassing all known cannon of which he dreamed. 'We had', he summed up modestly, 'made a beginning.'

2
TOWARDS PERFECTION

*So long as the war lasts, our most urgent task can only be the
rapid perfection of the rocket as a weapon.*

Major-General Dornberger, following the first successful test
of the A-4, 3 October 1942

By early 1933 the trend of German foreign policy was plain
for all to see. In January the Saar, taken from Germany in
1919, was reunited with what was soon to be called the Third
Reich. In March Hitler proclaimed the creation of a German
Air Force and the return of conscription, in open defiance of
the Treaty of Versailles. Meanwhile at Kummersdorf the
rocket experiments were visibly outgrowing the existing facilities, and on safety grounds alone a move was overdue to a far
larger, more remotely sited, establishment. While Dornberger
concentrated on finding the money needed for equipment, 'an
impossible sum running into seven figures', von Braun searched
for a location on the coast, both to secure secrecy and because
'on safety grounds we must be able to fire out to sea and to
observe the entire trajectory from land'. While spending the
Christmas holiday with relations near the Baltic coast, he was
reminded that his father had once hunted duck on the remote
island of Usedom, near a fishing village called Peenemünde.
The young scientist's report brought Dornberger hurrying to
inspect it – and he was highly impressed:

The place was far away from any large town or traffic of any kind,
and consisted of dunes and marshland overgrown with ancient oaks
and pines, nestling in untroubled solitude behind a reedy foreland
reaching far out into smooth water. Big Pomeranian deer with dark
antlers roamed through the heather and among the bilberry bushes
of the woods right to the sands of the low-lying coast. Swarms of
duck, crested grebes, coots and swans inhabited this beautiful spot

23

undisturbed for years by the report of the huntsman's shotgun. The bustle of the watering-places strung along the coast like a necklace of pearls never invaded the lonely islet of Peenemünde. I thought there would be no difficulty in building a railway and roads and concealing the really important installations in the woods. . . . A small island. . . . faced the Peene estuary, the Greifswalder Oie. There we could carry out our experiments unnoticed throughout the year. We had a range of over 250 miles eastwards along the Pomeranian coast.

Now to raise the money. Dornberger had always believed in 'demonstrating our wares in front of the prominent people who sat on the money bags', and he now arranged a demonstration for General Wernher von Fritsch, Commander-in-Chief of the German army. Von Fritsch listened patiently to 'a short lecture illustrated with coloured drawings and many diagrams' and was then shown three static rocket engines at full thrust. 'Hardly had the echo of the motors died away in the pine woods', recorded Dornberger, 'than the general assured us of his full support provided we used the funds to turn our rocket-drive into a serviceable weapon of war. Bluntly and dispassionately he put the all-important question: "How much do you want?"'

By a master-stroke of military diplomacy, Dornberger next managed to interest the head of the Development Branch of the Air Ministry in rocket propulsion, describing 'in glowing terms the possibilities of using rocket motors for launching heavy bombers', and the latter next infected General Kesselring, Director of Aircraft Construction, with his own enthusiasm. In April 1936, a decisive date in the rocket story, both Luftwaffe men, plus Dornberger, von Braun and their own chief, General Karl Becker of the Army Weapons Office, met to agree terms for cooperation between the two services. The Luftwaffe Works Department, it was agreed, would build the station, but the army would administer it, and though there would be separate army and Luftwaffe divisions the running expenses would be shared. An Air Ministry official was immediately dispatched to negotiate with the owners of the site, the city corporation of the nearby town of Wolgast, and he telephoned that evening to say the deal was clinched at a price of 750,000 marks, £66,250 at the then rate of exchange.*

For Germany and the world 1936 was the year Hitler occupied the demilitarized Rhineland – and the Western democracies, by doing nothing to stop him, ensured him the wholehearted support of the hitherto hesitant German general staff. For the rocket team it was the year they planned the layout of Peenemünde, saw construction started, and mapped out the future pattern of their research. Already they had realized that to build a projectile large enough to accommodate the complicated motor, fuel and guidance systems they must 'think big' and, just as the A 1 had been replaced by the A-2 before the former had ever flown, so now they decided to press on to a more ambitious design still, the A-3, designed purely to give experience and information. This 'research' rocket was none the less an impressive sight, standing almost 25 ft (7.6m) high, 2 ft 5 in (0.75 m) in diameter, and weighing 1654 lb (750 kg). The motor developed a thrust of 3300 lb (1500 kg) burning the same fuel as the A-1, a mixture of liquid oxygen and alcohol, as here the research team were sure that they were working on the right lines.

Military and public relations considerations, too, argued in favour of omitting the usual small-scale stages of development, as Dornberger later recalled:

As we kept on pestering the army chiefs for money for continued development, we were told that we should only get it for rockets that would be capable of throwing big loads over long ranges with a good prospect of hitting the target. In our youthful zeal we promised all that was asked, never suspecting what difficulties would arise in consequence.

For professional reasons, too, Dornberger was eager to produce a missile of sensational range and power:

I had been a heavy gunner. Gunnery's highest achievement to date had been the huge Paris Gun during the First World War. It could fire a 21 cm [8.2 in] shell with about 25 lb [11.5 kg] of explosive about

---

*I have used a conversion factor of 11.32 Reichsmarks to £1 throughout this book. This is the middle figure for the exchange rate, 11.76 to 10.88 RM, on 31 August 1939.

80 miles. My idea of a first big rocket was something that would send a ton of high explosive over 160 miles . . . double the range of the Paris Gun.

Already by the spring of 1936 the main features of the real objective of the research team, an operational rocket soon to be known as the A-4, were emerging. Dornberger constantly reminded his colleagues that they were not engaged in a search for knowledge for its own sake, pioneering though their work was, but in producing a practical weapon in the foreseeable future. One essential was accuracy:

I stipulated a number of military requirements, among others that . . . for every 1000 feet of range a deviation of only 2 or 3 feet was acceptable, either too far or too short, and the same for lateral deviation . . . stricter than is customary for artillery.

Another need was mobility:

I limited the size of the rocket by insisting that we must be able to transport it intact by road and that it must not exceed the maximum width laid down for road vehicles. If carried by rail the rocket must be able to pass through any tunnel. These points determined the main dimensions, although we were all certain from the start that a slender body would involve less air resistance and give us greater range. It would be for the engineers to find the ideal flying shape.

Because of the lack of knowledge about how such a large object would behave at supersonic speeds, Dornberger and von Braun decided that they needed their own wind tunnel, and a far larger one than any so far built; up to now they had made do by borrowing the tunnel belonging to the Technical High School at Aachen. Even their most loyal supporter, Karl Becker of the Army Weapons Office, 'looked grave' when asked to find an estimated 300,000 additional marks (£26,500) but eventually agreed provided another of the twelve departments within the Army Research and Development Branch would share the cost. Dornberger tried them all and struck lucky with the very last. Soon the huge wind tunnel, 'expected to be the most efficient in the world', was adding its shape to the hitherto unspoiled skyline of Usedom.

The team now needed a wind-tunnel specialist and successfully 'poached' the academic who had helped them at Aachen. They also recruited the leading authority on rocket motors, Dr

26

Walter Thiel, who had formerly had a desk job at Research Branch headquarters and now moved to a test bench at Kummersdorf. Thiel, although 'extremely hard-working, conscientious and systematic . . . was', admitted Dornberger, 'tremendously ambitious and aware of his own worth. He took a superior attitude and demanded equal devotion from his colleagues. I had to smooth over a good deal of friction'. However, this proved a price worth paying, for this prima donna of the laboratories soon began to make a major contribution, including one immediate advance, 'the use of welded sheet-steel chambers' for the rocket motor instead of the light alloys previously considered indispensable.

Another valuable recruit, Dr Steinhoff, was spotted by von Braun at a conference and invited to visit Peenemünde, where, von Braun correctly anticipated, he would be captivated 'by the big-scale modern plant, the freedom to work, and the prospects of the rocket'. Dornberger found him wandering about Test Stand 1, and was astonished when this 'young man, apparently in his late twenties . . . seized my hands with every appearance of genuine enthusiasm and exclaimed "Sir, you must take me! I'm all yours! I want to stay!" ' Stay he did, not merely abandoning the academic post he was about to take up but drawing 'a whole train of skilled scientists after him'.

By May 1937 work on Peenemünde was sufficiently far advanced for most of Dornberger's team, now totalling nearly a hundred, to move there, though Dr Thiel and five of his assistants did not follow them until the summer of 1940. Ultimately Peenemünde was to cost the German taxpayer between £25 and £40 million, but little of this had yet been spent and conditions were still primitive when it was decided to test the first completed A-3 at the new test centre on Greifswalder Oie, the tiny island, five miles from Usedom and seven and a half from the nearest town, Rügen, which Dornberger had identified on his first visit as ideal for the purpose. A mere 1100 yards long by 300 wide, 'with a steep, loamy coast, lashed by storm and surf in winter', and standing only 60 feet above the surrounding waves, Greifswalder Oie in 1937 contained only a handful of houses, a lighthouse, linked to the main settlement by a single rough road, and an inn, presided over by an innkeeper of 'inexhaustible good humour', which doubtless increased still further as the island became 'like a swarming anthill', producing a sensational increase in his trade.

Dornberger was fully conscious of the drama which surrounded the successive tests of the rockets. For none were preparations more elaborate than for this first trial of the A-3 for all the facilities had to be brought by sea to this remote islet and the test stand had to be constructed under conditions more appropriate to the front line than to a sophisticated scientific research project. Dornberger's sharp eye noted, and recorded in loving detail, each new arrival in the 'tiny fishing harbour on the south-west coast' of Greifswalder Oie:

One day a number of small motor launches filled with building personnel and surveyors . . . arrived in the little harbour. Next came a large vessel of unusual appearance, such as had never been seen before in that part of the Baltic. She carried building materials and . . . had been a car and passenger ferry. . . . A typical example of mid-nineteenth-century shipbuilding, she possessed large cabins with decrepit furniture upholstered in red plush, a quantity of gleaming brass fittings and mountings, towering upper works and a high funnel. . . . The next to arrive were the harbour dredgers and barges.

All this was only the start of months of frenzied activity:

A bustle now began with which the island was wholly unfamiliar. The harbour was dredged. Berths and landing facilities had to be created for big vessels and heavy cargoes. The cart track to the uplands was given a firm surface of planks. In front of the storm-topped coppice that stood to the east of the track a square concrete platform went up. A pit was excavated opposite to it, at the edge of the forest, and a dug-out was built.

The builders and builders' labourers departed. Engineers and craftsmen took their place. Then came more builders. Lines and cable after cable were laid between the shelter and the central point of the platform. Dug-out, lighthouse and inn were connected by telephone. The dug-out was transformed into an observation post with lookout slits and gauges of all descriptions on the walls. . . . In the coppice immediately behind the shelter two big open clearings were made and levelled off. . . . Generators were unloaded at the harbour and brought to the coppice. Wiring was laid for electric light. Petrol, materials and tools arrived by sea. Weeks passed in a whirl of activity.

It was a red-letter day when the rockets themselves arrived:

One day at the end of November the ferry-boat delivered two large boxes painted dark grey. They were 21 feet long and 4½ feet in depth and breadth. These giants' coffins were unloaded with great care and cautiously conveyed in a heavy lorry to the tent. There they were guarded day and night. Shortly afterwards two further chests of this type were unloaded and taken into the tent.

Word of the forthcoming test had spread, and it had become a matter of prestige to be present, as well as one of genuine scientific curiosity:

In the end about one hundred and twenty men of science and engineers had assembled. Anyone connected in any way with our rocket wanted to be there. We had had to set a limit to the number, but . . . when I finally came to check the list I found that the telephone operators were doctors of physics and mathematics, the M. T. drivers qualified engineers, and the kitchen staff made up of designers and experts in aerodynamics. Even the humblest posts were occupied by technicians or enthusiastic executives. . . . Then it started raining. The rain poured down and the wind rose. It whistled over the island from the north, whipped the bare branches of the stunted trees and blew through the window crevices of the houses. It tore up the tent. It hurled gigantic waves against the island and thunderous breakers dashed over the stone walls of the harbour. The cold became intense. The bad weather forced us to postpone operations. But it went as quickly as it had come. The sky grew clear and the wind blew steadily from the east. The weather forecast sounded favourable. We made final preparations. . . We now had to work fast. The rocket would have to be launched before winter storms set in and the Baltic froze between the islet and the mainland. We baptized our missiles with liquid oxygen. Then at last we were ready for them. One of the chests was carefully hauled out of the tent and on to the platform. After the top and bottom had been removed the box was pushed against the overturned four-legged firing table and set upon it by means of a block and tackle. . . . Scaffolding protected by awnings gave access to the parts of the rocket which had to be serviced before launching. The checking began, but we were held up again and again by short circuits, insulating difficulties, trouble with the control gear, the reducing valve and the fuel valves. . . . The specialist engineers toiled, fetched missing spare parts from the mainland and checked over connections. . . . At last we were able to fix a time for the first launching. The ferry-boat delivered liquid oxygen. The rocket was tanked up and the control gear given current. The working scaffolding was taken down. . . . The rocket now stood in the vertical position on the firing table. Its slender, gleaming body in its aluminium skin was some 21 feet long, with a diameter of nearly 3 feet.

What followed on that December day in 1937, three years after the first research had started at Kummersdorf, proved a massive disappointment. The launching turned out such a failure that Dornberger could not bring himself to describe it and 'eyewitness accounts from the staff were wildly contradictory'. But Dornberger was not the man to give up at the first rebuff:

We decide to venture on a second launching. I watched, from the lighthouse, how the second rocket rose from the ground. The same thing happened again. Soon after the start it made almost a quarter-turn about its longitudinal axis, turned into the wind and, after climbing a few hundred feet, ejected the parachute. Then the motor stopped burning and the rocket fell into the sea near the precipitous east coast of the island.

Before they could try again, having decided to leave out the recovery parachute, the fog came down and the scientists crowded into the inn for a melancholy inquest on the recent failures. The moment the fog cleared they went back to the launching site:

According to the weather forecast, rain, snow, gales and a cold snap were to be expected within a few days. We had to hurry. But even the next two launchings gave no better result. Immediately after rising the rocket took the line of least resistance, turned into the wind and at a height of between 2500 and 3500 feet turned over and fell into the sea.

This premature splashdown, so different from the triumphant flight they had hoped for, left the rocket team depressed, and it was a sad voyage back to the mainland:

As we ran into the Peene estuary in our motor-boats late in the afternoon, when it was already getting dark and blowing hard, the icy north-westerly gale sent high black waves slapping down on the foredeck and away over the upper works. Rain and snow made visibility difficult. We were feeling subdued, almost despondent. But not hopeless. Despite all our failure we were still convinced that we should pull it off.

Already they had decided that the four A-3s they had tested

had simply been blown off course from the start by the stiff north-east wind and that what was needed was a tenfold increase in the power of the control gear and in the speed of the rudder vanes it operated. Like a general who, with centre and flanks crumbling, plans to attack, Dornberger decided to abandon the A-3 and press on to a far more ambitious model, the A-5, designed specifically to provide data applicable to their real goal, the A-4. The motor, the outstanding success of their work so far, remained unchanged, and efforts were now concentrated on the control mechanisms and the missile's aerodynamic properties. The famous Zeppelin aircraft works at Friedrichshafen provided a wind tunnel to test 'the stability of the A-5 with the new tail surfaces', the Graf Zeppelin Flight Research Institute at Stuttgart devised two new types of parachute to slow it down and return it to earth, while a draughtsman at Kummersdorf came up with a money-saving idea, making the rocket's external vanes of graphite instead of molybdenum, which cut the cost of this item from 150 RM to 1.5 (£13.25 to 13p). By the autumn of 1938 four A-5 rockets, complete except for the guidance mechanism, had been launched from Greifswalder Oie. All had reached a height of five miles and had approached the speed of sound without the A-3's instability; that was one giant hurdle climbed.

In March 1938 Austria was forcibly incorporated in the Reich, in September Britain and France were publicly humiliated at Munich, and in March 1939 the rest of Czechoslovakia was seized in plain defiance of the recent agreement. These events simply seem to have passed Dornberger and his subordinates by. Of far greater important to them was the Führer's visit that same month to Kummersdorf, though it was not an obvious success. Hitler said barely a word, even when watching the testing of a horizontally suspended rocket motor, which usually set visitors gasping in admiration. He did show a flicker of interest in the A-4 and asked how long it would take to develop – Dornberger was evasive in answer – but spoiled things by telling his hosts, over his frugal lunch of mixed vegetables and mineral water, that his only previous contact with the rocket world had been back in his Munich days, with a rocket enthusiast who was a hopelessly impractical dreamer. Hitler, Dornberger decided – a verdict from him which came close to disloyalty – 'had no feeling for technological progress', but he consoled himself with the knowledge that 'Colonel-General von Brauchitsch' – Fritsch's successor as army Commander-in-Chief – 'and the few others who had seen the demonstration had given . . . expression to their admiration and approval of what we had accomplished in so few years'.

Von Brauchitsch's support was now to prove all important. On 5 September 1939, two days after Britain and France had declared war on Germany, he agreed to give the A-4 project the highest possible priority, and Dornberger returned from his headquarters, jubilant, to witness the first A-5 tests on the Greifswalder Oie. It was a glorious autumn day on which the previously inhospitable island looked its best; permanent buildings had now replaced the tents and huts of two years before, and Dornberger looked around at these signs of progress with warm approval:

Facing north, in the direction of the firing point, stood the long and massive Measurement House, dazzlingly white in the sunshine, with its workshop, oscillograph room, offices, and flat roof reached by an outside stairway. There were concreted roads, concrete observation shelters, and a concrete apron of considerably enlarged size. The scaffolding which covered the awnings had been replaced by an armour-plated working tower which could be wholly closed in and lowered for the take-off. To bring the rocket, painted bright yellow and red, to the firing position, it was pushed through the detachable roof of the lowered tower and both were then raised by means of a cable winch.

What happened when the rocket was launched was also very different from that day of unhappy memory nearly two years before:

The first rocket shot up from the firing table. It rose vertically in the azure sky. It did not turn about its longitudinal axis and did not yield to the wind. The projectile rose steadily higher and higher, faster and faster on its course. . . . The backs of our necks ached as we stared aloft. . . . At a height of nearly five miles, after 45 seconds of burning time, the tanks run dry. . . . The speed of the rocket caused it to rise still higher, though it had lost its motive power. At last it reached the peak of its trajectory and slowly turned over. At that moment von Braun pressed the button transmitting the radio order for para-chute release and a tiny white point appeared close to the flashing, sunlit body of the rocket. This was the braking parachute. Precisely two seconds later von Braun pressed another button, which released the big supporting parachute. The rocket . . . glided slowly down, hanging quietly from the shrouds . . . and after a few minutes it dropped in the water outside the mole with a splash that glittered in the sunshine. . . . Our launch immediately left the harbour and in little more than half an hour the rocket, its bright paint easily seen among the dark waves, was hauled aboard.

The A-5 had achieved, on its first flight, a range of eleven miles and reached a height of seven and a half miles, leaving Dornberger well content:

What we had successfully done with the A-5 must be equally valid, in improved form, for the A-4. . . . I could see our goal clearly and the way that led to it. I now knew that we should succeed in creating a weapon with a far greater range than any artillery.

From now onwards Peenemünde, already the most advanced establishment of its kind in the world and soon to be the largest, was the heart and centre of the whole rocket enterprise. Administratively, as well as physically, the island was divided into two. The eastern half, or HVP, for Heeresversuchanstalt Peenemünde (Peenemünde Army Research Establishment), was Dornberger's province, with von Braun, a civilian, as his technical director, and an army officer, Colonel Leo Zanssen, as his 'camp commandant'. The western part of Usedom, Erprobungstelle Karlshagen (Karlshagen Experimental Station), which contained the airfield, was Luftwaffe territory. The two coexisted in comparative harmony. These were the golden years at Peenemünde. Research and development work went ahead smoothly, with virtually unlimited funds, a pilot factory already planned to study how the finished A-4 could be mass-produced, and even a target date, albeit an optimistic one, for the start of large-scale manufacture, December 1941. The real obstacle, but fortunately a remote one, was Hitler, who apparently believed that the rocket, if it worked at all, would arrive too late for the present war, and in the spring of 1940 Peenemünde was removed from the priority list for men and supplies. Von Brauchitsch's support now stood Dornberger is good stead and he connived at the creation of a new, and essentially fictitious, Northern Experimental Command, to which the 4000 men working at Peenemünde, from technologists to labourers, were transferred, supposedly for merely temporary duty in Germany, the only way to prevent their being called up for routine, front-line military service.

Around the same date there was a more encouraging development: on 21 March 1940 an A-4 motor was successfully tested for the first time. It required 284 lb (129 kg) of the propellant mixture of oxygen and liquid alcohol every second, and merely to provide this a wholly new type of pumping system had to be devised, making use of a turbine operated by steam released from hydrogen peroxide by calcium permanganate, 'a motor within a motor'; the cooling arrangements, which involved the use of a separate supply of alcohol, proved equally elaborate. Progress had by now also been made on the launching technique. The original intention had been to fire the rocket at an angle, pointing towards the target, but it proved unstable when fully loaded and the intention now was to achieve lift-off vertically, after which it would gradually tilt to an angle of 49° as it climbed upwards. When the rocket had sufficient thrust, the supply of propellant would be cut off, a radio signal at first being used for this purpose, though later a self-contained system, which operated automatically at a predetermined point, was substituted.

The myriad technical and design problems which every part of the increasingly complicated A-4 presented left the Peenemünde team little time to observe events in the outside world. While France fell, Russia was invaded, the armies in the Western Desert advanced and retreated, the Battle of the Atlantic was joined and British bombers flew over Germany in increasing strength, Dornberger's men remained obsessed with their own problems. On 18 March 1942 the first complete A-4 was ready for a static test. It proved a disaster, but component after component was doggedly tested and it was decided to go ahead with a full-scale launching, on Usedom itself. On the flat roof of the glittering new measurement house Dornberger stood on 3 October 1942, microphone in hand, observing a scene of which he wrote an almost minute-by-minute account:

It was noon and the arch of a clear, cloudless sky extended over

34

Towards Perfection

Northern Germany. My eye strayed out to the Development Works, gloomy in their camouflage, to the spreading pine woods and across the reedy promontory of the bay of Peenemünde, to the . . . Greifswalder Oie six miles away.

In the south, nestling in the evergreen forest, I saw the two big, bright concrete sheds of the Pre-Production Works, their northward sloping roofs covered with camouflage netting. In the west the low hills of the far bank of the River Peene were dominated by the redbrick tower of Wolgast Cathedral. The light blue contours of the oxygen-generating plant, the six conspicuous chimneys of the big power-station overlooking the harbour, and the long hangars of the Peenemünde airfield completed the picture I had grown to know so well. . . .

When I leaned over the parapet I could see a great deal of animation. In the avenues and paths between the widely scattered buildings of the Works, at the windows and on the roofs of sheds, workshops and offices, the entire staff seemed to be waiting and watching. . . . All wanted to witness the event they had striven for, one which would perhaps make history. . . .

There were still three minutes to go. . . . Their almost unbearable tension was repeated with every trial launching and they had come to be known as the 'Peenemünde minutes', so much longer than sixty seconds did they seem. . . .

'X minus 1.'

The tension mounted. . . . So far we had succeeded only twice in getting a rocket of this size off the ground at all. . . . If today's test failed . . . I should have to propose the transfer of all our armament potential to aircraft or tank construction. . . . I felt cold with suspense and excitement under the warm autumn sun. . . .

A smoke cartridge hissed into the sky. Its green track over Test Stand VII drifted sluggishly away before the wind. Ten seconds more! . . .

'Ignition!' . . .

After about a second thrust rose to 25 tons. . . . The gleaming body of the rocket rose vertically from the forest into the sky. . . . The flame darting from the stern was almost as long as the rocket itself. The fiery jet of gas was clear-cut and self-contained. The rocket kept to its course as though running on rails. . . . The first critical moment had passed. . . . Then it began, almost imperceptibly at first, to incline its tip eastwards. The tilt had begun. . . .

'Sonic velocity!' reported the loudspeaker at last. My heart missed a beat. . . . Now was the time – what if the white cloud of an explosion should appear in the blue sky?

Nothing appeared. The projectile flew on imperturbably. . . . At that moment on 3 October 1942 supersonic speed was achieved for the first time by a liquid-propellant rocket. . . . The reddish flame had vanished. The thick white vapour trail was forming no longer. Only a thin, milky streak of mist still followed the rocket as it raced away at a speed of over 3000 m.p.h.

For the rocket men this, far more than the later first operational firing of the A-4, was the real moment of triumph. Even the normally detached scientists and army officers who had achieved it were caught up in the excitement of the moment, not least Dornberger himself:

I couldn't speak for a moment; my emotion was too great. I could see that Colonel Zanssen was in the same state. He was standing there laughing. His eyes were moist. He stretched out his hands to me. I grasped them. Then our emotions ran away with us. We yelled and embraced each other like excited boys. . . . Everyone was shouting, laughing, leaping, dancing and shaking hands. . . . As I went out into the street half the technical staff came dashing towards me. There was a great deal of hand-shaking. I bundled von Braun into the car and we drove to Test Stand VII. As we shot through the open gate in the sand-built walls surrounding the great arena we beheld something like a popular riot. The test field crews had surrounded Dr Thiel and their chief engineers. . . . I can still see Thiel's face, with his shrewd savant's eyes sparkling behind his thick spectacles. . . . His response to my congratulations was a flood of new ideas and suggestions for improvement.

The actual splashdown, marked by sudden silence from the radio which had been transmitting a continuous note ever since lift-off, came as almost an anticlimax to the shouting, laughing crowd of scientists assembled round the loudspeakers. Young Dr Steinhoff, whom Dornberger had found wandering around the test area several years earlier, was sent off in a Messerschmitt to locate the precise spot, marked by brightly coloured dye in the sea, and returned with more good news: the missile had travelled 120 miles and come down only two and a half miles wide of its aiming-point. Already Dornberger had fulfilled one private ambition. 'Our rocket today', he told his excited audience at a celebratory party that evening, 'reached a height of nearly 60 miles. We have thus broken the world height record of 25 miles previously held by the . . . Paris gun.'

To Dornberger, the artillery-man and First World War veteran, this no doubt meant more than it did to the scientists around him, and just in case the day's success should set their minds moving again in the direction of that old dream, space travel, he added a stern reminder of their real purpose:

The development of possibilities we cannot yet envisage will be a peacetime task. . . . So long as the war lasts, our most urgent task can only be the rapid perfection of the rocket as a weapon.

3

TAKING IT SERIOUSLY

It looks as though we'll have to take these rockets seriously.

British Air Intelligence Officer, 27 March 1943

When the war began, the British government had no suspicion that the Germans might be developing long-range rockets, and the possibility was examined seriously only because of a mistake. Hitler's speech at Danzig on 19 September 1939 boasting that the Nazis might 'use a weapon which is not yet known and with which we ourselves cannot be attacked' led to a young government scientist, Dr R. V. Jones, being instructed to search the files of the Secret Intelligence Service for clues as to the identity of 'Hitler's secret weapon'. His report, 'The Hitler *Waffe*', running to six foolscap pages, submitted on 11 November 1939, identified seven 'weapons to which several references occur, of which some must be considered seriously', the fifth of these being 'long-range guns and rockets', although he concluded that in all probability 'Hitler's weapon was neither bluff nor novelty, but merely the extensive use of his air force'. This interpretation is now generally accepted as being correct, but 'The Hitler *Waffe*' remains important, since it marks the first systematic study of the rocket threat.

The secret-weapon investigation helped to make Dr Jones's unique role, which he regarded as essentially that of keeping an eye open for significant developments in German weapons, especially in the air, well known throughout Whitehall, and his name was constantly to recur whenever such matters were discussed during the next few years. Still only twenty-eight, he had taken a first in physics at Oxford, where he had worked in the Clarendon Laboratory under the famous Professor Frederick Lindemann, known as 'Prof' to his students and to his close friend, Winston Churchill. It was thanks to Lindemann that R. V. Jones first became involved in government research, while still doing postgraduate work at Oxford, though the £50 he received for equipment was somewhat less than the millions of marks the Germans were at that time spending on Peenemünde. He had entered the scientific civil service in 1936 with the salary, unprecedented for someone of his age, of £500 a year, and shortly after the outbreak of war had transferred to Air Intelligence Branch AI (I (c)), which was closely linked to MI6, known more commonly as SIS, the Secret Intelligence Service. In this capacity, while working at SIS headquarters at 54 Broadway in Victoria, he had constant contacts with 'Station X', at Bletchley Park in Buckinghamshire, which housed the SIS pre-war files and was to become well known as the centre of intelligence obtained from breaking German codes, including the Ultra material enciphered on the Enigma machine. Dr Jones also became personally acquainted with almost everyone else of importance in the intelligence war, including the 'Y' Section, responsible for intercepting ordinary German signals traffic, and the staff, military and civilian, of the Royal Aircraft Establishment at Farnborough, Britain's nearest equivalent to Peenemünde. All these links were to prove of crucial importance, and before long Dr Jones had acquired a well-qualified colleague, Squadron Leader S. D. Felkin, later famous for his skill in interrogating German prisoners. The British intelligence system lacked neither resources nor professional talent. Where it was sadly deficient was in scientific knowledge. 'The average SIS agent', Dr Jones wrote later, 'was a scientific analphabet' – i.e. he lacked even the ABC of that area of knowledge.

While still completing his secret-weapon study, Dr Jones found another problem literally dumped on his desk, the seven-page document known as the 'Oslo Report', left a week earlier at the British Legation in Norway, apparently by a German well-wisher to the Allied cause. Dr Jones took it seriously from the first, recognizing that it 'was obviously written by someone with a good scientific and technical background', dismissing the suspicions of some of his colleagues that it might be a German 'plant'. The Oslo Report mentioned, for the first time in any intelligence source, a research establishment at Peenemünde, and the development by the German army of rocket projectiles 80 cm (32 in) wide.

In May 1940 British military intelligence received information that a scientist called Oberth was collaborating with the Germans on producing a 30 ton rocket with a range of 160 miles at an establishment near Stettin. Most unfortunately it did not reach the Air Ministry, where Dr Jones at least would have recognized the name of Professor Oberth as the 'father' of German rocket research and an expert on liquid-fuelled rockets and could have identified the 'establishment near Stettin' as Peenemünde. Here the consequences of the intelligence service's lack of scientifically trained officers were strikingly demonstrated.

May 1940 was also the month in which Winston Churchill became Prime Minister and took into power with him his private crony and confidant, Professor Lindemann, as his scientific adviser, appointing him to the sinecure post of Paymaster-General. Lindemann's elevation meant that science was now represented at the very highest level of government, and that the voices of scientists, at least if they enjoyed Lindemann's highly selective approval, would be heard in Downing Street; but for this there was a high, almost disastrous, price to be paid. Lindemann was a bigoted, mean-minded, grievance-treasuring, malicious snob, and his German accent – he had been born in Baden-Baden in 1886, the son of a very wealthy German engineer who later became a British citizen – was all too likely to pour into Churchill's uncritical ear supposedly objective advice fatally warped by personal prejudice. It was typical of Lindemann that because he disapproved of the man his sister had married he refused to speak to her for the remaining forty years of his life, and his professional life was riddled with similar small-minded vendettas. Cold and aloof to outward appearance, beneath the surface, he was, according to an admiring biographer, 'a man alive and raw and quivering with authentic passions, nourishing love and hate with an intensity rare among men, revengeful in thought yet vulnerable to slights . . . his vision was somewhat narrow and his obstinacy impervious to argument'. His own judgement as a scientist too was often spectacularly faulty, and R. V. Jones, while working as a research student under Lindemann, 'found that he had been leading me up a garden path because he had made some erroneous assumptions he had not troubled to check'. When he disliked anyone – and he disliked a great many people – he was liable to disregard whatever they said, however soundly based; equally, and almost as misleadingly, he was intensely loyal to his friends and would unwaveringly support them even when wrong. His feud with the other major figure offering the government scientific advice, Professor Henry Tizard, had become notorious even before the war and was to have dire consequences during it, for in 1942 Tizard was virtually driven out of Whitehall back into academic life, so that for the whole 'rocket period' Lindemann reigned supreme and unchallenged. His response when R. V. Jones (for whom, as a former pupil, he apparently retained a grudging respect) attempted, with Tizard's agreement, to make peace between the two, was typically ungracious and small-minded: 'Now that I am in a position of power, a lot of my old friends have come sniffing around!' Equally revealing was his response to congratulations when, in 1941, Churchill created him a peer, and he took the name of that charming Oxford river, the Cherwell, 'a gleeful sneer', and the comment, ' "Of course . . . it wouldn't be any use getting an award if one didn't think of all the people who were miserable because they hadn't managed it." '

All allowances for Lindemann made, he remains, on the evidence of the documents as well as the recollections of those who knew him, a singularly unpleasant figure who was almost always wrong. His presence in Whitehall was generally disliked, and one former junior minister in Churchill's wartime government expressed a widespread view when he remarked in a broadcast long after the war that in his view the German-born scientist was the most repellent individual ever to have disgraced British public life and that he 'seemed to have crawled out from under a stone'. In the story of the rocket, however, as the Prime Minister's private, as well as official, scientific adviser he was to play an important part.

As one country after another was overrun by the Germans, and an increasing number of decent German citizens came to hate their own government, the problem for British intelligence became less one of too little information than of too much. Into Branch AI (I (c)) at 53 Broadway poured a steady flow of facts, rumours and – most troublesome of all – half-truths, from a variety of sources: the code-breakers at Bletchley, the 'Y' Service, the London 'Cage' where especially important prisoners were questioned, the numerous other centres where enemy prisoners or suspect arrivals from Europe were interrogated, the reports from agents on the ground in Europe, including an increasing number of slave-labourers, eager to harm the Germans but wholly untrained in intelligence work, and, probably most important of all in detecting new enemy weapons like the rocket, the Central Interpretation Unit, Medmenham, a large country house in Buckinghamshire where every week the thousands of photographs taken by RAF reconnaissance aircraft over Germany and Occupied Europe were scrutinized. As a result of the personal contacts he had established, Dr Jones was uniquely placed to assess the value of the reports that crossed his desk, for he often knew personally the pilot who had flown a particular sortie or the official who had compiled a specific report. Thanks to Lindemann's sponsorship – though this probably did him little good in the growing number of quarters where Lindemann was already detested – he had as early as 1940 found himself at a top-level meeting addressing the Prime Minister on the threat from German navigational beams. In February 1941 he became Assistant Director of Intelligence (Scientific Intelligence) at the Air Ministry, a post he combined with that of being scientific adviser to MI6, and thereafter his name became even better known in government circles, increasingly carrying an authority far greater than his rank suggested.

On 15 May 1942 a Photographic Reconnaissance Unit pilot in a Spitfire fitted with long-range tanks, on a routine mission to cover Kiel, also brought back some pictures showing a new airfield and buildings on the island of Usedom. The 'second phase' interpreter at Medmenham, concerned with developments not requiring immediate operational response, duly noted 'heavy constructional work', in the shape of large circular earthworks like open rings. The 'third phase' interpreter, to whom the pictures were then passed, a WAAF officer called Constance Babington Smith, whose job it was to look for long-term trends on the enemy side, mentally registered the name Peenemünde, which was new to her, before filing the photographs away. The Scientific Intelligence Branch of the Air Ministry, where it might have produced some response, was not informed.

The section headed by Dr Jones was in fact badly over-worked. Although it had expanded since 1939, he was still one of only five professionally qualified people trying to keep track of evidence of forthcoming changes in German weapons and equipment in the torrent of paper, amounting to an average of 150 foolscap pages, which descended upon them every day. On 20 November 1942 – a month after the Germans' first successful test of an A-4 – he wrote to his immediate superior, the Assistant Chief of Air Staff (Intelligence), pleading for more staff:

There is an extreme danger that something vital will be missed. In view of Hitler's recent statement that German inventive genius has not been idle in developing new weapons of offence against the country,* we cannot afford to relax our watch as we have been forced to do. . . . Unless some relief is forthcoming, the present Assistant Directorate cannot accept responsibility for surprises which are likely to be sprung upon us by the enemy without the timely warning which has been achieved in the past.

Dr Jones had always believed that a few outstandingly able recruits were more valuable than an army of indifferent intellects, not least because the best way of ensuring that one piece of information was correlated with another was the mind and memory of a single individual. His appeal rapidly resulted in his receiving some first-class reinforcements, including a physicist with pre-war industrial and defence experience who spoke German, French, Dutch and Russian; a former RAF intelligence officer with a science degree; and a professor of mathematics, appointed to his chair at the age of twenty-nine. A key position was that of Dr Jones's assistant, Charles (later Sir Charles) Frank, an Oxford contemporary of his own, and a chemistry specialist, who had worked for two years in Berlin. 'A theorist', in Dr Jones's judgement, rather than 'an experimenter', he had nevertheless, while in Germany, done a little unofficial spying on German radar developments at his friend's

---

*In his speech in Munich on 8 November 1942, during the annual celebration of the unsuccessful Nazi *Putsch* of 1923.

request, and had finally joined him at Broadway in November 1940. Charles Frank's special role was to study closely but critically the material that flowed into the office, including the often long but rarely very informative transcripts of the interrogation of prisoners of war, and the shorter, but not necessarily more reliable, telegrams that arrived from British representatives abroad.

Just before Christmas 1942 a telegram, dated 18 December, arrived from Stockholm reporting that a new source, soon afterwards identified as a Danish chemical engineer, had 'overheard conversation between Professor Fauner of Berlin Technische Hochschule and engineer Stefan Szenassi on a new German weapon. Weapon is a rocket containing five tons explosive with a maximum range of 200 kilometres, with a danger area of 10 kilometres square'. This was much more specific than the vague rumours from unnamed informants so often featured in reports from abroad and its implications were still being considered when a second message, dated 12 January 1943, arrived from Sweden. 'The Germans', it asserted, 'have constructed a new factory at Peenemünde, near Börfhöft, where new weapons are manufactured. . . . The new weapon is in the form of a rocket which has been seen fired from the testing ground.' As so often, the accuracy of the whole report was called in question because it included one detail too many, which seemed highly dubious. The rocket, it was stated, 'was previously tested in South America'. Nevertheless the informant seemed genuine, since he included photographs of German airborne radar aerials, of obvious value to the British, their authenticity being soon afterwards confirmed when a night-fighter equipped with them landed in Scotland, its crew having decided they had had enough of the war.

Between the second Stockholm dispatch and this unexpected confirmation of it, three other reports had also reached London, allegedly originating in Germany during February. One referred to both rockets and 'rocket guns', said to exist in large numbers. A second spoke of a rocket 50–60 feet in length, 13 to 16½ feet in diameter, with a warhead of 550 lb, already successfully tested at Peenemünde. A third claimed that a rocket with a range of 75 miles, built by Krupps, was 'being installed on the Channel coast'. This contradictory testimony, all too typical of the raw material of intelligence work, was sufficient merely to arouse suspicion, but other evidence, far more suggestive, was now to arrive from a far more promising source.

On the afternoon of Saturday, 27 March 1943, a comparative calm hung over the SIS headquarters at 54 Broadway. Several officials had left to enjoy the weekend, and Dr Jones and Dr Frank, who shared an office, were quietly catching up on their paperwork. Charles Frank was, as so often, reading the transcript of a conversation between German prisoners, but this was an unusual one. Prepared five days before, it recorded the exchanges between two German generals, brought together in a 'bugged' room after five months of separation following their capture in North Africa. The inadequate microphones of the time meant that the transcript included some frustrating gaps, but what General von Thoma had said to his old friend, General Crüwell, once Rommel's second-in-command, was still sufficient to arouse the suspicions even of someone not specifically looking out for references to the rocket.

Von Thoma, realizing that they were near London – probably in fact at Ham Common near Richmond, though he could not have guessed this – began by expressing surprise that they had heard no loud explosions, which suggested that 'No progress whatever can have been made in this rocket business'. He went on:

I saw it once with Feldmarschall Brauchitsch. There is a special ground near Kunersdorf [i.e. Kummersdorf]. . . . They've got these huge things which they've brought up here. . . . They've always said they would go 15 kilometres into the stratosphere. . . . You only aim at an area. . . . The major there was full of hope; he said 'Wait until next year and the fun will start!'

Von Thoma was, as R. V. Jones knew, the 'most technically informed' of the senior officers captured by the Allies, so Jones needed no convincing when 'Charles Frank . . . looked up and said, "It looks as though we'll have to take these rockets seriously!" ' However, much more information was needed before any worthwhile appreciation of the nature of the rocket threat could be made, and as, in his own phrase, 'a watchdog' on enemy activities he considered it essential not to 'bark' too soon, or too often. He therefore contented himself with informing Lord Cherwell of his anxieties and putting in hand 'a perfectly normal, if exhilarating' search for the truth, establishing which was 'a straight intelligence problem' involving recognized procedures:

Agents could be briefed; and in particular there was hope of information coming through the army of foreign labourers that had been recruited to work at Peenemunde. P.R.U. could be asked to photograph the Establishment there. . . . Felkin and his colleagues [who interrogated German airmen] . . . could also be briefed.

Dr Jones also tried 'one very long shot', asking Bletchley and the 'Y' Service to keep track of the movements of the 14th and 15th companies of the German Air Signals Experimental Regiment, likely to be called on if the rocket were to be tracked during trials by radar.

Unfortunately the same transcript was seen by the War Office, which, instead of believing that intelligence material should be kept until a complete picture emerged, favoured distributing the 'raw' sources to operational departments piecemeal, so that they could see the evidence, and not merely the experts' conclusions. As a result, while the Air Ministry was preparing quietly to gather all the information it could about the rocket, the War Office hastened to raise the alarm. On 12 April 1943 General Archibald Nye, Vice-Chief of the Imperial General Staff, informed his fellow Vice-Chiefs of the apparent danger, and, in the absence of the Chiefs of Staff abroad, they agreed that the Prime Minister and Herbert Morrison, Minister of Home Security, responsible for Civil Defence, must be told. General Nye had already consulted two eminent scientists, whose names were later to recur during the rocket investigation: Professor C. D. (later Sir Charles) Ellis, scientific adviser to the Army Council; and Dr A. D. (later Sir Alwyn) Crow, Controller of Projectile Development at the Ministry of Supply, the nearest Great Britain possessed to a Dornberger. The number of people who knew about the rockets now multiplied almost by the hour, for the War Cabinet Secretariat took a hand. One of its senior officials, Brigadier (later Major-General Sir Leslie) Hollis, a regular point of contact between the Cabinet and the Paymaster-General, urged that every department with any possible inerest in the subject ought also to be alerted, including the technical branches of the Air Ministry and the Ministry of Aircraft Production, and perhaps also the Scientific Advisory Council, a high-level panel of scientists from a variety of backgrounds. He also recommended that the Joint Intelligence Sub-Committee, on which all three services were represented and which reported to the Chiefs of Staff, should be asked to study the subject, thus removing it from the Air Ministry's exclusive concern. By background a soldier, not a civil servant, Hollis may himself have felt that all this might involve endless committee meetings and memo writing and little action, for he went on to make a further suggestion:

In view of the importance of the subject, the Vice-Chiefs of Staff might care to consider recommending to the Prime Minister that one individual, who could devote a considerable amount of time to the matter, should be appointed to take charge of the investigations, so as to ensure that no aspect is overlooked and that the work is pressed on with all speed.

The Vice-Chiefs went one better, arguing that the person selected should be drawn from outside the existing intelligence agencies, which ruled out the obvious, Air Ministry, candidate, Dr Jones.

On 15 April 1943 Major-General Sir Hastings ('Pug') Ismay (later General Lord Ismay), who was Chief of Staff to Churchill in his capacity of Minister of Defence, and his personal representative on the Chiefs of Staff Committee, gave formal recognition to the rocket threat in a note to the Prime Minister:

The Chiefs of Staff feel that you should be made aware of reports of German experiments with long-range rockets. The fact that five reports have been received since the end of 1942 indicates a foundation of fact even if details are inaccurate.

4

A DECISIVE WEAPON OF WAR

The Führer considers that this is a decisive weapon of war.

Albert Speer, German Minister of Munitions, 8 July 1943

The cheerful atmosphere that hung over Peenemünde after the spectacularly successful test of 3 October 1942 soon evaporated. To produce the A-4 on a large scale for operational use by December 1943, the earliest practicable date, it needed to be given super-priority at once, not merely for chemicals, machinery and a variety of ancillary items but, in Dornberger's words, for 'production planners, statisticians, designers and engineers'. The ordinary channels were quite inadequate to cope with a totally new weapon of this complexity. 'The state', wrote Dornberger, 'must either make up its mind at last to put the A-4 project into operation in earnest . . . or else work on the long-range rocket ought to be given up.' Dornberger pressed his case in memos 'to the highest authorities both civilian and military', prepared in octuplicate, no less, and made numerous 'begging expeditions' (as he called them) to Berlin, but, he complained, 'nothing was said about any raising of priority or orders to the Ministry of Munitions to give us all possible assistance'.

Dornberger's frustration was understandable, but he was not as ill used as he suggested. On 22 December 1942 Hitler signed a decree drafted by his Munitions Minister, Albert Speer, authorizing the mass-production of the A-4, though failing to give it special priority. On the following day the German War Office officially confirmed that the pilot factory at Peenemünde had as large a claim on German resources as any other 'giant industrial concern' and gave Dornberger plenary powers over its production both there and at Friedrichshafen, where the managers of the Zeppelin works had offered floor space for a production line. At a meeting in Berlin on 8 January 1943 Albert Speer promised on his own authority as head of the Todt organization, responsible for major constructional projects, to put in hand the building of launching sites on the Channel coast and, in his capacity of Minister of Munitions, assigned one of his most dynamic officials to take charge of A-4 production in cooperation with Dornberger – Gerhard Degenkolb, a successful businessman with little regard for established procedures, a German 'Beaverbrook'.

Dornberger took against Degenkolb the moment the latter entered Speer's office:

In came a man of middle height and middle age, with a well nourished appearance. In his round, sallow, face, the obliquely set, keen blue eyes darted restlessly hither and thither. Prominent swellings above his eyebrows and the clearly-marked veins in his temples were evidence of a hasty temper. . . . Degenkolb's completely bald and spherical head, his soft, loose cheeks, bull neck and fleshy lips revealed a tendency towards good living and sensual pleasures, while the restlessness of his powerful hands and the vigour of his movements were evidence of vitality and mental alertness. . . . Degenkolb shook hands with me and promised to work in the closest possible collaboration with me. Then he started telling me about his great successes as chairman of the locomotive production committee. . . . I found myself admiring his energy, his achievements and his ideas. . . . If only the indications of conceit and the repulsive complacency had not been so clearly evident! . . . Many of his phrases indicated a cynically unsympathetic attitude to any organization or scheme which he had not started himself. His claims to exclusive competence were brutally stressed. . . . I noticed that Degenkolb had an absent air and did not even listen to some of my remarks. . . . Degenkolb seemed to belong to that brand of industrialist who automatically assumes that everyone in uniform must be reactionary, narrow-minded and in need of enlightenment. I could already see some stiff fights ahead.

Degenkolb was, Dornberger admitted, 'outwardly most friendly'. His reception from the head of the central office of Speer's Ministry, Karl Otto Saur, was very different. Saur made no secret of his hostility to the whole rocket enterprise, and Dornberger considered him 'our greatest adversary', thanks to his contempt 'for all industrial work initiated or directed by the army'. Certainly on this occasion he behaved with a remarkable lack of discretion:

Just as I was going to my car, Saur appeared and accosted me.
'I suppose you think you've struck it lucky today. . . . But don't be too sure. . . . You haven't yet convinced or won me over, any more than you have the Fuhrer.'

On 11 January 1943 Dornberger attended a meeting at the Army Weapons Office in Berlin where an initial target of around 6000 missiles was agreed, half to be built at Peenemunde and half at Friedrichshafen, and on 15 January Speer formally nominated Degenkolb chairman of the new A-4 committee, responsible for equipping these two assembly plants and subcontracting out the manufacture of the individual components of the A-4. On 24 February the planning board which reported to Degenkolb's committee circulated its detailed programme, prepared by Detmar Stahlknecht, a former director of a division at the Ministry of Munitions with great experience of organizing the mass production of aircraft and the handling of high-quality steel and lightweight alloys. Unlike Degenkolb, he enjoyed Dornberger's confidence, and the figures he produced were sensible and realistic. The factory at Peenemunde, he proposed, should turn out five completed A-4s in April 1943, ten in May and twenty in June. Thereafter production would gradually be shared between Peenemunde and Friedrichshafen until each factory was turning out 100 a month, a rate that would rise to 200 in April 1944, 300 in May, 500 in June, 550 in August and 600 in September. This would see 5150 rockets delivered by the end of 1944, a respectable total if not the flood which Dornberger would have preferred. These figures were not, however, good enough for Gerhard Degenkolb, who had his reputation as an industrial miracle-worker to consider. 'He acted', Dornberger complained, 'like a burly, unendingly foul-mouthed and dreaded slave-driver', who refused 'to grasp that instead of engine bogies we were dealing with extremely delicate potentiometers' and having 'inspected the experimental missiles assembly hall and many workshops' threw off a stream of impractical suggestions for 'the improvement of working processes and . . . simplifying construction'. Degenkolb now raised the targets from 80, in

October 1943, to 300, and from 100, in December 1943, to 300, earmarking an additional factory for the purpose, the Rax works at Wiener Neustadt. This programme Dornberger considered 'a mere illusion' which could not possibly be reached, but it was by no means the worst of his troubles, all of which he now attributed to the hated Degenkolb. 'For him,' Dornberger complained bitterly after the war, while the memory still rankled, 'competent authorities, "channels" or any limitation of his scope did not exist. He negotiated over the heads of superiors with anyone he pleased and set people wherever it suited him without the slightest regard for any work they might be doing.'

Worse was to come. In February a mysterious professor – in Germany no one could get far without some form of academic title – turned up to propose turning the factory into a private limited company, run by some such concern as AEG or Siemens, with the state owning all the capital until the war was won.* Two weeks later another professor who was actually a director of AEG appeared, supposedly to inspect the electrical side of the plant, before re-materializing as chairman of a new development commission for jet-propelled missiles. Then four hitherto unknown engineers arrived, sent by Degenkolb to acquire experience of the A-4 before becoming directors of the test plants which would approve the rocket prior to its delivery to the army, though Dornberger believed they were part of a plot by his hated rival to turn Peenemunde 'into a private concern of his own'. Dornberger ultimately complained to Speer of Degenkolb's interference but got a dusty answer. Unable to get higher priority for the rocket, Speer explained, he had done the next best thing, provided a man of proven ability and strong temperament to make the best possible use of existing resources, and the two should have 'found some way of getting on together'. Meanwhile Dornberger was offered two consolation prizes, promotion to major-general, and the promise of an audience with the Fuhrer.

Hitler remained lukewarm about the future of the rocket.

---

*As Dornberger pointed out, the professor's valuation, of 1–2 million marks, was a ludicrous underestimate, the true figure being 'several hundred million'. Its annual budget alone was already 150 million RM (£13.2 million).

In January 1943 he had been enthusiastic when Speer had discussed with him plans for large bomb-proof bunkers in northern France to serve as both storage and launching sites for the rockets, but during a further visit, between 5 and 10 March, he told Speer, according to the official text circulated within the Ministry of Munitions, 'I have dreamed that the rocket will never be operational against England. I can rely on my inspirations. It is therefore pointless to give more support to the project.' Less used to Hitler's strange mixture of intuitive brilliance and credulous superstition than those closer to him, Dornberger, when he discovered this statement, was outraged. 'Not only had we to struggle with red tape and lack of vision in high places,' he wrote in his post-war memoirs, when it was safe to put such thoughts on paper, 'but also nowadays, with the dreams of our supreme War Lord', and, most incautiously, he made a similar remark to his heads of department at Peenemünde. Whether or not Hitler's dream ever happened – and it is possible that Speer invented the story to cover his failure to obtain higher priority for the rocket, though this seems unlikely – rocket manufacture went ahead and at least one new supporter in high places was secured, Fritz Sauckel, Reich's Director of Manpower, who paid a highly successful overnight visit to Peenemünde on 13–14 May 1943. He was greeted with a guard of honour and was wined and dined in the senior staff mess, and next morning the sun beat down and the sky was clear during the firing of an A-4 for the visitor's benefit. It functioned perfectly and a whole succession of VIPs followed, including Speer himself, Colonel-General Fromm, C-in-C of the German Home Army, and Grand Admiral Dönitz, over-lord of the German navy. Enormous care was taken over their entertainment, even down to written orders assigning responsibility for ensuring that there was soap in the cloakroom, and the A-4 gained many new champions. The real challenge to it came from nearer home, in the Luftwaffe Experimental Station at Peenemünde West, where ever since March 1942, a totally different long-range weapon, the flying-bomb, had been under development.

The flying-bomb, then known to the Germans at the Fi.103 or FZG 76, was everything that the rocket was not: cheap, easy to perfect, simple to manufacture – and likely to be ready for action soon. Dornberger was well aware that the rocket programme, for 5000 rockets, was threatened by this upstart rival, which cost a mere £125 a machine and could, it was predicted, he turned out at the rate of 5000 a month. He was relieved, rather than alarmed, when it was decided to demonstrate both together for the benefit of an audience of Nazi ministers and generals, being confident that the awe-inspiring sight of the A-4 rising dramatically into the stratosphere could not fail to impress all who saw it.

The strange shoot-off, regarded by all concerned as something of a sporting competition, took place on 26 May 1943 in front of most of the recent visitors to Peenemunde, plus Goring's deputy, Field Marshal Milch, and all the members of the Long-Range Bombardment Commission, headed by a recent less welcome visitor, Professor Petersen of AEG, which was supposed to oversee the production of both weapons. The day began with a wide-ranging discussion in the main Peenemunde mess of the relative merits of the two weapons on paper, in which, while acknowledging some of the flying-bomb's advantages, Dornberger did his best to stress the rocket's unique benefits:

The A-4 rocket could be freely launched in any direction with little difficulty . . . and, once launched, there was no defence against it. Dispersion, with proper servicing and testing before firing, was less than that of the Fi. 103. Because of the high speed of impact the effect . . . would be greater with the same load of high explosive. The impact would come as a complete surprise owing to the high supersonic speed. The launching site itself would be difficult or impossible to identify from the air.

He also candidly set out the case against the rocket.

Its disadvantages, in addition to higher costs, were vulnerable installations for testing and supply and the necessity for bomb-proof plants for liquid oxygen. Moreover, as a result of the high alcohol consumption and the low supplies of spirit available, output would be fairly low. Finally, in view of the complexity and delicacy of the components . . . spare parts would have to be available on a rather elaborate scale.

Rather than trying to denigrate his rival, Dornberger wisely suggested that there was room for both weapons in Germany's armoury, advice which the commission accepted, and they decided to recommend that both should be put into production with top priority. The party then moved out to the firing range, where, in bright sunshine, it was 3 October 1942 all over again. Both rockets behaved perfectly, achieving the remarkable flight of 160 miles. But there was one difference. This time the Luftwaffe's flying-bomb was tested too. The first to be fired crashed miserably into the Baltic after only a mile or two, and the second proved equally unsuccessful. Milch, leading the airforce team and a great advocate of the flying-bomb, put the best face on events that he could, clapping Dornberger jovially on the back, as he remarked: 'Congratulations! Two–nought in your favour.' Albert Speer was equally encouraging. 'I was convinced you would succeed,' he told Dornberger. Even more remarkable was the conversion of an old enemy, the head of the central office of Speer's ministry, as Dornberger described:

On the way to the reception room I ran into Saur. He shook hands with me.

'I never knew, I never even dreamed you'd get so far! . . . You have convinced me. From now on I shall be one hundred percent behind you. . . . Come and see me if you want anything, either alone or with Degenkolb.'

Saur's support was to prove more embarrassing than his opposition, for he now began to out-Degenkolb Degenkolb in his efforts to increase A-4 production. At a conference in (somewhat inappropriately) huts erected in the Berlin Zoo in July, Saur astonished a conference of 250 managers and technical staff from the major firms assigned contracts for A-4 components, by announcing that the Degenkolb programme, which Dornberger thought impossible to achieve, was to be raised dramatically 'from 800 to 2,000 units a month as from December'. While 'Degenkolb, beaming, shook hands with me,' wrote Dornberger, 'Professor von Braun . . . was giving me imploring and despairing looks, shaking his head again and again in incredulous astonishment' – as well he might. Even if, by some near miracle, the three existing factories, and a fourth now under construction at Nordhausen, could produce 2000 rockets a month, another great bottleneck, that of fuel supply, would remain, for 'oxygen-generating plant could not be conjured from nowhere', so that liquid oxygen 'could not be guaranteed even for 900 units a month', while 'how much alcohol we should have depended on the potato harvest'. But Degenkolb, in the chair, and Saur, now his ardent supporter, were deaf to all entreaties. Dornberger tried to reintroduce a note of realism by stressing that any increase in the supply of components at the expense of reliability would be worse than useless. 'Better', he urged, 'fewer rockets of first-rate quality than masses of inferior ones that cannot be used except as scrap.' But Degenkolb and Saur were interested only in production figures; they, after all, would not have to use the rocket in action. One manufacturer who attempted to explain his difficulties in increasing output of a key piece of equipment, the mechanism for feeding liquid oxygen to the A-4, was rudely interrupted. 'I am not interested in your difficulties,' Degenkolb told him, and when the industrialist replied that he must consult his staff before undertaking to meet the new schedule Saur also intervened, threatening to dismiss him from his post and to hand the firm over to trustees. Others who raised similar points met with the same treatment until, as Dornberger observed, 'opposition and objections grew weaker and weaker until finally the heads of firms, when asked whether they could meet the schedule, merely nodded resignedly'. They were, he decided, demoralized by being publicly reproved like naughty schoolboys and 'so completely convinced of the impossibility of meeting Saur's requirements that they believed there would be no harm in agreeing'.

Peenemünde now acquired an even more powerful and even less welcome friend than Saur, Heinrich Himmler, Minister of the Interior and head of the Gestapo, who invited himself for a brief visit early in April 1943. To Dornberger Himmler looked, as they talked in the Mess, 'like an intelligent elementary school-teacher' and he 'possessed the rare gift of attentive listening. Sitting back with legs crossed, he wore throughout the same amiable and interested expression. His questions showed that he unerringly grasped what the technicians told him.' Less reassuring, however, was Himmler's offer to protect Peenemünde 'against sabotage and treason' once Hitler had finally endorsed the A-4 programme, since the last thing the army wanted was a Gestapo presence there. The mere threat brought General Becker's successor as head of the Army Weapons Department, General Leeb, hurrying to Peenemunde, and Himmler was, for the moment, bought off by the tactful suggestion that he should declare 'a prohibited zone round Peenemunde' and should order 'a tightening up of security measures in northern Usedom and the adjacent mainland', a task entrusted to the police commissioner for Stettin, himself an SS general. For the moment the army was allowed to retain responsibility for security at Peenemunde itself, though Gestapo spies were installed in the nearby town of Zinnowitz, where the scientists went for recreation, with instructions, Dornberger suspected, to 'watch us rather than . . . local inhabitants and strangers'. More seriously, the official commandant of the whole establishment, Colonel Zanssen, was, on SS instructions, relieved of his duties on 26 April, after various vague but alarming charges had been made against him, and transferred back to Berlin.

On 29 June Himmler paid his promised second, and longer, visit to Peenemunde, entertaining the assembled scientists until four in the morning with an account of Hitler's racial theories and the Nazi plans to colonize Russia and Poland. Although Dornberger claims to have 'shuddered at the everyday manner in which the stuff was retailed' – 'We hardly ever discussed politics at Peenemunde,' he insisted – he and his colleagues seem to have been untroubled to discover the sort of New Order their work was helping to establish and to have been undismayed by Himmler's promise of 'severe punishments', at the first hint of sabotage or spying, for the foreign, forced labour he wished them to employ. Nor was he deterred from laying on the demonstration planned for Himmler's benefit next morning, a grey, overcast day on which everything went wrong. By now thirty-seven A-4s had been fired, twenty-three of them since the first major success on 3 October 1942, but number 38 proved what the launching team had nicknamed 'a reluctant virgin'. It had hardly left the ground when it plunged back to earth, this time on the Luftwaffe airfield at Peenemünde West, two miles away, where no one was hurt, though three aircraft were destroyed. Himmler, still in a good humour despite his late night, joked that he could now recommend the A-4 as a close-combat weapon, while one of the men from

Peenemünde, not to be outdone in wit, commented that it had also justified its description as a revenge weapon; only a few days before, one of the Luftwaffe's flying bombs had landed near the army's Development Works, also without casualties. A second test that afternoon,* however, went off perfectly, and Himmler parted from Dornberger on good terms, promising 'to put our point of view to Hitler', though adding 'that he could help us only if Hitler's decision were favourable.'

At last, on 7 July 1943, came the opportunity, promised months earlier by Albert Speer, for Dornberger and his colleagues to demonstrate their progress before Hitler in person. Dornberger prepared for the great occasion carefully, taking with him a whole range of visual aids that might capture Hitler's interest, including 'coloured sectional drawings . . . the manual for field units' and a large-scale model of the massive storage and launching site already planned for the Channel coast, complete with 'models of the vehicles one detachment required'. The star item was a film of a successful launching, for Dornberger attributed Hitler's lack of enthusiasm for the rocket so far to his never having seen, 'even in a photograph, the ascent of a long-range rocket' or 'experienced the thrill provided by the huge missile in flight'. To support him, Dornberger selected von Braun, the most impressive and articulate of his lieutenants, and the young and enthusiastic Dr Steinhoff now head of his Instruments, Guidance and Measurement Department, who was also a qualified pilot. Through the thick fog which blanketed eastern Germany Steinhoff groped his way, with radio help, towards Hitler's 'Wolf's Lair' at Rastenburg. Beyond the Vistula the skies cleared and 'below us, as far as the eye could see,' observed Dornberger, 'stretched the dark forests of East Prussia, plentifully adorned with glittering lakes and occasionally flower-decked meadows'. Having risked their lives to get there on time the little party now found their appointment had been postponed till 5 o'clock that afternoon and when Hitler finally appeared, escorted by

---

*Dornberger p. 186. David Irving, p. 74, places the second test at 10.10 a.m. The two sources also disagree about the weather in the morning, which Dornberger says was 'fine' but Irving describes as ten-tenths cloud. Both agree the afternoon was fine.

General Wilhelm Keitel, head of the Supreme Command, General Alfred Jodl, C-in-C of the army – their old friend von Brauchitsch had been dismissed in disgrace after the army's failure in Russia – Jodl's Chief of Staff, General Buhle, and Albert Speer, Dornberger was shocked by the deterioration in the Fuhrer's appearance since he had last seen him at Kummersdorf in 1939. 'A voluminous black cape covered his bowed, hunched shoulders and bent back. He looked a tired man. Only the eyes retained their life.' To Hitler the presentation was clearly just one more event in a wearying day. To the rocket men it was the unique, all-important opportunity of a lifetime, and Dornberger later recalled every detail:

After briefly greeting us he sat down between Speer and Keitel in the front row. . . . On to the screen came the historic ascent of the A-4 which had so enraptured us at the time and everyone who had seen it since. Von Braun spoke his commentary. The shots were thrilling. The sliding gates, nearly ninety feet high, of the great assembly hall of Test Stand VII opened. . . . A completely assembled A-4 rolled slowly out of the hall and over the great blast tunnel sunk in the ground. . . . The men in attendance shrank to nothing. . . . The rocket was loaded on to the transporter scheduled for field use, a *Meillerwagen*. Driving tests on the road and in cornering proved the remarkable ease with which the rocket could be carried. Soldiers operating a hydraulic crane set the rocket vertically on the firing table, so astonishingly simple in design. The *Meiller's* hydraulic machinery handled the 46 foot rocket . . . like a toy. Sequences showing fuelling and preparations for launching proved the missile capable for use under field conditions. Finally came the actual launching . . . followed by animated cartoons of the trajectory of the shot on 3rd October, indicating speeds, heights and range reached on that day. . . . The end of the film was announced by a sentence which filled the entire screen: 'We made it after all!'. . . . Von Braun ceased speaking. Silence . . . . No-one dared utter a word. Hitler was visibly moved and agitated. Lost in thought, he lay back in his chair, staring gloomily in front of him. When, after a while, I began to enter into some lengthy explanations he came to with a start and listened attentively. . . . At last . . . I stopped speaking and awaited questions. Hitler walked rapidly over to me and shook my hand. I heard him say, almost in a whisper: 'I thank you. . . . Why was it I could not believe in the success of your work? If we had had these rockets in 1939 we should never have had this war.'

As the team had foreseen, Hitler's imagination was particularly caught by the model of the proposed firing bunker, which must, he insisted, with his familiar obsession with detail, have a roof 23 feet thick; Dornberger's preference for small, mobile batteries he brushed aside. Within minutes a 'strange fanatical light' had flared up in his eyes and he was demanding 2000 rockets a month, each able to deliver a 10 ton warhead, and shouting 'What I want is annihilation!' Eventually, however, he calmed down and the meeting ended agreeably, with Hitler announcing that he had created von Braun a professor – though of what and where was not clear – while Dornberger was given an even more striking indication of the Führer's favour:

Halfway to the door, he suddenly turned round and walked back to me.

'I have had to apologise to two men only in my life. The first was Field-Marshal von Brauchitsch. I did not listen to him when he told me again and again how important your research was. The second man is yourself. I never believed that your work would be successful.'

He walked out of the room with his suite. We were left alone.

That evening, while Hitler, to universal relief, ate alone, Speer entertained the three scientists to a modest celebratory meal of soup, fish and sweet with a glass of wine, but coffee, brandy and cigars followed, and eventually they made a night of it, keeping up the celebrations till 7 a.m. Already Dornberger, a born worrier, had a new anxiety, for Hitler, he realized, expected the A-4 'to produce a turning point in the war', while Dornberger himself recognized that 'the military situation had long ceased to be such' that even 'launching 900 . . . a month' could snatch victory from defeat. He would have been even more troubled had he been present at the subsequent meeting between Hitler and Speer, as later described by the latter:

Hitler . . . was greatly impressed and his imagination had been kindled. Back in his bunker he became quite ecstatic about the possibilities of this project. 'The A-4 is a measure that can decide the war. And what encouragement to the Home Front when we attack the English with it! This is the decisive weapon of the war. . . . Speer, you must push the A-4 as hard as you can! Whatever labour and materials they need must be supplied instantly.'

For once, Hitler was as good as his word. The decree he was about to sign giving the highest priority to tank production was now amended to put the A-4 on a par with it. The effects were immediate, especially on the Luftwaffe's flying-bomb programme and its orders for other new weapons. A conference at the Air Ministry on 13 July heard one industrial representative complaining bitterly that companies who refused new A-4 contracts because they were fully stretched already were told bluntly 'You've got no option – this is DE production', i.e. it enjoyed super-priority, while a factory already making Wasserfall (Waterfall), a new and highly promising rocket-powered anti-aircraft missile, had simply been requisitioned to produce A-4 components instead. Even worse was the loss of specialist staff. The army, it was also learned, had simply absorbed into the A-4 programme 500 technicians lent it by the Luftwaffe to work at Peenemünde on Wasserfall. At a conference at the Air Ministry on 29 July 1943, in the middle of the RAF's devastating series of raids on Hamburg named Operation Gomorrah, the Luftwaffe men agreed to hang on to their skilled labour wherever they could, but four days later, on 3 August, both Speer and Milch were present at a further meeting at which it was reported that 'a man turned up at the Daimler-Benz factory and said that all 103 [i.e. flying-bomb] production is being shut down and that A-4 rockets will be manufactured instead'. Speer denied that his ministry was to blame and on 17 August issued a new directive stating that 'the Air Force's manufacturing programme is not to be interfered with by the A-4 programme', but inevitably the latter's demands were now being felt over the whole of the skilled engineering industry. The Heinkel factory at Jenbach, instead of making ordinary aircraft motors, was turning out the most complicated part of the whole rocket, its pump turbine, and in the Freiburg area alone 36 firms, each employing up to 200 workers, were making magnetos and control gear.

Even that scientific perfectionist, von Braun, and the usually pessimistic Dornberger, were reasonably content with the way things were going. They had flown back from the triumphant meeting with Hitler at Rastenburg in a mood of elation. Dornberger, as they crossed the coast over Zinnowitz and began the descent over Swinemünde Bay, was 'delighted . . .

with the view of Peenemunde from the air and the vast extent and magnificence of the Army and Air Force establishments hidden in its forest solitudes'. On the ground he took an equal satisfaction in the dedication and brilliance of the men around him, not merely the senior scientists like von Braun – though 'it was a never ending joy . . . to take part in the development of this great rocket expert . . . from his youth up' – but of more junior employees, like the cameraman whom he watched climbing up on a safety wall to film the explosion of a rocket which had come down only forty yeards away. ('I was', wrote Dornberger, 'filled with an immense pride. Only in this fashion, only with men like that, could we finish the job that lay before us.')

By mid-August everything seemed set fair for the rocket's future. Far away in France the construction of the great launching bunkers had already begun. The vehicles required for the mobile launching units to be based within it were on order, the troops who would man them were being selected, and, thanks to Saur and Degenkolb and the Führer's blessing, a large-scale production programme was under way. Even the Gestapo was proving cooperative; the exiled Colonel Zanssen had been cleared and would be returning to Peenemunde shortly. When his work allowed, Dornberger enjoyed wandering about the empire he had created on this peninsula hitherto given over only to woods and sand-dunes, and this was how he soothed his nerves, around 4 o'clock on the afternoon of Thursday, 17 August 1943, after a rare argument with his senior staff; they had threatened to resign *en masse* and return to academic life because they were finding the pressure from Degenkolb intolerable. He had managed to calm them down and attributed the tension in the air to the weather. 'For days the sun had been blazing down on the arid, sandy soil of the island of Usedom. We were longing for a cooling thunderstorm.' In any case there was consolation in his office, with its 'gaily printed curtains . . . handsome gleaming quantities of flowers, rugs and pictures' – the Germans did their scientists better than the Ministry of Works treated their British counterparts – and even more in the sight of the 'big assembly hall of the pre-production works', recently finished after a year's delay, where soon A-4s, hitherto built only in single units for test purposes, would begin to be assembled in their hundreds 'to cover a third of the Degenkolb Schedule':

I passed through a small door in the roughly boarded main entrance over 60 feet high into the hall, which rose to a height of 100 feet. The white roughcast walls gave the room, with its five divisions, its central aisle 200 feet wide and its four side aisles separated by pillars, an almost solemn appearance at this evening hour. I crossed the double rail-track leading into the hall and went up the ramp to the assembly hall proper, 80 feet high.

The view seen from here of the depth of the central aisle, over 600 feet long, hemmed in on each side by 16 strong, square and gleaming concrete pillars, foreshortened from this point, and the rear wall fading into blue mists, once again held me spellbound. I lingered a long time. Potent joy swept over me. This hall must be thronged with happy, contented workers. I must hear in it the roaring, pounding, whirling, whistling, humming, ringing, infinitely varied sounds of work in progress. I was more than ever certain that we should pull it off!

5

A DISTINCTLY UNPLEASANT PROSPECT

The prospect of these bombs with some 7–10 tons of high explosive falling at intervals in populated areas . . . is not at all a pleasant one.

Sir Stafford Cripps, Minister of Aircraft Production, to the Prime Minister, 16 June 1943

The paper the British War Office circulated on 'German Long-Range Rocket Development' on 12 April 1943, the first formal warning of the impending threat, was in some respects surprisingly accurate. Although it referred to a missile 95 feet long, its estimates of the rocket's all-up weight, 9½ tons, and its warhead, 1 ton, were remarkably close to the mark. Unfortunately, however, and getting the whole investigation off on the wrong foot, the document predicted that the rocket's fuel would be cordite, the standard even-burning propellant used in ordinary cartridges, and that it would be fired from huge projectors, a hundred yards long. Because the British had so far failed to develop a self-contained, liquid-fuelled projectile, the Germans, it was assumed, must have failed, too.

On 15 April the Vice-Chiefs of Staff not merely endorsed the proposal, originating within the Cabinet Secretariat, for a single individual to direct the search for evidence of the rocket's existence, and its likely nature, but actually submitted 'for your consideration the name of Mr Duncan Sandys'. No doubt soundings about its acceptability had been taken beforehand and the nomination was rapidly accepted.

Still only thirty-five, and a man of dynamic energy likely to keep his subordinates on their toes, Duncan Sandys, though relatively junior for such a responsible assignment, was on the face of it a sound but imaginative choice. After a conventional

63

background, at Eton, at Oxford and in the diplomatic service, he had entered the House of Commons as MP for Norwood in 1935, had served with an anti-aircraft battery in Norway and later, as a lieutenant-colonel, had commanded the first British rocket regiment, before being invalided out of the army after a car accident and becoming Parliamentary Secretary to the Ministry of Supply, responsible for its weapon research and development work. As the husband of Churchill's daughter Diana he was often in Downing Street and close to the Prime Minister, while, as a politician, he was supposedly free of bias towards any of the services. Lord Cherwell, however, who had not, surprisingly, been consulted on Sandys's appointment, was unenthusiastic about it. The Air Ministry Intelligence Branch was also disappointed. 'It did not seem to occur to the Chiefs of Staff', reflected R. V. Jones, when his old professor broke to him the news of Sandys's selection, 'that they already had a Scientific Intelligence component inside their organization.' To his assistant, Charles Frank, he commented 'that Sandys had been appointed to do a job that we already had in hand and for which our qualifications were much better'. Jones resolved that 'we would continue to keep an eye on everything so as to be able to step in if there were signs of a breakdown', but it was not a happy beginning.

As soon as he learned, on 20 April 1943, of Duncan Sandys's appointment, Lord Cherwell did his best to prejudge the results of the forthcoming investigation. On the following day he invited Dr A. D. Crow, then in charge of British rocket development and one of Sandys's own advisers at the Ministry of Supply, to his flat to hear his own views, which on the following day he set out in a minute to the Prime Minister. Cherwell had already made up his mind that a large solid-fuel rocket, fired from a projector, was unlikely:

Though this possibility cannot be ruled out . . . I have the impression that the technical difficulties would be extreme. . . . The firing point must obviously be in the neighbourhood of Calais. If the launching rails were above ground, they would be easily observed and not very difficult to destroy by bombing. If below ground, there would be terrible problems in bringing forward and handling these ten-ton projectiles especially as all the loading gear would have to be carefully insulated from the rocket . . . before the four tons of cordite [required to launch it] were touched off. The rocket would emerge at comparatively slow speed, so that accuracy would be severely impaired by wind. . . . Without hearing all the evidence my opinion is not worth very much, but, as at present advised, I should be inclined to bet against such rockets being used.

The search for the nonexistent rocket projector was to bedevil the rocket investigation for many months to come. On 19 April the first Air Ministry directive to the RAF team at Medmenham had urged them to look out for signs of a 'rocket launched from a tube'. As one historian has put it, 'basically the British were talking about an outsize firework rocket', of the kind familiar from peacetime Bonfire Nights, and were accordingly seeking something like a giant milk bottle from which it might be fired. Since no such apparatus existed none was discovered, but the first full-scale photographic cover of Peenemünde, commissioned on 22 April 1943, did produce some interesting results. A twin-seater Mosquito had been used, enabling the observer to concentrate on the photography while the pilot kept the machine straight and level, and the excellent pictures that resulted were soon under the stereoscopes of the industrial section of the RAF unit at Medmenham. They soon decided that *something* strange was going on, with two large factories to the south-east of the site, an 'elliptical earthwork', noted before but still unidentified, at the northern end, further earthworks to the south-west and, strangest of all, 'on photograph 5010, an object about 25 feet long . . . projecting in a north-westerly direction from the seaward end of the building. When photograph 5011 was taken four seconds later this object had disappeared and a small puff of white smoke or steam was issuing from the seaward end of the building.' On 24 April two acknowledged experts on rockets and explosives respectively came down to Medmenham to study enlargements of all the recent pictures of Peenemünde, but could offer no explanation of the earthworks on the tip of Usedom. In the existing state of knowledge, they could hardly be blamed for not realizing that these were in fact protective walls built round the A-4 launching pads or that the 'smoke or steam' came from liquid oxygen in contact with the air. On 14 May another Mosquito sortie came back with, had it been recognized as such, even more remarkable evidence. Flight-

Lieutenant Kenny, the 'third phase' officer directly concerned, discovered on a truck near the still unexplained earthworks a 'cylindrical object 38 feet by 8 feet', and, taking another look at the pictures taken on 22 April, discovered on them two small blurred white shapes, one of them on a wagon. They were also merely recorded as 'objects'.

That Friday night of 14 May Dr Jones happened to be staying at RAF Benson, where the Mosquito pilots of the Photographic Reconnaissance Unit were based, and was able to explain to them – many already being personal acquaintances – precisely why Peenemünde was so vital, and even the most rewarding angles from which to direct their cameras. It was a fortunate visit, for it led to the officers concerned turning a blind eye when in due course instructions were given 'that all photographs of Peenemünde were to go only to Sandys'.

Three days later Duncan Sandys submitted his first report to the Chiefs of Staff. It was a frank and sensible document:

I do not . . . consider that the evidence available is sufficiently complete or reliable to enable a firm and final opinion to be reached. Of the various reports received there is not one which can by itself be regarded as wholly reliable or conclusive. They contain, moreover, many points of conflict and divergence in matters of detail. . . . In view of the urgency of the matter and of the seriousness of this new menace . . . I have reached the following provisional conclusions:

(a) It would appear that the Germans have for some time past been trying to develop a heavy rocket capable of bombarding an area . . . from very long range. . . .

(b) The development of such a rocket, though extremely difficult, is technically quite possible. . . .

(c) The economic effort involved in the production and projection of such rockets, though very considerable, is not prohibitive when compared with the cost of dropping an equal weight of explosive from aircraft, allowing for the heavy losses which the German air force must now expect.

(d) Very little information is available about the progress of the development of the long-range rocket. However, such scant evidence as exists suggests that it may be far advanced.

(e) From scientific calculations and from the results of special prisoner of war interrogations it would seem likely that the weapon in question is a multi-staged, rocket-propelled projectile with the following very approximate characteristics:

A Distinctly Unpleasant Prospect

Length: 20 ft
Diameter: 10 ft
Total weight: 70 tons
Weight of HE head: up to 10 tons
Max. velocity: 6000 ft per second
Height at zenith: up to 40 miles
Propellant: new fuel with at least twice the calorific content
of cordite.
Range: 100–150 miles.

Duncan Sandys went on to warn that 'heavy attacks of this kind upon London, particularly if gas were employed, would undoubtedly have a very serious effect upon the machinery of government, upon production and upon civilian morale' and that 'it is possible that Portsmouth, Southampton and the larger towns along the south-east coast might also be attacked'. He was not optimistic about counter-measures once the rocket was launched, unless it turned out to be radio-controlled, or of detecting it in flight, and recommended a pre-emptive strike as more likely to be effective. 'The experimental establishments and factories which appear most likely to be connected with the development and production of this weapon . . . together with any suspicious works in the coastal region of north-west France, should', he suggested, 'be subjected to effective bombing attack.'

This report was the first of a long series on similar lines, as Sandys garnered more information and was able to update his conclusions. The pressure on all the departments concerned to produce new facts led to credence being given to some informants whom at other times might have been disregarded. The most famous was a former German army officer, 'Captain C.', later known as Mr Peter Herbert, after he had been given his liberty in return for changing sides and joining the Ministry of Supply. He claimed to have seen 'projectiles . . . weighing one hundred tons and over', and another, weighing 60 tons, actually fired from a ramp inside a launching pit, which had travelled 150 miles over the Baltic. Suspiciously, however, when asked the colour of the missiles' exhaust flame in flight he could only reply that he was colour-blind. Lord Cherwell, making no effort to separate the wheat from the chaff, although most intelligence reports contained both, dismissed Mr Herbert's

67

testimony out of hand. R. V. Jones, with more experience in this field, thought he did have some genuine knowledge to contribute. The claim by a German general to have seen an alcohol-fuelled rocket (probably in fact a Wasserfall) fired from the Greifswalder Oie was also dismissed out of hand; ironically, had he mentioned a solid propellant he might have been believed. A third informant, from a Luftwaffe experimental unit, testified that his CO, while visiting Berchtesgaden, had been assured by Hitler personally that rockets would be fired against England 'this summer', but the idea of the Fuhrer indulging in careless talk was too much for the sceptical British. Less defensibly, the British authorities also disregarded the implications of events in the United States, from which two of the Ministry of Supply's own rocket experts had now returned, having witnessed in May a demonstration of a rocket engine using liquid oxygen and petrol.

On 4 June 1943 the first report reached London from a foreign worker, in fact a scientist from Luxembourg, whom the Germans had conscripted to work for them inside Peenemünde. This was, though no one could have known it at the time, the first detailed and accurate piece of intelligence to arrive, for it referred to a rocket 10 metres long with a range of 150–250 kilometres, and included a sketch showing the location of Test Stand VII. It also – a vital clue – referred to 'bottles containing gas' being used to provide fuel. Lord Cherwell had probably not seen this latest message when, on 11 June 1943, he wrote a further memo to the Prime Minister casting doubt on the reality of the threat from the rocket, which he still assumed to be a 70 ton monster burning solid fuel:

There seems little doubt that the Germans have been working on long-range rockets, but what evidence there is also indicates that there have been serious difficulties. This is scarcely surprising. To construct jets which would stand for some 10 seconds the passage at about 1½ miles a second of the hot gases produced by burning 20 tons of cordite might well keep an engineering team busy for years. . . . To handle 70-ton projectiles and shift them from the railway to the launching rails, to insulate this gear from the terrific blast, etc., is no mean technical problem. If the projector is to be inconspicuous all this must be underground. . . . I cannot conceive that the Germans would carry out such elaborate installations in the neighbourhood of Calais without being observed and having their work nipped in the bud.

Cherwell, however, who hated being shown to be wrong, was careful to hedge his bets.

Jones, who you may remember is in charge of scientific Air Intelligence, has been following these questions closely, and I do not think there is any great risk of our being caught napping.

And, having argued that there was no danger from the rocket, Cherwell, somewhat illogically, endorsed Duncan Sandys's proposal for counter-measures against it:

Though I do not think for a moment that they are connected with rockets, I favour bombing, before they are completed, the new emplacements now being built in the Calais region. If it is worth the enemy's while to take all the trouble of putting them up, it would seem well worth our while – or rather the Americans' – to knock them down before their protective concrete roofs are finished.

The Air Ministry, obsessed with its area-bombing campaign against Germany, favoured delay, but Churchill was now under pressure from other quarters. On 16 June the Minister of Aircraft Production, Sir Stafford Cripps, a former member of the War Cabinet and the least alarmist of men, wrote to the Prime Minister pleading for early action:

The prospect of these bombs with some 7–10 tons of high explosive falling at intervals in populated areas with no apparent possibility of dealing with them is not at all a pleasant one and the casualties may be very heavy indeed. . . . I feel that the matter is potentially so serious that the whole question should be considered, particularly the counter-measures that may be possible, whether by bombing, paratroops, commandos, sabotage or any other way. May I suggest that you should initiate a small high-level committee to deal with this matter throughly?

Churchill's reply was reassuring. He was, he assured Cripps next day, 'thoroughly alive to the danger', even though 'Lord Cherwell is extremely sceptical of the practical application', and Cripps was 'welcome to talk to Duncan Sandys on the subject' pending a full-scale meeting at which it would be thrashed out. Meanwhile Dr Jones was, as Cherwell had promised, keeping an eye on the story as it unfolded, and on Friday, 18 June 1943 was studying the results of photographic sortie N/853, flown six days before, when he glimpsed through his stereoscope an object the experts at Medmenham had apparently missed:

Suddenly I spotted on a railway truck something that could be a whitish cylinder about 35 feet long and 5 or so feet in diameter with a bluntish nose and fins at the other end. I experienced the kind of pulse of elation that you get when after hours of casting you realize that a salmon has taken your line. . . . To [Charles] Frank I said in as level a voice as I could 'Charles, come and look at this!' He immediately agreed that I had found the rocket. . . . I went across to the Cabinet Offices and saw Lindemann before he left for the weekend at Oxford. . . . Very generously, I thought, Lindemann said that I should send a note to Sandys telling him that there was a rocket visible on the photograph, to give him a chance to react before I told anyone else.

This courteous gesture produced no response except an undated, supplementary report from Medmenham to the effect that 'the object' shown in the N/853 photograph 'is 35 feet long and appears to have a blunt point' resembling 'a cylinder tapered at one end and provided with three radial fins at the other'; no mention was made that it was Dr Jones who had first drawn attention to it. But on Wednesday, 23 June, a Mosquito of 540 Squadron brought back from sortie N/860 the best set of pictures so far, examined soon afterwards, with growing excitement, by WAAF Section Officer Babington Smith:

Two rockets – actual rockets – had been photographed, lying horizontally on road vehicles within the confines of the elliptical earthwork. . . . Above the rockets towered a structure resembling a massive observation tower and the steep encircling slope of the earthwork might have been some sinister Germanic stadium.

Already Dr Jones had prepared a rough sketch of the rocket's likely appearance which would have been instantly recognizable to anyone at Peenemünde, with its long, slim body, estimated at 35–38 feet long by 5–7 feet wide, its pointed nose and its dominant 10-feet-by-10-feet fins. Its weight he put at 'perhaps 20 to 40 tons', only to alter it after being invited to meet Duncan Sandys, who told him 'that our experts said that it must be at least 80 tons', a figure confirmed, when Jones demurred at it, by one of them by telephone. The latter insisted that any lesser weight was impossible in view of the 'fuel/carcase weight ratio, since the carcase' had 'to be of steel thick enough to stand the pressure of the cordite or other propellant burning in the jet', and, reluctantly and against his own better judgement, Dr Jones amended the already-cut stencil of his report to a probable weight of 'perhaps 40 to 80 tons'.

On 27 June 1943 the Chiefs of Staff circulated a massive paper – it ran to seventeen pages – entitled 'German Long-Range Rocket: Evidence Received from All Sources', which recounted in detail the results of the seven reconnaissance flights undertaken since 15 May, attaching a selection of photographs. Influenced no doubt by the same experts who had persuaded Dr Jones to change his report, the author warned that 'the total weight of the projectiles is between 60 and 100 tons, the probable HE content being 2 to 8 tons'. The estimated flight time was put at '3 seconds for a range of 130 miles and 2 seconds for 90 miles', a grotesque error; even a layman might have realized that 'minutes' would have been more likely. The paper concluded unequivocally that 'Long-Range Rocket development is taking place at Peenemünde' and that 'manufacture or assembly on a moderate scale will shortly be proceeding in the factory area and workshops'.

Duncan Sandys's Third Interim Report the following day, which revealed that in addition to Peenemünde itself nine other suspect areas were now under surveillance, confirmed that 'The German long-range rocket has undoubtedly reached an advanced stage of development' and that it could probably 'be put into operational use at a very early date' if the Germans were willing 'to accept a considerable loss in accuracy and effectiveness'. This was only too likely, warned Sandys:

Reports . . . indicated that Hitler sees in the long-range rocket a means of retaliating against England for the bombing of the Ruhr and that he is pressing for it to be brought into action as quickly as possible, without awaiting the completion of development.

A detailed analysis of the likely means of launching the rocket followed, based on the 'projector' theory; thirty projectors, it was estimated, were under construction of which fifteen had been completed. Far more alarming, however, were the forecasts of the casualties each explosion might cause, based on 'the Hendon incident' of February 1941, when a 2500 kg bomb, the largest so far used against Britain, had killed 75 people and injured 445, also destroying 196 homes, making 170 uninhabitable and inflicting lesser damage on 400 more. It was this section of Sandys's report, headed 'Effect of Rocket Attack upon London', which was to be the basis of most subsequent planning, for it set out in frightening detail what the Ministry of Home Security experts thought each rocket 'containing 10 tons of high explosive' might achieve:

They estimate that a single rocket of this size would cause damage to property over an area of 650 acres. Complete or partial demolition might be expected over an area of a radius of 850 feet and serious damage from blast over an area of a radius of 1700 feet.

The Ministry's estimate of casualties which might be caused by each rocket is as follows:

Killed	600
Seriously injured	1,200
Slightly injured	2,400
	4,200

One such rocket falling in the London area every hour for 24 hours might result in 10,000 killed and 20,000 seriously injured.

The grim prospect facing London was spelt out in even more depressing detail in an 'annexe' to Duncan Sandys's report, prepared by 'Sir Findlater Stewart's Committee', one of those powerful bodies whose very existence was unknown to the general public. Findlater Stewart himself had barely been heard of outside Whitehall but within it he was a highly influential figure, chief adviser on civilian matters to the Commander-in-Chief, Home Forces, and chairman of the Home Defence Executive, which coordinated all the departments involved in the civilian side of the war. An archetypal Establishment man – flat in Cheyne Walk, club, the Athenaeum, in Pall Mall – a civil servant for forty years, now aged sixty-four, he had, improbably, become regarded by Herbert Morrison (whose opinion carried great, if not decisive, weight) as his right-hand man. The advice tendered by the Civil Defence department of the Ministry of Home Security, to which Sir Findlater now lent his vast authority, made frightening reading.

It was, these experts thought, reasonable to anticipate 'one rocket per hour daily for four weeks' and an error of up to four miles in accuracy, so that 'taking the aiming point as TOWER BRIDGE the projectile might be expected to land within a circle bounded by CANNING TOWN on the east, DULWICH on the south, KENSINGTON GARDENS on the west and STOKE NEWINGTON on the north'. How would the Civil Defence services be able to cope with such a scale of attack? The best guide to what might happen was provided by the now famous Hendon Incident two years before:

At Hendon 22 Heavy Rescue Parties, 10 Stretcher Parties, 29 ambulances and 24 motor cars were continuously deployed for 70 hours. . . . On the Hendon analogy some 250 ambulances would be required. . . . A serious traffic problem arises if we envisage the deployment of some 250 vehicles at the incident.

But this traffic jam would be the least of the problems each rocket caused. 'It is probable', the committee thought, 'that at least 12 Incident Officers will be required, or approximately one for every 6 acres [of damage].' And even if these highly trained specialists, who took charge after every explosion and coordinated the response to it, could be mustered, the forces under their command would be inadequate, for twenty-four heavy and forty-eight light rescue parties would be needed 'for every three acres' while 'the wardens service', the backbone of the whole Civil Defence service, 'will be quite inadequate without organized reinforcement or assistance'. The London Region could, it was believed, cope 'with one incident every 12 hours . . . for 6 days and one every 24 hours for perhaps a fortnight . . . if the fall of bombs were reasonably dispersed over the four-mile radius'. By the end of that time all concerned 'would be completely exhausted' and thereafter, if the bombardment continued, the whole Civil Defence organization would be overwhelmed:

It took three days to close the Hendon incident. Assuming each incident due to the new weapon takes five days, then at one per hour we have:

After 1 day	24 active incidents
After 2 days	48 active incidents
After 3 days	72 active incidents
After 4 days	96 active incidents
After 5 days	120 active incidents

The cumulative effect of one such incident every hour for four weeks would be quite beyond the resources of London Region and would, in fact, entail the virtual destruction of the Metropolis. . . . Any extensive use of this weapon might make it quite impossible to carry on the government in London.

Moving ministers and their key officials would not be impossible; most ministries had already made contingency plans for just such an event. The real difficulty lay with the ordinary population. Reactivating official evacuation schemes for the 'priority classes' – mainly expectant mothers, mothers with infants under the age of five, and schoolchildren – would be relatively easy, but, warned Sir Findlater Stewart, 'no organized arrangements can be made for large numbers of aged, infirm, invalids, etc., or for the non-essential general population of London', although once the rockets started to fall 'it is anticipated that considerable numbers of persons will leave London and make arrangements to stay in the reception areas without assistance'. As for those who remained, there were places in 'domestic shelter . . . for 5,454,000 out of the night population of 6,540,000', but only 147,900 places in underground stations and new deep shelters proof against a direct hit, and these presented their own problem 'in that a certain number of people will want to get into them and stay there, and they will be difficult to eject if rockets are frequent'. The whole shelter situation was in fact worse than it had been during the blitz, for only the very briefest warning of a rocket's arrival was anticipated, or none at all. Both at work and at home, therefore, shelter needed to be near at hand, ready for 'a quick entry and a short stay'. But even if more shelters could be provided – and the committee recommended strengthening public surface shelters and ordering another 100,000 Morrison table shelters – people who remained in London faced an uncertain and highly disagreeable future, with far greater 'disruption of water, gas, electricity and sewer services' than anything so far experienced, and serious 'health problems . . .

74

if the damage was so extensive that proper repairs in a reasonable time became impracticable'. Above all, there was the danger to life and limb. As the rockets rained remorselessly down, troops patrolled the streets of the stricken capital and Civil Defence reinforcements 'from the North and Midlands' were assembled 'under canvas if necessary on the outskirts of London', its surviving citizens would be faced by a melancholy and more or less continuous procession of hearses and ambulances, for 'the casualties in 24 hours', it was predicted, 'might exceed 10,000 killed and 20,000 seriously injured' – and that was assuming the rockets 'were reasonably dispersed over the four-mile radius' and that the Germans did not improve their aim.

Faced with this depressing scenario, ministers might almost have been inclined to come to terms with Hitler on the spot, but Churchill was always inclined to discount the more gloomy predictions of his colleagues, while Lord Cherwell still did not believe in the existence of the rocket at all. The meeting of the War Cabinet Defence Committee (Operations) which assembled in the underground conference room in Great George Street at 10 o'clock on the evening of Tuesday, 29 June 1943, was therefore surprisingly cheerful. This was the most senior, and largest, body yet to consider the rocket menace, possessing executive rather than merely advisory powers, and everyone of importance was there, including Herbert Morrison with Sir Findlater Stewart, Lord Cherwell and Dr Jones, Duncan Sandys and his assistant, Colonel Kenneth Post, the Ministry of Supply's chief rocket expert, Dr Crow, the three Chiefs of Staff, plus General Ismay, and a positive galaxy of top-ranking ministers. They were being asked essentially to settle two questions: did the rocket exist? and, if it did, what could be done to counter it, or modify its consequences? Although so much – perhaps the whole outcome of the war – hung on the answers, the Prime Minister was, however, at his most mischievous. He was highly amused that Cherwell's protégé, Dr Jones, was one of the chief advocates for the reality of the rocket threat, and regularly interrupted his contribution with such jocular comments to Cherwell as 'That's a weighty point against you! Remember it was you who introduced him to me!'

The meeting began with Duncan Sandys recapitulating the evidence already circulated. 'The reports', he conceded, 'did not, of course, all tally, but they had sufficient common basis to lead one to the conclusion that the rocket was a fact.' He dismissed the suggestion that 'the whole affair was a fantasy or a hoax. . . . If it were a hoax, it was a hoax on an extremely big scale. . . . Peenemünde was a very important establishment and to choose it as the centre of a hoax which would invite the heaviest bombing seemed a very illogical proceeding'.

Lord Cherwell, however, was unimpressed by this argument, and made the most of the discrepancies and deficiencies in the evidence so far available. One prisoner, he recalled, had spoken of a powerful new type of fuel which 'was scientifically quite out of the question'; a highly significant interjection by Dr Cook that a greatly increased performance 'might not be impossible with a liquid fuel' went unanswered. Cherwell thought it 'extraordinary' that there were no reports of 'terrific' flashes of light being spotted by Swedish fishermen in the Baltic and 'curious that the rockets should be painted white and left lying about so that we could not fail to observe them'. He asserted flatly that '40 miles was the longest possible range for a single-stage rocket', that 'radio steering . . . would not be possible with a rocket' and was doubtful if a 60 ton rocket could be launched at all, or, if launched, steered. He summed up his views unequivocally:

The impression that he had formed was that the rocket story was a well-designed cover plan. . . . He thought it was almost incredible that the Germans should have got, without an intermediate step, to something which we could certainly not develop under five years.

Cherwell used one phrase which was to become notorious but which does not appear in the official minutes, when he described the object seen at Peenemünde as 'a great white dummy'. Even here, however, his remarks did not go unchallenged. Apart from the white-painted rockets, 'there was also a black one', it was pointed out. Sir Stafford Cripps, in peacetime an eminent advocate well used to assessing the value of evidence, came out, cautiously but decisively, against him. There was, he agreed, 'not enough evidence to warrant definite conclusions' about whether there was any immediate danger, but 'there was nothing inherently impossible in the rocket' and 'it was evident that the Germans had genuinely made great efforts to develop it. . . . We must', he advised, 'therefore assume that there was a grave possibility of the rocket being fired within the next few months'. The contributions of the other participants in the discussion were less helpful. Herbert Morrison, curiously for a professional democrat, wanted to know if the prisoners who had talked about the rocket were officers or Other Ranks, while, to Dr Jones's disgust, Sir Alan Brooke, Chief of the Imperial General Staff, actually confused the 'Paris Gun' with 'Big Bertha', a solecism which would also have outraged General Dornberger.

Jones's own opportunity came after Churchill had directly invited him to give his opinion, reminding the meeting that it was his discoveries, and his attendance at just such a meeting as this, which had established the existence back in 1940 of the German *Knickebein* navigational beams for their bombers. His verdict on the evidence was as decisive as Lord Cherwell's, though directly contrary to it:

Dr Jones said that he had very carefully studied the whole matter and he was of the opinion that the rocket was genuine. . . . The evidence . . . was considerably stronger than the evidence . . . about the use of beams by the Germans. . . . He could not accept the theory of the hoax. The Germans were not at all adept at deception and, moreover, a deception which would bring down a great attack upon one of the two most important experimental establishments which the Germans possessed would be highly absurd.

Although no formal resolution to this effect was discussed, and Cherwell and his supporters in the 'anti-rocket' party were to continue to question its existence for months to come, it was now tacitly agreed that the rocket threat must be taken seriously. The obvious, indeed the only, counter-measure available was to attempt to destroy Peenemünde, the one place where activity connected with the missile was known to be going on, and discussion now turned on how this could best be done. This was a straightforward military problem on which the Chief of the Air Staff now offered his professional opinion:

Sir Charles Portal thought it would be a mistake to act against Peenemünde until a really heavy attack could take place, which would not only destroy the experimental establishment but would also kill a large number of highly important scientists. Buildings were still being put up at Peenemünde . . . and the flak defences were comparatively few. If we attacked with Mosquitoes now, we might cause the Germans to move everything of value before we could launch a real assault.

This advice was accepted by the Prime Minister, and it was also decided to reduce the number of reconnaissance flights over the area to avoid alarming the Germans. In case the rocket should still survive, despite the bombing of Peenemünde, it was also agreed to increase the provision of shelters, and to draw up plans for large-scale evacuation of government departments and of 100,000 of the 'priority classes'. Preparations were also made for a new and more rigid form of censorship which would deny the Germans any news of the rocket's arrival. About the chances of securing an adequate period of warning no one was optimistic, but it was agreed 'that the manufacture and installation of the R.D.F. [i.e. radar] equipment required for detection of the firing points of long range rockets should be energetically pursued' and that 'plans should be prepared for immediate air attack on rocket firing points in Northern France as soon as these were located.'

This important meeting had left Duncan Sandys indisputably in charge of the rocket inquiry, on which he was now required to report weekly, but had also agreed that 'Dr R. V. Jones should be closely associated with him' in his parallel watch 'on the state of development of pilotless . . . aircraft in Germany'; in the rocket investigation he still had no special status. Churchill's latest 'midnight folly', as weary or unsympathetic participants called it, had also left Herbert Morrison convinced of the rocket's existence and he now became alarmed that not enough was being done on the Civil Defence side. In a memo of 13 July he urged Churchill to authorize the production of 100,000 more Morrison shelters and on 22 July begged him to overrule the Chiefs of Staff, who were demurring at the modest amounts of steel and manpower required. Meanwhile, partly no doubt generated by the demand for information on the flying bomb and the rocket, messages from Europe about new weapons – including 'liquid air bombs', 'atom-splitting explosive' and projectiles with ranges of up to 500 miles – were becoming more frequent and even more disquieting. In his fourth report, on 9 July, Duncan Sandys mentioned this proliferation of reports, which included one, on 3 July, suggesting that a large site at Watten on the French coast, where reconnaissance confirmed that major constructional work was in progress, was connected with 'German long-range rocket activity'. The fear that this was the dreaded 'projector' for which everyone had been searching, combined with references in some agents' signals to attacks beginning in August or September, caused something like panic in some quarters. Lord Cherwell reacted forthrightly, however, to the suggestion that parachute troops should be dropped to find out exactly what was happening, in a memo to General Ismay on 29 July:

I find it difficult to understand what information which cannot be got from photographs could be obtained by paratroops in these earthworks in half an hour in the dark. . . . No doubt before sacrificing 150 highly trained men the Chiefs of Staff will assure themselves that the evidence connecting these particular sites with the L.R.R. [long-range rocket] is consonant. But no doubt I am biased by the fact that I do not believe in the rocket's existence.

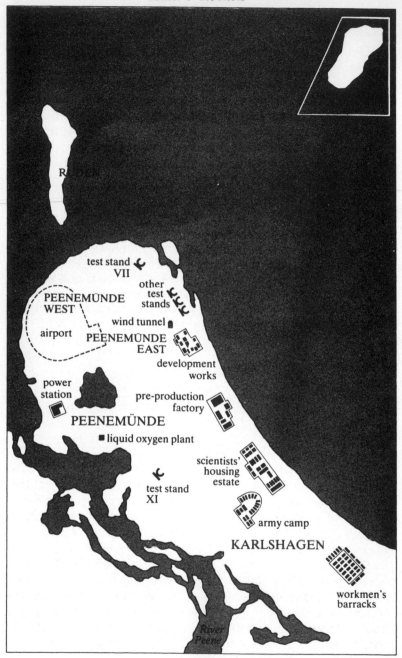

test stand VII

other test stands

PEENEMÜNDE WEST

wind tunnel

airport

PEENEMÜNDE EAST

development works

power station

pre-production factory

PEENEMÜNDE

liquid oxygen plant

scientists' housing estate

test stand XI

army camp

KARLSHAGEN

workmen's barracks

River Peene

6

POOR PEENEMÜNDE

My poor, poor Peenemünde

General Dornberger, surveying effects of RAF raid,
18 August 1943

On one of the conclusions reached at Churchill's 'rocket' meeting of 29 June 1943 everyone was agreed. As the minutes put it: 'The attack on the experimental station at Peenemünde should take the form of the heaviest possible night attack by Bomber Command, on the first occasion when conditions were suitable.' This meant waiting for the longer nights when the Lancasters and Halifaxes could reach and return from the Baltic in darkness, and moonlight was also considered essential to assist accurate bombing. On 8 July a planning conference was held at Bomber Command headquarters for Operation Hydra, as it was aptly named, the 'hydra' being defined as 'a water-monster with many heads, which when cut off were succeeded by others; any manifold evil'. Most unusually, 'Bomber' Harris's proposals were subsequently scrutinized by the Chiefs of Staff, Lord Cherwell, Herbert Morrison and the Prime Minister himself. Meanwhile new information about the target was still coming in. Ultra provided unexpected confirmation of its importance from a low-level routine document, listing the allocation of petrol coupons, which showed that it ranked second only to Rechlin, the German 'Farnborough', in priority for fuel supplies. The two reconnaissance flights in July, all that were permitted, both yielded useful intelligence. The power station, which had previously been thought to be not yet in commission – the Germans had in fact fitted smoke filters to the chimneys – was now recognized to be fully in use, and a decoy site, stretching over twenty acres, where fires would be lit to attract bombs in the event of a raid, was

81

correctly identified as such. More unwelcome confirmation of Peenemunde's significance came from the erection there of new anti-aircraft guns.

The level of accuracy acceptable in Bomber Command's normal area-bombing was not going to be adequate on this occasion, and for weeks before the raid crews found themselves sent to the bombing range at Wainfleet Sands in Lincolnshire to practise the new 'timed run' technique, whereby bombs were dropped a certain number of seconds after flying on a fixed course from some convenient landmark, far enough from the target not to be obscured by smoke. By constant practice, No. 5 Group, the Command's crack formation, cut down its average error from 1000 to only 300 yards wide of the aiming point. Another innovation was the use of a master bomber, a group captain, no less, who flew around the area throughout the raid directing the crews towards the most accurate markers dropped by the Pathfinders, while the new 'red-spot fire' flare, which burned for ten full minutes once on the ground, would, it was hoped, remain visible through the thickest smoke. To discourage 'creep-back' in the face of flak, and encourage the 'press-on' spirit, the crews were told at briefing that radar equipment for anti-aircraft use was being manufactured there, and that if the job were not completed the first time they would be sent back again and again, 'even if', one air-gunner recalls hearing, 'it meant wiping out Bomber Command'.

Harris had wanted to have only a single aiming point, the scientists' housing estate, but he was overruled and two others were added: the building believed to be used for development work and the two largest workshops, where actual manufacture was thought to be in progress. He was, however, given a free hand in planning the attack, and by 9 p.m. on Thursday, 17 August the first aircraft were beginning to take off under a rising moon for the long flight via Denmark. It began at low level in the hope of slipping below the radar screen; later the main force would climb to 7000 feet, still low enough, Harris believed, to ensure accuracy in what was essentially a precision attack. A tiny diversionary force of eight Mosquitoes was sent to Berlin, crossing the coast near Peenemunde but then flying on another 120 miles to the German capital, dropping 'Window', the reflector strips first used only three weeks before against Hamburg, to fill the German radar screens and suggest that a major attack on the capital was impeding. This feint attack, watched by Colonel Zanssen, still undergoing 'rustication' from Peenemünde, from the balcony of Dornberger's borrowed flat in Charlottenburg, was brilliantly successful. It followed the heaviest raid yet by the US 8th Air Force, against Schweinfurt, which had provoked Hitler's fury, and the Luftwaffe Chief of Staff, General Hans Jeschonnek, was now licking his wounds near Hitler's Rastenburg headquarters after being made painfully aware of the Führer's extreme displeasure.

This Thursday was intended to be a red-letter day in the Peenemünde calendar, for the scientists were entertaining the most famous woman in Germany, the legendary test pilot Hanna Reitsch. Dornberger had put behind him the disagreeable events of the afternoon when his staff had protested at the pressure being put upon them, and 'in the panelled Hearth Room lit by the festal glitter of brass chandeliers' – further proof of the establishment's lavish budget – von Braun, Dr Steinhoff and Hanna Reitsch were happily exchanging reminiscences.

Curled up in a deep armchair, this elegant, clear-headed and courageous woman told us about her life, work and ambitions. . . . Listening to the laughter of these young people, who cheerfully took all the surprises of technology in their stride . . . I felt less oppressed by the serious worries of the afternoon. . . . Towards half-past eleven [10.30 p.m. British time], tired out with the heat and the care and excitement of the day, I was walking the few steps that led to one of the residential houses when the air-raid warning sounded. It was not a new experience for us. The British airmen usually gathered over the central Baltic before they flew south with their load of bombs for Berlin. . . . Our A.A. had orders to fire only if we were actually being raided. All was quiet. The black-out was faultless. I got into bed and soon fell into a quiet, dreamless sleep.

Meanwhile, as so often, in the air things were not going according to plan. As the Pathfinders approached the coast, unexpected patches of cloud hampered identification of the surrounding islands, and the outline of Ruden, on the screen of their H2S ground-reflecting radar, was confused with the tip of the Peenemünde peninsula. As a result, some of their red markers were dropped two miles from the correct spot. Others, however, were correctly placed. At 0017 hours on Friday, 18 August 1943, 2317 hours Thursday, 17 August, British time, Master Bomber John Searby ordered the first main force to begin their attack, directed at the scientists' housing estate. Ten minutes later it was over. At least 150 of the 227 aircraft in the first wave had, it later appeared, dropped bombs on or close to the target. Many of the rest had, tragically, thanks to the Pathfinders' error, attacked a camp housing foreign labourers.

Dornberger, roused by his rattling windows, at first attributed them to the test-firing of an anti-dive-bomber weapon he had authorized, but was soon disillusioned as he recognized the sound of the local defences:

At intervals the light 2 cm guns barked from their elevated positions above the woods and from the roofs of the highest buildings. The 3.7 from the Gaaz harbour outpost was sending up many-coloured strings of pearls, with a 'plop, plop, plop' into the sky. . . . I sprang out of bed and had breeches and socks on in record time. Where the hell were my riding boots? . . . I had to make do with slippers. . . . The first window-panes tinkled out. Tiles came hurtling and clashing down the sloping roof, smashing on the ground. . . . For the moment, tunic over pyjama coat would do. Now for overcoat, cap, gloves and cigar-case.

Thus equipped, Dornberger set out to witness the attempted destruction of the place which, more than any other individual, he had created.

I was confronted, as though through a rosy curtain of gauze, by an almost incredible stage setting in subdued lighting and colours. Artificial clouds of mist rolled past me. . . . The moon shone through these fragile, cottony clouds, lighting up the pine plantations, the roads and the buses. . . . The buildings of the administrative wing, so far as I could distinguish them through the veiling mists, the drawing-offices, the development works and the canteen, appeared and disappeared at intervals through the rose-red fog like menacing shadows. Overhead was the star-strewn night sky with the beams of the searchlights whisking to and fro.

At 0025 hours, local time, the second wave, of 113 Lancasters, attacked. The original two-mile error by some Pathfinders had now been compounded, since the aiming point for the second wave was supposed to be some two miles from that assigned to the first. As a result, the aiming point was brought back to the scientists' housing estate instead of forward to the 'main workshops', which were in fact the pilot, pre-production factory. Luckily the master bomber realized what had happened and managed to direct many of the second wave's bombs to the proper spot, until, at 0033, the last second-wave machine turned for home.

By now the third, and most important, aiming point, the centre of the development works, was covered by drifting smoke, both from fires and from the smoke generators the Germans had installed for this purpose half a mile away. This was where the timed run was supposed to come into its own. At 0043 hours the third wave, 180 strong, began its attack. Their orders were to bomb visually if they could and many did so, though in fact only one load of target indicators had been dropped, as intended, amid the main laboratories and offices, and most had landed well to one side of the proper spot, and between the two earlier aiming points. Had more bombs landed near the development works they might well have claimed the lives of von Braun and Dornberger, who were in a nearby shelter, the latter now happily reunited with his riding boots which some unsung hero had fetched from his batman's room.

As the second wave of bombers withdrew, Dornberger emerged from his shelter to take charge. No one knew what had happened at the residential estate at Karlshagen or at the pilot factory, since the telephone lines were dead, but runners were dispatched to find out and to turn out the special 'labour service' contingents earmarked to give help in just such an emergency. Even in the few minutes Dornberger had been below ground, the situation had visibly changed for the worse:

Great fires were painting the ubiquitous fog, now thickened with stinking smoke, dark red. Bright flames were darting from many places on the roof of the drawing-offices. Glowing sparks whirled upwards in dense clouds of smoke. The attic windows shone red. Some rafters on the residential building roof were on fire. All round us, on the roads and in the grounds, the hissing thermite incendiaries shone dazzlingly white.

Von Braun was dispatched to try to save the drawing office or at least 'to get the safes, cabinets, records and drawings out' and Dornberger himself set off 'along the main avenue to the command shelter', a melancholy progress:

The old office hut, where the accounts department, the printing and binding trades and smaller ancillary businesses were still housed, was enveloped in flames and past all hope of saving. . . . I could see a small fire beginning on the roof of the boiler house. . . . I sent men up to the roof. . . . Flights of bombers were passing uninterruptedly over the Works. There was a distant, hollow rumble of many bombs falling, mingled with the noise of A.A. guns. . . . Alternately throwing ourselves down and leaping up again, we reached the west side of the Measurement House, containing the Instruments, Guidance and Measurement Department . . . the most valuable part of the Works. The windows were dark. Behind the building a big fire seemed to be raging. I rushed round the corner and beheld the Assembly Workshop on fire in several places. The big entrance gates, 60 feet high, were burning. Tongues of flame shot, crackling and hissing, out of the shattered windows of the wings. Iron girders, twisted and red hot, rose above the outer walls. Parts of the roof structure collapsed, crashing down into the interior. . . . I looked at the windows in the east facade of the Measurement House. Many of them shone brightly. . . . The heat . . . had set fire to the wooden sashes. I took my two men along and we divided the floors between us. Fire extinguishers hung in front of almost every door. In fifteen minutes we had saved the Measurement House and with it an indispensable element for the continuance of our work.

The huge display of flares over a supposedly thinly populated stretch of the Baltic coast had attracted the attention of many of the night-fighter pilots milling aimlessly about over Berlin, and some members of the 'freelance' 'Wild Boar' squadrons set off at once in their direction, wreaking havoc among the Lancasters and Halifaxes of the third wave. Realizing at last that they had been duped, the Germans also ordered up several squadrons of Messerschmitt 110s based near Copenhagen, and these harried the returning bombers on their flight home, usually the time when losses were heaviest.

Duncan Sandys had waited at RAF Wyton for the return of Group Captain Searby (who had himself to shake off a pursuing night-fighter on the way back) and the other Pathfinders of 83 Squadron and, on hearing their encouraging news, at once telephoned Churchill, at the 'Quadrant' conference in Quebec. Later that day the Air Ministry sent a confirmatory telegram:

586 aircraft dispatched to attack RDF establishment PEENEMÜNDE last night. 41 missing.* Weather was clear over target and preliminary reports suggest that a successful attack was made in spite of an effective smoke screen.

The loss rate, just under 7 per cent, though high, was acceptable for a once-for-all effort on a uniquely important objective, in which almost 1600 tons of high explosive and 250 tons of incendiary bombs had been dropped, and early that afternoon the interpreters at Medmenham found that the first post-raid pictures, taken by a Mosquito at 10 a.m., showed that the place at which they had peered through their stereoscopes through so many weary hours had changed almost beyond recognition:

There is a large concentration of craters in and around the target area and many buildings are still on fire. In the North Manufacturing Area some 27 buildings of medium size have been completely destroyed; at least four buildings are seen still burning. . . . Severe damage has been done to the buildings of the factory and laboratory type probably serving the supposed 'projection installations' and the aerodrome. The accommodation for personnel has suffered very severely.

Group Captain Searby was awarded an immediate DSO and received a congratulatory letter from 'Bomber' Harris, whose tactics had been brilliantly vindicated: only one Mosquito had been lost over Berlin, of the nine which had tied up virtually the whole German night-fighter force. An analysis of the 400 photographs brought back by the Peenemünde raiders revealed that 'it is probable that nearly all aircraft bombed within three miles, and the majority within one mile, of the aiming point'. On 21 August, when Duncan Sandys submitted his tenth report to the Chiefs of Staff, he was soberly confident:

There is every indication that the raid on Peenemünde was most successful. . . . A large part of the living quarters were annihilated and many buildings in the main factory area were destroyed. From

---

*The official history gives the number dispatched as 597 and the losses as 40.

preliminary assessments of damage it would seem unlikely that any appreciable production will be possible at PEENEMÜNDE for some months.

The Chief of Staff had already, two days earlier, turned down a generous offer by the US 8th Air Force to finish the job off in daylight. There was, they believed, nothing worthwhile left to destroy.

This indeed was how it must have seemed to Dornberger on the miserable, smoke-wreathed morning of Friday, 18 August. He had seen his own 'stamp collection . . . shotguns and hunting gear' lost in his burning house and the great establishment he had virtually created destroyed around him. But, as always, action lifted his spirits. When 'the canteen manager . . . appeared . . . hatless, in torn clothes, hurt and singed by phosphorus bombs', he was instructed 'to go and get coffee and soup ready at once', and Dornberger set off on a tour of inspection by bicycle. Things, he soon discovered, were not quite as bad as they had seemed during the night. 'The waterworks were undamaged.' So, too, was 'the assembly hall for experimental rockets'. Even more important 'the big assembly hall of the pre-production works' was still standing, though 'nine 1000 1b bombs and many phosphorus and stick incendiaries had penetrated the concrete roof and exploded or burnt out in that huge place. . . . Machines and material had been hit by bomb splinters. There were hits in the outer side aisles, big holes in the masonry of the walls. But the damage was not really serious.'

As it became light Dornberger reached 'the settlement', the residential estate for the German staff, and here, as he put it, 'Death had reaped a rich harvest', among those who had not fled along the coast to Zinnovitz when the bombing started:

Soldiers of the Northern Experimental Command, Labour Service men and some of the staff were feverishly working to open up buried cellars, clear slit trenches, rescue furniture from burning houses and remove fallen trees, beams and other wreckage. I saw the bodies of men, women and children. Some had been charred by phosphorus incendiaries. I hurried along the beach road to Dr Thiel's house. It had been destroyed by a direct hit. The slit trench in front was just a huge crater.

It was a scene which, thanks to Dornberger himself, was soon to be repeated on a far larger scale in southern England, but this thought does not seem to have crossed his mind as, 'shaken to the very soul', he hurried to the school being used as a temporary mortuary and 'stood before the remains of Dr Thiel, his wife and his children'. Thiel had been one of the inner circle of rocket researchers ever since 1936, and, wrote Dornberger, 'my heart overflowed with gratitude for all he had done for our project'; without his work on developing its motor and perfecting the mixture of propellants there might, indeed, have been no A-4. However, to a soldier death was commonplace. 'I pulled myself together. The most important thing now was to help the living.'

With von Braun beside him Dornberger flew over the site by air in a light Storch aircraft, their first view of it by air since the triumphant return from the visit to Hitler a month earlier. He was 'struck to the heart by this first comprehensive view of the destruction' and 'on landing . . . could only mutter wearily: "My poor, poor Peenemünde!" ' But the arrival that morning of Albert Speer, who flew on to report to Hitler on what had happened, helped to cheer him up, as did the discovery that 'material damage to the works, contrary to first impressions, was surprisingly small' and that 'the test fields and special plant such as the wind tunnel and Measurement House were not hit'. The damage that had been done, he turned to his advantage. Once the main administration building had been made usable again, burnt timbers were laid across the roof to mislead subsequent reconnaissance sorties and, where they did not actually block a road, craters were not filled in. 'We maintained the effect of complete destruction for nine months, during which we had no more raids,' he later recalled – a vital nine months, for 'the project could not be prevented now from coming to fruition'.

What was the true balance sheet for the Peenemünde raid? To set against the 40 heavy bombers and one Mosquito missing in action, at least 39 German fighters had been lost, 9 of them shot down and the rest victims of each other, of their own anti-aircraft guns, and of collisions on the ground, owing to the chaos that had developed in the skies over Berlin and on the airfields around it. This fiasco also brought the RAF its most distinguished victim of the night, General Hans Jeschonnek, for whom the news around 7 a.m. that Peenemünde had apparently been destroyed proved the last straw, after being harangued by Hitler the previous day and bawled at in the early hours by Göring. He wrote a reproachful, but still loyal, suicide note before shooting himself. 'I cannot work with Goring any more. Long live the Führer!' Of 12,000 people living on the Peenemünde 'campus', 8000 of whom, including dependants, were directly concerned with rocket production, 732 had been killed. Only 120 were German; the rest, in Dornberger's words, 'consisted of Russians, Poles, etc.' The British were to pay a heavy price for the mis-aimed bombs which had killed them. Previously these forced labourers had been a valuable source of intelligence, a source which now wholly dried up.

The loss of accommodation on Usedom was rapidly overcome by billeting bombed out people all over the surrounding area and collecting them by special transport. No premises not absolutely essential were repaired, thanks to a captured airman cheerfully passing on to his interrogators the information he had been given at briefing that Peenemünde would be bombed again and again until it was destroyed. The immediate effect on rocket testing was slight, for Test Stand VII had not been seriously damaged by the few stray bombs that had landed near it. Nor was production seriously interfered with, thanks to the foresight shown back in March when it had been ordered that 'production blueprints, special tools and so forth' should be maintained elsewhere. But the cumulative effect of the raid, and of the loss of life and general disruption it caused, was substantial, undoubtedly justifying the lives and effort devoted to Operation Hydra. Winston Churchill, in his post-war memoirs, considered that 'The attack on Peenemünde . . . played an important part in the general progress of the war' and that 'but for this raid Hitler's bombardment of London by rockets might well have started early in 1944'. This is to claim too much. Dornberger put the delay in resuming work at 'only four to six weeks', though no doubt to achieve full production took longer. Goebbels, in mid-October, made a similar estimate. 'The English raids. . .', he wrote, 'have thrown our preparations back four or even eight weeks, so that we can't possibly count on reprisals before the end of January.' R. V. Jones, reviewing all the evidence long after the war, concluded that 'the raid must have gained us at least two months' – 'very significant' months, as he points out.

The bombing of Peenemünde, although much the most serious, was not the only blow to befall the A-4 programme that summer. On 22 June 1943, six weeks before Operation Hydra, sixty Lancasters had been sent against the former Zeppelin works at Friedrichshafen on Lake Constanz, in the belief that early-warning radar installations were being built there. The attack, carried out without loss, was spectacularly successful, though undertaken for the wrong reason. The factory was in reality being converted to turn out 300 A-4s a month, a target now unlikely to be achieved. On 13 August 1943, four days before the great Bomber Command assault on Peenemünde, the US 9th Air Force had made an equally fortunate mistake, sending a heavy force of Liberators to destroy the Messerschmitt works at Wiener Neustadt in Austria as part of its long-standing campaign against German fighter production. Only after the war was it learned that Wiener Neustadt was manufacturing rocket components.

7

REVENGE IS NIGH

Our hour of revenge is nigh!

Adolf Hitler, broadcasting from Munich, 8 November 1943

Less than a week after what Dornberger described as Peenemunde's 'flaming night' Speer and Himmler spent a long session with Hitler discussing the A-4 programme. Speer's report, on Sunday, 22 August 1943, made a deep impression on Hitler, even though he had never visited the place,* and he now ordered that the 'pilot factory' there should not be expanded for mass production, as intended, but that manufacture of A-4s on the site should continue only until a safer location had been developed. Pre-production work on the A-4 would be taken over by a new plant at Traunsee in Austria, code-named 'Cement', and the principal testing range for rockets would be transferred from Usedom to Blizna, a small village near Debice in Poland, and about 170 miles south of Warsaw.

The name Blizna now began increasingly to feature in the intelligence reports about the A-4 reaching London. Before 1940 it had been notable only as the site of the confluence of the River Vistula and River San, but then the inhabitants had been evicted to make way for a huge SS training camp, 20 kilometres square, the work being done after 1941 by Russian prisoners of war, deliberately worked and starved to death, and by the occupants of a small concentration camp now set up in the area, known as Heidelager, or 'the camp on the

---

*Churchill's statement in his memoirs that Hitler 'inspected Peenemunde about the beginning of June 1942' is wrong and rests on an inaccurate intelligence report.

heath', a name now transferred to the whole establishment. The decision to move rocket research to Blizna led to its being expanded still further. The existing railway siding, linked to the main railway line from Cracow to Lvov, was lengthened, new roads and barracks were built, and, after a visit from Himmler on 28 September 1943, a full-scale programme of camouflage was put in hand. 'The outlines of cottages and outbuildings', a Polish historian noted, 'were brought from Germany; fences were erected and linen hung on them; dummies of men, women and children stood around, and flowers were sown.' But there was one sinister addition to this idyllic picture. 'At the railway siding trains began to arrive composed of long flat trucks, covered with canvas, hiding long objects', a development rapidly reported to the Cracow District of the Polish Home Army by the Poles of the Forestry Commission, allowed by the Germans to remain in residence when the rest of the population were deported. Apart from them it was now a solidly German area, with no fewer than 16,000 troops in the main barracks. Another 400 were stationed six miles away, with SS officers to keep an eye on them, near what had been earmarked as the main A-4 launching and test site. Blizna reminded Dornberger of Kummersdorf, where the rocket programme had begun: 'in the thick woods of fir, pine and oak' there was 'a big clearing measuring a little over half a square mile. A small, stone-built house and a dilapidated thatched stable stood there in complete isolation'. Under SS General Hans Kammler, however (of whom much more will be heard), in charge of the building programme, no time was wasted in creating a new, if more modest, Peenemünde in Poland. 'A concrete road, built in a few weeks, led from the nearest main highway to our testing ground. . . . During October and November, huts, living-quarters, sheds and a large store were erected close by.'

The whole rocket programme was now coming increasingly under the control of the SS, that 'state within a state' – originally set up to protect the Nazi regime against disaffection – which had steadily spread its tentacles over every part of the nation's activities. Speer, for all his professed innocence of the worst aspects of Nazism, raised no objections to Himmler's invasion of his own specialist field, munitions production. 'The

Führer orders', he noted loyally in his office diary after the meeting of 22 August 1943, 'that, jointly with the SS Reichsführer [i.e. Himmler] and utilizing to the full the manpower which he has available in his concentration camps, every step must be taken to promote both the construction of A-4 manufacturing plants and the resumed production of the A-4 rocket itself.' Speer seemed delighted with the turn events had taken. 'The A-4 men', he told a conference in Berlin approvingly on 26 August, 'have met with the strongest support from the SS in accelerating rocket production.'

On 9 September 1943 the Long-Range Bombardment Commission, set up to advise on the manufacture and use of both main secret weapons, under the chairmanship of Professor Petersen, and with Dr Saur of the Ministry of Munitions, now, in his own words, 'a fanatical disciple of this project', in attendance, tried to tie von Braun down to firm delivery dates for the operational version of the A-4. Hitherto only rockets with dummy warheads had been fired, and Petersen dealt briskly with von Braun's reluctance to bring the 'live' trials forward from mid-November to mid-October, observing that though 'the most unexpected surprises might crop up . . . the earlier we invite these surprises, the more quickly we shall be able to overcome them'. This pressure for results probably reflected the growing faith of all the Nazi leaders in the rocket. A mass turnout of Nazi ministers and senior officers, summoned to the Wolf's Lair on 10 September 1943, heard Hitler predict that the bombardment by both secret weapons could begin in February 1944, but it was the A-4 on which he set the highest hopes. 'The Führer', observed Goebbels in his diary, 'is hoping for great things from this rocket weapon. He believes that in certain circumstances he will be able to force the tide of war to turn against England with it.' That month Dornberger was formally appointed Commissioner for the A-4 programme, responsible to the C-in-C of the Home Army, Colonel-General Friedrich Fromm, for any remaining development of the rocket that was needed and for 'the formation and final training of field units for operations'.

Meanwhile the arrangements for rocket manufacture, in which Dornberger had little say, were being finalized. Ultimately a group of factories known collectively as the Southern

Works, incorporating the Zeppelin factory at Friedrichshafen, the Henschel Rax works at Wiener-Neustadt, and various other firms around Vienna and throughout Austria would receive A-4 contracts, and there were also plans for an Eastern Works, another umbrella title covering several concerns, near Riga. The chief, and at first the only, source of finished rockets, however – the many other factories involved were merely producing components – would be the so-called Central Works, occupying a site selected by the dynamic Degenkolb, carved into a peak called Kohlstein in the Harz mountains in the very centre of Germany, a location often referred to in the German documents as Hammersfeld, though the nearest town was Nordhausen. The place was remote and secure both from air attack and from prying eyes, and soon the highly disciplined labour battalions of the Waffen SS were extending the caves and tunnels used before the war to store sensitive chemicals for the Industrial Research Association into the largest underground factory in the world.

Central Works Ltd came formally into existence on 11 September 1943 and took over from Peenemünde responsibility for meeting the contracts previously placed there. Many sub-assemblies would also be manufactured at Nordhausen, but it was primarily an assembly centre to which the many thousands of parts making up each A-4 would be brought for transformation into a complete missile. The factory consisted primarily of two spacious tunnels, a mile and a quarter long and about three-quarters of a mile apart, with forty-six smaller galleries connecting them – a layout which lent itself to a highly efficient production-line system, based on a railway track along which each missile moved as new components were added to it. The engineer supervising the installation of machinery had formerly been in charge of the pilot factory at Peenemünde and, once it was in operation, quality was maintained by constant inspection at every stage. A mobile force of a hundred army officers would overcome any bottlenecks, being given unlimited powers to take charge on the spot to get the assembly lines moving again.

Gauleiter Sauckel, the Reich's manpower director, now amply repaid the care devoted to entertaining him at Peenemünde. On 30 September 1943 Hitler agreed that prisoners

95

with scientific qualifications could be sent there, irrespective of nationality, while the bulk of the workforce was to come from slave-labourers from eastern Europe. Himmler, via General Kammler, offered to provide 16,000. They were to be kept in order by an SS officer, Major Förschner, who was deputy to the General Manager, Dr Kettler, a scientist, though in April 1944 a Director-General was brought in over his head. Förschner was in charge of five SS men, who were responsible for beating and bullying the assembly-line operatives into working themselves to death and for preventing any of the German craftsmen supervising them from treating their work-mates with normal decency.

The earliest contingents to reach Nordhausen came largely from Buchenwald where, 'during the second half of August 1943', a Polish historian has recorded, 'the news went around . . . that a small transport would be going to set up a new sub-camp in the Harz mountains'. In the end '107 Poles, Russians and Germans were chosen' and set off, escorted by forty SS, on 27 August, being followed a few days later by another '1,223 prisoners, mostly French, Polish and Russian'. During September the total rose to 3300, housed in tents while they built a barracks for their SS guards. Soon there were also Belgians and Italians in the makeshift camp, at first known as Mittelbau, but later called Dora. The Italians were former soldiers, hitherto allowed to wear their own uniforms and be commanded by their own officers. When they protested at being treated like ordinary political prisoners and being expected to work on the A-4 assembly line, six were shot, the first clear indication of what the regime at Nordhausen would be like.

Even the contingents sent from Buchenwald had not wanted to come, reasoning that any change the Germans made must be for the worse, and their fears soon proved well founded, as the Polish prisoner* previously quoted has recorded:

After two months of living in tents, towards the end of October the whole sub-camp *Dora* was transferred underground. The prisoners were shoved into chambers . . . still in a raw state, dark, damp and

---

*He was himself detained in Auschwitz, not Buchenwald, but has based this account on the evidence of eyewitnesses.

full of an irritating dust. Normally . . . the bunks were three-tiered; here four tiers were set up. They worked and slept in two shifts; when one went to work the other lay down on the same filthy litters and covered themselves with the same damp blankets. There were no latrines at all; empty carbide barrels, cut in half, were used; it was necessary to walk about a kilometre to the water-taps.

As the work made progress the nature of the prisoners' duties changed:

In the beginning 70–80% of the prisoners were employed in unloading, transporting and setting up the machines. About 1,500 worked at building the camp. . . . [Most of] the rest drilled the rock. From the end of November . . . all the prisoners, except for those building the camp, were employed at assembling rockets. Since after twelve hours of hard labour a further six and a half hours had to be spent on roll-calls, getting to work and standing in a queue for food, as well as finding a place to sleep, barely five and a half hours were left for rest. There was very poor and insufficient food, brutal treatment and constant very hard work, so the mortality rate was high.

On 23 September 1943 Hitler kept Goebbels up into the small hours at a late-night tea party at the Wolf's Lair while he held forth on the transformation the A-4 was about to achieve in the whole war situation. 'The Führer thinks that our great rocket offensive can be opened at the end of January, or early in February,' noted Goebbels in his diary. 'England must be repaid in her own coin and with interest for what she has done to us. . . . The Giant rocket-bomb weighs fourteen tons. What an awe-inspiring murder weapon! I believe that when the first of these missiles screams down on London, something akin to panic will break out among the British public!'

A week later, on 1 October, Degenkolb officially asked the German War Office to issue a contract for the installation at the Central Works of 1800 A-4s a month, but at a subsequent conference with representatives from the factory it was agreed to scale down the target figure to more realistic proportions. On 19 October 1943 the general responsible personally signed War Contract No. 0011–5365/43, for 'the manufacture of 12,000 A-4 missiles at a rate of 900 monthly, not including electronic, warhead or packing material'. The price was set at 40,000 RM (£3520) each, later raised, in the light of experience, to 100,000 RM (£8800) per rocket for the first thousand and, by gradual reductions, to 50,000 RM (£4400) after 5000 had been delivered.

The repercussions of this order, still far higher than could conceivably be met, on the slave-workers at Nordhausen were immediate:

They were driven to work with sticks, they were not allowed to rest for a single moment, any negligence was regarded as sabotage. . . . Their output fell and the mortality rate rose. *Dora* did not yet have its own crematorium, so trucks carried hundreds of corpses to Buchenwald more and more frequently.

By November Nordhausen had already overtaken Peenemünde as the main source of finished rockets, and on 10 December 1943 it was visited by Albert Speer, whose ministry in theory, he later wrote, 'remained in charge of manufacturing' though in practice 'in cases of doubt we had to yield to the superior power of the SS leadership'. His office diary recorded what happened in a notable example of euphemism, if not Orwellian double-speak:

Carrying out this tremendous mission drew on the leaders' last reserves of strength. Some of the men were so affected that they had to be forcibly sent off on vacations to restore their nerves.

Speer's own account was more informative:

In enormous long halls prisoners were busy setting up machinery and shifting plumbing. Expressionlessly, they looked right through me, mechanically removing their prisoners' caps of blue twill until our group had passed them. . . . The conditions for these prisoners were in fact barbarous. . . . As I learned from the overseers after the inspection was over, the sanitary conditions were inadequate, disease rampant; the prisoners were quartered right there in the damp caves and as a result the mortality among them was extraordinarily high. The same day I allocated the necessary materials and set all the machinery in motion to build a barracks camp immediately on an adjacent hill. In addition, I pressed the SS camp command to take all necessary measures to improve sanitary conditions and upgrade the food. They pledged that they would do so.

On 25 January 1944 Werner von Braun also visited Nordhausen, where by now nearly 10,000 prisoners were at work and the installation phase was almost complete. 'The young engineer', noted the watching Poles, 'walked all round the corridors in silence and left despondent.' In fact, thanks to Speer, conditions at Nordhausen were already undergoing a remarkable improvement. The workforce's living quarters had originally occupied only 5000 square metres of the Central Works' 96,000, which eventually increased to 125,000, some of it devoted to flying-bomb production. All of this was underground, but immediately after Speer's visit a hutted wooden camp began to be built outside the factory and by the end of the year half of the 11,000 men, with a few women, so far sent to Nordhausen were, by concentration camp standards, luxuriously housed.

The camp was set up in a mountain valley less than a kilometre from the entrance to tunnel B, to the south. All the living quarters were wooden, but well supplied with sanitary and heating appliances. Each barrack was divided into a sleeping compartment with two-tiered bunks occupied by two prisoners and an eating compartment with tables and stools. There was always running water in the barracks and the prisoners could also take showers. The domestic buildings were of brick, with modern equipment for the kitchen and laundry. A hospital was also built, consisting of eight barracks with equally modern equipment; there was also a cinema, a canteen and a sports-ground with a swimming pool. The ground for the roll-calls and all the roads in the camp were cemented. . . . There also existed a special psychological and vocational selection unit, with modern equipment, to determine the professional qualifications of the individual prisoners. . . . Speer's intervention also brought about an improvement in the food in a way quite exceptional for German camps. Within the camp there were pigsties and the prisoners began to get soup with macaroni and pieces of pork.

Eventually the amenities at Nordhausen even included a brothel, but the camp's inmates, as this Polish writer was well aware, remained slaves, who could be maltreated or murdered at any moment: 'Naturally there had to be a crematorium and a camp prison . . . and the whole camp was surrounded by high-tension wires and guard towers.'

Dora eventually became an independent camp under the name KZ (Konzentrationslager) Mittelbau, with its own network of sub-camps, and, ironically, since its ultimate purpose was mass murder, to be sent there came to offer the chance of life. The mortality rate, due to overwork, neglect and sickness rather than deliberate brutality, reached at its peak 15 per cent. At Auschwitz, excluding those murdered on arrival, it was 84 per cent. Some Jews already en route to extermination camps were diverted to Nordhausen, so great was its need for labour; the A-4 had saved their lives.

If it was Dornberger who had developed the rocket, and Degenkolb who had got it into production, the man who more than any other now ensured that it was used in action was SS Gruppenführer Hans Kammler, often referred to by his equivalent army rank of major-general. In the autumn of 1943, Kammler already had, at forty-two, a spectacular career behind him and, it seemed, an even more glittering one in front. Speer at first rather took to him, for, like himself, he 'came from a solid middle-class family . . . had been "discovered" because of his work in construction and had gone far and fast in fields for which he had not been trained'. Later, his admiration waned. Kammler, Speer decided, more closely resembled that other young man whom Himmler had picked out for rapid advancement, Reinhard Heydrich, known to the Allies as the 'butcher of Bohemia', and both, considered Speer, 'were surrounded by an aura of iciness like that of their chief', as well as being 'always neatly dressed'. Later Speer was to modify this first impression of Kammler:

In the course of my enforced collaboration with this man, I discovered him to be a cold, ruthless schemer, a fanatic in pursuit of a goal, and as carefully calculating as he was unscrupulous. Himmler heaped assignments on him and brought him into Hitler's presence at every opportunity. Soon rumours were afloat that Himmler was trying to build up Kammler to be my successor.

Kammler had, since the spring of 1942, been responsible for SS construction work, which extended from the gas chambers at Auschwitz to the great training camp near Blizna, and he made his appearance on the rocket scene at the conference called by Speer after the bombing of Peenemünde. He worked with Saur and Degenkolb on producing the scheme to replace Peenemünde by Nordhausen and on 1 September formally took charge of the resulting building programme. Dornberger, always ready to resent anyone else's intrusion into what he regarded as his private domain, disliked him from the first, though recognizing the young brigadier's (he had not yet been promoted) impressive appearance:

He had the slim figure, neither tall nor short, of a cavalryman. . . . Broad-shouldered and narrow at the hips, with bronzed, clear-cut features, a high forehead under dark hair slightly streaked with grey and brushed straight back, Dr Kammler had brown, piercing and restless eyes, a lean and curved beak of a nose and a strong mouth, the underlip thrust forward as though in defiance. That mouth indicated brutality, derision, disdain and overweening pride. The chin was well moulded and prominent. One's first impression was of a virile, handsome and captivating personality. He looked like some hero of the Renaissance.

Along with Kammler's good looks, however, went a less than attractive personality, as Speer was also to discover:

After a few moments he captured the conversation. . . . His first concern was to show you what a splendid fellow he was, how boldly he spoke his mind to his opponents and superior officers, how cleverly he pushed his partners on and what exceptional influence he had at very high levels. There was nothing for it but to let him talk. He was simply incapable of listening. . . . He had no time for discussion or reflection. . . . It was quite out of the question to get him to change his mind.

Kammler briefly endeared himself to Dornberger by dismissing the latter's own old adversary, Degenkolb, as 'a hopeless alcoholic', but his other judgements soon proved equally severe. Colonel Zanssen, he decided, was 'unacceptable for collaboration with the SS' and he was now removed from the rocket project for good. Kammler described von Braun as 'too young, too childish, too supercilious and arrogant for his job', but he had to put up with him. By November 1943, however, Kammler seemed to be ubiquitous, like Degenkolb before him. 'He took part in conferences as Himmler's representative,' grumbled Dornberger, 'and came to the launching tests without being asked. He talked to individuals, listened to opinions and differences of opinion . . . started playing one man off against another.'

There was ample room for his intrigues, for the final stages of the development programme, testing the model of which mass production was about to begin, were going badly. Up to now all the launching tests had taken place over the sea and, though there had been numerous failures on or soon after lift-off, 'we were', wrote Dornberger, 'of the firm opinion that the end of the trajectory left nothing to be desired'. Now they learned that many rockets were exploding in flight, often as they re-entered the earth's atmosphere, though many did not get so far.

Troubles now came thick and fast. Shot after shot went wrong. . . . Some rockets rose barely sixty feet. Vibration of some sort would cause a relay contact to break, the rocket would stop burning, fall back to earth and explode. . . . Other rockets made a good start, but then unaccountably exploded at 3,000 to 6,000 feet or even higher. The rocket was destroyed and with it all the evidence of the cause. Others, again, made a perfect flight, but over the target area a white cloud of steam suddenly appeared in the sky, a short, sharp double report rang out, the warhead crashed and a shower of wreckage fell to earth. The rocket, after covering 160 miles, had unaccountably blown up at a height of a few thousand feet. Only 10 to 20% of the rockets launched reached their target without a hitch. I was in despair.

Dornberger sought, and obtained, permission to fire rockets from one range to another over the heads of any remaining Polish civilians living below the flight path, though, disquietingly, the matter was first referred to Himmler. With von Braun he spent many hours that autumn and winter crouched in a slit trench somewhere below the point where the latest A-4 should begin to plunge to earth, staring skywards with binoculars. In case launching a rocket was, as some of the staff at Peenemünde had all along contended, too complicated for ordinary soldiers to handle, engineers and technicians from Peenemünde joined the firing crews, but there was no improvement. Was, they wondered, a particular fault creeping in, either in the rockets still coming from Peenemünde or in those now coming off the production lines at Nordhausen? But this theory was soon, quite literally, exploded. 'We had the same failures with all of them.' While conference followed conference, 'visitors from headquarters drove away with long faces', but eventually the causes of the premature explosions, which proved to be due to a variety of reasons, were identified and cured. Meanwhile some rockets were 'fitted with the new measurement data transmitters . . . which would reveal danger points while the rocket was in flight', the resulting information being transmitted by radio. Dornberger had apparently forgotten that famous slogan, *Feind hört mit*, 'The enemy is also listening'. At last six rockets resulting in 'six impacts' were launched in a single day, the longest run of success so far. The A-4 as a warhead-delivery system was as near perfect as they were going to get it in the time available and, as Dornberger put it, 'we thought ourselves justified in devoting time to increasing the explosive effect'.

All the A-4s so far fired had been loaded with nothing more lethal than sand, though even these did a formidable amount of damage, for 'the sheer momentum of a rocket weighing over 4½ tons and travelling at 1500 m.p.h.', they had established, 'caused a crater 30 to 40 yards wide and 10 to 15 yards deep even without a high explosive charge'. Dornberger would have liked to install a proximity fuse to explode the warhead 'about 60 feet above the target . . . to get the maximum lateral effect', but for once 'it proved impossible . . . to get such a device manufactured in Germany'. They were also compelled slightly to reduce the weight of explosive used, having to fit ¼ inch steel over the warhead in the nose in place of the scarce light alloys they would have preferred. However, even the 1650 lb (750 kg) for which they finally settled – within a warhead weighing 2200 lb (1000 kg) – exploding 10 feet from the ground or even, as Dornberger anticipated, on impact, should prove impressively destructive. They also consoled themselves for the continuing tendency of the rocket to break up on re-entry into the atmosphere with the evidence that 'in hundreds of cases . . . the warhead and the adjoining instrument compartment flew on alone . . . and reached the ground undamaged' so that 'we could expect to achieve some effect even with the 30 per cent that disintegrated'.

The need for continued testing meant that consignments of rockets had regularly to be shipped from Peenemünde and Nordhausen to Blizna, providing useful experience of the problems that would arise when finished A-4s were shipped straight from Nordhausen to the munitions dumps supplying the launching units. The whole procedure was studied in detail, and eventually it was found that it would take six or seven days for the rockets to complete their journey, travelling in pairs on flat wagons, with five or ten wagons to a train. The usual labels and documentation were omitted, the curious or bureaucratic being repelled by the detachments of soldiers who travelled with each trainload.

A realistic target had now been set – an output of fifteen A-4s a day from the beginning of April 1944, rising to twenty-five by the middle of the month. The real bottleneck was the liquid oxygen supply, calculated to be sufficient for only twenty-eight firings a day, though a substantially higher rate of fire would be possible if sufficient missiles were available. Already two detachments or *Abteilungen*, each of three batteries, had been formed to use the A-4 in action. One *Abteilung* would be mobile and was expected to fire off up to nine A-4s per battery in each twenty-four hours, a maximum of twenty-seven. The other, based in a permanent bunker, was expected to launch more than fifty, giving the two *Abteilungen* together a capacity of nearly eighty missiles a day, considerably more than the one per hour which the British experts regarded as intolerable. Later, when supply permitted, a third *Abteilung* might be formed.

The first battery actually to be set up was No.444 (Experimental and Training), designed to test rockets under field conditions and to work out the 'drill' on which the instructional manuals could be drawn up for later units. It was formed at Koslin on the Baltic in the summer of 1943 and in October moved to Blizna. Here, while Dornberger was, most unfortunately as it turned out, 'detained in Berlin by some conference', it gave its first demonstration of a mobile unit in action.

On 5 November 1943, with the temperture nearly 10°C below zero, the first launching test took place. . . . The experimental battery had so far fired only a few test shots and was still inexperienced. At the first practice at Blizna it had been assumed that loose sand, the surface frozen over to a depth of only half an inch, would be adequate as a base. Owing to some unfortunate carelessness, the blast deflector plate of the firing table was not set firmly on the ground at ignition time. The gas jet thawed out the ground and burrowed down into the sand. One leg of the firing table sank slowly into the soil during the preliminary burning time. The rocket rose diagonally, lost control and crashed into the woods two miles away.

Even worse than Dornberger's absence was the unlucky presence of the senior artillery officer recently selected to command the rocket and flying-bomb launching batteries in action.

That would not have been so bad if General Heinemann . . . had not been watching a rocket launched for the first time. From this false start, due entirely to the inexperience of the man in charge, the conclusion was drawn that only firm concrete platforms would serve for front-line operations. For over six months manpower and material were wasted on the erection of these concrete emplacements in the battle area. . . . The first impression stuck.

Dornberger's own preference had always been for 'a bit of planking on a forest track, or the overgrown track itself', but here he was up against Hitler's passion, as an architect *manqué*, for huge and grandiose constructions, preferably made of concrete. Hitler had always favoured large bunkers combining storage facilities with firing platforms for both the A-4 and the flying bomb. The first 'large site' (as the Allies called them), intended specifically for the rocket, had been selected as long ago as December 1942 in woodland near Calais, one and a half miles from the nearest railway station at Watten, by which name it became known. The site was also conveniently close to main roads, a canal and electric grid lines, and Dornberger, bowing to the inevitable, thought it could also be used to accommodate a liquid oxygen plant, as well as 108 A-4 rockets and the troops to fire them. The prodigious amount of concrete needed for 'North-West Power Station' (as it was code-named), 120,000 cubic metres, made the scheme irresistibly attractive to Hitler, when Speer presented it to him on 25 March 1943. It was then anticipated that the structure, though not its wiring and plant, would be ready by the end of July 1943 and on 4 May the army asked for it to be complete and fit for operations by 1 November.

Unknown to the Germans the photographic interpreters at Medmenham had, as already mentioned,* been keeping a sharp eye on what was going on at Watten and various other points in the Pas-de-Calais, though most of the activity they detected was related to flying-bomb launching and storage

---

*See page 65.

sites. As early as 17 May Medmenham drew attention to 'a large rail- and canal-served clearing in the woods, possibly a gravel pit', and as the work progressed a scale model of the site was prepared. On 3 July Lord Cherwell candidly admitted in a note to the Prime Minister that he was as much in the dark as anyone about 'these very large structures similar to gun emplacements' but repeated the view he had expressed three weeks before that 'if is worth the enemy's while to go to all the trouble of building them it would seem worth ours to destroy them'. On 6 July an agent's report described the area as a centre of 'German long-range rocket activity', and Watten's fate was sealed. The head of one of the country's most famous construction firms, Sir Malcolm MacAlpine, advised that the best moment to attack would be before the concrete had set and was still surrounded by planking, and on 27 August the job was duly undertaken by 185 Flying Fortresses of the US 8th Air Force, all of whom 'made it' home. They left behind a scene of ruin. The 'launching shelter', Dornberger lamented, was now 'a desolate heap of concrete, steel, props and planking. The concrete hardened. After a few days the shelter was beyond saving. All we could do was roof in a part and use it for other work'.

Watten was in fact converted, with remarkable ingenuity, into a virtually impregnable factory for producing liquid oxygen, by building a roof 10 feet thick on top of the surviving 12 foot walls and then hoisting it up hydraulically and building up the walls beneath it. The Germans were left, after the roof had been strengthened, with a vast concrete cavern 300 feet long by 150 feet wide, beneath 23 feet of concrete, and the Todt organization engineer responsible, Xavier Dorsch, now produced an even more imaginative plan for a second 'bunker' at Wizernes near Boulogne, originally intended merely as a storage dump. Dorsch's plan, as he told Dornberger, involved 'placing a bell of concrete 20 feet thick on the top of the quarry' already there, beneath which a huge network of tunnels were to be hollowed out, including workshops, storerooms, barrack rooms and even a hospital. At the heart of this vast complex, which would require a million tons of concrete, would be a huge chamber where the rockets were prepared for firing, before being trundled into the open air along two passageways, whimsically named 'Gretchen' and 'Gustav', protected by 5-foot-thick steel doors.

Dorsch decided that a scheme of this magnitude required Hitler's approval, and he and Dornberger were duly invited to Rastenburg on 30 September 1943 to meet the same galaxy of generals as had watched the A-4 film back in July. Dornberger was 'shocked' at the deterioration in the Führer's appearance even in those few weeks. 'He seemed to me to have aged. . . . I particularly noticed the unhealthy, yellowish . . . greenish-yellow colour of his complexion and . . . the ghastly pallor of his face.' As he signed the necessary orders, which also empowered Field Marshal von Rundstedt, C-in-C, West, to make 'preparations for action throughout France', Hitler's 'hand trembled slightly' but when 'Dorsch began to speak Hitler at once brightened up . . . immediately captivated by the grandiose plans Dorch described and . . . enthusiastically consented'. Hitler also listened to Dornberger's counter-plan for 'putting the A-4 into action from motorized batteries', though he ruled against it, but was perhaps more impressed than he admitted, for a few days later he told Albert Speer that he was doubtful if the Wizernes battery would ever be finished. It was a perceptive comment. Although the workforce on the site was built up from 1100 in April 1944 to nearly 1300 in May and 1400 in mid-June, most of them German, progress was slow because of the constant air-raid warnings, which stopped work no fewer than 229 times during May alone.

In addition to Watten and Wizernes, the Germans also built a large though somewhat less impressive bunker at Sottevast, eight miles due south of Cherbourg, and another at Équeurdre-ville on its outskirts, misleadingly known to the Allies as Martinvast, a town four miles away, though Équeurdreville was later allocated to the flying bomb. A number of other, much simpler, small sites were also built, consisting of two sunken parallel roads on either side of an existing tree-lined road, so that camouflage nets could be strung from the branches, with three small platforms built across it. The launching crews would emerge from the side roads to set up their missiles on the platforms, then go back into hiding. The only known site of this type actually built was near the Chateau du Molay, west of Bayeux, but other places were earmarked for similar use.

By 8 November 1943 all these preparations were sufficiently far advanced for Hitler, broadcasting fcom the Munich beer-cellar which was one of the shrines of the Nazi movement, to proclaim to his wildly applauding audience, 'Our hour of revenge is nigh!' At the beginning of December the elderly Lieutenant-General Erich Heinemann, who had watched the disastrous test at Blizna the previous month, was appointed commander of Army Corps 65 (LXV in German army numbering), which was to launch both secret weapons, with, in charge of the A-4 component, a hitherto obscure artillery officer, Major-General Richard Metz, henceforward known as HARKO (from the German abbreviation for Senior Artillery Commander) 91. Control of Peenemünde was soon afterwards taken away from Dornberger, against his wishes, nominally so that he could concentrate on 'the formation and training of field units'.

The new year brought fresh problems. On 15 March 1944, in response to a telephone call in the small hours, Dornberger reached Berchtesgaden after a nightmare journey 'delayed by snowstorms, icy roads and the havoc of a heavy air raid on Munich' to be told that von Braun and two other senior engineers had been arrested by the Gestapo for alleged sabotage. They had, he learned from Field Marshal Keitel himself, been overheard 'in company at Zinnowitz', presumably by the spies planted by Himmler, boasting 'that it had never been their intention to make a weapon of war out of the rocket' but only 'to obtain money for their experiments in space travel'. What had happened, he decided, was that remarks to the effect that the A-4 was 'only the first tentative step' towards 'voyages in space' had been misunderstood, perhaps deliberately, as part of Himmler's campaign to take over the whole enterprise. Next day Dornberger pleaded his subordinates' case at the Gestapo head office in Berlin, where he was not much comforted to be asked 'Do you know what a fat file of evidence we have against you here?' and to be told that it 'would have to be gone into eventually'. His incautious criticism of Hitler's dream that the rocket would never be used was, he now learned, held to have 'exercised a harmful pessimistic, almost defeatist influence' on his staff, and he was also held responsible for the general 'delay in the development of the A-4'. He was, however, allowed to leave, being 'still regarded as our greatest rocket expert', and a few days later von Braun and the others were also released, the whole episode having apparently been designed to warn them to watch their step – and, perhaps, to demonstrate their loyalty by getting the rocket into action at last.

On 1 June 1944, much against Dornberger's wishes, the main part of the development works at Peenemünde was converted into a commercial concern under a managing director from the great electrical engineering firm of Siemens, who was, Dornberger complained, 'practically a stranger to our work'. Nor were things going well at Nordhausen, where a new man, Alben Sawatzki, who had made his name in speeding up output of the Tiger tank, had been seconded from another firm, Henschel, to take charge of production planning. The inevitable delays were attributed by Degenkolb and his fellow engineers and industrialists from the commercial world to defects in the development work. 'Major difficulties are cropping up . . . now that mass production is starting,' he had told a meeting presided over by Speer on 8 November 1943, and it was not till New Year's Day 1944 that the first three A-4s left Nordhausen. During the whole month, which was to have seen the start of the rocket offensive, only 50 were delivered, and in February only 86, a long way short of the 300 called for under the Degenkolb–Saur programme and even further short of the 1000 that Saur had asserted to be possible. In March the figure was better, 253, and in May better still, 437 – a total that would have been higher if constant demands for major changes, with all the retooling and redrawing of blueprints they involved, were not still arriving from Blizna and Dornberger's own headquarters at Schwedt, 80 miles from Peenemünde and 250 from Blizna, to which he flew ceaselessly back and forth in his beloved Storch. By now, although the training and equipment of the launching batteries was going smoothly, the earliest possible date for a sustained A-4 bombardment was early September. On 13 June 1944, while General Metz – holding the post Dornberger thought should have been his, as operational commander of the A-4 batteries – waited for his first missiles to arrive, his colleague Colonel Wachtel, in command of Flak-regiment 155 (W), armed with flying bombs, opened fire on London. The Luftwaffe, coming on the secret-weapon scene long after the army, had got its missile into action first.

Hitler's reaction was immediate. Flying-bomb production, he ordered, should be increased at the expense of rocket manufacture, and on 6 July he directed that the second underground A-4 factory, Cement, now being built at Traunsee in Austria, should instead be earmarked for tank production. The rocket-manufacturing programme was already in trouble, however, because of the constant modifications still being made to the production model, which cut the output figure from May's 437 – not all that far short of the 600 a month that Albert Speer considered reasonable – to 132 in June and only 86 in July. But Goebbels remained enthusiastic. 'If we could only show this film in every cinema in Germany,' he told his officials, after Speer had invited him to see an updated version of the now classic documentary which had previously impressed Hitler, 'I wouldn't have to make another speech or write another word. The most hardboiled pessimist could doubt in victory no longer.'

The rocket men also had other troubles than the loss of Hitler's support. Having fled to Blizna to escape the British bombers, they now had to move again to escape the advancing Red Army, deserting Heidelager (Heathcamp) for the equally romantically named Heidekraut (Heather) 10 miles east of Tuchel and about 160 miles north-west of Warsaw. Here they struggled with the rocket's continuing tendency, in spite of earlier modifications to blow up on re-entering the earth's atmosphere, a fault finally, or at least largely, cured by fitting the fuel tank with a steel 'sleeve' which made it better able to withstand vibration. By now, however, perfecting the missile was becoming an end in itself and, after 65,000 modifications to the original design, both von Braun and Dornberger seem to have felt there was always time for one more. Kammler, anxious to get the rocket into action, had no patience with this approach, but seems himself to have been losing faith in the missile, as Dornberger discovered in a humiliating public confrontation:

On 8 July 1944 I was described by Kammler, in the presence of

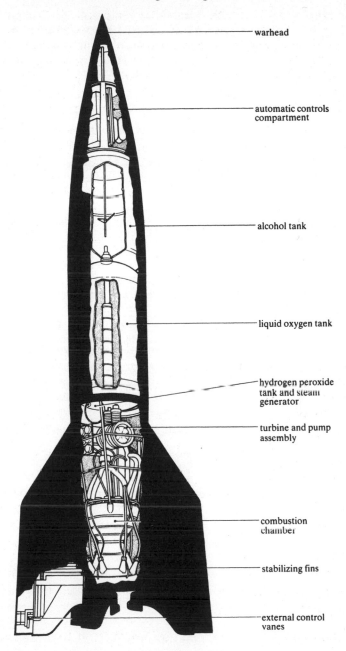

warhead

automatic controls
compartment

alcohol tank

liquid oxygen tank

hydrogen peroxide
tank and steam
generator

turbine and pump
assembly

combustion
chamber

stabilizing fins

external control
vanes

111

General Buhle and two other generals, as a public danger. He said I ought to be court-martialled . . . [and that] for years I had been weakening Germany's armament potential by tying [up] . . . both . . . men and material. . . . It would be a crime to devote another penny to so hopeless a project.

On 20 July there came the attempt on Hitler's life, in the aftermath of which the SS seized an even closer grip on the whole war machine, including the rocket. Dornberger's ultimate superior, General Fromm, C-in-C of the Home Army, was arrested and his post taken over by Himmler. Promotion for Kammler soon followed. He became a lieutenant-general in the Waffen SS and, on 8 August, special commissioner for the whole A-4 programme, the post Dornberger had 'been fighting for years to obtain'. It was, even for the naturally doleful Dornberger, a particularly gloomy period:

Thus, after nearly all the obstacles to the tactical employment of the A-4 had been overcome, a complete layman took the leadership, a man who only a month before had clearly professed his disbelief in the project. . . . The first two months after Kammler's appointment were hard and bitter ones. I had to endure a whole series of humiliations. I had to submit to a chaotic flood of ignorant, contradictory, irreconcilable orders from this man who was neither soldier nor technician. They took the form of a hundred telegrams a day. . . . In those two months I reached the limit of man's endurance. But I had made rockets my life's work. Now we had to prove that their time was come.

8

NO IMMEDIATE DANGER

No serious attack by rocket . . . was likely, at any rate before the New Year.

Minutes of War Cabinet Defence Committee,
18 November 1943

On 27 August 1943, while the American Fortresses were bombing the suspected 'projector' at Watten, Duncan Sandys issued his eleventh interim report. It included the full text of a message that had recently arrived from 'a quite unusually well-placed and hitherto most reliable source', which at last dispelled, or should have done, the confusion surrounding the whole secret-weapon investigation. It began by stating categorically that 'there are two different rocket secret weapons under construction' and after referring to a 'pilotless aircraft' went on to give by far the fullest account yet of the rocket, including its correct German name:

A-4 is 16 metres long and 4.15 metres in diameter. . . . The explosive charge is stated to have an effect equivalent to the British four-ton bomb. The A-4 is launched from a projector . . . [and] has vanes at the rear end like a bomb. The range . . . is 200 kilometres, with maximum altitude approximately 33,000 metres. . . . So far approximately 100 A-4 projectiles have been fired and a further 100 are at present in hand. The accuracy of aim is most unsatisfactory. . . . The construction of parts . . . is distributed throughout Germany. . . . Assembly and tests . . . are carried out . . . near Peenemünde. . . . Some concrete emplacements for A-4 projectors are now ready near LE HAVRE and CHERBOURG. More are under construction. These concrete emplacements are for protection but are not essential as the projectors can be placed in open fields if necessary. . . . About June 10th Hitler told assembled military leaders that the Germans had only to hold out, as by the end of 1943 London would be levelled to the ground and Britain forced to capitulate. . . . October 20th is at present fixed as zero day for rocket attacks to begin.

113

In his covering note Duncan Sandys reported confirmatory evidence, of a kind, from Stockholm. A Swedish engineer recently back from Germany claimed 'to have been present at a trial firing of the long-range rocket in July'. Sandys made no comment on either report but, in an appendix, listed the plans already agreed to meet the rocket threat, to which had now been added a 'Confusion Plan . . . employing smoke and flash simulators . . . with the object of making it difficult for . . . reconnaissance planes to make accurate observations'.

Four days later, on 31 August 1943, the Chiefs of Staff, with various ministers and Dr Jones in attendance, heard from Air Chief Marshal Portal that it was estimated that it would take six months to make good the damage at Peenemünde, while Sir Malcolm MacAlpine, when shown the post-raid picture of Watten, had commented that 'it would be easier for the Germans to begin again elsewhere' than try to repair the wrecked site. Meanwhile Lord Cherwell once again repeated that 'he was still sceptical' about the whole affair. 'Many of the reports were inconsistent and some of them scientifically incorrect.' The chief 'pro-rocket' advocate among senior ministers was now Herbert Morrison, who would, he said, 'feel happier if he could construct a further 100,000 Morrison shelters and press on with the reinforcement of surface shelters'. So far all he had been able to do was warn 'Regional Commissioners to move Civil Defence workers to London if required. . . . If serious bombardment started,' he warned, 'a move of the seat of government might have to be contemplated.' This prompted the committee to agree that the Chancellor of the Exchequer, who, as head of the Treasury was responsible for the civil service, should 'examine and report on the implications of reviving the "Black Plan" ', which covered this contingency.

On 14 September Kingsley Wood duly did so, though the tale he had to tell the Defence (Operations) Committee was not encouraging:

A large proportion of the accommodation at one time earmarked in connection with the 'BLACK' plan had now been taken up for various purposes. This and other difficulties . . . made it practically impossible to revive. . . .

It was generally agreed [recorded the Minutes] that the plan should not be revived but that the 'Citadel' accommodation available in London should be reviewed and arrangements made to ensure that the essential work of government departments could continue to be carried out in London.

Soon afterwards the Prime Minister made his first, distinctly veiled, reference to the whole matter, in the House of Commons on 21 September:

The speeches of the German leaders contain mysterious allusions to new methods and new weapons which will presently be tried against us. It would, of course, be natural for the enemy to spread such rumours in order to encourage his own people, but there is probably more in it than that.

The danger of attack by pilotless aircraft was now increasingly dominating the secret-weapons scene and, despite all the evidence to the contrary, there was a tendency to assume that this must also be the 'rocket weapon' to which so many reports referred. Lord Cherwell in particular was determined to discredit belief in a separate long-range missile and on 15 September, after consulting Dr Crow, also a known sceptic in the matter, drafted a list of seventeen 'loaded' questions designed to be put to Dr Crow and three other leading scientists. The first was typical: 'Could a range of 160 miles possibly be obtained with a single-stage rocket?' The questionnaire purported, quite falsely, to have been drafted by Duncan Sandys and Herbert Morrison. When Cherwell sent this dubious document to Ian Jacob at the Cabinet Office, the latter, very properly, sent copies of it first to its two supposed authors, who had never seen it before. Morrison's response is not clear, while Duncan Sandys neatly outmanoeuvred the Paymaster-General, proposing that if the questionnaire were put to anyone it should be to his own 'Bodyline' Scientific Committee, nineteen strong. Cherwell rejected this idea as 'hardly . . . practical' and when his questionnaire was not sent to its intended, and supposedly sympathetic, recipients, complained of 'gross negligence to say the least' within the Cabinet Office.

Meanwhile the 'pro-rocket' party were also active. On 29 September 1943 the head of the Secret Intelligence Service, known as 'C', circulated a document entitled 'German Long-

Range Rocket. Report on Reliability of Evidence Collected',
which came in fact from the fertile and convincing pen of his
scientific adviser, Dr Jones. The paper selected a number of
'keystones' in the case for the rocket's existence, particularly
the report from the 'unusually well-placed' source recently
circulated by Duncan Sandys – the informant was, he now
revealed, on 'the staff of a high officer in the German Army
Weapons Office'. Dr Jones first disposed of those twin night-
mares of all intelligence officers, that they might become the
victims of a hoax or a deliberate 'plant' of false evidence:

For the rocket story to be a hoax, it is necessary to suppose that
information . . . has been planted upon many of our secret sources
and upon German prisoners of war, over a long time and in many
places. In addition, the effort of building a fake establishment . . .
would have been enormous and beyond human thoroughness. . . . If
the rocket story is a complete hoax, it is the most consummate ever
conceived. Such a hoax could only be played for a very important
object.

What could such an object be? 'It has been suggested', went
on Dr Jones, 'that long-range rockets are a cover for radio-
controlled pilotless aircraft.' But was this really likely?

While looking for the one we should almost certainly stumble across
the other. Supposing that we believe in the threat of a bombardment
by pilotless aircraft, then those reports which mention both rockets
and aircraft are confirmed by this belief. . . . Much of the critical
evidence points to both weapons and it is at least plausible that while
the German army is developing the one there is keen rivalry with
the air force developing the other. . . . There are obvious technical
objections which, based on our own experience, can be raised against
the prospect of successful rockets, but it is not without precedent for
the Germans to have succeeded while we doubted.

Here was the stumbling block which so many eminent scien-
tists found it hard to overcome, including some members of the
'Bodyline' Scientific Committee, reporting to Duncan Sandys,
which included many outstanding physicists, among them the
'father' of British radar, Robert (later Sir Robert) Watson-
Watt. To assist this large and imposing body, a smaller Fuel
Panel was set up, on which sat Dr Crow, in whose judgement
Lord Cherwell placed so much faith. By its third meeting, on

4 October, it had concluded that 'the necessary range cannot be achieved by a single-stage rocket and that the possibility of such a development in Germany can be ruled out'. A multi-stage rocket, in which one missile lifted another into the sky, was also agreed to be impractical. A suggestion from the panel's chairman, Sir Frank Smith, an electrical engineer, that it should consider the practicality of 'a rocket with a range of one hundred miles or more and an explosive content of one ton', as well as the 60 ton monster with the 10 ton warhead on which Cherwell had poured such scorn, was never really pursued. Even more strangely, the panel does not seem to have grasped the significance of the information provided by the country's two leading authorities on liquid-fuelled rockets, Isaac Lubbock – a Cambridge-educated engineer employed by Shell International, who had successfully experimented, though only on a test stand, with a rocket motor burning high-octane petrol and liquid oxygen – and his assistant, Geoffrey Gollin. Lubbock was one of the scientists who had, as mentioned earlier, recently returned from America – he had in fact been summoned back by Gollin specifically as an expert in this area. With help from Duncan Sandys' assistant, Colonel Kenneth Post, and other experts, he had immediately sketched out the possible design of a long-range rocket burning liquid fuel based on the photographs brought back from Peenemunde. Far from being welcomed by the scientists on the Fuel Panel, at its meeting on 11 October there were complaints that this new evidence had been introduced without warning. More attention was paid to a drawing prepared from the Peenemunde photographs. Dr Crow suggested that the torpedo-shaped objects seen there on heavy-duty wagons were obviously 'inflated barrage balloons' – prompting Colonel Post to ask, since they were being carried by rail, if they were heavier than air. The chairman summed up the opinion of the meeting as being that, 'having seen the sketch submitted to us, we are of the opinion that it may be a rocket', whereupon Lord Cherwell walked out.

At Duncan Sandys's request, Isaac Lubbock went on to prepare a more detailed blueprint for a long-range rocket, four-fifths of the weight of which would be fuel, very close to what the Germans had in fact achieved. Dr Crow considered such a missile impracticable, but eventually the 'Bodyline' Scientific Committee, of which the Fuel Panel was an offshoot, produced a compromise report. Twelve of its members, including Lubbock and Gollin, signed it. The report examined the possible range and warhead weight of both a solid-fuel multi-stage rocket and 'a single-stage rocket using existing American technique for liquid jet motors' and concluded that an improved version of the latter was possible and 'that a rocket projectile . . . possessing the performance estimated . . . could have the dimensions of the object seen at Peenemünde'. Dr Crow agreed to the estimates concerning the solid-fuel rocket but added a dissenting note to the effect that he did not 'consider the performance given' in the two liquid-fuelled version 'to be possible'. The two other members of the committee refused to sign the report at all. A majority of the committee, consisting of the best-qualified men in the country to consider the matter, had, however, decided that the rocket could be a reality and they also attempted an assessment of its accuracy:

We consider it reasonable to assume that half the rounds fired would fall within a circle of about five miles radius round the Mean Point of Impact at a range of 100 to 130 miles. The dispersion would be proportionately greater at longer ranges.

On 24 October 1943 this important report was circulated to members of the Defence Committee (Operations), which met on the evening of 25 October. Lord Cherwell's was the rudest, and most dominant, voice heard that evening. Isaac Lubbock, who was present and who unquestionably knew far more about rockets than Cherwell, was dismissed to his face as a 'third-rate engineer' whose views should be ignored, and Cherwell repeated his conviction that 'At the end of the war, when we knew the full story, we should find that the rocket was a mare's nest'. Churchill proved more open-minded. He asked the South African leader, Field Marshal Smuts, a former lawyer, who happened to be present, for his opinion. 'The evidence', replied Smuts, 'may not be conclusive, but I think a jury would convict!' The Prime Minister himself was clearly beginning to come round to the same opinion. That day he sent a private signal to President Roosevelt about the rocket. 'Scientific opinion . . .', he admitted, 'is divided, but I am personally as yet unconvinced that they cannot be made.'

Cherwell's hostility to the rocket remained unrelenting, even when evidence was forthcoming of the very kind he had himself suggested should exist. When a number of German airmen who had actually been stationed at Peenemünde described seeing 'very large, dark objects' accompanied by a 'flaming yellow mass' rising slowly and almost vertically into the sky – just what he had argued that Swedish fishermen should be reporting – he ignored the information. Those witnesses who could not simply be disregarded he did his best to suborn and at midday on 28 October 1943, shortly before the meeting of the Defence Committee scheduled for 6.30 that evening, called a meeting in the Cabinet Offices in Great George Street of the 'Cherwell Four', the scientists to whom he had previously unsuccessfully tried to have his questionnaire submitted.

The group was highly impressive. Beside that already unwavering opponent of the rocket, Dr Crow, it included a highly distinguished engineer, Sir Frank Smith, and two former Cambridge academics, both Fellows of the Royal Society, Professor Geoffrey Taylor and Professor Ralph (later Sir Ralph) Fowler, both authorities on the application of mathematics to ballistics and engineering. No doubt under pressure from Cherwell they now agreed, as Cherwell reported to Churchill's meeting that evening, that 'there were many formidable difficulties in the way of accepting the object photographed at Peenemünde as the long-range rocket, and that no adequate solution of these difficulties had yet been put forward'. At the same meeting, for good measure, Cherwell mustered a whole series of reasons to 'prove' to his non-scientific colleagues that the rocket was a technical impossibility. He doubted if 'the ratio of two-thirds fuel to one-third weight in metal', necessary if the rocket was to reach London, 'was practicable since it was far in excess of anything our experts had been able to achieve'. Even if some breakthrough in fuel had been made, he questioned whether 'the metal of which the combustion chamber was made could withstand the very high temperatures which would be necessary'. It would be impossible for such a rocket to lift off under its own power, but a projector would 'be very difficult to aim' and would have to weigh 700 tons 'in order to stand the force of recoil'. If launched, the rocket could not be kept on course, since 'no gyroscopic method of control was likely to be effective', while if kept on course it could do no damage, since 'it would be extremely difficult to fit a warhead to the hemispherical nose'. 'In view of the difficulties. . .', the minutes recorded, 'he did not agree that the object photographed at Peenemünde was, in fact, a long-range rocket.'

Perhaps Cherwell had overstated his case. At all events the most prominent scientist present, the scientific adviser to the Army Council, Professor C. D. (later Sir Charles) Ellis, who had been first consulted as far back as April, now said flatly that 'he believed in the possibility of the rocket', while Isaac Lubbock bravely pointed out that 'his calculations' about the possible form a liquid-fuelled rocket might take 'did not substantiate any of the criticisms made by Lord Cherwell'. The Prime Minister refused to come down firmly on one side or the other, but summed up that 'unless it could be shown scientifically that a rocket was impossible we could hardly ignore the existence of unexplained facts'. He proposed to set up a special Committee of Inquiry to settle the matter once for all, starting work the following day, and invited Lord Cherwell to chair it, but the latter, affronted at having his opinions rejected, walked out, pleading a previous engagement for the time proposed. The job was then passed to Sir Stafford Cripps, who was asked to begin work at 9.30 the following morning.

On 1 November Cripps submitted his interim findings. The rocket was, he advised, 'theoretically possible', and the still-unexplained earthwork at Peenemünde might be the 'giant mortar' for which everyone had been seeking. A little later the Ministry of Supply produced some highly imaginative drawings suggesting what it might look like – they envisaged an 80 foot object not unlike a giant milk bottle, poised on a giant seesaw or trundled into position on a trolley to be raised to an acute angle for firing – and searching for these totally fictitious structures now added an extra burden to the work of the interpreters at Medmenham. On the same day as Cripps's first report Cherwell reaffirmed in a private memo to Churchill his belief 'that we shall not suffer from rocket bombardment, certainly not on the scale suggested', adding a barbed postscript: 'As I am often believed to be responsible for giving you scientific advice, it would perhaps be well to mention the fact that I am sceptical about this particular matter.'

Churchill's response to the two contradictory memos of 1 November was to ask Cripps, on the following day, to

hold a short inquiry, of not more than two sittings, into the evidence, as apart from the scientific aspects, of the long-range rocket. At the same time it would be well to assemble what arguments there are for and against:

  (a) the pilotless airplane, and
  (b) the glider bomb operated by a directing aircraft from a distance.

These two latter requirements were, inevitably, to divert the investigation from giving a clear answer to the single question concerning the rocket. Equally unfortunately, but also perhaps inevitably, he decided to invite Lord Cherwell to form, with himself and Duncan Sandys, a three man tribunal, before which witnesses could be cross-examined, the tribunal being assisted by a scientist and an engineer hitherto unconnected with the inquiry. This quasi-judicial procedure did not appeal to that least judicial of men, Lord Cherwell, and he now set out to prejudice what might have been called the court of appeal, the Prime Minister, by writing privately to him before the Cripps inquiry had even met. 'It appears', wrote Cherwell, 'that the Ministry of Aircraft Production' – i.e. Cripps's own department – 'is now planning measures even more far-reaching than were envisaged in 1939 in order to meet a danger whose existence is not certain.' He also tried to throw doubt on the credentials of the man he considered the chief 'prosecution' witness for the rocket. If Cripps, commented Cherwell, preferred 'to accept the assurance of Mr Lubbock – who has not hitherto been conspicuously successful in rocket design . . . against the view of Dr Crow, who has made successful rockets . . . there is nothing more to be said'.

The 'trial' of the evidence for the rocket's existence began on 8 November 1943 in a room in the Cabinet Offices, with one witness after another, including a three-man contingent from Medmenham, traversing the now familiar ground. The 'case' had hardly opened when it took an unexpected turn. Wing Commander Kendall revealed the discovery of a whole new series of concrete ramps in the Pas-de-Calais, all pointing towards London, and Cripps immediately adjourned the proceedings to allow more photographs to be studied. The following day was, as it happened, that of the Lord Mayor's Luncheon (to which the traditional annual pre-war banquet had now shrunk), and Churchill took the opportunity in his speech at the Mansion House to remind the nation of the secret-weapon danger:

We cannot . . . exclude the possibility of new forms of attack upon this island. We have been vigilantly watching for many months past every sign of preparation for such attacks. Whatever happens they will not be of a nature to affect the final course of the war.

The following day the Cripps inquiry heard that more possible launching sites had been discovered, and these dominated its further discussions and its second report, submitted on 17 November: 'There is no doubt that the Germans are doing their utmost to perfect some long-range weapon . . . though there is no evidence of its materialization before the New Year at the earliest.' As for its nature, the 'court' put the 'Rocket A-4' fourth and last in its 'order of probability', after 'glider bombs, pilotless aircraft' and 'long-range rocket, smaller than A-4'. Even this heavily qualified acceptance of the rocket, however, infuriated Lord Cherwell. 'What can you expect from a lawyer who eats nothing but nuts?' he grumbled to his staff, an odd comment from a man who, in the absence of his favourite Port Salut cheese, lived largely on stewed apple and rice.

With the Cripps report the rocket inquiry was shunted into a siding. On 18 November, with his own agreement, since his ministry had its hands full with pre-D-Day problems, Duncan Sandys's special inquiry came to an end, though it was agreed he would attend whenever secret weapons were on the Chiefs of Staff's agenda. The Joint Intelligence Committee, reporting to the Cabinet's Defence Committee, would continue to keep an eye on the whole secret-weapons field, but this was only one of its responsibilities and Dr Jones doubted if this would be adequate. 'My section', he had written to the committee's chairman on 15 November, when he learned what was proposed, 'will continue its work, regardless of any parallel committees which may arise, and will be mindful only of the safety of the country.' In fact his section too, before long, was to have an even more urgent responsibility than hunting down the rocket – that of deceiving the German radar stations in the area where Operation Overlord was soon to fall. The Defence Committee, the senior policy-making body below the War Cabinet, formally endorsed, on 18 November, Cripps's conclusion that 'no serious attack by rocket . . . was likely at any rate before the New Year', and also agreed 'that there was a reasonable prospect of our receiving at least a month's notice before any heavy attack could develop'.

On 27 November 1943 the former secret-weapon code-name, 'Bodyline', most commonly applied to the rocket, was replaced by 'Crossbow', which was used principally about the flying bomb. On 2 December the flying bomb's triumph over the rocket, at least in London, became complete with the discovery of a pilotless aircraft on a ramp at Peenemünde identical with those discovered in France, and seeming to point to an imminent attack of this kind. On 28 December Herbert Morrison's Civil Defence Committee, taking another look at the formerly dreaded rocket, decided that 'on the new appreciation the weight of attack is very much less' than that previously contemplated and Morrison himself, previously the chief alarmist in the government, argued 'that it is undesirable to make plans for any more extensive evacuation of priority classes than is absolutely necessary'. By the end of the year the rocket was definitely in eclipse. 'It is now thought', the committee learned on New Year's Eve, 'that the form of attack likely to be used first by the enemy would be pilotless aircraft, although the possibility of long-distance rockets being utilized, probably at a rather late stage, would certainly not be ignored.'

Once convinced that the rocket existed, Herbert Morrison had all along taken the danger from it more seriously than his colleagues and at the first meeting of the Civil Defence Committee in the new year, on 18 January 1944, he raised the question of a public warning system – essential, he thought, both to reduce casualties and to maintain morale. He was a good deal more confident than the Air Ministry experts that radar would detect each missile as it was fired, or at least before it arrived, but recognized, in the draft public announcement he had prepared, that the interval between warning and impact would be desperately short:

There will be no time for preparations. People who can reach their shelters in less than a minute should go to them immediately. Failing such protection – in a corridor or stairway away from windows, under a strong table or bed or stairs. People caught in the street should, if there is not a shelter handy, run into the nearest building or lie down flat in the gutter or beside a low wall. Get under the best cover immediately.

Owing to the nature of the attack no 'Raiders passed' signal will be possible. Each . . . warning should be regarded as lasting for five minutes and after this time has elapsed work may again be resumed.

Until Air Defence of Great Britain (formerly, and later, known as Fighter Command) was able, via a special electrical system, to give a simultaneous alarm in the endangered areas, it was proposed that 'four rounds will be fired in quick succession from light anti-aircraft guns from a selected number of battery sites', but this crude and temporary system would be replaced as soon as possible by 'a number of maroons fired simultaneously'; sounding the sirens would take too long. Morrison also proposed that, just before the attack was expected to start, people should be warned of the necessity of keeping the Germans guessing where their missiles had landed:

The public are warned not to communicate, by word of mouth or otherwise, any information as to whether [rocket] shells have fallen, where they have fallen, or the extent of the damage done by them. The enemy will be anxious to obtain such information as a guide to the range and accuracy of his weapon and even quite general statements, if they fall into his hands, may assist him.

All this seemed sensible enough, but the Civil Defence Committee were dubious. Even a preliminary announcement at this stage was ruled out, on the grounds it might cause needless alarm, and there were doubts about the value of a short-term warning. A headlong rush to take cover might, it was feared, cause a disastrous crush in the narrow tube-station entrances, production would be interrupted, and some timorous workers, once underground, might 'remain there indefinitely or even fail to come to work at all'. For the moment the preparations stayed secret.

Meanwhile the Chiefs of Staff were trying to decide whether the 'ski sites' discovered in northern France – so called after the shape of their most prominent building – which were rightly associated with the flying bomb, or the 'large sites' detected earlier, assumed, in most cases correctly, to be connected with the rocket, presented the more urgent problem. At a meeting on 25 January 1944 a sharp differences of opinion emerged. The Chief of the Air Staff, Sir Charles Portal, 'considered that SIRACOURT and WATTEN should be attacked on the highest priority, the necessary effort being at the expense of attacks on "ski" sites, and that SOTTEVAST and LOTTINGEM should be raised to the highest priority' a little later. 'Sir Alan Brooke', meanwhile, the minutes recorded, 'queried the wisdom of diverting effort from the attack on "ski" sites to large sites at this juncture', while Lord Cherwell, no doubt present because secret weapons were on the agenda, made a typically unhelpful, and grotesquely wrong, contribution. 'He was not convinced that the large sites were in fact rocket projectors for the attack of targets in this country. Possibly they were some form of anti-invasion defences' designed to put down a 'heavy concentration of gas on the beaches'. It was also decided to look into the possibility 'of capturing for cross-examination purposes technical personnel concerned with the construction of large sites', to try to establish just what the Germans were up to, and of 'staging commando raids against "CROSSBOW" sites'. These last ideas never in fact came to anything, but bombing was something the Allies *could* accomplish, and between the start of the major 'Crossbow' bombing effort, on 5 December 1943, and 12 June 1944 more than 8000 tons of bombs were to be directed against all four 'large sites' so far mentioned, plus another three examined later.

On 10 February 1944 the Ministry of Home Security sent a 'Most Secret' letter to the Regional Commissioners of the six Civil Defence regions most likely to be affected – they included the cities of Southampton, Portsmouth, Bristol and Plymouth – setting out the arrangements for reporting suspected 'Crossbow' incidents, now subdivided into those caused by 'Diver', the new code-word for pilotless aircraft, and those attributed to 'Big Ben' (officially one word, but usually typed as two), the cover-name for the rocket. The need for continuing secrecy was stressed, with even wardens and police officers being kept in the dark, so that 'reliance must be placed on [Civil Defence] Controllers and Chief Constables picking out and investigating any report which suggests the possibility of CROSSBOW attack'.

Two weeks later, on 22 February 1944, perhaps in deference to the Home Secretary's wish to alert the public to the coming danger, Churchill specifically referred to both secret weapons in the middle of a long review of the war situation in the House of Commons:

There is no doubt that the Germans are preparing on the French shore new means of attack on this country, either by pilotless aircraft, or possibly rockets, or both, on a considerable scale. We have long been watching this with the utmost vigilance. We are striking at all evidences of these preparations, on occasions when the weather is suitable and to the maximum extent possible without detracting from the strategic offensive against Germany.

Following this speech Morrison's civil servants diligently redrafted the announcement to be issued at the appropriate moment and the Civil Defence Committee spent a happy session on 27 April 1944 in that most agreeable of occupations, rewriting someone else's draft, making such amendments as substituting 'excessive alarm' for 'panic'. There was some opposition, too, to the whole idea of a widespread warning, on the grounds this might 'involve the stoppage of work throughout, say, the whole London area for five minutes every time a single rocket was fired'. It would, it was thought, be helpful to consult trade unions and employers on the subject, though how this was to be done without breaching the security that enshrouded all rocket preparations was not explained. That no warning might be possible does not seem to have occurred to anyone, and the substance of Morrison's announcement was left intact, promising the citizens of London – slightly different arrangements were proposed for Portsmouth, Southampton and Bristol – a display at once noisy and colourful:

When it is known that a rocket is on its way the special warning for London will be a number of maroons fired simultaneously and their short, sharp explosions will be accompanied by whistles and red flares which will shoot up to about one thousand feet. The flares will burn for about eight seconds and will be visible by day or night. A single short wail like the first wail of the Alert will at the same time be executed on the air-raid sirens. . . . There is no occasion for panic or alarm. People in the areas affected have already stood up to far worse bombardment than anything the enemy can achieve by his new weapon; its employment is in the nature of a 'last throw' and steps are being taken with all possible speed to eliminate it or reduce it to negligible proportions.

The warning system planned by the government might have been even more impressive than the authorities envisaged if the reminiscences of an airman placed in charge of one improvised maroon on a site in the Fulham Road are typical:

This appliance consisted of something like mortar barrels, a supply of canisters containing firework mixtures similar to Roman Candles and firework rockets combined – one made the flare, the other made the bang. It was to be fired by a car battery and wires leading to the barrels. I give thanks that we never had to fire these things. . . . It would, to my mind, have been . . . disastrous to us standing around such a contraption.

For his men, too, the non-arrival of the rocket at this period provided an unexpected bonus:

My crew at that time consisted of three North Country lads who asked if I would let them have leave to go along the road to watch Fulham Football Club. I gave them a certain spot to stand so that I could get them recalled should an 'operation' occur, [but] we never had cause to 'operate'.

9

WE HAVE BEEN CAUGHT NAPPING

In reply to a suggestion by the Prime Minister that we had to some extent been caught napping, Sir Charles Portal said that . . . the evidence had been most closely watched.

Minutes of the 'Crossbow' Committee, 18 July 1944

With the arrival of the flying-bomb in mid-June and the rapid escalation of the first few uncertain shots into a continuous major bombardment, it finally became clear that when they boasted about their secret weapons the Germans had not been bluffing. For the moment the Civil Defence Committee was preoccupied with the effects of this new attack, which included the possibility of a disastrous hit on 'one of the Charing Cross tunnels' of the London Underground beneath the Thames, which could result in a destructive tide of water flooding through 57 miles of low-lying tunnel at a speed of 15 m.p.h., which, Herbert Morrison warned in a note to the Prime Minister on 23 June, might 'put the tubes out of action for months'. A rocket was even more likely to pierce a vulnerable tunnel, and this was to be a recurring fear in the coming months. The vast exodus from London, estimated at one and a half million people, which followed the arrival of the flying bombs made planning for what might happen if 'Big Ben' followed 'Diver' a little easier. But to Morrison the outlook still seemed dark, and on 27 June 1944 he spelt out his fears in a long memorandum on 'The Flying-Bomb and the Rocket':

I am apprehensive of what might happen if the strain continues, and, in addition to flying-bombs, long-range rockets are used against the metropolis. . . . I have a high degree of faith in the Londoners and . . . will do everything to hold up their courage and spirit, but there

128

is a limit and the limit will come. . . . Some installations which . . . seem to be destined for firing the weapon are nearing completion and may be operational in a matter of a fortnight or so. No very accurate estimate of the scale of attack is available but a theoretical calculation on admittedly scanty information gives a maximum of some 700 tons every 24 hours. . . . In the heaviest attack London ever experienced (May 1941) about 450 tons of HE only were dropped in a night and the Civil Defence personnel . . . much more numerous than they are now, were severely strained and could not have held the position much longer. . . . German propaganda . . . has in this context promised 'a further turn of the screw'. We must neglect no possible method of preventing it.

Morrison's suggestions ranged from 'commando raids' on suspected launching sites to threats of reprisals against selected German towns 'or the use of gas', but when the Cabinet discussed the paper that day practical objections were put forward to all of them, although there was one ray of hope. The army was already succeeding where, at least in the case of the flying bomb, the RAF had failed, for of seven 'large sites' believed to be intended for launching rockets two had already been captured and a third had been abandoned. The remaining four, though frequently bombed, might, it was thought, still be used. Typically, Cherwell seized the opportunity to try once again to discredit the rocket's existence. The 'large sites', he suggested, might be designed for 'a larger type of pilotless aircraft', but, also typically, he left himself a loophole. 'The Paymaster-General', the minutes recorded, 'said that the production of a rocket on the scale suspected would be extremely uneconomical. It did not follow, however, that the enemy would not adopt this form of attack.' On 30 June Cherwell sent Churchill a long and detailed paper to prove – contrary to the true facts – that he had been right in every particular in his predictions about the flying bomb and therefore, by implication, that he was right about the rocket. A long and time-wasting inquest followed, tactfully ended by Ian Jacob in a note to the Prime Minister on 14 July:

Lord Cherwell consistently challenged the possibility of such a weapon, whereas the Chiefs of Staff and the Joint Intelligence Committee equally consistently held that the rocket should be taken seriously. . . . It is a bit early yet to say who was wrong.

During the opening months of 1944 the most urgent preoccupation of all the military departments had been Operation Overlord and most secret-weapon intelligence had concerned the flying-bomb. The radar watch that Dr Jones had set up on signal activity around Peenemünde had yielded evidence of only 'an occasional attempt to plot the track of a rocket', but the fortunate move of the main A-4 testing centre to Blizna now began to produce a steadily increasing flow of information. The Polish Home Army, though it operated in secret and underground, was well organized, with its own intelligence departments and scientific advisers. Its attention was directed to Blizna after it was learned that a carload of German secret-weapon specialists killed in a road accident in Warsaw came from that area, and by January 1944 rockets, their warheads filled with sand so that large fragments of the missile often survived the impact, were coming down over much of the countryside to the north, north-east and west of the little village, and some as far north as the River Bug. As members of the Forestry Commission, still able to move fairly freely, reported, these mysterious objects demolished buildings and uprooted trees, as well as causing craters 20 metres wide, and the Polish historian previously quoted has described the clandestine war which now developed in this sparsely populated corner of eastern Europe.

Motorized patrols stationed in the countryside . . . would rush to the scene of the explosion, seal it off and gather up all the fragments and parts of the mechanism. . . . Patrols of the Home Army did the same and almost every day a race took place between the Germans, acting openly, with every technical facility at their disposal, and the underground army, which had to operate in secret but was on its own territory and received willing assistance from the local population. In the fight to get there first, shots were exchanged several times.

Ultra intercepts, emanating from Bletchley, also drew attention to Blizna, for one signal revealed that the Germans were seeking details of a crater near Sidlice, 160 miles north-west of it, too far to have been made by a flying-bomb. A subsequent reconnaissance on 5 May, however, merely confused the issue, for the photographs revealed a flying-bomb launching ramp, not a Peenemünde-style 'earthwork' and, with D-Day approaching, there was no immediate response to Dr Jones's request for further flights.

Realizing the importance of their discoveries, the Poles conceived two somewhat desperate plans: to seize the Blizna base by force and hold it long enough for the accompanying scientists to learn its secrets; and to hijack a train near Blizna, transfer the rocket on board to a lorry and remove it to a secret hideout in the Lower Carpathian mountains, where it could be examined at leisure. Fortunately neither operation proved necessary, for at dawn on Saturday, 20 May 1944, a rocket landed, almost undamaged, in swampy ground on the bank of the River Bug, near the village of Klimczyce, close to the town of Sarnaki, eighty miles east of Warsaw. The Poles managed to get there first and pushed their treasure deeper into the bog, till it was totally covered. A few days later three pairs of horses, aided by 'troops' of the 22nd Regiment of the Polish Home Army, dragged it from the mud and transported it by cart to a local barn where it was dismembered by the flickering light of candles and hurricane lamps, under the direction of an engineer who had been in Auschwitz, like the head of the Research Committee of the Home Army, and, most exceptionally, been released. For ten days he commuted between his home in Warsaw and the village of Holowcyze-Kolonia, where the rocket was hidden, until, by ill-chance, he was arrested by the Gestapo for a totally different offence, though he survived this experience too. Meanwhile a professor specializing in radio research, and another who was an authority on propellants, had studied material brought to them by couriers and made two important discoveries – both promptly relayed to London – that at some stage the rocket was radio-controlled and that it contained concentrated hydrogen peroxide, a well-known source of oxygen.

While work was continuing on the rocket held by the Poles and plans were being worked out to transport the essential parts of it to London, the first A-4 fragments had already reached London from a totally different source. Just after 4 p.m. on Tuesday, 13 June 1944, exactly twelve hours after the first flying bomb had landed in Kent, an A-4 fired from Peenemünde to test the Wasserfall anti-aircraft missile installed in it went spectacularly astray and blew up over open countryside at Knivingaryd, near Kalmar,* on the Baltic coast of Sweden, about 200 miles south-west of Stockholm and about 190 north-east of Peenemünde. A man directly below was blown from his horse and the main part of the rocket carved out a 13-foot-wide crater in a cornfield. The first reports, relayed to London via the Air Attaché in Stockholm and based partly on the Swedish press of 15 June, confused the rocket with the flying-bomb, of which a specimen had also recently gone astray, but those in the know soon realized the truth. 'The projectile exploded in mid-air and released a bomb weighing about 500 kg, which caused a tremendous crater in the soft ground,' ran the first account. 'A local farmer who managed to recover fragments . . . before the military arrived on the scene stated that they contained Swedish ballbearings . . . while part of the radio mechanism was made in Italy.' Further details followed two days later, including a reference to 'two electric motors driven by accumulators'.

The Kalmar rocket caused tremendous embarrassment all round except to its real beneficiaries, the British. Owing to some understandable confusion, because it was a Wasserfall missile that was being tested not an A-4, Peenemünde at first denied responsibility for the incident and when the truth came out Dornberger was 'summoned to the Führer's headquarters to receive a reprimand, with the consoling comment that Hitler was in a towering rage'. By the time Dornberger got to Rastenburg Hitler, in his unpredictable way, had changed his mind. 'It was', he told General Jodl, who passed the comment on to Dornberger before sending him away again, 'quite a good thing for the Swedes to realize that we could bombard their country from Germany; they would be more inclined to be co-operative in negotiations.'

But international times had changed. 'There is no reason', suggested *Afton Tidningen (Evening News)*, 'why Sweden should oblige the Germans', and, alarmed by the public revelation that the rocket included Swedish-made components, the Swedes cordoned off the crater and refused to let any Germans past to recover the fragments. According to one account a

---

*Not near Malmö, which is nearly 200 miles south-west of Kalmar, as several previous accounts have stated.

German detachment tried to get to the crater by posing as undertakers' men, complete with hearse, while the mishap was variously ascribed to the controlling engineer being so astonished by his first sight of an A-4 taking off that he had jerked the main lever in the wrong direction, and to his not knowing what to do when he lost visual contact with the missile in cloud.

The end of the affair was even more colourful. Precisely what bargain the Swedish government struck remains uncertain: according to one report it secured two squadrons of brand-new tanks in exchange for two tons of miscellaneous wiring and scrap metal from the shattered rocket. At all events, the Air Attaché in Stockholm managed to dispatch photographs of some of the components to London and, pending the arrival of the two plane-loads of parts, in mid- and late July, two Air Technical Intelligence Officers were flown to Sweden to provide an interim report. This proved in some respects misleading, for it seemed at first that the costly and complex electronic control equipment would be uneconomic unless it was part of a delivery system with at least a 4½ ton warhead. The discovery of radio equipment, in fact linked to the Wasserfall rocket being carried as a 'passenger', suggested that the A-4 would be radio-controlled, while the presence of hydrogen peroxide seemed to bear out the reports from Poland that this would be the missile's fuel. However, at least the rocket's dimensions now seemed settled, for a message from Poland, on 27 June, which put them at 40 feet (12.2 metres) by 6 feet (2.7 metres) agreed with those of the 'objects' detected at Peenemünde and with calculations based on the pieces retrieved from Kalmar. The return of the officers sent to Sweden yielded an important piece of new evidence – that one of the pumps used to feed the combustion chamber was lubricated by the liquid it was circulating, which pointed unmistakably to liquid air or liquid oxygen as the rocket's fuel.

Further study of the photographs from Peenemünde and Blizna now at last began to throw light on the continuing mystery of how the rocket was launched. The presence in the latter of a rocket lying horizontally on a trailer and the absence of any tower-type construction, such as had previously been seen at Blizna, led Dr Jones to scrutinize the surrounding area closely, revealing 'a square about 35 feet wide' linked to the rocket workshop by a gentle curved road. This he correctedly identified as the rocket's launching pad, from which it would take off unaided. The supposed 'projector' was merely the frame – in fact, though this was not yet known, part of the *Meillerwagen* – which surrounded the missile while it was prepared for firing. The 40-foot-high columns observed on earlier pictures of Peenemünde were now explained: they were rockets waiting to be fired.

As so often, one discovery was rapidly followed by another, for, as the Allied forces broke out in Normandy, both prisoners and intended launching sites fell into their hands. One soldier admitted that his unit had been responsible for selecting and building small sites for storing and launching rockets and one – of the 'sunken road' type – soon afterwards fell into British hands at the Chateau du Molay, west of Bayeux. In contrast to the 'large sites' to which so much attention had been directed, the whole platform, including hard standing for the launch vehicles, measured only 69 feet (21 m) by 33 feet (10 m) and a sketch, prepared on the spot by a team sent for the purpose, cleared up another long-standing puzzle. A strange pattern 'laid out on the sands at Peenemünde' now appeared to have been built 'to see whether the proposed curves in the loop roads' serving the launching platform 'could be negotiated by whatever transporters were to carry the rockets'.

With his family having gone away to Cornwall to escape the flying-bombs, and D-Day safely past, Dr Jones now had leisure in the evenings to puzzle over another outstanding and important question, the likely scale of attack. Ultra intercepts referred to the sending back of 'apparatuses' to Peenemünde from Blizna and these, he now guessed, were rocket warheads. As No. 17053 had been dispatched on 17 June and No. 17667 in early July (i.e. 614) the total of rockets likely soon to be ready for use, allowing for the period not covered, was probably at least 1000.

On 16 July 1944 Dr Jones had written an interim report on his findings, which within the next day or two, so fast was information now coming in, was in some respects, he realized, inaccurate, but of the reality of the rocket threat there could no longer any doubt. 'I did not want', Dr Jones later wrote, 'to destroy my old professor', nor put him in a position where 'he might try to argue to the end and . . . Churchill would be torn between the facts and a loyalty to his most trusted friend.' He therefore warned Cherwell privately of the accumulating evidence before the crucial meeting of the 'Crossbow' Committee scheduled for 10 p.m. on Tuesday, 18 July 1944, in the Cabinet War Room, at which his recent report was the main item of business.

The Prime Minister, it rapidly appeared to Dr Jones's now experienced eye, 'was clearly in a . . . mood . . . to test every piece of evidence submitted to him' and 'briefed to "gun" for the Air Staff', reflecting the current public discontent at the government's failure to prevent the flying-bomb arriving. The minutes of the discussions were, however, discreet and detached:

Although there had been considerable fragmentary intelligence regarding the German Long-Range Rocket for a year or more . . . it was only within the last fortnight that it had become possible to establish definitely which intelligence referred to the rocket. . . . It was believed that about 150 experimental rockets had been manufactured and that perhaps up to 1000 production models had been made. . . . Evidence from Poland suggested that 50 per cent of the rockets fired might fall within a circle of ten miles radius. . . . The maximum range appeared to be about 200 miles, but it was probable that the effective range would not exceed 150 miles.

At the mention of a possible stockpile of a thousand rockets, Churchill, Dr Jones recalls – though the minutes omitted this dramatic detail – 'exploded and started to thump the table'. Even the minutes reveal his evident displeasure:

In reply to a suggestion by the Prime Minister that we had to some extent been caught napping, Sir Charles Portal said that . . . the evidence had been most closely watched and all action that could be thought of had been taken so far as could be done without harming the essential interests of OVERLORD.

The unfortunate Dr Jones, less culpable than anyone, now faced the Prime Minister's full fury, patiently explaining the reasons for his conclusions and that, having had to attend seven meetings that day, he had not yet had time to inform Lord Cherwell of his discovery, made only a few hours before, that 'the projector', on which hopes had been pinned of detecting and destroying the launching sites, was a myth. Eventually, to Dr Jones's relief, the Prime Minister calmed down, giving him a reputation among his colleagues as the man who 'had shut Winston up'. Herbert Morrison 'urged that every possible counter-measure should be taken to prevent the attack', but his intervention was hardly necessary, for Churchill himself was now firmly in the 'rocket party'. 'The highest priority', it was agreed, should be given to bombing the nine major German hydrogen peroxide plants, and to developing means of jamming the rocket's supposed radio control system, though 'control might well be automatic'. 'Marshal Stalin', Churchill reported, 'had agreed to render us all assistance to obtain information from Debice [i.e. Blizna] when the Russian forces capture that area' and the US Air Force had that day 'carried out a heavy attack on Peenemünde'. If both allies agreed, the British government were prepared 'to threaten the enemy with large-scale gas attacks in retaliation should such a course appear profitable'. With this cheerful prospect before them, the participants in the meeting filed out into Whitehall in the small hours to get what sleep they could, punctuated by the explosions of flying-bombs, now arriving in a more or less continuous procession.

10

THE BATTLE OF LONDON IS OVER

Except possibly for a few last shots, the Battle of London is over.

Duncan Sandys, MP, 7 September 1944

Churchill's late-night meeting of 18 July 1944 brought the subject of the rocket to the top of 'Pending' trays throughout Whitehall and two days later prompted a long essay in self-justification from Lord Cherwell. 'I am', it began untruthfully, 'most reluctant to waste your time (or my own) in arguing to what degree on past occasions I was right or not', and went on to claim that he had, of course, been right. 'I did not', insisted Cherwell, 'assert that the rocket was impossible . . . but it seemed to me extraordinary, when . . . the pilotless airplane was available, that the enemy should divert the huge effort required to develop an immensely more difficult alternative method. And if he has, I do not think he has employed his scientists to the best advantage.' This remained Cherwell's contention throughout the coming months – as though in some way people killed or injured by a rocket would be consoled to learn that the Germans were using their resources inefficiently – and, no doubt in the hope of causing more trouble, he added that, 'not having been shown all the secret evidence', he could not 'offer a view on the likelihood of attacks in the near future'. The totally false implication that Cherwell was being kept in the dark brought an angry inquiry from Churchill, and during the next month numerous officials were drawn into the argument, only ended by a note from Ian Jacob to the Prime Minister on 25 August assuring him that 'No secret information is withheld from Lord Cherwell.'

137

On 20 July, Herbert Morrison was also busy writing to the Prime Minister:

It is clear, I think, that there is something wrong with the Intelligence side. It was a surprise to me, as it appeared to be to you, that we should have been told for the first time on Tuesday that the scale of attack envisaged was four or five times greater than had previously been contemplated. . . . We are having to deal with a potential menace of great gravity, which may materialize at any moment, on the basis of evidence which is both scanty and conflicting. It might be worthwhile to consider whether there is not an undue number of official and other meetings about the organization of our counter-measures which may leave insufficient time for those with executive responsibilities to get on with their jobs.

Churchill discussed this note with Duncan Sandys that afternoon, but on 26 July Herbert Morrison circulated another paper, uncompromisingly entitled: 'Long-Range Rocket. Need for Re-Examination of Government Plans':

Nearly a year ago, and in an atmosphere of scepticism, the Cabinet instructed that paper plans should be drawn up for dealing with attacks on London by long-range rockets of heavy explosive content. . . . With the emergence of the flying-bomb . . . the plans . . . were put on one side. Last week, however, we were advised by Intelligence that 1000 rockets with a range of possibly 200 miles were believed to be in advanced state of preparation and that the warhead weighed probably 7 tons. . . . The latest theory is that no elaborate launching sites are necessary and . . . that the enemy will mount an attack on a fairly considerable scale.

On the basis of flying-bomb experience, and scaling up the casualties caused by its one-ton warhead, Morrison calculated that, if 60 per cent of the rockets landed in Greater London, 'about 30 per projectile would be killed', producing 18,000 dead 'from the assumed stock of 1000 rockets'. The number of seriously injured he put at three times that figure. To meet this need, if the London hospitals were cleared of other patients, as in 1939, and treated as 'casualty reception units', with patients being evacuated after initial treatment, 'about 4000 cases could be handled per day . . . just double the worst day in the 1940/41 blitz', but 'the strain on staff would, of course, increase with each successive week' and 'it is . . . possible that the hospital service would be swamped'. As for house damage,

138

Morrison forecast that 'each rocket . . . would be likely to produce A and B damage' (i.e. houses demolished or having later to be pulled down), 'within a radius of 600 feet, C damage' (houses uninhabitable until given maajor repairs) 'up to 1200 feet and D damage' (where the occupants could remain but with 'appreciable discomfort' up to 2400 feet, with 'a considerable amount of minor damage to roof coverings, odd windows, etc.' beyond that area. Inevitably, thought the Home Secretary, there would be a mass flight from London:

> The exodus might reach such proportions as to present a completely unmanageable problem both for the police and for the railways and the pressure of evacuees by bus, tube or on foot on the north and west perimeter of London might result in the complete breakdown of the emergency accommodation and feeding arrangements. . . . Many workers would leave London with their families in order to make sure that their families were settled in a place of safety. . . . It is quite impracticable to devise any system of control which would effectively secure that the people who ought to stay, stay, and the people who ought to go, go.

As for morale, one of Morrison's official responsibilities, this was already suffering from the flying-bomb and would grow worse:

> The British public will accept hardship, suffering and casualties that are due to unpreventible enemy action. They will be less ready to submit even to inconvenience which they judge to be due to government inactivity or lack of preparations. . . . As the areas of sheer devastation grow under continuous bombardment, I fear the public will become angry. . . . In my view the rocket attack must from now onwards be regarded as a major effort by the Germans to avoid sheer defeat. It must be met by us by a corresponding effort, both in active attack and passive defence, and not regarded as fatalistically inevitable.

A Cabinet meeting that day gave Morrison the opportunity to underline these points in person and to strengthen them by reporting the effects of the flying-bombs: 16,000 dead or seriously injured in London alone in six weeks and 700,000 houses damaged. Cherwell now weighed in with his view 'that the assumptions made by the Home Secretary as to the scale of attack were unduly pessimistic' and that 'he doubted whether the available stocks of rockets were as large' or 'whether the size of the rocket warhead would be as great as had been suggested. Again, the estimates of damage and casualties were based on a degree of accuracy which the rocket was unlikely to achieve'. These were all perfectly sound comments, but by now Morrison's alarm had infected his colleagues. Duncan Sandys said that 'the probable scale of attack' might be 'considerably heavier' than the Home Secretary had described, the Minister of Health admitted he was planning, if necessary, 'to clear the London hospitals completely', the Minister of War Transport was ready to move 250,000 people a day up to twenty miles out of London, and the Chancellor of the Exchequer spoke of the need for protected accommodation for up to 55,000 civil servants. The Minister of Production was already dispersing some manufacturing effort, while even Morrison's traditional adversary, Ernest Bevin, Minister of Labour, had a helpful suggestion to offer – that Double Summer Time, due to end on 13 August, should be extended. This was agreed, and on 3 August it was announced that the nation could enjoy its second extra hour of daylight until 16 September.

Meanwhile Morrison's right-hand man, Sir Findlater Stewart, had been discussing with other departments how 'to prevent information on the fall of shot reaching the enemy', and his proposals were circulated by the Chiefs of Staff on this same day, when rocket fever reached its peak. The restrictions, the Chiefs of Staff commented, were 'more stringent than those proposed for OVERLORD and would include . . . the suspension of diplomatic mail and telegrams . . . other than American and Russian', a total ban on all overseas travel, except for servicemen and government officials, and the virtual cessation of telegraph and postal services, at least for the first forty-eight hours. Telephone calls, especially to Ireland, would be monitored and be liable to be cut off. So drastic was the scheme for depriving the Germans of any hint where the rockets were falling that even Sir Findlater Stewart himself was doubtful if it could be kept up for much more than 'a week or ten days', but the Cabinet, on 28 July 1944, nevertheless accepted it, against the opposition, so far as diplomatic communications were concerned, of the Foreign Secretary, Sir Anthony Eden (later Lord Avon). Eventually he got his way in the case of the United States and Russia, partly on practical grounds 'since the United States Embassy possesses direct lines not under our control and the Soviet Embassy has a private wireless transmitter'. He would instead make a private approach to 'the two ambassadors not to send any information about rocket attack by this means'.

Elaborate plans also went ahead for mass evacuation, largely in the hope of anticipating the panic flight which seemed the likely alternative. People leaving, it was proposed, would make their way on foot along eighty-seven preselected routes to a number of assembly points such as cinemas, where buses would be waiting to take them the short distance required to remove them from the target area. The Ministry of Home Security also made its own private preparations. 'A new map of Greater London', an internal memo announced, 'is being mounted in the Map Corridor on which BIG BEN incidents will be plotted', with the numbered coloured pins at present used to mark incidents being replaced by others in black once the rocket was known to be responsible. That day, too, the Cabinet set up a new Rocket Consequences Committee, presided over by Herbert Morrison, the other regular members being the Ministers of Labour, Production, Health and War Transport, with additional ministers being invited as necessary.

This was also a busy time for Air Intelligence. The industrious and daring Poles had by now compiled a massive 4000-word document on the rocket, 'Special Report 1/R, No. 242', accompanied by eighty photographs, twelve drawings, a sketch map of Blizna, a list of all known rocket firings – and, they now proposed, eight* large parcels of rocket parts, which could, if London agreed, be collected by a Dakota flying from southern Italy. With typical effrontery they proposed to use an abandoned German airstrip at Tarnow, 200 miles from where the rocket had crashed, to which the key items were transferred by bicycle. The operation, on the night of 25 July 1944, proved even more hazardous than anticipated, for two German Storch aircraft were using the airfield – fortunately they took off again

---

*As in most details concerning the Poles, the sources disagree. Dr Jones refers to only one container, which included some parts from other rockets.

– and after the British aircraft had landed safely it proved reluctant to leave the ground:

The engines roared, the aircraft vibrated, moved forward a few inches and stopped. It had been raining for the last few days and . . . the wheels had sunk in and made take-off impossible.

Flight Lieutenant Szrajer [the Polish co-pilot and interpreter] . . . ordered all the passengers to get out and the baggage to be unloaded. . . . The soldiers of the reception team were ordered to dig small trenches in front of the aircraft's wheels and fill them with straw. . . . The plane still refused to move and once more the door was opened and everyone ordered to get out. . . . Flight Lieutenant Szrajer . . . decided to make just one more attempt. The soldiers ran to the carts, brought over boards and laid them under the wheels. For the third time the wretched passengers were told to board . . . and the luggage was loaded on. Eighty minutes had passed since the aircraft had landed and the short July night was beginning to brighten into dawn. This time, at last, the Dakota began to move and its take-off was accompanied by the joyful shouts of the underground soldiers who ran alongside waving their weapons and caps.

The arrival of the rocket parts, at Hendon, on 28 July, was also not without drama, for the Pole in charge of them, who knew no English, refused to hand the cargo over to anyone except General Bor, commanding the Free Poles in the United Kingdom, or a Polish colonel whom he knew. When British intelligence officers tried to persuade him he drew a knife, and everyone was relieved when General Bor finally appeared. The information the suspicious messenger had brought, when finally in the hands of Air Intelligence, proved very useful, providing, among much else, the first news of the airbursts which had so troubled Dornberger, which seemed to confirm that it was not yet ready for operational use.

On 31 July the Joint Intelligence Sub-Committee dealing with the rocket issued a paper entitled 'Imminence of Attack by BIG BEN', which was circulated to the Cabinet two days later. It was far from reassuring:

It might well be that about a thousand of these rockets exist. . . . Launching sites exist, are of simple design and easy to construct. Plants for producing liquid oxygen in France and Belgium . . . are known to have been constructed. . . . Personnel have been trained in handling these weapons and at least a skeleton organization exists in the west.

Why, then, had the rocket not yet been fired? The Germans might, it seemed, be waiting till they could 'launch the operation at greater intensity'. But this was only a respite:

In mid-July a well-informed high-ranking officer told a usually reliable source that BIG BEN would probably be used within two or three months' time. . . . [There was also] a report from a usually reliable source . . . that BIG BEN would be launched by the beginning of September. . . . We therefore feel that a heavy and sustained scale of launchings against this country is unlikely to develop during August.

Meanwhile Dr Jones was hot in pursuit of the rocket's remaining secrets. One valuable prize was a wooden replica, full-size as was confirmed later and as seemed probable at the time, of an A-4 – Cherwell's 'great white dummy' in reality*– found in a quarry at Hautmesnil, between Caen and Falaise, abandoned by the fleeing Germans. This, Dr Jones guessed, 'had clearly been used to give the troops experience in handling the missile around the bends in the tunnels'. The same site yielded a heavy trolley, correctly assumed to have been used to transport the real missile, enabling its dimensions to be calculated beyond argument and from the slope of the nose cone, deduced from the curve of the front section, an informed guess to be made about its weight, the most vital clue to its likely range and explosive payload. The total weight was now, around the end of July, put at 24 tons maximum, which Dr Jones still suspected to be on the high side.

Identifying the rocket's fuel was also important, both in indicating its possible performance and as a guide to Allied bombing policy. Information from the Swedish and Polish rockets, along with signals, intercepted by Bletchley, between Peenemünde and Blizna, all referred to each A-4 requiring 4.3 tons of '*A-Stoff*', and to another fuel known as '*B-Stoff*'. This led Dr Jones to the conclusion that the former was probably liquid oxygen and the latter might well be alcohol. This hypothesis made immediate sense of much that had hitherto been contradictory and on 6 August Dr Jones reviewed all the

---

*See page 76.

existing reports on the rocket, eliminating any that did not refer to liquid oxygen or liquid air. Only five survived, three from agents and two from prisoners of war, and, in contrast to the rest, they showed a remarkable amount of agreement. Even more significant, all were to some extent validated by their pointing to a rocket from 9 to 16 metres long and around 1½ metres in diameter which, from the recent, quite independent, discoveries, was now known to be correct. This in turn suggested a fuel weight of about 8 tons, in line with the Ultra evidence, and an all-up weight of up to 10 tons, with a warhead of between 1 and 2 tons, the lower figure appearing in four of the six reports. The latest interrogation report was only two days old, and Dr Jones and his assistant drove out to see the prisoner concerned and decided his information was reliable. It was borne out, too, by another fruit of Bletchley's eavesdropping, a mention of one-ton 'elephants' being shipped between Peenemünde and Blizna. What more likely than that the 'elephant' was a rocket's warhead?

Oddly, having earlier faced up to the appalling prospect of 70 ton rockets carrying a 10 ton load of high explosive, none of the ministers or scientists on the 'Crossbow' Committee was now ready to see the threat reduced to more familiar and manageable proportions. A meeting on Thursday, 10 August, with Herbert Morrison in the chair, was unimpressed by the new evidence Dr Jones laid before it and concluded 'that it was too early to draw a firm conclusion regarding the smaller size of the warhead of the rocket'. Next day Lord Cherwell, now proved right in rejecting the 'giant rocket' but concerned that Jones might have 'cut it down to size' too drastically, telephoned Dr Jones to advise him to leave himself some 'loophole of escape' over the rocket's weight. 'They are all waiting for you to make just one mistake and I am afraid that you have made it now!' he warned his former pupil. But Cherwell himself, who on his way to Oxford for the weekend called at Farnborough, where the captured A-4 trolley was being studied, and the Swedish and Polish rockets were being pieced together, was convinced. On the Monday, 14 August 1944, he wrote to Churchill stating that the one-ton warhead was an established fact, but adding, very typically, that the rocket remained such an uneconomic means of delivering this weight of explosive that 'Hitler would, I think, be justified in sending to a concentration camp whoever advised him to persist in such a project'.

Dr Jones faced one last hurdle in getting what he was convinced were the true facts accepted, for the engineers rebuilding the Kalmar rocket reported that the design pointed to a warhead of only 1300 to 1500 lb, so he had now 'to convince the Farnborough experts that their estimate was too low', owing, it soon appeared, to 'a segment missing, which . . . would have increased the size of the [nose] cone significantly'. The warhead was now finally put at 2000 lb, or just under a ton (2240 lb) – a remarkably accurate estimate. The true figure, as we now know, was 2200 lb, of which 1650 lb (750 kg) was high explosive, and the rocket's total weight 12.65 tons (12,900 kg) against Dr Jones's calculation of 'about 12 tons'.

On 21 August 1944 the Air Ministry updated its 'Standing Instructions for Duty Group Captain . . . in the event of Rocket Attack'. The 'use of a considerable number of alternative firing points of simple design' was now anticipated, known sites being identified by the singularly inappropriate name 'Pop Gun'. Although 'a constant watch for rockets at certain specially equipped radar stations on the south coast' was now being maintained, 'the firing of rockets', it was acknowledged, 'may not be detected by . . . radar . . . in which case incidents will be reported by the Ministry of Home Security'. The precise wording for this dread message had already been laid down and had a curiously ecclesiastical ring: 'This is Home Security War Room speaking. Big Ben has been confirmed!'

On 26 August 1944 Dr Jones completed a 30,000-word report setting out in detail the facts about the rocket, and the evidence and reasoning that had established them. The range he now put at '200–210' miles; the German figure was in fact 207. The total stocks he estimated at 'perhaps 2000' – the actual figure was 1800 – and monthly production at 'about 500'; the average for the period the campaign lasted proved to be 618. Of overwhelming interest to the Civil Defence authorities was the 'intended monthly rate of fire', which he calculated to be 'about 800'; the German target was 900. This last figure was based on a series of deductions, a classic example of how intelligence could postulate the unknown from the known. A map showing the location of both genuine and 'decoy' sites west of the Seine had been captured, and it seemed likely that the tidy-minded Germans would follow the same ratio of real sites to dummy ones east of it. The same map indicated the storage capacity of the real sites and the likely rate of fire was worked out from flying-bomb experience, where captured sites had shown the German practice was to keep two weeks' consumption in hand.

A bombardment of 800 tons of high explosive a month, though exceedingly unpleasant, was substantially less than Londoners had managed to endure and the Civil Defence services to cope with during both the blitz and the flying-bomb assault. Why, then, had the Germans gone to so much trouble and expense to produce such a modest return? To the rigidly limited mind of Lord Cherwell the rocket's uneconomic cost/destruction ratio had proved an insuperable stumbling block, but Dr Jones, in his report, proved more imaginative:

A rational approach brought us nearest the truth regarding the technique of the Rocket. When, however, we try to understand the policy behind it we are forced to abandon rationality, and instead to enter a fantasy where romance has replaced economy. . . .
Why, then, have they made the Rocket?
The answer is simple: no weapon yet produced has a comparable romantic appeal. Here is a 13 ton missile which traces out a flaming ascent to heights hitherto beyond the reach of man and hurls itself 200 miles across the stratosphere at unparalleled speed to descend – with luck – on a defenceless target. One of the greatest realizations of human power is the ability to destroy at a distance.

Forty copies of the report were circulated, including a highly accurate sectional drawing of the A-4, but were immediately withdrawn, on Duncan Sandys's insistence, as unfair to some of the experts he had consulted. With its issue, however – for the main facts about the rocket were now established beyond argument – 'my Intelligence task', Dr Jones later wrote, 'was over'. One important gap in the picture remained – where the rockets were being made – for the British knew only that the main factory was located 'somewhere in central Germany . . . operating in conjunction with a concentration camp "Dora" '. Its location, at Nordhausen, was only discovered on 31 August, but made little difference, since it was virtually impregnable to air attack.

About the small sites earmarked by the Germans for launching rockets nothing could be done, but with the 'large sites' suspected to be connected with the offensive – though some were, we now know, intended for other, though equally dangerous, purposes, such as storing flying bombs or (at Mimoyecques) housing a new type of long-range gun – it was a different story. On 6 July Watten, first devastated a year earlier and now intended to house a liquid oxygen plant, was wrecked again by a 12,000 lb 'Tallboy' bomb, able, as 'Bomber' Harris testified, to 'penetrate 12 feet of concrete' and set off an earth tremor producing earthquake-like effects. A 'Tallboy' also literally raised, and then brought down, the roof of another suspect construction, at Siracourt, in fact intended for flying bombs, not A-4s, while the Todt organization's masterpiece, the 'roofed-in' quarry at Wizernes, fulfilled Hitler's prediction that it would never be finished. 'Persistent air attack with heavy and super-heavy bombs so battered the rock all round that in the spring of 1944 landslides made further work impossible,' complained Dornberger. Work was in fact restarted, only to attract more bombs. 'The construction itself has not been hit by the new six-ton bombs,' it was reported to him on 28 July, 'but the whole area around has been so churned up that it is unapproachable.' The Americans loyally joined in, on 4 August sending four battered Flying Fortresses loaded with 9 tons of high explosive, against Watten, Wizernes, Mimoyecques and Siracourt, the crews baling out while the 'drones', as they were known, were directed on to their targets by radio, but the results were disappointing. Two more, sent on a further sortie against Watten two days later, also achieved nothing.

A considerable proportion of the Allies' bombing effort was now being directed against 'Crossbow' targets, including – always more acceptable to the 'bomber barons', since this could be fitted into their long-term area offensive – factories believed to be connected with rocket manufacture. The first successful blow of this kind, as mentioned earlier, had come by accident, when an A-4 factory at Friedrichshafen was bombed in the belief that radar parts were being manufactured there; and during the Gomorrah raids on Hamburg in August 1943 a factory making special vehicles for the A-4 launching units was, by lucky chance, also destroyed. Hydrogen peroxide plants were singled out for bombing when this was still believed to be the rocket's fuel, and the US 8th Air Force bombed two at Ober Raderach and Düsseldorf, between 2 and 9 August 1944, as well as one at Peenemünde itelf. On 24 August American aircraft dropped nearly 300 tons of bombs on a factory near Weimar believed to be making rocket components and in the following week two suspected 'radio beam' stations and – now that the rocket's true fuel was known – five liquid oxygen works were similarly harassed. But most of the effort was still against the 'large sites', the air marshals preferring targets near at hand which seemed to be definitely connected with the rocket, rather than more distant factories whose use was uncertain. In the fourth week of August 1764 tons of bombs were directed at rocket-linked targets, but only 266 tons of this total were aimed at 'industrial and production centres' believed to be connected with rocket production, plus 223 tons directed at liquid oxygen production, probably the most worthwhile target, and 41 tons designed to knock out the 'radio beam stations', wrongly supposed to guide the rocket to its target. The rest, 1234 tons, was devoted to 'large sites'.

This vast effort reached its peak around the end of August. On 31 August and 1 September Bomber Command dropped nearly 3000 tons of bombs on supposed storage bunkers, bringing to 118,000 tons the total dropped by both Allied air forces on all secret-weapon targets since the first attack on Peenemünde twelve and a half months earlier, of which 20,000 had been directed at places primarily connected with the rocket. More than 82,000 tons had been delivered since mid-June, of which about 8000 had been 'rocket-orientated'. The price for the whole campaign, most of it incurred between then and the end of August, had been 450 aircraft lost and 2900 aircrew. Most of these were British, but the US 8th Air Force had lost 63 Flying Fortresses or Liberators in more than 16,000 sorties. These were far from negligible figures and put in a different perspective Cherwell's constant cry that the rocket was uneconomic, for they had been incurred before a single A-4 had been fired in anger and when the total German dead amounted to only a handful of scientists and their families.

The new, and much less frightening, forecasts for the rocket's destructive power and rate of fire, and the dwindling away of the flying-bomb nuisance to one or two a day, until none at all arrived between 1 and 4 September 1944, led to a marked relaxation of tension in Whitehall, encouraged by the excellent news from across the Channel. In those heady days when the Allied armies were racing across France and Belgium towards the very frontiers of the Reich, and the war seemed likely to end, as had long been hoped and planned, in September, it was hard to believe that a whole new type of bombardment might still begin. Herbert Morrison's Rocket Consequences Committee, once the chief dispensers of gloom, now led the premature rejoicing, and the committee's report to the War Cabinet on 5 September 1944 struck a cheerful note:

Since the date of our appointment the position has undergone a fundamental change, as a result partly of the latest intelligence about the rocket and partly of the progress of the Allied armies. . . . The possible average weight of combined rocket and flying-bomb attack . . . is up to 80 tons of HE a day falling in London Region, which should be compared with the average of 48 tons a day experienced during the worst week of flying-bomb attacks. Rocket attack may start at any time from now onwards, but the enemy is unlikely to be able to launch rockets or flying bombs against London on any appreciable scale after the Allied armies have crossed the Franco-Belgian frontier. . . . We have therefore directed that . . . plans . . . to meet the contingency of severe rocket attack should so far as possible be kept on a paper basis.

The committee went on to report encouragingly on all the problems that a few weeks earlier had seemed so formidable, such as creating 'Citadel' accommodation for civil servants, providing hospital beds, preventing news of the first rockets' arrival reaching the Germans and, above all, evacuation, where the problem now was not so much the fear of a panic flight from London as of 'a drift back . . . as a result of . . . the rapid growth of optimism about the end of the war'. They urged, none the less, that there should be 'no relaxation of offensive action' to prevent 'the initiation by the enemy of rocket attack during the probably short time left to him in which to do so'. The Vice-Chiefs of Staff, however, decided on the following day, in the official historian's words, 'that rocket attacks on London need no longer be expected', endorsing the view expressed four days earlier by the Joint 'Crossbow' Priorities Committee, which selected targets for attack, that the rocket menace would disappear once (as was about to happen) 'the area in northern France and Belgium 200 miles from London was "neutralized" by the presence of our land forces'. It was left to Air Marshal Sir Roderic Hill, alerted by his chief intelligence officer, to point out that western Holland was well within rocket range of the UK and still in Nazi hands. But no suspicious sites had been detected there and his voice went unheeded.

The flying bombs had come as an unwelcome shock to the public, and the politicians had been dismayed at their resulting unpopularity. Everyone wanted to believe that it was now all over bar the shouting, and though when the Germans had coined the term 'V-1' (*Vergeltungswaffe* or Revenge Weapon No. 1) for the flying bomb back in July, the prospect that it would be followed by V-2, the rocket to which Churchill had publicly referred back in February, now seemed remote. 'Allies nearing Nazis' reprisal weapon depots. We may soon wrest secret of V-2 from enemy,' asserted the *Evening Standard* on 25 August. The Allied advance might 'stop . . . Hitler's chance of ever using the much boasted V-2 rockets,' suggested its fellow London evening newspaper, the *Star*, on the same day. The *News Chronicle* struck an equally cheerful note in a front-page story on Monday, 4 September. 'V-2 may never start,' it predicted. 'Can it be fired from inside Germany? It is thought improbable.' The *Daily Express*, always a paper to look on the bright side, was even more encouraging next morning. 'The Germans were known to have four V-2 launching sites in northern France. They are all now either captured or in the range of our massed guns. Are there other V-2 launching sites in Germany? This is considered unlikely. And there is substantial evidence to indicate that the rockets may never be sent against Britain.'

So similar and detailed were the press stories – the *Daily Express* even carried an account of the captured quarry at Hautmesnil and of the Germans' problem with airbursts during rocket trials – that it seems likely they were reflecting official guidance. Up to now the Ministry of Information had been involved mainly in preparations for intensifying the existing censorship if and when the rockets started to fall. It had also, as the Chief Censor himself described,

prepared complete plans for carrying on the work of the news and the censorship divisions continuously in the basement of the Ministry. . . . Accommodation had been provided there for the representatives of the British press and for the Dominions and United States correspondents and we were expecting to be marooned there while London was being devastated by the huge twelve-ton rocket.

Now that it had a happier tale to tell, the Ministry made the most of it and, far from restraining the more optimistic statements by members of the government, did its best to secure them the widest possible publicity.

Although it was Duncan Sandys whose remarks were to be most widely quoted and remembered, it was in fact Herbert Morrison who led the rejoicing and first used a phrase about 'the Battle of London' that was soon to become notorious. Morrison, Lambeth-born, had always considered himself a Londoner first and foremost and on 6 September delivered a long and jubilant statement in praise of his native city:

London has been in the front line in the final victorious phase of the greatest war that history has ever known. . . . There may conceivably still be trials in store for us before the Allied armies have rooted out the last of the vipers' nests, but Hitler has already lost the Battle of London as surely as he has lost the main battle of France. . . . The day has come when London can openly rejoice in the great part she has played in the overthrow of Nazism.

That day Morrison advised the Cabinet that no further action was needed on any of the recommendations made by the Rocket Consequences Committee, and on the following morning Duncan Sandys held an even more widely publicized press conference, which seemed to establish beyond question that the secret-weapons danger was over. Behind the scenes this had already caused a great deal of ill-feeling. The Air Ministry, which had borne the brunt of the public's and, even more, the Prime Minister's criticism over the flying-bomb, was naturally anxious to take the chief credit for defeating it. It proposed that the Secretary of State for Air, Sir Archibald Sinclair, or his deputy, the Parliamentary Secretary, Harold

Balfour, should preside, assisted by a suitable air marshal who, it was learned, had actually asked Duncan Sandys for his notes. Churchill was furious. Sinclair, he pointed out in an angry memo to Ian Jacob on 4 September, was away and Balfour had not been involved in 'Crossbow'. 'I forbid the slightest change', wrote the Prime Minister categorically, 'in the arrangements which have been made by the Ministry of Information. . . . A statement to the press can only be made by the chairman of the committee set up by me with Cabinet authority.'

Although one Air Ministry official protested to Ian Jacob that it was their minister who was responsible to parliament for air defence, Churchill, perhaps fortunately for the civil servant concerned, never saw this letter, since he was by now on his way to Canada. It was therefore, and very justly, Duncan Sandys, who got most of the limelight when the reporters assembled in unprecedented numbers in the largest conference room that the Air Ministry headquarters, at Senate House in Gower Street, could provide on Thursday, 7 September 1944. The Minister of Information, Brendan Bracken, was in the chair, and the C-in-Cs of Ack-Ack Command and Air Defence of Great Britain, Frederick Pile and Roderic Hill, sat beside him, but it was Duncan Sandys whom everyone wanted to hear. His opening statement, 'Except possibly for a few last shots, the Battle of London is over', made headlines everywhere, often with its qualifying phrase omitted. Even less attention was paid to his brief exchange with an unidentified journalist which still survives in the official transcript of the proceedings:

Question: Is there a V-2 weapon, sir. . . ?
Mr Duncan Sandys: . . . I am a little chary about talking about the V-2. We do know quite a lot about it . . . which perhaps is more than you have at the moment, but in a very few days' time I feel the press will be walking over these places in France and they will know a great deal more about it than we do now.

This occasion brought Duncan Sandys firmly, for the first time, into the public eye and was a personal triumph. That evening he held a celebratory cocktail party at his flat in Vincent Square at which Dr Jones, who had not been invited to the press conference, was a guest, and next day, Friday, 8 September 1944, Brendan Bracken, like Sandys and Cherwell a close and trusted confidant of the Prime Minister, sent him an enthusiastic account of the occasion and its subsequent coverage, duly enciphered as signal 'Cordite No. 23':

Duncan Sandys held the largest press conference I have seen since I came to this ministry. His account of how the government handled the flying-bomb menace was beyond praise. He spoke for more than an hour and answered many questions and at the end he was cheered by the press and, as you know, the press are a hard-boiled lot. The newspapers are full of Duncan's praise and his speech has been reported in every part of the world.

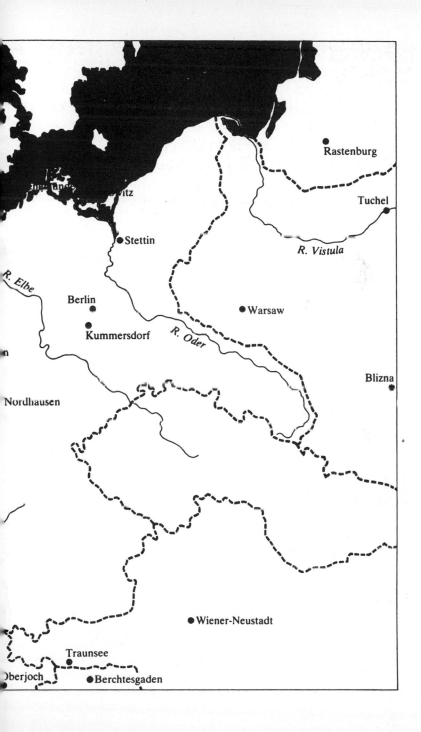

Rastenburg

Tuchel

Stettin

R. Vistula

R. Elbe

Berlin

Kummersdorf

Warsaw

R. Oder

Blizna

Nordhausen

Wiener-Neustadt

Traunsee

Oberjoch

Berchtesgaden

itz

11

IGNITION!

'Ignition!'

Firing order to German rocket units, 8 September 1944

As one by one the dates on which the rocket was to make its operational debut approached and slipped past, it began to seem that it would never be used in action. But at last, after a demonstration at Blizna in May 1944, its future commander, General Metz, fixed what everyone felt to be a realistic target – September. On 31 August General Dornberger, still resenting his displacement by Kammler, was present at a final planning meeting in Brussels presided over by the elderly and amiable General Heinemann, commander of 65 Corps, but the real power, it soon became clear, belonged to his much younger and more forceful Chief of Staff, Colonel Eugen Walter, of the Luftwaffe: the corps headquarters, responsible for both secret weapons, 'interleaved' army and air-force officers. Nominally General Metz, recently brought back from the Eastern Front, was in charge of A-4 units, but it was Kammler who had called this late-night meeting and he soon demonstrated that he considered himself (as special commissioner for the A-4) in charge of everything to do with the rocket, from research to launching. Colonel Walter, who for practical purposes had ousted his own superior, General Heinemann, was now pushed aside in his turn. He first consulted Supreme Headquarters on Kammler's status then asked to see his written orders, but a man enjoying Himmler's support was not to be defeated. Kammler, Dornberger complained later, had 'never done a single day's military service nor enjoyed any military instruction whatsoever' but he now ignored his superior officers and countermanded Metz's instructions. The

156

rocket attack, which should have started on 5 September, was postponed while they made a further appeal to headquarters, and General Jodl and his staff tried to save the face of their subordinates before capitulating. They failed. On 2 September Colonel Walter was told that Kammler would direct the A-4 offensive and would not be answerable to his nominal superior, General Heinemann, an arrangement personally confirmed by Hitler. Metz, a general without an army, now dropped out of the picture.

So much time had been lost that events had overtaken the elaborately worked-out plans to use the rocket. The original intention had been to bombard not merely London, Bristol, Southampton and Portsmouth but, rather strangely, Aldershot and Winchester. The Germans contemplated a front about 160 miles long, in a direct line, but covering about 250 miles of coastline, from Cap Gris-Nez, midway between Calais and Boulogne, to the Cotentin peninsula, round Cherbourg. There would be giant 'bunkers', at Sottevast and Wizernes, and another forty-five unprotected smaller sites, supplied through seven main storage depots, La Meauffe, Hautmesnil and Elbeuf in Normandy, Mery-sur-Oise, near Paris, Tavannes and Savonnieres, some 200 miles inland, and, much further north, Hollogne, near Liège. Four field storage depots near the launching sites had been planned, at La Motte, Thiennes, Bergueneusse and Fransu, in the Pas-de-Calais, and six transit dumps, scattered over the whole area. Liquid oxygen was to be manufactured in France, at seven centres, which would supply a large storage depot, at Rinxent, near Boulogne, and another at Saint-March d'Ouilly, near Falaise, for the six small sites, and the giant Sottevast bunker, beyond the Seine. Alcohol was to be manufactured in Germany, but stored at Tourcoing, near Lille, for the main launching area, with eight forward sites, one of them in Normandy, between Caen and Saint-Lo, the rest between the Somme and Calais.

This whole elaborate supply structure now had to be replanned, since every site concerned was in Allied hands. The same cause had upset the original German Order of Battle, which had envisaged some fixed detachments based in bunkers, with other, mobile ones, moving about between the smaller sites. When Kammler took over his headquarters were at

Kleve, about 15 miles south-east of Arnhem and just across the German border with Holland. His men were organized into two formations. Group North, under Colonel Hohmann, consisting of two batteries of 485 (Mobile) Artillery Detachment (*Art. Abbt.* (*mot.*) 485), was at Kleve but was now ordered forward to The Hague. Group South, under Major Weber, consisted of two batteries of 836 (Mobile) Artillery Detachment and also of the former 444 (Training and Experimental) Battery, now promoted to an operational role. On 8 September 1944 this was at Euskirchen in Germany, about 15 miles south-west of Bonn and about 25 from the Belgian frontier. The SS was also supposed to be forming another unit, known as SS Werfer Batterie 500.

The loss of the bunkers had forced the Germans back on what Dornberger had always considered the proper tactical use of the rocket, its discharge by mobile units from constantly changing sites. Each launching team required only a small convoy of vehicles. It normally consisted of three *Meillerwagen*, each carrying a rocket and drawn by a half-track lorry, which also transported the crew. With these large, low-loading trailers came three tankers, for alcohol, liquid oxygen and other fuels, a generator truck, an armoured command vehicle and a number of staff cars. The tankers were made of a special aluminium, at once strong and light, but the real triumph of German ingenuity lay in the *Meillerwagen*, which served as rocket transporter, inspection gantry and firing frame. On reaching the launching site it was tilted upwards into a vertical position by hydraulic jacks, which took about 15 minutes, leaving the rocket resting on a solid, cone-shaped metal plate, on an open, four-sided frame, this launching base being known to British intelligence, from its shape, as 'the lemon squeezer'. It was designed to deflect the rocket's burning jet sideways and protect the ground or platform beneath. The erect *Meillerwagen* frame also provided a platform, 40 feet high, on which the soldier setting the gyroscope near the nose could stand, while others, at lower levels, filled the fuel tanks and checked the electrical circuits. The *Meillerwagen* was then moved away and lowered back to the horizontal, to be used another day.

All this took little more than an hour, during which time the rocket had been linked to the command trailer by electric cables, and the non-technical troops who formed part of the unit had been digging a slit trench. At an announcement by the officer in charge – 'X minus three minutes. Counting down' – everyone took shelter and the actual firing sequence was initiated, with vapour from the liquid oxygen beginning to stream out of the vents in the fuselage in a fine mist. At 'X minus one minute' the vents were closed by remote control, the mist ceased and, as a final warning, a green flare was fired. If everything seemed in order the order came: 'Ignition!' As the control button was pressed by one of the other occupants of the command vehicle, a stream of sparks began to burst from the rocket's tail, which settled down into a jet of red and yellow flame. A second button cut off the rocket's outside fuel supply and switched it to its own batteries, and a third brought into action the pressure pump forcing 33 gallons per second of alcohol and liquid oxygen into the combustion chamber. Slowly, trailing a flame its own length behind it, the rocket hoisted itself into the air, while inside the command lorry the seconds since lift-off were counted aloud. If all went well, after 4½ seconds the nose would tilt in the direction of its target; at 23 seconds those on the ground ceased to hear it, for it was travelling faster than sound; by 30 seconds they considered themselves safe, for if it did come down it was likely to fall several miles away. By 35 seconds, now six miles up and travelling at twice the speed of sound, it might still be visible as a dot, through binoculars, thanks to its trail of liquid oxygen, gleaming white against the sky, and nicknamed 'frozen lightning'. The crucial moment came about 54 seconds after ignition, when the commander announced 'All burnt!' The rocket had now consumed all its fuel and was travelling on its own from the velocity it had built up, at 3200 feet per second, nearly 2000 miles an hour. It became the custom at this stage for the officer in charge and the propulsion engineer who had actually pressed the firing buttons to engage in a ritual handshake, perhaps with some Germanic heel-clicking, before the launching platform was re-installed on the *Meillerwagen*, which trundled off to be loaded at the nearest storage depot with another A-4, while the fuel tankers headed for the liquid oxygen and alcohol supply points. What had by then happened to the rocket they had just launched they could only speculate, but, if all had gone well, it should have reached a maximum speed of 3600 m.p.h. and a height of 50 to 60 miles, before plunging to earth at some 2200 to 2500 m.p.h., likened by Dornberger to the impact of fifty 100 ton railway engines colliding with the same spot in London at 60 m.p.h. He took pride, too in the missile's elegant and graceful appearance, whether in the silver-grey aluminium of some of the earliest models, the contrasting black and white or red and white squares, sometimes with fins picked out in contrasting shades, of many of those fired at Peenemünde – a livery designed to make them easier to follow in flight – or the standard Wehrmacht greenish-grey of most of the operational missiles. Now at last the rocket was to be used in action.

On 7 September 1944 Kammler had twelve launching units at his disposal, three of them from 444 Battery and the other nine from 485 – a total of about 6000 men and 1600 vehicles, including supporting technical units. 444 Battery, on German soil at Euskirchen, had the honour of firing the very first A-4 launched at an enemy. The target was Paris, and two rockets were fired in rapid succession, at 10.30 a.m. and 11.40 a.m. on Wednesday, 7 September 1944. Both were total failures, falling back on to the firing table. After two days' frantic examination the cause was located – a malfunctioning mechanism had prematurely cut off the rockets' fuel supply – and at 7.28 a.m. on the morning of Friday, 8 September (8.30 British time) the unit tried again. This time they succeeded. The rocket climbed into the sky and shortly afterwards plunged down into the suburbs of Paris, but, curiously, no one seems to have realized the significance of the explosion, nor to have passed the news to London.

444 Battery was now ordered to move to Walcheren Island in Holland, while the honour of firing the first round against the real enemy, England, went to its sister battery 485. During Thursday, 7 September, the occupants of three pleasant tree-lined suburban streets in The Hague – Nonijnenlaan, Koekoekslaan and Lijsterlaan, all in the residential area of Wassenaar – found German lorries outside their door and louts in SS uniforms banging on their doors, but, to their relief, the occupants were merely ordered to pack up and move elsewhere, leaving doors unlocked and windows open.

The start An A3 rocket, the forerunner of the A4, on the test stand at Kummersdorf, 1936

Above: **The Führer's blessing** Hitler at Kummersdorf, March 1939. Dornberger (then a colonel) is on Hitler's left, with Dr Walter Thiel, Germany's leading authority on rocket motors

Success in sight An A4 on the test stand at Peenemünde, to which from 1939 most research was transferred

Peenemünde, which ultimately cost the German taxpayer at least £25 million, in all its glory.
Top: The recreation block, part of the establishment's lavish facilities. *Above:* The main production
hall, intended, once the design had been perfected, to be the main centre of A4 manufacture

Retribution *Top:* Test Stand 7, the heart of the development programme, after the RAF raid of August 1943. *Above:* The giant bunker at Watten in France, intended by the Germans as a rocket storage and firing point after bombing in the same month

'Peenemünde in Poland.' After the bombing of Peenemünde most research was transferred to much more modest quarters, at Blizna in Poland. The hut on the left is the SS mess hall; on the right is the latrine block

After Blizna was overrun by the Russians a mission was sent to investigate its secrets. Allied officers studying the remains of a rocket combustion chamber found by the River Bug

The men who made the rocket The scientists: a picture taken in Vienna in 1942. Dornberger is on the left, with, on his left, Colonel Zannsen, Camp Commandant of Peenemünde, and (carrying hat in right hand) Dr Thiel, later killed in the RAF raid. Von Braun (carrying raincoat) is on the far right

The organizers Karl Otto Saur (left), head of Albert Speer's Technical Staff, who at first opposed the rocket programme; Gerhard Degenkolb (centre), the dynamic industrialist who got the rocket into mass production

The Commander SS General Hans Kammler, a dedicated Nazi, who directed the use of the rocket in action

The defenders *Below* (from left to right) Herbert Morrison, British Home Secretary, who from the first took the rocket threat seriously; Sir Stafford Cripps, Minister of Aircraft Production, asked by Churchill to establish whether the rocket really existed; Lord Cherwell, Scientific Adviser to the Prime Minister who believed the rocket to be 'a mare's nest'. *Bottom* (from left to right) Dr R. V. Jones, of Air Ministry Scientific Intelligence, who constantly warned of the coming danger; Duncan Sandys MP, appointed by Churchill to assess the evidence about German Secret weapons and plan counter-measures; Group Captain J. H. Searby RAF (photographed when a Wing Commander, who led the attack on Peenemunde

In full production. Rockets on the production line in the underground Central Works at Nordhausen

The final test. Rockets awaiting firing at Blizna in 1944. Note the Meillerwagen, at once transporter and mobile launching platform, in the foreground, and the other vehicles of the firing units in the background

Ignition!

Once they had gone, the Germans laid cables to provide an extra electricity supply from the adjoining roads of Rijksstraat-weg and Rust en Vreugdlaan. Next morning, Friday, 8 September 1944, a convoy of six trucks and a *Meillerwagen* rolled in, followed by others, rockets were set up at either end of Koekoekslaan, and the launching procedure began. The missiles were aimed to land 1000 yards east of Waterloo Bridge, the heart of a closely built-up area of south-east London, the precise spot selected being – though the Germans can hardly have known this – the site of the National Fire Service station in Southwark Bridge Road, SE1. At 5.38 p.m. local time, 6.38 in England with its extended Double Summer Time, the 'Ignition!' order was given for both missiles. The rocket bombardment of the United Kingdom had begun.

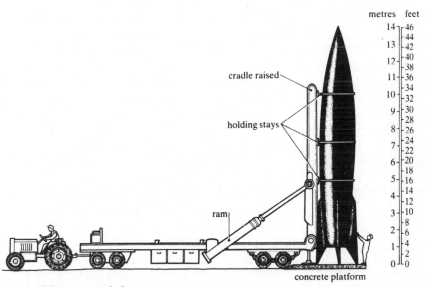

How the Meillerwagon worked

12

INCIDENT AT STAVELEY ROAD

*An enemy missile dropped in the centre of the concrete
roadway, forming a crater about 40 feet across.*

Ministry of Home Security report, prepared on
11 September 1944

Friday, 8 September 1944 had been a typical autumn day in
southern England. After a cold night, the morning was bright
and sunny, but during the afternoon the skies clouded over,
and rain followed. In spite of the weather there was much to
feel cheerful about. On Saturday, 26 August, the papers had
reported a turning point in the campaign in Europe. 'Gen. de
Gaulle enters liberated Paris. Last Germans surrender after
ultimatum,' ran the *Daily Telegraph* headline, while down-
column was recorded 'A US Forecast. End of war by October'.
'London's buildings quickly broke out into a flutter of
tricolours,' reported the *New Yorker*'s excellent correspondent,
Mollie Panter-Downs, on reaction to the news from France.
'Nobody appeared to mind when one confused building superintendent ran up the Dutch flag instead.' The ringing of the
church bells added to the general sense of jubilation, for those
of St Paul's had not 'uttered a sound since June, when it was
decided that the bells might drown out an approaching robot'.
The 3rd of September revived many poignant memories, for it
was not merely the fifth anniversary of the outbreak of war
but, like that earlier 3rd of September, a Sunday, and also a
National Day of Prayer. For Londoners, even more significantly, it was explosion-free. 'The peace of these last few days
passed belief,' wrote Vere Hodgson, in Notting Hill. 'I have
been out twice today and never had to listen for danger.'

The following week the good news continued. On Tuesday,
5 September, a corner of *The Times*'s front page, otherwise
devoted to advertisements – 'No Coupons. Rust tweed suit,

unworn: £15', 'For sale, Excellent indoor shelter, steel arch, £25' – contained the small announcement, 'Allies enter Holland'. On the main news page one cheerful item jostled with another: 'Antwerp captured', 'Pressing on in Italy', 'Cease Fire in Finland', even 'Standing-Down of the Home Guard'. The impending replacement of the blackout by a dim-out, with thinner curtains permitted and even some street lighting restored, due on Sunday, 17 September, added to the feeling that it was all over except the flag-waving. The *Daily Herald* on Wednesday, 6 September 1944 described events in the capital the previous day:

Rumour upon rumour swept through London yesterday: Germany had capitulated; the King was to broadcast; Parliament had been recalled. Not one of these rumours was true but they spread from London to the suburbs, from the suburbs to the provinces. People left their suburban homes and came to town to join in the celebrations. There were taxis full of singing soldiers. There were stories that barricades were being put up in Piccadilly to control the overjoyed crowd. . . . Brussels radio had announced that 'foreign stations' had announced at 9.30 that morning news of the capitulation of Germany. A little later . . . the message was 'killed', but the report had got a flying start.

The next morning, Thursday, 7 September, the press carried Herbert Morrison's cheerful 'Hitler has lost the Battle of London' speech of the previous day, but one man at least remained unconvinced. 'It appears that Civil Defence is ending,' wrote the borough librarian of much-flying-bombed Croydon in his diary. 'There is a sort of dizziness in the news; it is so good that one wonders if all is really well.' On Friday Duncan Sandys's press conference was splashed across every newspaper, often accompanied by congratulatory leading articles. All this made pleasant reading that Friday evening, when there was not much to tempt anyone out. The two films which had just opened, *Wing and a Prayer*, with Don Ameche winning the war in the Pacific, and *Take It or Leave It*, about an American sailor on leave, were, on the kindest interpretation of the reviews, undistinguished, while the theatre had not yet recovered from its doodlebug doldrums. The current bestsellers, G. M. Trevelyan's *English Social History* and Somerset Maugham's *The Razor's Edge*, were hard to come by and the most popular occupation in London that Friday evening was probably listening to the radio. On the Home Service one could hear Jack Payne's Orchestra, *American Commentary* and *As You Like It*, interrupted by the great event of the day, the *Nine O'Clock News*. It was a typical evening's listening for what seemed all set to be a typical wartime evening.

The London Borough of Brentford and Chiswick, formed in 1932, lay just outside the London County Council area, but well within that of the London Civil Defence region, being served by both the Underground and the Southern Railway – Chiswick Station to Waterloo took twenty minutes. Its wartime experience had been 'middle of the road'. Chiswick was fifty-fifth in the 'league table' of V-1 incidents suffered by the 95 boroughs in the London Civil Defence Region, with 13 flying-bombs, and it had, to 8 September 1944, endured 635 incidents, inflicted by two parachute mines, 359 HE bombs and some 7000 incendiaries.

Close to the river, which formed Chiswick's southern boundary, lay Staveley Road, a 'middle-middle-class' district, with semidetached, and a few detached, houses. At first, when the area was developed in the 1920s, they had enjoyed the social cachet of names alone – Westcourt, Elsmere, Dunrobbin – though further building had led to their being numbered. Although it now included a 'council school' for eleven- to fourteen-year-olds, the road still contained some vacant plots and was quiet and spacious, renowned for the cherry trees which lined it; every spring the King's mother, Queen Mary, came to look at their blossom. But on the evening of Friday, 8 September 1944, Staveley Road was a dismal place, with the few people about hurrying home to get indoors before the drizzle that was just beginning settled down into a steady downpour.

At 6.34 p.m., totally without warning, a huge hole appeared in the middle of the roadway opposite number 5. Houses on both sides of the road collapsed and for hundreds of yards around walls cracked, tiles clattered to the ground and windows shattered into lethal fragments. All that anyone heard was a 'plop' and a sudden rumble, though many felt the force of the explosion, like the caretaker of Staveley Road School who had been crossing its playing field and suddenly found himself hurled twenty feet to the ground. 'I picked myself up', he told a *News Chronicle* reporter, in an interview destined not to be published till a whole year later, 'and staggered to the nearest wrecked house; a woman – I later learned it was Mrs Harrison – crawled out of the wreckage and died in my arms.' Mrs Harrison, a sixty-five-year-old housewife, had been sitting by her fireside with her husband. In the same instant died a young soldier, Frank Browning, walking down the road to visit his girlfriend, and a three-year-old infant, Rosemary Clarke, killed in her cot. Dornberger and von Braun had claimed their first victims.

Thanks to the evacuation after the flying-bombs, and because some people had not yet arrived home, the casualty list was surprisingly light: 3 dead (although the official figure at the time was 2), 10 seriously injured, another 10 slightly hurt. Three wrecked houses, numbers 24, 26 and 28, had all been empty. A fifteen-month-old girl living next door to the dead baby survived; her mother, the wife of an airman, had taken her to safety in North Wales a few days before, although, as she recalled bitterly, she and her husband had only just finished paying for their now ruined home. This was only one of many families with new reason to hate the Germans; 11 houses had been demolished outright, 15 more had to be evacuated for extensive rebuilding, 12 more had been seriously affected and 556 more had suffered 'minor damage', though a far larger number of people had been inconvenienced, for there was, the official account noted, 'a very large crater 20 feet deep in the middle of the road', and the water and gas mains had been broken.

Brentford and Chiswick coped well with incident no. 636 – it was to suffer only one more, a very minor one, during the rest of the war. A rest centre, on 'St Thomas's playing field' – the areas was full of sports-grounds and pavilions – was promptly opened, and provided shelter for sixteen people, until closed on 15 September. Ultimately fourteen families were rehoused and three individuals found private billets. An incident inquiry point, opened on Saturday, was needed only for a day, since everyone affected was soon accounted for.

What was for Chiswick almost the end of its war was for

the British government the start of a new and particularly troublesome campaign. By some strange acoustic quirk the explosion, which was barely heard near at hand, echoed over London and was easily audible in Westminster, seven miles away. The double bang – the sound of the impact following a split second after the sonic boom as the missile re-entered the earth's atmosphere – rapidly became the rocket's trademark. Among those alerted by it that Friday evening was R. V. Jones, busy in his office with his assistant. 'He and I looked at one another and said almost simultaneously, "That's the first one!" ' he later recalled. Duncan Sandys, a few hundred yards west of Broadway, in his office in Shell Mex House on the Embankment near the Savoy, instantly telephoned the Home Security War Room to find out where the rocket had fallen and then called for his car. Within an hour Staveley Road was full of VIPs, including Herbert Morrison, in his invariable dark overcoat and black Homburg, accompanied by the even more unmistakable figure of his red-headed Parliamentary Secretary, Ellen Wilkinson. The regional commissioner for London, Admiral Sir Edward Evans (famous as a First World War hero, 'Evans of the *Broke*') was soon there, resplendent in his naval uniform, and several senior officials from Group 6, the regional sub-headquarters responsible for Chiswick. So, too, were the Civil Defence controller for the borough, and the borough engineer, in charge of the rescue service. It was immediately clear to all of them that Big Ben had made its historic debut in Chiswick, and one of Morrison's officials recorded the facts in impressive detail:

Incident Staveley Road, 8 September 1944, 1845 hours. The area was not under the 'Alert'. An enemy missile dropped in the centre of the concrete roadway, forming a crater about 40 feet across × 10 feet in depth, causing damage of gas services, the demolition of 7 houses, damage beyond repair to 5 other houses, together with major blast damage to about 600 other houses within a radius of 600 yards from the crater, including the school on the south side of Staveley Road.*

The area is a dormitory one with 2-storey semi-detached houses –

---

*For obvious reasons, small discrepancies almost always occur between local and central figures for casualties and damage, especially when compiled at different dates.

on a density of about 8 to the acre – erected in 1920, of reasonably good construction with 9 in. walls, wood floors and tiled roofs.

The size of the crater was that usually associated with 1000 kg bombs from piloted aircrafts, but a feature was the penetration of the reinforced-concrete roadway. Blast damage was on a more limited scale than that experienced by fly bombs. The size of the crater was such that blast took an upward passage and the open areas in the vicinity of the incident helped in its dispersal.

Rescue operations were under the direction of Mr Skinner, Deputy Rescue Officer, with 3 Heavy and 5 Light Rescue parties, assisted by NFS personnel and voluntary helpers. At the time of visit the incident was much overcrowded by workers, who were standing on live debris [i.e. liable to move if people walked on it]. I instructed Mr Skinner to call off all workers other than the Rescue Service and form chains of men with baskets so as to allow the rescue personnel to work from the lower levels. . . . At 2015 hours the incident was cleared of all known casualties, 1½ hours after the fall of the missile.

The noise of the explosion left most of those who had heard it puzzled. An American civilian working for the US Office of Strategic Services was told by his taxi-driver in Piccadilly that a bomber had crashed. Vere Hodgson, nearer the scene, in Notting Hill, having just rejoiced at a whole week of nights spent in bed instead of on the office floor, decided that as there was 'No Warning on . . . it could not be the new secret weapon' and that 'perhaps it was an explosion at a munitions factory'. Another diary-keeper, the wife of a former barrister, living in West Hampstead, was more perceptive:

An hour or so ago, I was listening to the wireless with Bob [her cat] on my lap, when he gave a great start and sat up, my chair shuddering at the same time. Ralph came running in: 'Had I heard *that one*?' He says there was a very loud report indeed and from their behaviour passers-by in the street seem to have heard it too. They just stopped dead and stared about – it was just a single very loud crack, or report, something like a gun. Ralph rang up Mr T. [a friend in the Post Office], who said he had also heard it. . . . Presently he rang us to say . . . his office in Whitechapel . . . said it was 'gun-fire at an unidentified aircraft'. I just wonder if it is some munition works explosion; or the heralded 'V-2'!

Surprisingly few people, however, in spite of Churchill's recent hints, seem to have realized what this latest 'big bang' meant. The usual explanation, though it rapidly became something of a joke, offered a non-military reason for the sudden noise. One member of the staff of the West Middlesex Hospital in Isleworth, on seeing Civil Defence ambulances arriving, telephoned the main gate to ask 'what was happening. I got the reply "Gas main explosion" '. The same rumour was current among the crowd which gathered in Staveley Road, as one member of it, a Royal Navy petty officer home on leave, discovered. But he was unconvinced. 'If that's a bloody gas main,' he told his father, 'I don't know what Hitler's messing about wasting his time on bombs for!'

Even those on the site when the rocket landed did not at first know what had happened. Among them was an engineering worker, alone in a house in Wilmington Avenue, parallel to Staveley Road and about 200 yards from it. Having just got home from work, she had 'put on the kettle for a cup of tea . . . and put down a bowl of food for the family cat, Billy . . . large and white and not particularly friendly':

I left him happily eating in the kitchen and went into the lounge to put a match to the fire. I was . . . waiting for it to burn up when Billy came into the lounge and tried to jump on my lap, as I crouched in front of the fire. This was a very unusual thing for Billy to do, so I stood up and lifted him up in my arms. He was quite still for a second, then suddenly he leapt from my arms and rushed out of the lounge and through the cellar door, which was just outside. . . . Before I could gather my senses there was an almighty explosion, quite the biggest I've heard. I remember seeing the half-alight lounge fire blow out at me as my legs carried me out of the lounge door to the safety of an inside corridor between the lounge and kitchen. I remember looking back at the partly boarded windows and the outside door of the lounge as I ran and they were crumping into the room. I crouched in the corridor hiding my face in the coats hanging there for a few minutes, wondering what the hell had happened. . . . Soon I ventured out to survey the damage. Every door had burst in or out, practically all the back windows, even the boarded-up ones, had been broken, the lounge fire miraculously had caused no damage. . . . It must have been sucked back into the grate where it was burning away merrily. The cat would not come up out of the cellar, not even for his food. . . .

I don't think I was particularly frightened, mystified maybe. I couldn't think what had caused such a tremendous explosion. Neighbours were gathering in the road, saying 'What was it?' I went out of Wilmington Avenue and towards Staveley Road, where I thought the explosion had come from, but there were ARP squads setting up barriers and turning people back. . . . Presently I went to a phone box to phone my fiancé, who was on a 24-hour [pass] from the RAF and from the box I saw a very large black official-looking car drive towards Staveley Road. . . . Then I knew it was really something unusual.

Sixteen seconds after the explosion in Staveley Road, Chiswick, a second occurred in Epping, 18 miles north-east of Whitehall, and more than 20 miles from Chiswick, destroying some wooden huts. It attracted less attention than the Chiswick incident for no one was hurt and no real damage done, but the fragments of the missile were duly collected up and taken to Epping Police Station, where they were later inspected by some of the officials who had earlier been to Chiswick. The party, less high-powered than earlier, reached the site around 9.30 and the historian of the Chiswick incident now chronicled his second rocket of the day – though, oddly, it appears in the official records as the very first:

Incident Parndon Wood, Epping Long Lane. . . . The area was not under the alert and an enemy missile fell in a wooded part of the open country, forming a crater about 30 feet across and 16 feet in depth. Blast caused considerable damage to undergrowth and trees but there were no casualties.

Although, for reasons which will be explained shortly, no reports of what had happened at Chiswick or Epping appeared in the press or in wireless news bulletins, news of them rapidly crossed the Atlantic. Lord Cherwell was in Quebec, too far away to hear his 'mare's nest' explode, but an informant in Downing Street sent him a detailed account in a style calculated to appeal to him:

I was showing a visitor out and when I got to the door the policeman and guards were saying 'Was that thunder?' and another said 'It sounded like bombs'. When I got back I found Room 59 had heard two explosions, close together, one slightly fainter than the other, but both loud. . . . There is going to be criticism of Morrison and Sandys for having crowed too soon.

13

A PLUME OF BLACK SMOKE

The explosion is usually described as giving a reddish flash and a large plume of black smoke.

Ministry of Home Security report, 24 September 1944

The immediate response of the British government to the arrival of the rocket was to keep dark about it. The 'sealing off' of the country for which such elaborate plans had been prepared did not take place, but internal censorship was immediately imposed. The explosions in Chiswick and Epping brought both photographers and reporters flocking to the scene, but none of the pictures taken then appeared at the time. One reporter in Staveley Road who asked if a new type of bomb was responsible was told 'It might have been a gas main' but he was not deceived and, as the Chief Censor, Admiral Thompson, later recorded, 'The Press Association reporters at those places telephoned reports of the incidents within a few minutes to their Head Office, who submitted them to censorship.'

I suspected that at long last we were now having a taste of the much talked-of rocket and I accordingly instructed the censors to hold the reports and requested editors not to mention anything about the explosions pending further notice. The Minister of Home Security soon afterwards approved the action I had taken and informed me that he felt no doubt that the incidents had been caused by rockets.

On Saturday morning the authorities, with the Deputy Prime Minister Clement Attlee in charge, endorsed the 'silence' policy, as Admiral Thompson discovered:

Next day I went out to see Mr Morrison who requested me to inform editors that for the time being absolutely nothing should be published about the explosions which had undoubtedly been caused by some form of rocket shell fired from Holland; that these two explosions might well be ranging shots and that it was quite posible the enemy didn't even know they had arrived in England, much less in any particular area. I accordingly informed Mr Will, Chairman of the N.P.E.C. [Newspaper Proprietors Emergency Council], of the request I had made to editors and soon received the reply that his Council were in entire agreement.

The no-publicity policy had one unforeseen, offbeat result: it nearly ruined a wartime wedding, as one photographer with a Fleet Street news agency learned that morning. He had agreed to act as best man for a friend, a *Daily Mirror* cameraman due to get married that Saturday at the 'journalists' church' of St Bride's, Fleet Street:

At about 9 a.m. that morning his bride-to-be telephoned me in a most agitated state as her husband-to-be, who had been on night duty at the *Mirror*, had not put in an appearance that morning as had been arranged. I telephoned the *Mirror* and they also were confused as it appeared they had sent him out to the Epping incident on Friday night and he had not returned. The next hour was spent in telephone calls to many sources . . . and it was ultimately discovered that my colleague was in an Epping police cell, having been arrested the night before for photographing the V-2 crater in the open field . . . by some type of Reserve policeman . . . although my colleague had all the official photographic permits. . . . However, he was released and arrived at the church for his wedding with a few minutes to spare.

Already it was clear that hopes of any warning system being possible were unfounded; radar had failed to detect either missile. The only possible counter-measure was to try to stop the rockets at source and that Saturday the Vice-Chief of the Imperial Staff, another of the 'second eleven' left behind while the 'top brass' went to Canada, sent a MOST IMMEDIATE signal to the recently promoted Field Marshal Montgomery at the Tactical Headquarters of 21 Army Group:

2 rockets, so called V-2, landed in England yesterday. Will you please report most urgently by what approximate date you consider you can rope off the coastal area contained by ANTWERP–UTRECHT–ROTTERDAM. When this area is in our hands the threat from this weapon will probably have dispersed.

The Vice-Chiefs of Staff decided that weekend – they met on

both Saturday and Sunday – to install new radar equipment in British-held areas of the continent. To lend point to their deliberations, rocket number 3 arrived, at 9.29 on the evening of Sunday, 10 September, at North Fambridge, near Maldon, in Essex, abut 40 miles east of London. It caused no damage or casualties, while the next two were also innocuous. The fourth rocket arrived just after 9 a.m. on Monday, 11 September, at Chelsfield, near Orpington, in Kent, 16 miles from London, causing a spectacular explosion just above the ground after the warhead had hit a tree. The fifth, half an hour later, was 25 miles away, at Magdalen Laver, near Harlow, in Essex, confirming that the missile's accuracy left much to be desired: these first shots had been spread over an area 50 miles square. Next day the Cabinet concluded that the Germans had no means of controlling their rockets in flight or of detecting where they landed and that the policy of press silence should therefore continue.

The most serious incident so far – and the first involving an industrial target – followed, at 6.15 in the morning of Tuesday, 12 September 1944, when a rocket plunged down into the Chrysler vehicle works in Mortlake Road, Kew, a mainly residential area. Eight people were killed and 14 seriously injured and the damage to property was enormous, but, though the busy Mortlake Road, now part of the South Circular Road, ran through the very centre of the area, still the secret was kept. Thereafter the rockets went on arriving at an annoying and increasing but not, so far as the Civil Defence services were concerned, an intolerable rate. There were three more on the 12th, one on the 13th and three on the 14th, of which the first landed in the centre of Walthamstow, the start of what was to be a long series. It came down, like many of the most destructive of its successors, in the early morning – in fact at 4.55 a.m. – causing the largest crater so far, 50 feet across and 10 feet deep, and demolishing, or leaving fit only for demolition, 13 houses within a 100 feet radius of the point of impact, and badly damaging another 39 up to 250 feet away. Luckily only one side of the road was built up at this point, but even so 6 people were killed outright, one of the 10 badly hurt died later, and another 54 had lesser injuries.

The rocket at Farnan Avenue caused much ill-feeling in

north-east London, where the lack of warning – for which the government was not to blame – and the conspiracy of silence about the rocket danger – for which it *was* responsible – were blamed for the loss of life and other suffering. The Civil Defence controller for Walthamstow, a local alderman, was scathing about the official policy in the wartime history which the borough published a year later:

At the end of August . . . Mr Duncan Sandys . . . fatuously and prematurely announced 'the Battle of London is over'*. . . . The next government pronouncement was to the effect that the second Battle of London was 'won but not over'. What exactly this meant in English it was difficult to decide, but, as the speaker was Mr Willink, the Minister of Health – responsible for evacuation – it had the to-be-expected but lamentable result of causing thousands of evacuees to come back to London. It also unfortunately inclined people to abandon the habit of sleeping in shelters. . . . I drew the attention of the Regional Commissioner to this when he visited us. I suggested that the policy of secrecy on the one hand, and the fatuous optimism of government speakers on the other, ought to be debited with these six deaths.

Walthamstow, a robustly independent, mainly working-class area, was not at all impressed by the arguments in favour of secrecy:

From the beginning . . . local authorities were variously advised by London Region to announce to their citizens that the explosions were those of gas mains, ammunition wagons or delayed action bombs. This, of course, was absurd and one of our own people dealt with the situation very adequately when, looking at a 50-foot crater in Farnan Avenue, he said solemnly to the Regional Commissioner, who had enquired the time of the incident: 'The Delayed Action Bomb fell at 04.55 hours, sir'.

The rocket bombardment once again put the families of many servicemen in greater danger than their menfolk, and exposed those who did have a dangerous job to new risks while on leave. On the day before Walthamstow had its first brush with the V-2s, and with the government, one young radar

---

*This account dates Duncan Sandys's speech wrongly and also describes him as Secretary of State for War, but these mistakes do not affect the subsequent criticism.

operator had arrived home in Farnan Avenue while his ship, HMS *Leeds*, was in dock for boiler-cleaning:

I walked to the shops with my mother and spoke to many of her neighbours who were about their various cleaning activities on our street. The topic of conversation seemed to be the mysterious explosions that had occurred in the London area . . . and there was talk about the official explanation, which was reported as gas explosions.

This scepticism was now to be vindicated:

I woke in the early hours of the next morning to a terrific explosion, which I imagined as my boat being torpedoed. I saw a large hole and imagined this to be a gap in the ship's side. It was only when I realized I was in bed, I remembered I was at home. I . . . attempted to go to sleep again when my parents insisted I should get up because the road was on fire. I quickly dressed and walked between the ruins of the houses adjacent to my own home. There were large piles of rubble by the side of the road and the gas main was burning furiously. Water was cascading down the footway from broken water mains.

I was one of the first in the road and there were a number of cries from the debris. I was joined by one other person and . . . we uncovered the head and shoulders of a young man who said he was a New Zealander training with the Royal Navy in the North-East Polytechnic, which was situated nearby. We were unable to remove him . . . as a slate penetrated his side between his ribs. . . . At this point the rescue team arrived and we left him to them. I next recall seeing an elderly man still in his bed on the remains of an upper floor in a room with only one wall standing. As we went to reach him, he cried out that there were younger members of his family in the wreckage. . . . He asked if we would rescue them first. We were able to trace their position by their cries and clear the way to a mother and daughter who were together in bed and trapped by heavy timbers across their legs. I recall that this young girl, who was in the ATS, explained that her army skirt was underneath the mattress and was therefore being very adequately pressed! . . . We joked about the situation in which they found themselves, trapped in bed, with a body of men trying to release them . . . . I recall one woman being dead in the branches of a tree, her chow dog being dead at the base of it. . . . I did not return to my own home till about 4 p.m.

Even men in Ack-Ack units, who had been the first to learn about the flying bombs, had no knowledge of this new danger.

A Plume of Black Smoke

One Bofors gunner, on leave in Croydon from the Kent coast, was astounded by the discovery:

I had previously written to an aunt saying how glad I was she was at last having peace and quiet and she wrote back and said 'I like your idea of peace and quiet. Things are popping off all over the place!' I took this to mean she was still being troubled by flying-bombs. . . . My wife said nothing to me about rockets, probably because she didn't want to spoil my leave and didn't wish to worry me. Next day, however, I was chatting to my neighbour over the garden fence and he said:

'What do you think about the rockets?'

'Rockets?' I said. 'What rockets?'

'Didn't you know?' he said. 'Haven't you been told?'

I was speechless. At that very moment there was an almighty explosion and slowly a huge column of black smoke rose in the sky in the direction of Catford.

'There you are,' he said. 'That's one!'

I was flabbergasted and very worried. . . . All that effort and suffering on the gun sites for nothing. No wonder they hadn't told us troops. It would have shattered our morale.

Kammler's twelfth rocket landed three hours after the one in Walthamstow, in Dairsie Road, Woolwich, with very similar results, followed by a harmless 'airburst' – of the kind that had earlier so much troubled Dornberger – over Rotherfield in Sussex at lunchtime, and the fourteenth met a watery grave in a filter bed of the Metropolitan Water Board works at Sunbury, at 4 a.m. on Friday, 15 September. This was the point at which the Ministry of Home Security undertook its first stocktaking, in a report circulated ten days later:

Out of the 14 projectiles reported crossing the coast, 8 fell in London Region. This is a slightly higher ratio than was obtained in the early days of FLY attack. The mean aiming error so far, however, appears to be larger. . . . A curious feature of the distribution so far obtained is that, of the incidents outside the London Region, all were very close to the correct line or to the correct range for London. The beaten zone [i.e. the area affected by V-2s] is thus approximately in the shape of a cross, as if . . . it were possible to control either line or range but not both.

The early assumption that, because it plunged deeper into the earth, the rocket would be less destructive than the flying-bomb was not borne out by this larger sample. The four rockets in residential areas had destroyed all houses within an 85 foot radius, compared to 72 feet for the V-1, had made others uninhabitable up to 108 feet, compared to 102, and caused serious damage up to 181 feet, against the V-1's 172. The death rate per missile for the first week of the attack was identical, at 2.7 for each V-1 or V-2, though this figure had dropped to 2.1 for the V-1 'as evacuation took effect and more people took shelter'. The V-1 had, however, seriously injured slightly more people per incident than the V-2 – 9.1 against 8.5 – but on crater size the rocket was an easy winner, the average being '34½ ft diameter by 9½ ft deep, the maximum being 50 ft by 10ft' compared to 'an average crater size of 17 ft by 4 ft for FLY'.

Only two rockets were definitely known to have broken up in the air, though others might have done so, the report writer suggested, but about its arrival on the ground there was now all too much evidence:

Two loud reports are commonly heard . . . presumably associated with the 'shell-wave' due to the arrival of the projectile and with the detonation. . . . Other sounds of long duration, rumbling or crackling, may also be heard and are presumably due to air disturbances in the wake of the projectile. The rocket is infrequently seen with the unaided eye, particularly at night, when it is usually described as glowing red or orange. . . . Several persons claim to have seen the projectile. They describe it as long and narrow ('about the size of a Spitfire without wings') and travelling very fast . . . nearly east to west. The explosion is usually described as giving a reddish flash and a large plume of black smoke.

By now others had suffered the same experience as some of the residents of Staveley Road, Chiswick, in not hearing the explosion which had wrecked their homes. The Civil Defence controller of Walthamstow later offered an explanation:

This so-called 'zone of silence' was a marked feature of rocket incidents, persons within a range of even up to 250 or 300 yards not hearing the explosion although they would, of course, feel the earth tremor when the rocket burst on the ground. The zone of silence was apparently caused by the terrific speed of the out-rush of the blast driving the air before it and in . . . a practical vacuum, no sound could travel.

The silence was not always total. One woman who lived almost opposite a house which suffered a direct hit recalls a noise 'like a heavy sigh, or a rapid intake of breath', while other reported a sudden pressure in the ears. As the bombardment went on, such experiences became daily more common. After lunch on Friday, 15 September, another rocket landed in the water, this time in the Thames Estuary at All Hallows in Kent, and there were five more on the 16th and another five on the 17th, until Kammler reached his quarter-century just before 7 o'clock in the evening of 17 September, nine days almost to the minute since his first successful strike. Rocket number 25, in Adelaide Road, Brockley, in south east London, was one of the worst so far, with 14 dead and 41 badly injured, illustrating once again the capricious nature of the missile, for 14 of the first 25 had caused no casualties at all and many had done no worse damage than set a corn-rick on fire or destroy a patch of brambles. On 18 September – marked by a solitary rocket which scored a direct hit on a church at West Norwood – the Cabinet decided to postpone a decision about publicity until 24 September.

It had previously been agreed that once the Germans publicly claimed to be bombarding London with rockets some form of 'official statement' would have to be made, and the Germans now put out what the Chief Censor considered a 'fishing report' on Berlin radio to the effect that an unspecified secret weapon had destroyed Euston Station. It was agreed, however, that this hardly qualified, and a meeting of ministers where Admiral Thompson represented his minister, Brendan Bracken, decided that their lips should stay sealed.

Mr Herbert Morrison pointed out that the rockets were causing no panic nor any real anxiety among the population. And I reported that editors were in full agreement with the policy of silence. It was therefore decided to ignore the German report and that I should inform editors that they were to continue to report nothing about the rockets. . . . Our policy of complete silence mystified the enemy, who could not be sure even that his rockets were landing in England.

One reason for the government's decision was the expectation that the whole nuisance would soon be over, for on 17 September Operation Market Garden had been launched, to secure a bridgehead at Arnhem and thus, it was hoped, end the war by a quick thrust into Germany itself. At the very least Holland might be liberated and the known launching sites be overrun. No lack of information existed about their general area, for the Dutch hated the Germans with a loathing second only to that the Poles felt for 'the master race', and information poured in from informants in The Hague. The trouble was that, by the time the bombers arrived, the birds had flown, while, even when their location was known, identifying the sites from the air was extremely difficult. Storage sites were an easier target and on 14 and 17 September Bomber Command dropped around 200 tons of bombs on suspect estates, at Raaphorst and Eikenhorst, in the suburb of Wassenaar, reserving a third, Ter Horst, for later attention. Holland was within range, too, of the fighters of ADGB, which flew constant 'interdiction' patrols, firing on any vehicles and troops they spotted. This effort produced no visible (or indeed any real) results and efforts to locate the rockets when fired had little more success. Special teams were formed to try to spot the flash as a rocket was fired, and to fix its position by sound-ranging equipment. The 10th Survey Regiment, Royal Artillery, was sent to Belgium as part of a new formation, 105 Mobile Air Reporting Unit, stationed at Malines near Brussels, while the 11th Survey Regiment was established near Canterbury, as a form of long stop, but neither proved able to provide even the minute or so's warning essential if anyone was to get into shelter in time.

On 25 September 1944, by now aware that the great gamble at Arnhem had failed, the Chiefs of Staff formally reported to the Cabinet on the rocket menace. The V-2's normal maximum range, they advised, seemed to be 200 miles, and this could probably be extended without any basic change to 240 miles, increasing the need to occupy the whole of Holland. But they still opposed any public announcement, since once the subject could be mentioned at all 'we should have difficulty in restraining the press from publishing information of value to the enemy, such as we experienced in regard to flying-bomb incidents'.

At a separate Cabinet meeting later that day the Minister of Information endorsed this policy and Stafford Cripps, a 'prorocketeer' in the past, agreed they should take their cue of silence from the Germans. Herbert Morrison dissented, arguing that a public statement was overdue, but he was over-ruled, and the only action decided on was to ask the US Chiefs of Staff to discourage any reference to the explosions in London in the American press.

The policy of secrecy resulted in the emergence in the capital of 'three nations': those who knew about the rockets, those who guessed the truth, and those who, conscious that they had been told about conventional raids and the flying bombs, assumed that no announcement about the V-2s meant that none had yet arrived. To the first category belonged those like the American OSS official who had accepted his taxi-driver's story of a 'bomber crashing' to explain away the mysterious explosion on 8 September. By the following Tuesday he was reporting 'all sorts of rumours . . . at Buck's club' and acknowl-edging that 'It was an eerie sensation to know that such explosions are happening and to have them ignored'. By next morning a better-informed colleague had taken pity on him and told him that 'the recent explosions were caused by 1100-pound rocket bombs that plummeted out of the sky from heights estimated to approach fifteen miles'. The barrister's wife in West Hampstead who had correctly guessed the cause of the 'Friday night explosion' learned the following day that it had occurred in Chiswick, only to be misled that afternoon by another informant who explained that it 'came from the explosion of the power station there' – a nonexistent insti-tution. By Tuesday, 12 September, however, the same helpful friend to whom her husband had applied for information on the Friday, an assistant postmaster in an East End borough, was able to provide an up-to-date bulletin. "Some enemy weapon, V-2,' he said, 'had demolished some thirty houses in Dagenham this morning." Such a weapon', the diarist commented, nicely confusing the truth, 'would account for the blowing up of the Chiswick power house.'

The Dagenham rocket, the seventh in the series, which seri-ously injured 14 people and slightly hurt another 70, though happily it killed no one, was much talked about in the area: it had landed on a school for crippled children, in Marston Avenue, doing considerable damage and starting a fire. It also meant for one small boy one of the most frustrating experiences of the war:

At about 8 o'clock in the morning I had got up and made my parents a pot of tea in bed when [in fact at 0819 hours] there was a loud bang and clouds of smoke rising from across the roof tops about half a mile away. Since there had been no siren or aeroplane or flying-bomb engine noise my parents dismissed it as a gas main explosion. Soon after I walked down our street to meet the milkman when I saw a large piece of metal in the gutter. It was similar to the metal used in aeroplane fuselage and was hot to touch. Another boy joined me but as we were discussing the 'spoils' an air-raid warden came up on his bike and claimed it for 'the authorities' and eventually cycled off with it under his arm.

There was, this informant recalls, 'an air of mystery at first about what had happened', and an electrician in Ilford was told that the explanation for the explosion in the neighbouring borough was that 'some secret war work in Fords had blown up', leaving – just the sort of nice, circumstantial touch in which rumour-mongers delighted – 'a very large crater which would hold quite easily two double-decker buses'. Frustratingly, too, some of those 'in the know' found less well-informed people eager to mislead them. The West Hampstead woman quoted earlier recorded in her diary for Thursday, 14 September, the conflicting information pressed upon her, following the Farnan Avenue incident:

Our peace has been short-lived. We now exist under another cloud, V-2 rockets. There was another loud explosion this morning. The barber at the club told Ralph some enemy missile had hit Walthamstow and done considerable damage. So Ralph range up Mr T., who very much knew all about it as one of his post offices had been hit. . . .
While out this morning, I ran into Miss D., who assured me that the explosions we were having came from guns across the Channel.

Such explanations were given little credence in fly-bombed Croydon. 'Explosions now believed by public to be either long-range shells or rockets,' noted one seventeen-year-old schoolboy in his diary that week. But at Clapham, not far away, it was still possible to remain in blissful ignorance. 'My wife explained there had been lots of these explosions,' recalls a then RAF electrician, puzzled by the constant bangs while they sat in the 'pictures'. 'The rumour was that the army and the ARP were blowing up dangerous buildings damaged during the V-1 raids.'

Aware of the marked improvement in morale which had followed the first full statement about the flying-bombs, Herbert Morrison was probably right in arguing that, whatever its military merits, his colleagues' insistence on tacitly denying the rockets' existence was having an adverse effect on the public. Although, as will be described, spirits were to sink even lower later in the winter, they began to decline significantly during the late autumn, with Arnhem a failure and the near certainty that the war would drag on into another year. Even Civil Defence workers were not immune, either from ignorance or sagging morale, as one woman then working as a 'control' telephonist at Welling in Kent recalls:

No one told us what they were. We were left guessing and yet they were the most devastating thing that had come our way. We were all terrified and nervy. The weather was very foggy at this early stage, which added to the nightmare. People started talking about poison gas as they had in 1939.

The prevailing gloom is vividly remembered by a woman then working as a student nurse in a North London hospital, where the staff could only judge what was happening by the broken victims they treated of a weapon which officially did not exist:

The stories that filtered into the hospital left a picture of Highgate Hill and Hampstead looking like the white cliffs of Dover, with nothing between them and us in Holloway. I had a particular fear of being left suspended in a bed overhanging a gaping hole.

When they did realize the truth there was a grim satisfaction for Londoners in seeing visitors from other parts of the country wake up to it too, as a wartime resident of Woolwich observed:

Some of the repair men coming into London thought that it was line-shooting when they heard of explosions caused by rockets . . . but they were not in London long before they were convinced of the truth. . . . A joke that went the rounds was that one man on the train, having refused to believe that such a thing was possible, arrived at the terminus at the same time as a rocket. . . . so turned round and took the next train back.

Even more frustrating was to be the bearer of a truthful 'bomb story' that no one would believe. 'We were all very sceptical of what she said,' remembers one woman who worked in a City bank of a colleague who arrived hotfoot from Chiswick with news of the first V-2, 'particularly when she stated it had brought a great deal of ice with it.' A Mottingham man remembers the story of a large hole containing 'parts of a German machine ALL COVERED IN ICE' being 'dismissed as the best rumour yet', no doubt inspired by the famous First World War story about the Russians with snow on their boots. In fact, of course, the liquid oxygen the rocket carried, at temperatures of up to minus 200°C, *did* often vaporize on landing if not consumed during the flight.

The 'gas main' story had a long run – so long that some credulous people are said to have applied to local gas companies for compensation for their damaged homes, and a few now believe, wrongly, that it was broadcast by the BBC. Within a few weeks, however, as explosions multiplied, 'flying gas mains' became an 'in joke' among Londoners. Among the men working on armoured fighting vehicles in Park Royal, one of them remembers, any explosion became greeted by a reference to 'another Chiswick gas main', while a man living in Streatham Hill recalls that when a distant bang interrupted a lunchtime drinking session in the garden of the Horse and Groom, general laughter greeted the observation that 'another gasworks had gone up and it was surprising that there was any gas left for cooking'. Even children's faith in the official 'cover story', much favoured by parents, rapidly weakened. A then sixteen-year-old schoolgirl in Raynes Park finally decided 'that there were not that many gas mains', while a fourteen-year-old in Brockley had reasoned out a similar conclusion. 'After all, the gas mains had behaved themselves perfectly for many years so why should they suddenly take to exploding without warning?' Eventually even the censor seems to have decided the story had worn thin. A man from Tooting Bec recalls a cartoon showing the manager of a gasworks remarking to a visitor: 'I suppose they'll be saying that explosion was yet another gasworks gone up in smoke.' Behind his back the plant could be seen through a window to be on fire.

The Arnhem operation, although it had failed, did give

London a temporary respite. Kammler's batteries, after occupying two streets, had then taken over the whole Wassenaar district of The Hague. From 10 to 12 September a large house known as the Beukenhorst residence was the firing area, and from 13 September a newly cleared road, the Oud Wassenaarse. The air-drop at Arnhem on 17 September exposed the whole of Abteilung 485 to the risk of being cut off, and its two batteries were now withdrawn to Overveen near Haarlem and then to Burgsteinfurt, north-west of Münster, about 40 miles inside Germany, while Kammler moved his headquarters from Nijmegen to the same area. Battery 444, 'Dornberger's own', had hardly reached Walcheren Island after its abortive attack on Paris from Euskirchen, on 14 September, when, around 17 September, it had to take the road again, to Zwolle, 36 miles north of Arnhem and about 10 miles inland. By now the three batteries combined had fired 35 rockets, of which – though Kammler did not know this – only 9 had exploded harmlessly in mid-air or plunged into the North Sea. On Tuesday, 26 September, the last survivors of 1st Airborne Division on the far side of the Rhine were withdrawn and, though the British still held a salient 60 miles deep on the south bank, the Germans occupied, securely it seemed, most of Holland, from which they could bombard both Antwerp, the major port on which the Allies depended, and Great Britain itself.

The Russians, who had clamoured for a second front to relieve the pressure on their armies, showed little gratitude now it had been established. Blizna, while still in use as the main V-2 development site, had not been bombed by the Russian air force, and – as the Germans had guessed – the Russians refused to allow Allied aircraft to attack it from Russian soil. By 27 July the Germans had abandoned it and on 29 July the party of British experts sent to study any material left there was on its way, a roundabout journey via Cairo, Teheran – where they were kept waiting for Russian visas – and Moscow, where they were kept waiting again, on the totally untruthful grounds that Blizna had not yet been captured. Only on 3 September, after the personal intervention of Anthony Eden, did they finally reach their destination, to find the research site deserted but undamaged, though fighting was still going on five miles away. The Germans had removed most of their equipment, but much useful information was gained from local informants and crater measurements, as well as from items left behind by the Germans, including a fuel tank, a useful pointer to the rocket's range, and, in a latrine, part of an A-4's test record, which clearly identified one of its fuels as oxygen, while other evidence confirmed that '*B-Stoff*' was alcohol, which several Poles recalled smelling in the remains of crashed rockets.

A little earlier all this information would have been invaluable; now it had been overtaken by events, and the expedition ended in anticlimax. By 22 September its members were on their way home, but when, a little later, the crates they had so carefully loaded arrived it appeared that their contents had, on the way, undergone a mysterious change into ordinary aircraft scrap. The material from Blizna remained in Russian hands, for the Russian rocket scientists and engineers to study at their leisure.

14
A SPLASH IN THE MARSHES

We . . . saw only a kind of waterspout as they fell in the marshes.

Member of Anti-Aircraft battery, recalling service in Norfolk, October 1944

The opening of the rocket offensive, so long delayed, delighted Hitler, who now suffered another of his volatile changes of mood. 'The Führer considers', noted Albert Speer in his office diary of 23 September, 'that the resumption of A-4 production at peak capacity – i.e. rapidly rising to nine hundred – is urgently necessary.' Already Kammler had launched a secondary offensive, on 21 September, against a number of continental cities, principally Antwerp, though Liège, Lille, Tourcoing, Maastricht, Hasselt, Tournai, Arras, Cambrai, Mons and Diest were also to be the target, at various times, for from two to twenty-seven rockets. The campaign benefited Great Britain by absorbing many missiles that would otherwise have been aimed at London, but the main cause of the reduced weight of the attack after its impressive opening fortnight was technical failure. 485 Battery, of Group South, based in Germany and bombarding French and Belgian cities, suffered more than the units in Holland. Several missiles during the last ten days of September crashed back on to the launching pad, or plunged to earth within a mile or two of it, one particularly notorious rocket even setting off back into Germany, until blown up by an emergency radio signal. Kammler had no doubt that defects in manufacture, for which Dornberger could ultimately be held responsible, were to blame. Dornberger in his turn was equally convinced that it was poor handling in the field that caused the trouble. 'Storage and rain caused the bearing bushes to swell in the trimming servo-mechanism. Replacements were not forthcoming.' The truth was that the liberation of France had thrown out all the Germans' elaborate plans for rapidly conveying the rockets from factory to firing point, via main storage dumps and forward supply depots. The vast bunkers in which highly trained speciaalists tuned up every missile into perfect condition shortly before it was launched were now heaps of rubble, and in Allied hands. Instead the rockets had been parked in temporary transit dumps, exposed to wind and weather, so that the highly sensitive electrical and mechanical components had become corroded – and only one of several thousand parts needed to fail for the whole missile to become unreliable.

Once he had diagnosed the source of the trouble Dornberger took energetic measures to put matters right:

Rockets ceased to be stored in the ammunition dumps. Immediately they came off the production line at the Central Works, express transport took them to the front and they were fired within three days. . . . Technical teams were detached from Peenemunde to the operational units to help in assembling newly introduced components. The first echelon of my staff . . . went to the operational area. It looked after transport, delivered the rockets to the batteries and ran the supply of spare parts. After this there were hardly any breakdowns.

The new supply arrangements, known as *Warme Semmel* (Hot Cakes), meant that rockets, though still transported to the launching area by rail, were then taken on by road to an assembly and testing point, where they were immediately inspected, and then sent on to the launching site. At the same time, Kammler and Dornberger managed, at least to some extent, to bury their differences. On 30 September 1944 the two men came to a formal understanding, enshrined in a written agreement which both signed:

Kammler took over field operations and had power of decision on fundamental questions. I was not made subordinate to him. . . . I was his permanent representative at home; as inspector of long-range rocket field units I had control of their formation and training; as his technical staff officer, vested with his own powers, I ran development and supply.

By now the central works was turning out 600 rockets a month and, as Dornberger was aware, 'the conveyor belt equipment . . . could have doubled this figure without any trouble', but the real bottleneck was fuel. The output of alcohol was barely sufficient even for the present production of rockets, while liquid oxygen, he complained, 'also became a restricting factor after the big underground generating plants at Liege and Wittringen in the Saar had been overrun'. The figures spoke for themselves. The total supply 'did not exceed the output of 30 to 35 generators', each of which could produce about 9 tons of liquid oxygen, but by the time 'the oxygen had been transferred from the factory storage tanks to the 48 ton capacity railway tankers' and 'thence to the 5.8 ton road tankers', there had been a substantial loss through evaporation and another 5 lb per minute disappeared through the same cause while the rocket stood waiting to be launched, so that the original 9 tons had shrunk, by the moment of lift-off, to only just enough – 4.96 tons – to fill its fuel tank. This powerful but hard-to-handle liquid, which had proved the key to the rocket's success, was also, therefore, its Achilles heel, and its lack affected development work as well as operations. His teams had, Dornberger considered, a totally inadequate number of rockets available – 5 to 7 a day – 'for experiments and acceptance tests', leaving '28 to 30 rockets per day for operations'. To Kammler, he was aware, 'the only important thing was the number of operational launchings. He wanted to report as many as possible to higher authority and whether they were effective seemed for the moment to be a matter of indifference.' Dornberger, by contrast, a scientist before he was a soldier and an artillery man before he was a general, remained a perfectionist, eager to produce an accurate as well as a long-range missile – and, in his view, the A-4 was 'still not fully developed':

Dispersion was too great, effect was unsatisfactory because of the insensitive fuse, and a few rockets still blew up towards the end of the trajectory. We had to eliminate these weaknesses and also to devise optical, acoustic and radio means of recording the impact, which could no longer be observed from aircraft over the target areas. . . . Success in the experiments depended on a reasonable supply of rockets for the purpose. . . . A single series of launching tests lasted for weeks. Alterations and improvements took months to

187

come through. On the other hand the front cried out for faster delivery and higher production.

Dornberger had one powerful card to play in seeking more rockets for deveopment, for 'the withdrawal of the front called for longer ranges', and here the scientists' work bore rapid dividends:

We were able by making some minor improvements in the standard rocket . . . and by slightly increasing the contents of the tanks to increase the range of operational missiles to 200 miles. Some trial missiles with even larger propellant tanks achieved a range of 300 miles when launched from Peenemünde.

All this boded ill for the British, for it would mean that the Midlands, as well as the ports of south-east England, would be exposed to attack, provided Kammler retained his foothold around The Hague. This, however, began to seem uncertain. The Arnhem offensive threatened to cut off his troops, and he ordered a hasty retreat northwards. Between 19 and 25 September no rockets at all were fired against England, while 444 Battery re-established itself on the mainland north of Zwolle, near Staveren in Friesland, the promontory between the Zuider Zee and the North Sea. The only British cities now within his reach were Norwich and Ipswich, of which the former was the more attractive target, though its size – it had a peacetime population of about 130,000 – meant that he had little hope of hitting it except by chance. Nor were missiles falling wide in the surrounding county likely to cause many casualties. Norfolk was the third largest county in England, with a mere half a million inhabitants spread over 1.3 million acres. Ipswich, with its 110,000 residents, was even smaller than Norwich, while east and west Suffolk combined were not much more densely populated than Norfolk, with 400,000 people to 900,000 acres.

The rocket campaign against Norwich was such a fiasco that probably few of its occupants even realized they were under attack. Norfolk was ultimately credited with 29 incidents within the county boundaries, though the Germans are believed to have aimed 43 V-2s at its county town. The first, a harbinger of those to follow, came down 20 miles from its intended target, and in the wrong county, at Hoxne in Suffolk, at 7.10 p.m. on

Monday, 25 September 1944. It was not even audible in Norwich, where people for the first time heard the double bang, now so familiar in London, the following afternoon. The explosion, according to a local historian, caused bewilderment in the city, since 'no information could be otained as to its origin'. The rocket had in fact landed 8 miles to the north-east in an area well known to holiday-makers on the Broads, as the incident sheet in the county Civil Defence War Diary recorded:

26 Sept	**Ranworth**	*Casualties*:	*Damage*:
1630 hrs BIG BEN		1 slight.	Slight.
			2 windows at
			Ranworth church.

Next morning, another explosion in a village 6 miles to the north produced more puzzlement. Again the War Diary tells the facts:

2/ Sept	Suspected Botany Bay	*Casualties*:	*Damage*:
1048 hrs BIG BEN	Farm	Nil.	Nil.
	Horsford		

As yet even the police and Civil Defence workers on the spot were uncertain about the reason why the rich Norfolk soil was suddenly erupting into the air. The Horsford incident – its original name, 'Horse-ford', was a reminder of the rural nature of the area – was at first reported merely as 'Double explosion and column of smoke' and was not correctly identified until an hour later. Kammler's next shot, landing ingloriously in a sewage works while disturbing the teatime peace of rural Whitlingham, was also not immediately recorded for what it was by 'Control' in Norwich:

27 Sept	Suspected Sewage works	*Casualties*:	*Damage*:
1625 hrs BIG BEN	**Whitlingham**	Nil.	Damage to 5
			houses.
			1 Converted
			Railway carriage.
			Whitlingham Farm.
			2 Pea Stacks
			destroyed.

The destruction done, though annoying, was hardly of a kind likely to bring the British government to its knees; nor was that which 444 Battery accomplished an hour and a half later, 9 miles east of Norwich:

27 Sept	Suspected	Acle Hall	*Casualties*:	*Damage*:
1944 hrs	BIG BEN	Farm	Nil.	Damage to farm.
		Beighton		Telephone wires down on railway. Also damage to sleepers and fence on railway.

Lunchtime had always been a favoured period for the flying-bomb bombardment of London and perhaps the Germans imagined that the people of rural Norfolk conformed to the same pattern, for their next rocket landed at 11 minutes past 1 p.m. on 29 September, carving out a 12-foot-deep crater at Hemsby, 16 miles north-east of Norwich and hurting no one. Six civilian houses and shops were damaged and about 60 military and naval bungalows, the nearest to a military objective the Germans had yet hit in East Anglia. By now the nature of the attack was beyond doubt and Big Ben struck twice again that day. At 1942 hours, as the War Diary recorded, two people were slightly hurt and 27 houses damaged, at Coltishall, a town of about 1000 inhabitants 8 miles north of Norwich; and at 2041 hours a rocket landed at Thorpe, 16 miles in the same direction. This now became almost the standard pattern of the bombardment, with one or two rockets a day landing well wide of the target and causing only minor, local inconvenience. On 30 September, eight houses, a farmhouse and a barn were damaged at Acle, but no one was hurt; on the following day a farmhouse was badly damaged, and five houses lost slates or windows at Sycamore Farm, Bedingham, rendering six people homeless, some of them evacuees who had sought safety in the depths of rural Norfolk, while three adults and two children were slightly injured.

The peak of the offensive, such as it was, came early in October. Between 3 and 5 October eleven rockets landed in the county, but between them they injured only one man seriously; ten adults and four children were slightly hurt. The great majority of the V-2s fell on farmland, creating a crater up to 15 feet deep and 35 feet across, but curious locals who came

190

to stare probably did more damage than most of the missiles, though sometimes a church or a few farm outbuildings were mildly battered. At Acle on 5 October the road was briefly blocked by debris, at Surlingham an airburst blew down electric cables and telephone wires, at Shotesham All Saints, on 6 October – a relatively serious incident by Norfolk standards – 20 houses, the church and the school were all damaged, but only one person was slightly hurt. Norfolk's twenty-eighth rocket, at Ingworth, at 0740 on 12 October, was really the end of this phase of Kammler's campaign. It slightly injured two men at Welbourne, and inflicted damage on farm buildings, the school and twenty houses. By now the local Civil Defence personnel were so efficient that Region had heard of the rocket's arrival within four minutes and had a full account of the incident by early afternoon. Even Norfolk's modest establishment of wardens and rescue parties had proved easily able to cope with the bombardment; the whole 28 rockets had not killed a single person, had seriously injured only one, and had inflicted minor injuries on another 56 – a clear demonstration of the futility of using the rocket against anything except a built-up area. Most of the casualties, including the one serious injury, occurred in a single incident, which could easily have become a major tragedy, at 1341 hours on 4 October, when a V-2 landed near the village school, hurting 34 children and 2 adults, one very badly, at Rockland St Mary. Minor damage was done to the School Institute and 23 houses, and more serious, but still reparable, damage – with nice impartiality between God and Mammon – to the rectory and public house. The village was doubly unfortunate, being the only place in Norfolk to be hit by two rockets; the other, at 1051 hours on 11 October, damaged 14 houses but harmed no one.*

The Germans' second objective, apart from killing or maiming the maximum number of British civilians, was to damage property. A post office and village institute, a public house, two shops, three schools and six churches were affected,

---

*The historian's difficulties in recording facts accurately are nicely illustrated by these incidents. The county 'Incident-Sheet' record, compiled by people on the spot at the time, gives two different versions of the village's name – Ruckland St Mary and Rocklands St Mary – and both are wrong.

plus about 750 dwelling houses, most of them by the only V-2
that landed near Norwich, on the north side of the Hellesdon
Golf Course, at 1950 hours on Tuesday, 3 October. 'The whole
city was shaken', according to a local observer, but only one
person slightly hurt. The Germans also succeeded in destroying
a few haystacks and – no doubt the most spectacular victim –
a glasshouse. Seven farms and five other farm buildings or
barns were damaged, and an acre of sugar beet rendered uneat-
able. Two cows were also injured, at Bedingham on 1 October.
It was, by any test, an unimpressive record for such a sophisticated weapon.

The people of Norfolk needed no story of exploding gas
mains to explain away those loud but distant bangs. The county
was the great airfield of the British Isles, and crashing Allied
aircraft, or objects inadvertently dropped from them, had
become a feature of daily life. But some people inevitably
knew, or suspected, what was happening. Ice-laden or other
fragments of missiles were sometimes picked up, and occasionally a missile was glimpsed as it hurtled to earth from the wide
Norfolk skies. One woman then serving in a heavy Ack-Ack
battery on the Norfolk coast remembers the frustrations of
those weeks. 'Some [V-2s]', she recalls, 'fell on the marshes
behind Caister and Yarmouth. . . . We were not involved as
we had no defence against them and saw only a kind of waterspout as they fell in the marshes.' At least another five came
down in the sea near enough to the shore to be visible. These
melancholy splashes, harming no one, provide a fitting
commentary on the whole Norwich campaign, though the
county was to suffer from one more V-2, on 6 March 1945, at
Raveningham, 10 miles south-west of Norwich, a 'stray' which,
like its predecessors, did little harm.

Only one V-2 is believed to have been aimed at Ipswich,
unsuccessfully, and the thirteen rockets that landed in Suffolk
were all, with this exception, probably intended for Norwich.
They caused no deaths or serious injuries and aroused so little
interest that the County Record Office contains no information
concerning them, though one local resident secured a more
tangible souvenir, in the shape of a fuel tank found at Hopton,
near Lowestoft, on 2 October. The same man also recalls how
'On several clear mornings in 1944, from a vantage point near

the police station in London Road, Beccles, I saw the zigzag vapour trails of V-2s climbing from Holland, the zigzags being caused by differences in direction and velocity of the wind in successive air layers.'

If the Norfolk campaign was not a victory for Kammler, it was also hardly a triumph for the British. It was some time before Friesland was identified as the source of the rockets now landing in the eastern counties – it was, of course, more thinly populated than The Hague, with fewer potential agents – and, when it was, it became realized that the town of Sneek, the suspected railhead serving the launching sites, was not within range of United Kingdom-based fighters. 'Policing' the area was now entrusted to the 2nd Tactical Air Force, based on the continent, and an RAF mission from England, to discuss the arrangements, was surprised to learn that already more than fifty rockets had been fired at targets in France and Belgium. Meanwhile the attack against London had ceased, so that the urgency had gone out of plans to protect it. An additional Mobile Air Reporting Unit, which offered the best hope, though still a slim one, of detecting rocket launchings by radar, was assigned instead for use against sites firing on continental targets. Roderic Hill's 10th Survey Regiment was sent elsewhere, and its sister unit, the 11th, moved from England to Belgium to replace it. Hill, recently promoted to Air Chief Marshal and now C-in-C of Fighter Command, which had replaced the short-lived Air Defence of Great Britain, thus found himself in mid-October with depleted resources to meet what he, though apparently no one else, feared might be a growing attack.

On 30 September, with the recent danger to his units now passed with the collapse of Operation Market Garden, Kammler ordered one battery of 485 Abteilung back to The Hague. On 12 October 444 Abteilung also ceased fire from Friesland and around 22 October, along with the other battery of 485 Abteilung, also arrived back in The Hague. Thus for the first time Kammler had three full batteries available to him for the campaign against London, which, on 12 October, Hitler had ordered should be the sole British target, though the bombardment of Antwerp was also to continue. It was this diversion of effort, violating the basic military principle of concentrating one's strength, which alone reduced the number of V-2s reaching England, for British counter-measures were still proving totally ineffective. In the five weeks beginning mid-October, about 600 anti-rocket-site sorties were flown by United Kingdom-based fighters, and Bomber Command was asked to attack two places on the southern outskirts of The Hague suspected of sheltering rocket units. Mosquitoes of the 2nd Tactical Air Force, based on the continent, were sent against a third site and the two railway stations at Leiden, through which rockets were believed to reach the *Meiller-wagen*. None of this effort had much real effect. For the moment, as had so often happened in the history of war, the advantage lay with the side which had developed a new weapon, and the defence lagged behind.

15

THE LIAR ON THE THAMES

*The liar on the Thames has withheld from the world the fact
of the German V-2 bombardment until today.*

Commentator on German radio, 10 November 1944

The bombardment of London had been resumed even before
the attack on Norwich had ceased. On 3 October 1944 rockets
again began to be directed at the capital, though not at first
with much success. In the week ending 4 October, the final
phase of the Norwich offensive, 14 V-2s reached the United
Kingdom. Between 4 and 11 October the number rose to 23,
then between 11 and 18 October dropped to 14, and in the
week ending at noon on 25 October to 12. Of the total of 63
only 6, less than 10 per cent, reached the London Civil Defence
Region.

The government's continuing insistence on concealing the
rocket's very existence was by now having some curious results.
'Complete secrecy was kept as to the nature and effects of the
bomb,' wrote Croydon's war historian of its first V-2, on the
evening of Friday, 20 October – more will be said of it later –
but the next of kin of those affected still had to be informed,
like a sergeant then serving in the Royal Army Ordnance Corps
at Dunstable:

I was having a shave in the ablution shed when an orderly called,
saying that a police message had been received to the effect that my
house . . . had been bombed, but that my wife and baby son were
'still alive'. I was dumbfounded by this, and frankly sceptical, as there
had been no report on the radio of any enemy activity on the previous
night. . . . A friend of mine at HQ . . . promised to contact the War
Office in London to confirm whether there had in fact been any
bombing . . . and he later told me there had been none. This
reassured me somewhat. . . . However, I was given leave to proceed

195

home and I arrived at South Norwood about 11.0 a.m. and on approaching my road I was no longer in doubt.

Kammler was now beginning to step up both his rate of fire and its accuracy. In the week ending at midday on 1 November 1944, 26 V-2s landed in London, against only 8 elsewhere, a success rate of 76 per cent, though the 'wides' were a long way off target, one landing in a field at Barley, near Royston, in Hertfordshire, well to the north of London, and another the next day ploughing up Windsor Great Park, near Egham, to the west. An increasingly high proportion, however, were landing on built-up areas like Walthamstow, Bermondsey, West Ham and Camberwell, and a few had done quite serious damage to transport or industry. At 6.45 p.m. on 26 October a rocket landed directly in front of a stationary train at Palmers Green Station in north London: 15 people were seriously hurt and another 38 suffered cuts or bruises. The following week began disastrously. On a single day, 30 October, V-2s hit the Becton Gasworks in Barking, knocking out 7 retort houses, the Victoria Docks in West Ham – where, the official summary acknowledged, there was 'heavy damage [to] No. 2 and 3 sheds and RE [Royal Engineers] equipment' and 'a small fire [in] No. 7 shed' – and Hermitage Wharf, Wapping, where 150 feet of dock wall was demolished and warehouses were seriously damaged. At 2.56 a.m. next morning, Tuesday, 31 October, the Swedish Yard of the Surrey Commercial Docks in Bermondsey suffered a direct hit, 'exposing wheat to weather', and there were four more rockets that day, at places as far apart as Hendon – an airburst which distributed fragments over an area a mile wide – and Orpington. 'The public', noted one seventeen-year-old in his diary in neighbouring Croydon that night, '[are] becoming alarmed by explosions' – as well they might be, for still the government, by implication, denied that anything was amiss.

In the absence of fact, speculation flourished. Even so well-informed a figure as the art historian James Lees-Milne, in Chelsea, was reduced in his diary for Tuesday, 31 October 1944, to recording rumour:

Several loud crumps during the night, which woke me up. Several more today. They are becoming worse. . . . They say they come

196

from inside Germany, even from the Tyrol. Nancy Mitford saw one descend in a ball of fire, like the setting sun. Even she had a cold sweat and was riveted to the ground.

As always, the poorest districts of London suffered most. At ten past two in the morning of Wednesday, 1 November, seven people were killed in Eglington Road, Woolwich, and people all over south-east London were roused again at ten past five by an even worse incident, in Friern Road, Camberwell, where a rocket landing behind a row of houses killed 24 people and seriously injured another 17. This casualty list was in turn surpassed that evening in Shardeloes Road, Deptford, where a rocket plunged into the centre of the street at 6.30 p.m., just as people were on their way home from work, wrecking houses up to a hundred yards away and inflicting much the worst toll of casualties so far, 183, of whom 31 were dead and 62 others needed hospital treatment as in-patients.*

This was the start of the worst week so far. In the seven days ending at midday, 8 November, 15 rockets landed outside London and 12 inside it, the former being in many cases well 'grouped', i.e. close together. Even more alarmingly, the last two rockets had come down within a mile or two of what the Ministry of Home Security already suspected to be Kammler's aiming point, somewhere in the Tower Bridge area – a deduction, as will be seen later, not too wide of the mark. By eliminating all V-2s which were obviously miles off target and drawing on a map a pattern of lines linking up the rest, a mean point of impact had been calculated, and any landings within 15 miles of the supposed aiming point were considered, in view of the size of Greater London, to be roughly 'on target'. By this test 50 of the 70 rockets arriving between 2015 hours on 20 October and 1458 hours on 6 November were accurate, and almost all the 'misses' belonged to the first half of the period. Between 20 and 30 October the figures were 18 'on target' out of 33, while of the next 47 rockets only 5 failed the '15-mile test'.

From the beginning of November the pattern of incidents –

---

*As often, the records disagree on the detailed figures. Another report gives the total of seriously injured at Friern Road as 16 and at Shardeloes Road as 47, though agreeing on the number of dead.

still officially not happening at all – settled down at between three and five a day, with an average of about one airburst in every ten rockets, though these could also do damage: one struck the trees outside a mental hospital at Banstead at 5 p.m. on 2 November, killing 3 people and seriously injuring another 11. 'Airbreaks', where the warhead fell to earth intact after the rocket itself had disintegrated, proved very few. Clearly much depended on chance. The first three disastrous rockets on Wednesday, 1 November, which had killed 62 people and seriously injured another 90, were followed by a fourth which landed harmlessly on a gun site at Wanstead Flats, Woodford, and a fifth, in a gravel pit at Dartford in Kent, where only one person was badly hurt. Three of the following day's four rockets, though causing five serious injuries, killed no one, the exception being the Banstead rocket just mentioned. One fell on a railway embankment at Esher in Surrey, another burst in the air over Upper Sydenham Station in south-east London, and a third plunged into the Thames off the Garrison Jetty at Dartford.

There were, similarly, good days and bad days. Sunday, 5 November, which in more peaceful times would have been disturbed only by the Roman Candles and Catherine Wheels of Bonfire Night, was a bad day. It began with a rocket at 35 minutes after midnight at Collier Row in Essex, continued with another, at Penshurst in Kent, an hour later, followed by a third, on Tooting Bec Common, at 7.45 a.m., got really into its stride with a direct hit on an iron bridge in Southwark Park Road, Bermondsey, at 10.45, which tore up 250 feet of railway track, and continued with a disaster at Grovedale Road, Islington, at 1713 hours, which caused 249 casualties, 84 of them serious and 31 of them fatal. Two minor incidents, in Rainham, Essex, and at North Romford, were still to come. This was a single Sunday in London after five years of war, leaving 32 British citizens dead, 121 badly hurt, 150 more nursing minor wounds – and thousands of others homeless. It was not as bad as the 10 ton warheads pounding down at the rate of one an hour, feared a few months earlier, but it was bad enough.

Almost all the really bad incidents occurred in London, at which only one had to go on firing missiles to be sure eventually of hitting some vulnerable target, but there were a few exceptions, and one was now about to occur 30 miles away in Bedfordshire. Just before 9.50 a.m. on Monday, 6 November, one of Kammler's crews, refreshed perhaps by a weekend pass in The Hague or Amsterdam, launched a rocket which dropped miles off course, into Biscot Road, Luton, a town famous in peacetime for hat manufacture but now in wartime largely devoted to vehicle production. The explosion wrecked 17 houses and damaged another 1500. The steel-strengthened walls of the Commer-Karrier factory nearby – the V-2 had come down close to its dispatch department – stood up well to the blast, though it wrecked the canteen on an upper floor, opened at a cost of £25,000 only a week before – and did other damage to the works. More seriously, 19 people, according to local records, were killed and 196 injured. (The Home Office records show 16 dead, 31 seriously injured, plus 79 minor casualties.) This was to remain the second-worst industrial incident of the whole campaign; the other, in London, was not to occur until its very end.

Within an hour or two of the much talked-about, but still strictly censored, disaster at Luton, two more rockets had arrived in England, at Yalding and Bexley, both in Kent. About thirty were now landing every week, excluding those which came down in the sea, and they were doing a great deal of damage and causing many casualties: the 150 recorded as arriving up to 8 November had killed 235 people and seriously injured another 711 – a casualty rate of more than 7 per rocket, and a death rate alone of 1.6. The prospects were bleak, for, with no warning possible, there was no reason why the number of casualties should decline; indeed, it was likely to get worse. Between 3 and 26 October, while Kammler's men were in Friesland, many missiles had tended to fall short and the north-eastern side of London had escaped relatively lightly. Now they were back in The Hague, accuracy was improving and likely to get even better as they became more expert.

In the circumstances it was remarkable that the government had managed to suppress all references to the rockets for so long, especially after an unfortunate, and irresponsible, 'leak' in an American newspaper. 'Yesterday *New York Times* Hanson Baldwin talks of rocket attack on UK,' an Air Ministry

199

representative in Washington cabled London on 7 October. But, the Cabinet decided two days later, the ban would remain in force, and their decision proved justified; the Germans, it seemed, did not read the *New York Times*.

The continuing deletion from all reports submitted for censorship of any references to the sufferings of the rocket-afflicted areas caused growing friction between the newspapers and the Ministry of Information. A new policy was now tried by the Chief Censor of letting through 'reports of both flying-bomb and rocket incidents provided the total number of reports released did not exceed the total number of *flying-bomb* incidents and that there was nothing in the published report which indicated whether the incident had been caused by a V-1 or V-2'. This ingenious compromise, taking advantage of the Germans' continuing use of nocturnal, air-launched V-1s, pleased no one, as Admiral Thompson sadly concluded:

Both the press and the censors . . . heartily disliked the new scheme. Indeed the reports had to be so heavily censored that some newspapers didn't think it worthwhile publishing them. It entailed the deletion of all such statements as 'I heard the engine of the bomb cut off . . .', or, 'I was having my breakfast when I heard a tremendous explosion', indicating that it was daytime and a rocket.

At a meeting on Monday, 16 October, the Cabinet minutes recorded, 'the Minister of Information asked whether it would be possible to release the ban on the mention of rocket attacks against this country', but Herbert Morrison argued against any change and his view prevailed. Behind the scenes, however, some MPs were growing restive, and one, the recently elected W. J. Brown, an Independent, had, the Cabinet noted on 23 October, put down a private notice question asking for information about German rockets. There was some discussion about whether the Prime Minister should cover the subject in his forthcoming review of the war situation on 27 October, but the Chief Whip thought this might lead to a demand for a debate, and on 30 October Churchill reaffirmed his unwillingness to make any announcement about it.

In the end the Germans forced his hand. The curious compact of silence which had developed between the two sides was finally broken at 2.19 p.m. on Wednesday, 8 November

1944, in the regular daily communiqué broadcast on the German Home Service and picked up and circulated by the BBC monitors at Caversham:

The German High Command announces: The V-1 bombardment of the Greater London area, which has been carried out with varying intensity and only brief interruption since 15 June, has been supplemented for the last few weeks by another and far more effective explosive missile, the V-2.

The same announcement was issued soon afterwards by the German News Agency and at 7.15 the Germans were treated to a morale-boosting commentary about the new weapon from Heinz Rieck, allegedly a reporter at the Front:

Not quite five months ago, the High Command communiqué startled the world on the employment of a novel explosive missile; this is the case again today. Once again, everyone is burning to hear details, and the questions 'What is it?' and 'What is the effect?' . . . are on everybody's lips. . . . The thanks of the homeland today go out to the innumerable hands which have worked on V-2, to the German inventors and workers who, despite enemy terror, in unending and self-sacrificing labour, and by the strength of their organizing ability, created this weapon, tested it, collected experience and finally, with the help of our soldiers, put it into use. . . .

All our thoughts go out to those soldiers who have been chosen to send out this explosive missile. . . . They know the sufferings of the homeland under enemy terrors. . . . Now they stand with clenched teeth . . . playing their part in the great plan of this war.

To the great annoyance of Dr Goebbels the British press next day reported the German claims without comment. 'Nothing speaks more eloquently of its devastating effect than the silence on the other side of the Channel,' claimed one German report, making the best of things. The V-2s, it was suggested, had 'literally taken London's breath away'. Not, however, for long. On 10 November the Prime Minister at last revealed to the House of Commons what was now becoming an open secret:

For the last few weeks the enemy has been using the new weapon, the long-range rocket, and numbers have landed at widely scattered points in this country. In all the casualties and damage have so far not been heavy. The reason for our silence hitherto is that any announcement might have given information useful to the enemy.

We were confirmed in this course by the fact that, until two days ago, the enemy had made no mention of this weapon in his communiques. Last Wednesday an official announcement, followed by a number of highly coloured accounts of attacks on this country, was issued by the German High Command. I don't propose to comment upon it except to say that the statements in this announcement are a good reflection of what the German government would wish their people to believe, and of their desperate need to afford them some encouragement.

May I mention a few facts?

The rocket contains approximately the same quantity of high explosive as the flying bomb. However, it is designed to penetrate rather deeper before explosion. This results in somewhat heavy damage in the immediate vicinity of the crater but rather less explosive blast effect around. The rocket flies through the stratosphere going up to 60 or 70 miles, and outstrips sound. Because of its high speed no reliable and sufficient public warning can in present circumstances be given. There is, however, no need to exaggerate the danger. The scale and effect of the attacks have not hitherto been significant.

Some of the rockets have been fired to us from the Island of Walcheren. This is now in our hands and other areas from which rockets have been or can at present be fired against this country will doubtless be overrun by our forces in due course. We cannot, however, be certain that the enemy will not be able to increase the range, either by reducing the weight of the warhead, or by other methods.

Doubtless the enemy has hoped by his announcement to induce us to give him information he has failed to get otherwise. I am sure this House, the press and the public will refuse to oblige him in this respect.

The Germans had been waiting with growing annoyance for some reference to the V-2 from the other side of the Channel and responded to Churchill's statement with alacrity. 'In accordance with his tactics, the liar on the Thames has thus withheld from the world the fact of the German V-2 bombardment until today,' declared a political commentator on the German Home Service at 12.35 p.m. By 2.53 p.m. the German Telegraph Service was assuring the world that the speech amounted to an admission of the new weapon's effectiveness, and at 4.36 it revealed a remarkably accurate knowledge of the security measures affecting foreign diplomats over which the British Cabinet had agonized three months earlier. At 6.35

The Liar on the Thames

the Germans put out an article, in English, for any overseas paper or radio station that cared to use it:

For three weeks now V-2, which according to British sources seems to be a kind of monstrous rocket-bomb, has been hurtling silently down out of space to deal death and destruction in addition to that caused by V-1. Naturally the German authorities are not interested in making public any particulars regarding the construction of V-2. They are content to listen to what the British say about the effect. And this effect is such as to make H. G. Wells wonder whether one of his 'things to come' hasn't prematurely come to life in Germany. The most remarkable thing about V-2 seems to be its enormous speed, which exceeds that of sound waves. The result is that V-2 crashes down without preliminary warning. There is no way of defence. . . . A period of horrible and silent death has begun for Great Britain. England is reaping the reward of its merciless slaughter of German civilians in countless German towns and cities.

After its long period of enforced silence the British press made the most of its belated freedom. Churchill's statement made front-page news everywhere and in the *Daily Herald*, for example, it was the lead story, accompanied by photographs long held up by the censor and a graphic account of a recent incident:

I have just come away from a district recently hit by a V-2. It dropped at teatime. It hurtled through a house, exploded and dug a deep crater. Several people were killed. Children at a birthday party in a tiny, old house, died as they sat at their table with the cake and its candles fascinating them. People poke around the debris. Cranes are at work. Men with torn hands are scratching away to find an old woman who is buried deep down in the piled-up wreckage of her home. The local Rest Centre is busy. . . . The local parson moves about saying a kind word to the people who are suffering again in the sixth year of war. . . . I am writing this in the front line. There is no siren warning now. No time to take shelter. For this is the most indiscriminate weapon of this or any other war. It is a sinister, eerie form of war.

But the reporter could not withhold his admiration for the Germans' technical ingenuity and achievement:

The rocket has been described to me by a scientist as a 'superb piece of invention. Its craftsmanship is magnificent'. . . . Each component I have seen has been wired delicately and intricately – even fine-spun

203

glass has gone into the lining of the units. . . . Another unit is frosted when found. It contains liquid air. In a field today I stood ankle-deep in mud to examine a massive urn-shaped component weighing 15 cwt, which had buried itself deep in a crater between the bean rows. It looks like an old-fashioned kitchen copper.

One of these 'coppers' crashed into a front garden of a house in a suburb. . . . A 69-year-old woman and her married daughter were at home, saw it coming down, slammed the front-door – and were spattered with mud and broken glass.

'We had a miraculous escape,' they told me. 'It seemed as if Hitler was chucking the whole of the kitchen at us.'

Not all restrictions on reporting incidents were lifted, but the press agreed to 'stagger' reports so that, as the Chief Censor explained, 'the report of an incident on Monday would be released on Wednesday and so on', to prevent the Germans 'having any idea which rocket had caused any particular incident'. The fact that one could now acknowledge their existence made the rockets more bearable – but not much. By 23 November 1944 more than 200 had landed on the English mainland, of which more than half had reached the London Region, and around 500 people had been killed. That day Duncan Sandys advised his colleagues that it had proved impossible to jam the rocket's radio guidance system; in fact only 20 per cent of rockets had been fitted with radio at all, and the proportion was decreasing. The prospect of finding a warning system seemed equally remote, for though, very occasionally, the survey teams installed on the continent or the east coast did manage to identify a rocket by radar as it took off such successes were too few to form the basis of any general scheme.

And so the rockets went on descending unannounced and in what must have seemed to those concerned intolerable numbers. Orpington, for example, already hit three times by 17 September, suffered another V-2 in October, while a further three landed there, or in adjoining Bromley, in the first half of November, followed by the worst yet, at 9.15 on 19 November, when the bars of the Crooked Billet in Southborough Lane, Bromley, were crowded with Sunday evening drinkers. A V-2 in the car park destroyed both the public house and surrounding premises, so that 23 people were killed, 63 others

204

had to be detained in Farnborough and Bromley Hospitals and 34 more needed first-aid treatment. It was the worst casualty list so far – but not for long.

The week of 15 to 22 November had seen 36 V-2s arriving; the next week, 22 to 29 November, it rose to 40, with, on the 22nd, another bad incident in the East End, when 25 people were killed and 44 badly injured in Totty Street, Bethnal Green.

At 8.30 p.m. on Friday, 24 November, another East London street, McCullum Road, Poplar,* suddenly erupted into flame and flying debris. When they had subsided 18 more East-Enders lay dead and another 53 badly hurt, the start of the worst weekend of the whole offensive. Around midday on Saturday, 25 November 1944, Kammler succeeded in landing two rockets in heavily built-up areas. The effects of the second will be described in detail later. The first, at 11.15 a.m., shattered a combined block of flats and offices in High Holborn, close to Chancery Lane, in the very heart of London. Six people were killed and an enormously high number, many of them no doubt caught in the street, seriously injured: 292. Among them was a young newly married secretary to a solicitor, who had just moved into a vacant flat owned by the firm, having 'had enough of south-east London' after being plagued by flying bombs in New Cross. Her husband, on leave from the RAF, was with her when 'without any warning whatsoever . . . we were both buried in the rubble'; three of her office friends and a young mother in the flat below were killed. Both she and her husband later realized that they were lucky to have survived:

I remember thinking as they lifted my husband clear, 'I didn't know this was a red brick building' and then I realized it was blood soaked into his uniform tunic. Afterwards he told me *he* thought, 'What a way to die, just me and Gym in a heap of rubble'.†

Not far away, in Fleet Street, a staff sergeant in the US Signal Corps suddenly discovered what it meant to be in 'a war zone':

---

*As so often, the names are wrongly recorded in the official Ministry records, appearing as 'Totly Street' and 'McCullam Road'.

†For a full account of this couple's rescue see my anthology *The Home Front*.

I was knocked clean off my feet by the concussion. I picked myself up outside Mooney's pub and went into the bar for a Guinness. The half-pint helped, so I ordered another. Halfway through my second drink, my hand began to tremble. I could not hold the glass.

This incident, much witnessed and much discussed, left behind the usual trail of tragedies, major and minor. One actor, then living in Streatham, who was walking in Theobalds Road, about 200 yards away, is still uncertain to which category the scene he now witnessed belonged:

Windows fell out of the shops I was passing and, with a shrill whistling sound, a small piece of metal, almost certainly part of the V-2, fell at my feet. After it had cooled down I picked it up. . . . I remember seeing a man with blood streaming down his face and a little boy clinging to an empty pram, crying uncontrollably, but no one seemed to be comforting him, perhaps because no one knew what to say.

16
DISASTER IN DEPTFORD

A Long-Range Rocket detonated at 12.25 hours on the 25th
instant on the north side of New Cross Road. . . . The
Casualty List was very heavy.

Report by London Region Casualty Services Officer,
29 November 1944

The Holborn rocket, right in the centre of the capital and in a previously inviolate, commercial, area, was the most 'public', but was to be totally overshadowed by another which landed an hour later in the working-class borough of Deptford on the far side of the Thames. In the history of the V-2s Deptford has a unique place. Other boroughs were to be hit by more rockets, but the dead of Deptford were to be far more numerous than those of any other place, outnumbering those of every other community in London and of all the eleven rocket-affected counties outside London put together.

In New Cross Road, in the very heart of Deptford, and in the middle of its modest shopping centre, stood Woolworths, which that Saturday morning was even more crowded than usual. The confectionery counters were besieged by children eager to spend their 'personal points' on sweets, the hardware section was at the end of a long queue of housewives waiting to buy a saucepan. Under wartime regulations non-perishable goods could not be wrapped, so news of the arrival of a consignment of these rare items had spread rapidly. It had even reached Romford, as one woman then living there remembers:

I had word via the grape-vine. . . . I was a very young bride of a couple of years, with first baby of about two months, so . . . I promptly thanked my informer, dressed my baby daughter in her outdoor clothing and put on my coat and hat and set off armed with my handbag for a hopeful purchase.

The streets around Woolworths were also exceptionally busy, but just after 12.20, observed a former police sergeant then living in Brockley, 'the traffic lights at the Marquis of Granby road junction released three stationary lines of traffic, including crowded tramcars'. This, he later realized, was to be New Cross's solitary piece of good fortune that day; by 12.25 the passing flow of vehicles outside Woolworths was no heavier than normal. At that moment the young mother from Romford just quoted reached the same road junction:

I had walked as far as the turning opposite the Marquis of Granby on the corner of Lewisham Way. The road was very steep at this point and I walked up the road on the right-hand side, with my bag in the right hand and my baby on my left arm. At that point there came a sudden airless quiet, which seemed to stop one's breath, then an almighty sound so tremendous that it seemed to blot out my mind completely.

To anyone watching it must have seemed as if Woolworths had been struck by a giant hammer, followed by a volcano-like eruption of rubble and bodies flung skyward, before they sank, slowly it seemed, back to earth, landing with a series of clatters and crashes. Then, as the last of these died away, there seemed to be a moment of silence, before it was broken by the screams and groans of the dying and injured, invisible beneath the tall column of dust that hung over the mound of shattered brick and timber that a minute earlier had been a busy store, and the sobs and cries of frightened children calling for their mothers. Those involved were slow to realize what had happened, like the Romford woman waiting to enter Woolworths:

When I came to seconds later I found myself over the road, pinned to the wall. . . . After a second or two I was released and slid to the ground. . . . I turned to continue my journey and a horse and cart, with its driver's legs waving in the air, came wildly rushing round from Lewisham Way. . . . I was laughing hysterically. I gradually quietened down and then looked at my child and then myself. Our clothing was undone. Buttons, ribbons, etc., all loose and clothing twisted and untidy. My baby's bonnet was twisted grotesquely and hung round her neck. Her hair was blown back tightly as if she had none. She was staring at space, not comprehending. Neither of us was hurt, so we continued up the hill, and round the corner a rescuer

208

stopped me and asked where I was going. I said, 'Woolworths, for a saucepan.' He gently turned me round and said, 'Not today, my love. Go home and try tomorrow.'

Everyone in New Cross knew what a sudden explosion meant. Living then in New Cross Road itself was a young railway worker who, only three months earlier, had been injured when a flying bomb, which had killed nine of her neighbours, had blown in the kitchen window. Now, it seemed, it was about to happen all over again:

Our windows came in and there was smoke and dust everywhere. I went to see what was going on. I knew that my younger brother had gone swimming with two of his friends and always went into Woolworths to have a hot drink on the way home. My mother and I went along New Cross Road and what we saw was horrible, people were lying on the road, some dying. There was a No 53 bus and all the people were sitting . . . most of them dead from the blast. The police then roped off the whole road. We had to go back to our house and wait for news of my brother, who had [still] not returned home. We then knew that something terrible had happened to him.

In fact, as the family later learned, 'he was one of the lucky ones':

He was standing waiting to be served with a hot drink [when] he was buried for six hours, [but] got out alive and taken to hospital with a broken collar bone. His two friends standing next to him were killed.

There was equally sad news for many people in New Cross that day. Everyone, it seemed, knew someone – a relation, an acquaintance, a workmate – whom they would now never see again. The experiences of a postman living in Peckham who heard the news after returning to the sorting office after making his noon collection were typical:

New Cross sorting office had telephoned that a V-2 had dropped on Woolworths opposite. I had a great many friends there and . . . it being the end of my duty, I cycled to New Cross. Ropes were across the road at New Cross Gate station and no one was allowed through [but] being a postman the police waved me on. The road was strewn with masonry, glass and timber. Woolworths had ceased to exist. In its place was a skeleton of jagged brickwork and hanging timbers. . . . I went into the sorting office and found them all shocked, with little recollection of what had happened. Only a few were in the office at the time. . . . Those that were just heard a loud blast and felt the whole building shaking. They said the whole earth trembled as if an earthquake had occurred. I asked if anyone was hurt. One driver on his way to the office had his leg broken and the overseer had not arrived for duty. He never did arrive. His hand, with a ring recognized by his wife, was the only clue that he had been in Woolworths.

The ripples of the tragedy spread far and wide through south-east London and beyond. One man then aged fourteen remembers how the 'devoted mother' of five children living close to them in Brockley 'went out shopping that Saturday morning and never returned'. Further afield, in north-west London, a young woman born in New Cross, but now working as a milkman in Stanmore, was waiting for her mother to join her in Harrow until her father, injured by a V-1, came out of hospital.

My address was pinned behind her door so that I could be notified in any such emergency. Unfortunately the police had the wrong address and they didn't notify me until the Tuesday. I had to go up to New Cross to identify my mother after I had done my morning milk delivery. The bodies were in such a very bad state that I could only identify my mother from a piece of clothing.

The Civil Defence authorities in Deptford knew at once that they had a major catastrophe on their hands and responded energetically. Within minutes the bells of the NFS appliances and ambulances, and the horns of the rescue-party lorries, could be heard approaching and, such was the scale of the problem, two incident officers were appointed to take charge of different sections of the affected area, and their chequered white and black flags were soon waving in the thin dust-obscured November sun. It was immediately obvious that outside help was needed, and within two hours officials from group and regional headquarters were on hand to coordinate these efforts and the deputy chief executive officer of the LCC heavy rescue service, since it was clear this would be 'a rescue and casualty job'. By now it was known this was much the worse incident so far, with 40 dead and 84 seriously injured casualties already recovered. Many, many more were still buried, but '4 mobile cranes, 16 heavy and 8 light rescue parties, assisted by about 100 NFS personnel', were already at work, noted a regional officer, and other helpers were still arriving.

Darkness fell early that winter day, about 5.30, but in New Cross Road the 'dim-out' was ignored as the NFS set up mobile lights, group headquarters sent in its floodlighting set, an Ack-Ack unit provided a searchlight and the US forces a mobile generator. The work of rescue went on all night and at 10.45 on Sunday morning, when a visitor from group headquarters came to inspect progress, was still 'proceeding for the release of an unknown number of trapped persons'. But the Monday morning journey to work had to go on and 'it was agreed . . . to clear parts of buildings which were dangerous in New Cross Road during the afternoon in order that tram services could be re-established . . . to allow factory employees to reach the Woolworth area'.

Four days after the rocket had struck, the casualty services officer from regional headquarters set out, in strictly professional prose, how the consequences had been coped with:

The missile caused complete destruction of Woolworths store of three and four storeys, of half the adjacent Cooperative Store premises, and of a draper's establishment on its other side. On the south side almost complete destruction by blast of five houses was caused at the junction of St James's with New Cross Road. . . . Amongst the many premises partially damaged by blast was Deptford Town Hall. . . .

Occurring as it did at a very busy time of day, the casualty list was very heavy, including a very large number of dead . . . many bodies being completely dismembered. . . .

The whole of the rescue services of Deptford (5 HR [heavy rescue] and 7 LR [light rescue] parties) were employed, assisted by 8 HR and 1 LR parties from neighbouring boroughs. . . . Assistance was also rendered by about 100 NFS personnel. At one time no less than five mobile cranes were in action.

A WVS inquiry point and mobile canteens were in operation.

The heavy mobile first-aid unit, in charge of Dr Knight, from Barriedale FAP [first-aid post] was called at 12.38 . . . and arrived within a few minutes of that time. . . .

Early in the incident casualties were conveyed by passers-by to the town hall, where an improvised collecting post for casualties and first-aid point came into being. . . . A number of cases had been dealt with at New Cross Station and the tramway depot, both of which are nearby. . . .

Two of them were childen who had so impressed people with their unselfish fortitude that the staff had written a letter of praise to the parents. At New Cross Station 8 cases had been treated and . . . the attendant . . . was very proud of himself for having dealt with a severe case of haemorrhage from the carotid artery. . . .

I then went on to Miller Hospital, Greenwich . . . 63 casualties had been received, of whom 29 had been admitted. . . . The admissions included 3 cases of fractured skull and . . . two cases requiring amputation (thigh and foot respectively). . . .

The original mortuary having been destroyed, a temporary mortuary was established at the premises of Pearces Signs, to which bodies and fragments of bodies were taken. Help was asked for and received from Lewisham and Bermondsey, who sent their staff to assist. Identification was likely to cause considerable difficulty in view of the extreme degree of mutilation and/or dismemberment of many bodies.

At one time there were seven first-aid posts in action in New Cross, and the more serious cases were passed on, or transported direct, to no fewer than five hospitals: St John's, Lewisham, the LCC Hospital, Lewisham, Guy's Hospital, St Alfege's Hospital, Greenwich, and the Miller Hospital, Greenwich. The final figures showed 160 people killed, 77 seriously injured and – undoubtedly an underestimate because of many 'unofficial' helpers whose records were incomplete – 122 slightly hurt. The number of dead surpassed the total killed by the famous 'Hendon bomb' on which so many calculations had been based and made clear that if Hitler's dream of firing off a hundred rockets *a day*, instead of the five or six he actually achieved, had been realized, life in London would have become intolerable. As it was, the prevailing secrecy aided rumour. Some people still believe the true death roll was 300 or more, and there were stories locally of people remaining buried for weeks, while one boy was said to have been recovered 'in a standing position by a wall' still alive after eighteen days.

Thanks to the relaxation of censorship, the press carried descriptive accounts of what had happened at New Cross in their Monday morning editions on 27 November 1944, giving no hint of the location or casualty figures, though it could have been deduced that these were heavy. The *News Chronicle* spoke of 500 rescuers toiling throughout the night with the help of four cranes and reported that '30 hours after the bomb had fallen' – it was not, of course, identified as a V-2 – 'bodies were still being brought out of the ruins'. The *Daily Express* story was even more evocative:

Ambulances stood silently by as rescuers worked with hydraulic cranes. Nearby lay a little pile of children's fairy stories, nursery rhymes and painting books. Beside them, salvaged intact, were rows of tumblers, bottles of lemon squash, tins of evaporated milk, packets of envelopes and assistants' invoice books. Price cards were scattered over the road and trodden underfoot.

The excellent local newspaper, the *South London Press*, carried a first-hand account from the assistant chief warden of Deptford, identified only as 'the borough':

On the roadway and pavements were bodies, some terribly injured, including some very young children. Yet in all this hell I never heard a murmur. Those spared and comparatively free from injury were all running to help others, soon sizing the terrible situation up and doing what good they could. . . . The control room [of the borough Civil Defence services, in the town hall] itself was full of smoke. It was barely possible to breathe, yet everyone was calm, and the work of restoring some order and putting the vital services into organization proceeded with efficiency.

There is no record of Lord Cherwell visiting New Cross, and almost certainly he was, on that fatal Saturday, enjoying his usual weekend break at Christ Church, Oxford. Two days before, however, he had written to the Prime Minister to suggest that the rocket, which he had – though this he did not recall – stated to be scientifically impossible, was not proving a very fearsome weapon. With 960,000 acres of London in which it could fall, one's chances of being killed or injured, on existing data, were, suggested Cherwell, only 1 in 384,000, a calculation which the Deptford disaster made out of date. In that unlucky borough, indeed, the risk of death or wounding was very much higher. All told, Deptford was to suffer nine V-2s, far less than some other places, but no fewer than five caused 'outstanding incidents', so that Deptford's toll of dead and seriously injured, 625 (297 of them killed) far surpassed that of any other borough, and, though nothing that happened later was to match the horror of the Woolworths rocket, the story of its ordeal may conveniently be given here.

Deptford's first bad incident, on 2 November, had left 31 people dead; its fourth, on 2 February, killed 24. But far worse was to come, at 3 o'clock on the morning of Wednesday, 7 March 1945, when a V-2 landed in the courtyard of a group of seven three-storey blocks of tenement flats known as Folkestone Gardens, built forty years before to replace slum-style back-to-back housing. The rocket pitched to earth between two blocks, which were demolished, brought down an air-raid shelter between them, and badly damaged the remaining five blocks. Another 25 two-storey terrace houses in Trundleys Road, which ran past the site, 'of poor construction . . . with 9″ walls in lime mortar, wood floors and slated roofs', were also, as a Home Security official who visited the incident at 5.30 that morning recorded, wrecked, and the first rough estimate was that 'total casualties might be in the neighbourhood of 160', reckoning four occupants in each of the 40 flats destroyed.

As dawn broke over Folkestone Gardens the ruined flats formed a huge mound of debris, over which, in the light of the searchlights, three huge cranes cast their weird shadows, as twenty rescue squads and a small army of firemen struggled to extract the dead and injured. Folkestone Gardens was apparently regarded as a model incident, for a whole string of VIPs were brought to see operations in progress, including an American admiral (duly greeted by the mayor of Deptford) and 'Madam Wellington Koo', representing the Chinese government. Eventually 52 bodies were recovered, and 32 badly injured patients were detained in hospital, making this, in terms of dead, the third-worst incident of the whole campaign so far, surpassed only by the Woolworths incident in November, and another at Islington, in December, to be described shortly.*

Deptford's misfortunes helped to inflate the total casualties for the Civil Defence area of which it was part – 'Group 4', which was made up of five boroughs – to 526 dead and 1078

---

*For an account of the Folkestone Gardens incident from the point of view of a rescue party officer, see p. 331.

seriously injured, caused by 83 V-2s. Its neighbours got off more lightly. Bermondsey, with 7 V-2s, escaped with 14 deaths and 117 serious injuries; Lewisham, with 12 V-2s, had 67 deaths and 233 other serious casualties; Greenwich, hit by 22 rockets, suffered 81 fatal casualties, 198 badly injured; Woolwich, with more rockets, 33, had fewer deaths, 67, and almost the same number of badly wounded, 201.

To those living in the area these totals must have seemed at the time even larger. This is what one woman, then aged eleven and living in Charlton, remembers of one of the Greenwich V-2s:

There was an awful explosion and the doors leading from our class-room on to the playground were blown out. All we children just ran into the playground in panic until the teachers quietened us and made us line up in rows. Some children had to go to the first-aid post for attention to cuts. Then I saw my mother. She was covered in soot, where she had been cleaning out the fire. She thought the school had been hit and did not realize she had run past the actual site where the rocket had dropped. She kept saying, 'The school, the school!' A man stopped her at the end of the road and said to her, 'The school is all right. Look! Look!'. . . . My grandmother had pieces of glass in her back. She had been pickling red cabbage and the place looked like a slaughterhouse with red cabbage everywhere. My mother had . . . been sewing a new coat for me by the window and the large doors in that room were found in the road. . . . After the rocket attack my mother, grandmother, young cousin and myself were evacuated to Wrexham in North Wales. We went to the cinema and in the newsreel were pictures of the damage the rocket had done in our road at home.

Greenwich was the scene of two 'outstanding incidents', on Shooters Hill, at 6.30 p.m. on 11 November, when 24 people were killed, and at one o'clock in the morning of 30 November, when 23 others died in Sunfield Place. Its riverside neighbour, Woolwich, did not feature on the 'outstanding incident' list, but was the second-worst hit borough in the country, in terms of the number of rockets landing within its boundaries. They became so frequent that people began to sleep in the shelters again, as one man whose own nights were mainly spent at work at Woolwich Arsenal remembers:

My father . . . when he was alone during my night shift used to go

215

to the underground shelters at Danson Mead and to take my dog with him. . . . She was a beautiful dog with charming manners and used to go round the bunks to see that the children were tucked in and to kiss them goodnight. This . . . calmed them no end, for, as the mothers pointed out, if Tony [the dog] was not afraid, why should they be? Unfortunately, some people . . . complained to the warden who, much against his wishes, had to order that the dog must not come back the next night, so my father stayed away, too. . . . The next night was bedlam, for the children were crying for the dog . . . the parents were rowing with the warden, [and] the people who had started the trouble . . . found themselves so unpopular that they had to remove themselves to another hole.

To one woman who travelled up each day from Maidstone to a tall office block near Waterloo, the whole area seemed to be under continuous bombardment:

We heard the boom . . . and saw the column of smoke rising high into the sky. From my desk I had a wonderful view of the Surrey Hills and many fell between us and the hills. When they fell in the Lewisham–New Cross area, I would pick up the telephone and ring my cousin, who worked there. If the phone rang following an explosion, her boss would say to her, 'You had better answer. It's sure to be your cousin to see if you are safe.'

17

CHRISTMAS IN ISLINGTON

Among the damaged buildings was a public house which was crowded at the time of the occurrence and which took fire.

Report by regional casualty services officer on incident in Islington, 26 December 1944

Even without the rockets it would have been a miserable Christmas. The war seemed to have been going on for ever. Children were now starting school who had never lived in peacetime, and thousands more had not seen their fathers for four or five years. The replacement of the black-out by the dim-out, on 17 September, had had little effect; such extra light as there was served to show up how shabby everything had become. 'London really is a frightful spectacle of damage and dirty buildings,' commented one sympathetic American resident after a walk through a normally fashionable residential area on 8 October. He had no illusions about the state of morale. 'People are shaking their heads over the approaching winter,' he confided to his diary on 31 October, having long since learned about the rockets. 'If London is to be peppered with V-2s it will be a grim experience.'

By now the Minister of Food had unveiled the contents of what one paper called his 'Christmas box': an extra half-pound of sweets for everyone aged up to eighteen in the four-week ration period beginning on 10 December, an extra half-pound of sugar for everyone, an extra 8d. worth of meat for Christmas week only, bringing the ration up to 1s. 10d. (9p) worth, even 'a few thousand turkeys', for the very fortunate, and some dates, peanuts and sultanas. The prospect did not do much to raise spirits, lowered by bad weather. 'Early snow does not mean hard winter,' the *Daily Telegraph* assured its readers on 14 November, but it was soon proved wrong. By 10.30 p.m. on the following evening, the normally cheerful Mrs Gwladys

Cox in West Hampstead was distinctly despondent as she made her daily diary entry:

Colder than ever! I am writing this lying on my bed, fully dressed. The V-1s and V-2s are so frequent we never know! However, if a rocket bomb did hit this block we should simply disappear, together with all our possessions. We Londoners are certainly going through a time of terrible strain.

Even those hoping to see a new social order after the war were infected by the universal miasma. George Orwell encapsulated the prevailing pessimism in his weekly column in *Tribune*, published on 1 December 1944:

I am no lover of the V-2, especially at this moment when the house still seems to be rocking from a recent explosion, but what depresses me about these things is the way they set people talking about the next war. Every time one goes off I hear gloomy references to 'next time' and the reflection: 'I suppose they'll be able to shoot them across the Atlantic by that time.'

The flying bombs had dictated a whole new pattern of life in southern England, in which you avoided loud noises and kept an eye open for the nearest shelter. 'Dodging the doodle-bugs', as the more flippant referred to it, had in its way been stimulating. There was nothing stimulating about the unavoidable, ever-present rocket. How indeed, when you heard that alarming double bang echo across the sky, should you respond? The publisher Philip Unwin recalls leaving the Haymarket Theatre one evening to find 'everyone standing about looking shocked and awed' revealing 'a sudden consciousness that something horrible had happened'. The then editor of *Woman's Own* faced a similar problem while entertaining her ATS sister, when she heard 'the unmistakable crump of a V-2. . . . We didn't mention it in case, perhaps, it bothered the other. We just went on talking and had tea.'

In the week ending at midday on Wednesday, 6 December 1944, 40 rockets landed, the same as the previous week, which had been the worst so far. The casualty figures for November were by a long way the highest since August, with 716 men, women and children killed and 1511 badly injured, though these totals included some flying-bomb victims. The new 'rocket week', starting at noon, made a disastrous start, with the first rocket so far in the West End – not, in fact, particularly bad in casualty terms but, because of its location, far more talked about, and causing more widespread apprehension, than much more serious incidents in less well-known areas.

The 'Duke Street rocket', as it became known, landed at 11 p.m. on the corner of Duke Street and Barrett Street, just off Oxford Street, the capital's main shopping thoroughfare, all along which windows were blown out, scattering such modest Christmas displays as they contained. A local resident, a BBC producer, noted next morning how houses in wealthy Wigmore Street had lost their windows, among them those of that great resort of upper-middle-class ladies up from the country, the Times Book Club. His wife, called out of bed in the small hours to man a WVS incident inquiry point in a 'school in a side street', found it 'rather a grim business . . . one room utilized for the WVS and the room opposite . . . converted into a mortuary'. Among the items brought in for the WVS to care for – its owner no doubt dead or in hospital – was 'a woman's shopping bag' full of 'odds and ends obviously intended to be Christmas presents' along with 'three little Union Jacks, bought . . . in readiness for the peace'.

The roping off of the approaches to Selfridges just as the Christmas shopping rush was starting spread news of the incident over a wide area, not always received with overmuch regret. 'Being a woman with a strong hatred of the well-to-do and employing classes, Mrs W. could ill conceal her pleasure that the West End had been hit,' observed the American OSS official quoted earlier of his maid's reaction. 'Mayfair, after all, nearly escaped the flying bombs. To have it immune from V-2 would be more than Mrs W . . . could bear.' More Americans suffered in the Duke Street incident than from any other rocket. Much of the blast had been taken by an annexe to Selfridges being used as a canteen by US government employees, while a passing taxi had been blown into one of Selfridges' windows, and some of its GI passengers were never found. All told, 8 Americans were killed and 32 injured; 10 British civilians also died, with seven badly wounded. Among the dead was a woman who had been walking quietly with her husband when the rocket exploded and 'simply disappeared, whisked from his side', her body being 'afterwards found at the back of Selfridges'.

The Duke Street explosion shook the whole West End. At the famous American forces canteen, Rainbow Corner, in Piccadilly Circus nearly a mile away, it set the chandeliers swinging. In a studio in Broadcasting House, a little nearer, it caused a gramophone needle to jump from its groove as the presenter of the American forces programme closed down with a disc of 'The Star-Spangled Banner'. The noise was also heard several miles away, often creating the illusion it came from close at hand. One actor living in Streatham while rehearsing an ENSA production of *Yellow Sands* found that 'the whole house shook, the curtains blew in and the plastic sheeting in the windows rattled', only to find himself greeted next morning by a fellow member of the cast with the remark, 'We had a V-2 in St John's Wood last night' – the same 'Selfridges' rocket, they rapidly realized.

December, having begun badly, got no better. 22 rockets arrived in the week beginning on 6 December, 12 of them reaching London, and the proportions remained roughly the same in the following week, with 20 V-2s between 13 and 20 December, 9 of them in the London region. In the following week, which covered Christmas itself, running from 20 to 27 December, there were 25, though only 6 reached London, and in the five days which rounded off the year, from 27 to 31 December, 21, again with 6 in London.

The war news, meanwhile, had taken a sharp and totally unexpected turn for the worse. The *Nine O'Clock News* on Saturday, 16 December 1944, reported a heavy German counter-attack in the Ardennes area of Belgium, and though an official spokesman described it in Monday's newspapers as 'a last throw, like March 1918', the public was not so sure. The rockets, an American historian has commented, had 'reinforced Hitler's "bogey-man" image. No matter how often Germany was bombed they could always come up with a new and nasty surprise, just when everybody thought the war was finally over.' The Ardennes offensive seemed to confirm this fear and sent spirits, already low, plummeting still further. 'Did I tell you,' asked a Bethnal Green Evening Institute worker, in a letter to her soldier husband on 18 December, 'that poor

Miss C. had had her home destroyed by a rocket? She reached home, at Eltham, one evening, to find her house gone and both her parents in hospital. Her mother has an unrecognizable face, from which both eyes have had to be removed, and is practically cut to pieces.' Social worker Vere Hodgson, in Notting Hill, had an equally melancholy tale to record in her diary the following day: 'Mrs S. [an office colleague] phoned us details of her bomb. Twelve people were killed. Every slate is off her roof. Her chimney is cracked. . . . Merry Xmas to all.'

On 26 December, after a lull enforced not by goodwill but by the needs of the battle in Belgium, the Germans returned to their familiar pleasure of trying to kill English civilians, and in Islington that Boxing Day they succeeded with one of their most destructive missiles yet. Islington, as yet 'ungentrified', was then a solidly proletarian borough, containing row upon row of small, mainly unmodernized houses in often attractive terraces and squares, just north of the great railway area around Kings Cross. Every group of streets had its 'local', and typical of these was the Prince of Wales, on the corner of Mackenzie Road and Holloway Road, which was crowded on that holiday evening, a little island of cheer and jollity on a particularly wretched night; a dense fog, of Dickensian thickness, had been blanketing London on and off for weeks.

At 9.26 p.m. a rocket burst in the concrete roadway just outside, causing two craters, one 40 feet across and 12 feet deep, the other 10 feet by 4 feet. The impact shattered the gas and water mains, so the main crater was soon flooded, adding to the hazards facing the first wardens and rescue men as they struggled to reach the scene through piles of rubble, hidden by the fog and by the smoke from the several small fires which had broken out. The first reports showed that some 22 or 23 storey houses and shops had been destroyed, and another 20, damaged beyond repair, would have to be cleared. One end of a brick surface shelter, luckily empty – on Boxing Day people were celebrating in their homes or in the pub – had been brought down by the blast, helping to block the road still further. The centre of the devastation, however, presenting a classic problem to the rescue men, was the Prince of Wales itself, for the cellar, normally the safest place in any building,

221

had become a death trap. It had been in use as a bar and crowded with drinkers, nearly all of whom were killed or badly injured as the roof and the debris above crashed in upon them, while to add to the horror fire broke out, so that some of the bodies were charred, when recovered at last.

The first reports, at half past midnight on the morning of 27 December, spoke only of 8 dead and 81 injured, but by 6 a.m. on Thursday, more than thirty hours after the rocket had landed, the total had risen to 64 killed, 86 seriously injured, 182 lightly injured and 4 still trapped. The publican, his wife and a barmaid, all serving on the ground floor, were carried out with minor injuries, and, the regional casualty services officer learned 'one lad . . . trapped for over nineteen hours' was removed to hospital, 'suffering from multiple minor injuries, but . . . stated to be doing well'. A woman trapped in the burning cellar was less lucky. A doctor had managed, at great risk, 'to get into the cellar and was able to administer morphia', but she 'was subsequently extracted dead'.

The timing and nature of the incident, as much as its high casualty figures, which finally reached 68 dead and 99 seriously injured, caused it to be remembered with particular indignation. 'We were surprised because it was normal to have a truce during the Christmas holiday,' remembers a man, then a boy aged twelve, who lived in the Caledonian Road in the same area.

Having ruined Boxing Day in Islington, the Germans also marked New Year's Eve with the borough's second 'outstanding incident', which occurred at 20 minutes to midnight on 31 December in Stroud Green Road and Stapledon Hall Road, Crouch Hill, at the northern end of its area, close to the boundary with Finsbury. This time 15 people were killed and 34 badly injured, and 15 more families started the New Year with their homes destroyed. It was the 382nd rocket to reach the United Kingdom and the last of 1944, which everyone saw vanish without regret. The only ray of hope was that Field Marshal von Rundstedt's last great offensive was now seen to have failed, but for Londoners this meant that Kammler's attentions would now be again directed even more vigorously against themselves. During December, including a few flying-bomb casualties, 367 people had been killed – 64 of them children – and 847 – 121 of them children – seriously injured. For their families it must have been a melancholy Christmas, and 1945 seemed to promise little better. James Lees-Milne, on his way home to Chelsea with a friend, observed the curious mixture of celebration and danger typical of the time:

We walked in the moonlight. At Hyde Park Corner we heard a crash, followed by the roar of a rocket that made our hearts beat. Then we laughed. Just before midnight I left him at Sloane Square station and continued homewards. Crowds were singing in the Square. . . . There were sounds of merriment from lighted windows. They seemed forced to me. There were no church bells.

The 'crash' was that of the missile descending on Crouch Hill, and one woman living in Birmingham who telephoned her parents in Croydon, on the other side of London from Islington, heard 'over the phone the distant explosion of a V-2 while wishing them "A Happy New Year" '. Much nearer was Gwladys Cox in West End Lane, NW6, who had spent the last few minutes of 1944 listening to a religious service on the BBC:

After the watch-night service at St Paul's, I felt the familiar vibration of a rocket bomb and could swear that during the pealing of the bells I also heard an explosion. Then Big Ben struck midnight and we heard 'Auld Lang Syne' sung by wounded servicemen, nurses and doctors, accompanied by the Band of the Welsh Guards, at the Royal Herbert Hospital, Woolwich.

A few hours later she learned that her ears had not deceived her:

A disastrous New Year for our old friend Miss G. of Crouch Hill! She sits today shivering in the kitchen, with all the windows in her house blasted, for the second time. . . . The top floor of her house is uninhabitable. It has been freezing all day. . . . So we begin the New Year.

It was a miserable New Year's Eve for the Foreign Minister of the Polish government-in-exile, awaiting the liberation of his country. In his diary diplomatic discretion could be forgotten:

The end of the war is not yet in sight. In autumn it seemed near and it is all the more depressing that the struggle continues, with more

223

slaughter than before. . . . A gloom has descended on the allied camp.

For Kammler's men it had been a busy evening. After the successful launching of the missile which killed 15 people in Crouch Hill they fired two more A-4s 'to wish Londoners a happy New Year', but one failed to achieve lift-off and the other, having staggered into the air, came down on a nearby German barracks. One Dutchman living in the area, on learning what had happened, opened one of his hoarded bottles of gin to drink at midnight to more such 'successes'. It was a toast which, as 1945 began, millions of people in southern England would have echoed.

18

WORSE THAN THE V-1s

*The V-2 has become far more alarming than the V-1, quite
contrary to what I thought at first.*

Chelsea resident in his diary, 3 January 1945

In the summer of 1944 the belief had been widely held that
nothing could be worse than the flying bomb. The rocket
proved it wrong. Debating which of these two achievements of
German technology was the more unpleasant provided one of
the few recreations of the winter and even, in December 1944,
occupied George Orwell in *Tribune*:

People are complaining of the sudden unexpected wallop with which
these things go off. 'It wouldn't be so bad if you got a bit of warning,'
is the usual formula. There is even a tendency to talk nostalgically of
the days of the V-1. 'The good old doodlebug did at least give you
time to get under the table,' etc. Whereas, in fact, when the doodlebugs were actually dropping, the usual subject of complaint was the
uncomfortable waiting period before they went off. Some people are
never satisfied.

The question is one that still interests those who lived
through both menaces. What might be called the pro-V-1 case
was put by a man then living and working in Woolwich, with
close personal experience of the effects of both weapons:

Personally I found that the evil you could not see far less trying than
the evil you could see coming towards you. . . . With the rocket there
was simply nothing that you could do, but with the doodles there was
plenty of time to watch its approach and to wonder if all that could
be done was done. . . . There was nothing for it but the basic philosophy of the soldier in the First World War. . . .. 'If you don't hear
the bang and are not alive then you can't worry', which was the only
way to regard something that was utterly beyond your control.

A Chiswick woman, whose house was damaged by the very first rocket, shared this attitude. 'There wasn't that moment of fear before they landed,' she recalls. A Streatham resident regarded the V-2 as belonging to the same category as a thunderbolt. 'By the time it had arrived,' she reflected, 'you were either dead or it had missed.' A third woman, living at Abridge near Epping, put the same point more succinctly: 'No build-up. Just bang or oblivion.' Technically minded males – the technically minded female was a rare being in 1944 – were sometimes so lost in awe of what one calls the 'tremendous technical mastery' demonstrated by the Germans that they almost overlooked the associated danger. 'One felt one was moving into a strange new age with these things rising 130–140 miles up above the earth,' recalls a then agricultural scientist living in central London. To him their arrival brought back memories of his childhood in a quarrying area of Wales, with 'the crack of the blast followed by the rumble of the falling rock face'.

But these were minority views. Most people would have agreed with the conclusion reached by Gwladys Cox in West Hampstead as early as mid-September:

The rockets, if less frequent, are a worse affliction than the flying bombs, as their entirely silent approach cannot be heralded by sirens and clear weather does not deter them. Travelling faster than sound, they are well-nigh impossible to stop.

Four months later James Lees-Milne in Chelsea was expressing similar sentiments:

The V-2 has become far more alarming than the V-1, quite contrary to what I thought at first, because it gives no warning sound. One finds oneself waiting for it and jumps out of one's skin at the slightest bang or unexpected noise, like a car backfire or even a door slam.

A weapons-design draughtsman, living in Mottingham, reached the same conclusion, even though the family home, in Lee, had been wrecked by a flying bomb:

The V-2s were far more frightening than the V-1s. . . . One didn't know what was happening until it had happened; and so life became a 24-hour-per-24-hour stint of realizing that 'It can happen now, this instant; but since it hasn't, perhaps it will when we've counted twenty, but it didn't so let's forget it. . . .' And then it happens a mile away and you start all over again. After a while you think you've forgotten it, but in fact you're subconsciously waiting for it all the time.

A fifteen-year-old schoolboy in Dagenham decided that 'after the takeover by the V-2s' the flying bombs 'seemed almost like old friends', and made an interesting comparison, based on his cinema-going:

If the V-1s were like the 'great Big Saw' always drawing nearer to the heroine in Saturday morning matinees, the V-2s were a bit like being under sniper fire for six months at a stretch. . . . The V-1s were old-fashioned melodrama, the V-2s were a threatening horror from outer space, abstract, unreal.

A then ten-year-old boy, living in Crayford, Kent, also chooses a metaphor appropriate to his age-group at that time:

The poor old doodlebugs . . . were somehow familiar. One could watch them chugging comfortably along. The difference was the same one feels about 'good old steam engines' and the anonymous new modern locomotives, streamlined and unfamiliar.

A woman living in Leigh-on-Sea on the Essex coast considered, like many other people, that the V-1s had been almost 'sporting' in contrast to their successors, 'a far more insidious and dirty weapon . . . you had no chance of avoiding'. It was this, and the fact that there was evidently no defence of any kind against the rockets, that was so unnerving, as is explained by a woman who was then a nineteen-year-old in Walthamstow:

When going about your daily chores you were rocked out of your skin by the sound of these explosions just coming from nowhere. . . . These really did shake our morale and . . . had they continued . . . a large proportion of the population would have lost their sang-froid.

A then ARP instructor in the City of London acknowledges the difference between one's superficial calm and inner fear:

We were often in bed when we would hear this ominous rumbling and the windows would rattle.My wife or I would say something like 'Oh dear! There is another of those things.' [But] if they had gone on a little longer I expect I should have been a casualty . . . or taken to the madhouse, because they were really getting me down and I was nearly reaching the state of surrendering, Churchill or no Churchill.

This was a more widespread reaction than was ever admitted. Dedication to the Prime Minister in the solidly Labour areas which had borne the brunt of every German bombardment had never been quite as solid as the newsreels like to suggest, and public confidence in its leaders reached a new low point that winter. One man then working on war damage repair in the Lambeth and Brixton areas remembers seeing 'women praying in the street for them to stop the war', something he had never observed at the height of the blitz or the buzz-bombs. Even hardened servicemen found the new danger hard to bear. One sailor, whose home was in Ilford, experienced 'a feeling of utter helplessness in the face of this new form of attack' – even before his own house was damaged by it. This was the reaction, too, of a 'regular' artillery officer, in Chiswick when the first V-2 arrived, aware of the success his battery had had against the flying bombs. 'To say he was frightened was an understatement,' recalls a woman then living in Lee Green of the response of her husband, newly back from the Middle East, after a rocket had brought down the kitchen plaster on the gooseberry pies she was making. 'He admitted that Rommel's guns and army . . . hadn't scared him so much.'

Horror of the V-2s affected all ages. One man, already an adult in 1944 and now looking back in his sixties, regards the rocket months, when he was living in Carshalton and working in Southwark, as 'the most nightmarish part of [my] life. . . . I'm sure many of my age-group will agree that these silent monsters were the most frightful weapon of all.' Even a V-2 seen in a museum after the war he found 'absolutely terrifying' and, he believes, if the Germans had possessed it in 1939 the war would have ended as soon as it had begun, for 'the public would have demanded a cessation of hostilities'. A then thirteen-year-old, living in Waltham Abbey – then part of the borough of Waltham Holy Cross – and attending school in Chingford, sees in retrospect that this was the moment when he grew up in his attitude to war:

Until the V-2s came it was all rather fun and just part of everyday life. . . . The V-2s were the first thing in the war to frighten me despite going through the blitz and the buzz-bombs. For the first time I really felt the Germans were not playing fair.

228

The flying bombs had prompted many jokes and attracted nicknames. Apart from the derisory 'flying gas main', aimed at the government rather than the enemy, of the early days, no nicknames are on record for the rocket, and only one joke, reported from Woodford and supposedly based on the doostep conversation of two Cockney-type housewives. 'Just fancy, you might be blasted into maternity at any minute,' one has remarked to the other, who responds: 'Yus. And you'll never know who done it.'

The official renaming of the pilotless aircraft as the flying bomb and its unofficial renaming as the doodlebug had helped to defuse some of the V-1's terrors, as had the growing public familiarity with its appearance and effects. The rocket, by contrast, seemed all the more horrific the more one learned about it. The government, from the moment its existence was officially admitted, had done its best to remove the veil of secrecy surrounding this new weapon. As has been seen, a reasonably accurate account of its main features had appeared in the press along with Churchill's statement of 10 November 1944, and a few days later the first 'artist's impression' was published, followed by a remarkably accurate drawing of a launching site in the *Illustrated London News*, which reached a much wider audience when reproduced in the *Daily Express* on 4 December. On Saturday, 9 December, the newspapers carried cut-away drawings showing how the rocket was constructed under such captions as 'The V-2 gives up its secrets', the fruits of earlier research by Air Intelligence and of the 'scavenging' expeditions of RAF officers at the sites of the first incidents. The twentieth rocket, which had broken up in the air into a few large fragments, scattered among the trees at Dagnan Park, Noak Hill, Romford, had proved particularly useful, but eventually the British experts had more than enough pieces for their 'jigsaws' and the amount of scrap left behind by many V-2s became an embarrassment. One man remembers how, even after several loads had been removed, portions of rocket casing and mechanism still littered the area surrounding his firm's head office at Danbury, near Chelmsford, and in the most rocket-plagued areas even schoolboy collectors eventually had their fill of souvenirs. 'Remains of V-2s were easy to come by,' remembers a then seventeen-year-old engineering apprentice in Essex, 'fairly large pieces of engine and exhaust nozzles and glass wool being found round the bombed site,' and often the combustion chamber lay around for weeks, being too heavy for removal by bicycle. (The tail fins, or perhaps the whole rocket, seen sticking up in the mud off Shoeburyness, visible only at low tide, defeated even the most ardent souvenir hunters.)

To oberve the signs of a rocket taking off was not, especially for those professionally concerned with counter-measures against the missile, an uncommon experience. A pilot based at RAF Newchurch on the Kent coast found it 'very frustrating', when sent against suspected launching sites in Holland to arrive just 'in time to see these large rockets climbing up and away from us, leaving long trails of white smoke against the dawn sky'. A gunner stationed at Maidstone watched another V-2 'like a golden thread climbing high into the sky' in the distance over Holland, 'the exhaust trail lit by the early sun'. A wartime soldier, stationed in the Welsh mountains, saw a speck of light far to the east, around Christmas 1944, very different from the star appropriate to the season, for 'it looped up, reached its zenith and plunged down – a V-2 falling on London'. A soldier serving near the Rhine in the closing stages of the war was intrigued to see 'many miles in the distance a rocket . . . rising . . . a straight white trail in the sky, which on dispersing became a zigzag line. I remember thinking that it might land on my home' – though it was more probably aimed at Antwerp.

On a clear day or night a rocket's trail might be briefly glimpsed from a hundred miles away or more – indeed, the government's original, and abortive, plans for a warning system had relied on such visual identification. In the event, the Royal Observer Corps plotted many such sightings, though to no purpose, by linking the reports from various posts. One ROC member stationed at Cranleigh remembers spending many hours that winter gazing in the direction of Holland for this reason and another Observer, stationed at Rainham in Kent, now realizes that the 'spiralling vortex trails' he could see on exceptionally bright moonlight nights before the attack began must have been V-2 test flights over the Baltic. Even ordinary civilians sometimes shared such experiences. A seventeen-year-old apprentice, walking across Mitcham Common on his way to work, found himself studying 'silhouetted against the dawn glow the gilden stream of a vapour trail rising from below the horizon . . . to the stratosphere', and the wide reaches of the Thames also favoured such observation, as a man working in the heavy-gun shop at Woolwich Arsenal discovered:

It was not strictly true to say that the rockets were undetectable, for if one was looking down river at the right time it was possible to see what appeared to be a shooting star climb upwards and you knew that in Robb Wilton's classic phrase 'I've only got three minutes'. Also at the point of re-entry into the atmosphere if the sky happened to be clear it was possible to see a vapour trail, but most of those claimed . . . were left by high-flying aircraft.

A few people believe they saw a rocket itself in flight. A man living in Warlingham recalls 'a Scots caber or telegraph pole hurtling through the sky, not straight like an arrow but turning over and over like a boomerang'. 'Like a telegraph pole with a vapour trail behind it,' thought a young man watching from a factory roof in Mitcham. 'A long black object like a thick telegraph pole with a dull red flame coming from the back,' agrees an artillery NCO, then stationed in Kent, of the missile he saw approaching the ground. 'A shooting star falling to earth . . . followed by a flash' is the description of a man then aged fifteen whose 'first and only sighting of a V-2' occurred as he left his youth club in east London.

More common were claims to have sensed a rocket's approach, but a Ministry of Home Security report, compiled late in 1944, was sceptical.

There have been isolated reports, from persons near the site of the incident, of a short 'swish' just before the explosion and several reports of a 'feeling of pressure' or a premonitory instinct of impending disaster immediately before the explosion. It is possible that this may be due to confusion of time in the memory afterwards.

The evidence suggests, however, that a few – a very few – people may have reacted in this way, like the wife of a warden in Croydon, who was, he realized, 'possessed of hearing equivalent to a wild animal's', a gift which proved useful when the area's first V-2 arrived. 'Suddenly she made a dive under the table. "What the hell is the matter?" I said. She replied: "It sounds like an express train flying through the air." A split second later I heard a huge explosion.'

Similar, and more widespread, claims were made for family pets, who had certainly shown a more than human facility to detect flying bombs. A young nurse living in Balham observed that the family cat, Junior, 'asleep on a chair . . . suddenly leaped up in the air, gave a wail of terror and rushed under the sideboard in the corner of the room', just before the 'terrifying explosion' of the first local V-2, and he was to repeat the performance 'on two more occasions'. Usually, however, the first sign of a rocket's arrival was a bright flash, a phenomenon made use of by a Mitcham family, where the son of the house, whose bedroom faced over London, went to bed before his parents. When a flash lit up his room he would bang twice on the floor with a shoe to warn his parents that in a few seconds they were likely to hear the roar of the explosion as the sound wave reached them. A then eleven-year-old has vivid memories of the 'big, blue flash' which preceded the destruction of her home in Dalton Lane, Hackney on St Valentine's Day 1945. 'There was', she remembers, 'no bang, only everything falling on us and my dad saying "Hello, Jack. This is your lot!" ' Fortunately it wasn't. The upper half of the house was 'smashed to nothing', but the family were all downstairs and unhurt. And some of those very close to an exploding V-2 did not even see the flash. One Walthamstow woman whose husband was working as a welder in a factory building outside which a V-2 landed – he was, he believed, 'only about fifty feet away' – 'did not hear a thing, only saw a white haze and then the debris falling all round him', memories on which he had ample time to reflect during his subsequent three months in hospital.

The sound of a rocket detonating rapidly became familiar to millions of people in Greater London and Essex, and a Ministry of Home Security report in December confirmed the interim description compiled in mid-September. The sharp 'crack', as the warhead exploded, was, the ministry agreed, followed by 'a drawn-out rumbling sound, caused by the passage of the missile through the air faster than sound . . . described as "more echoing and more prolonged than a flying bomb, like a peculiar peal of thunder".' The report also endorsed what many people had already discovered for themselves – that

the ears provided an unreliable guide to locating the point of
impact:

Sounds seems to be no indication of either the distance or of the
direction of the explosion. Explosions have been heard distinctly
twenty or thirty miles away. At ten miles that has been loud enough
to give the impression that the incident is very close, yet to people
within half a mile of the incident it has sounded too far away to be
of their immediate concern.

The ministry had also assembled much evidence on the
nature of the craters caused by the V-2, some of it obtained,
as at least one document hinted, by unwelcome calls to busy
officials made in the small hours. However, the duty of
garnering every possible scrap of information was not shirked.
'Craters . . .', the ministry advised regions with as yet no first-
hand knowledge of the V-2, 'are generally . . . steeply cone-
shaped or saucer-shaped. The cone-shaped craters are anything
between 20 and 45 feet across and between 6 and 20 feet deep.
Those of saucer shape are from 3 to 5 feet deep and from 30
to 45 feet across. . . . The deepest craters seem to be found
where the missile has struck the hardest surface, such as a
concrete roadway.' It was such impacts which produced the
'earthquake' effect sometimes felt several miles away, and able
to bring down buildings over a wide radius. This experience of
being physically shaken many people found the most alarming
aspect of the whole campaign. 'The whole building seemed to
sway,' remembers one woman who had been sitting in the
Brixton Palladium watching *Rebecca*. 'I was very scared and
. . . wanted to go home but my sister would not leave and said,
'It's down now''.' 'I felt the floorboards shudder beneath my
feet, the fire shifted and various small things in the room moved
or rattled,' recalls a Croydon woman of a similar occasion. A
man then aged fourteen remembers his astonishment when
cycling with a friend past a shop in Lee Green when 'the blind
suddenly gave a double flap', explained seconds later as 'the
long rumbling roar' of an explosion two miles away 'caught up
with it'. An AFS woman had an even more disconcerting
experience at a bus stop in Streatham. 'The legs of my trousers
started to move as though shaken by invisible hands', while

233

warm air rushed up her legs, from a V-2 which 'had exploded the other side of the Common'.

It was not always clear whether, as here, it was blast which was to blame or the tremor of the explosion spreading through the earth. One actor who was walking along Regent Street towards Broadcasting House observed 'the glass windows in a building just ahead . . . shaking like fury' while still 'reflecting the blue of the sky'. A Wandsworth woman treasures the memory of one of the oddest sights of the period, seeing a huge ball of dust and debris blowing over her house in which she could distinguish a cloud of feathers – whether from a ruined mattress or some unfortunate flock of hens she never discovered. As with sound, distance seemed to bear little direct relation to damage outside the immediate vicinity of the explosion. One American noted that the Duke Street rocket had not even knocked off the hat of a friend near enough to it to be 'conscious . . . of a sheet of flame' and to endure 'for a minute or two following the explosion . . . a rain of minute particles of glass', although 'windows in buildings a mile and a half distant were blown out'.

What it felt like to be on the distant fringes of an explosion is vividly recalled by a man then working in the New Kent Road who was waiting for a train at the Elephant and Castle Station when a V-2 landed in St George's Circus, nearly a quarter of a mile away:

I stood on the station leaning over the parapet awaiting my train . . . when this awful tearing draught occurred, the sky lit up by a myriad of colours, a bright mauve being predominant, followed by an explosion that . . . [left] my ears affected for days. The station parapet, a massive stonework affair, literally lifted quite six inches, pushing my hands in the air – then dust, smoke and an acrid smell in the nostrils. I felt shaking in my limbs. It was so silent: no whistle like a bomb, or the throb of a doodle, but this awful draught.

Of all the manifestations of the rocket, to those not directly harmed by it, the most spectacular was the airburst, which, to Dornberger's despair, had become such a common sight over the Blizna rocket range. One wartime schoolboy remembers his newspaper round in Tottenham being enlivened by 'an enormous explosion in the sky . . . like an enormous firework,

234

or a whole boxful of rockets going off together, with all the colours of the rainbow'. An RAF dental officer at Biggin Hill watched 'a succession of fine curved black lines emerge from behind a cloud at a very great height, fanning out across the blue sky . . . as though a pebble was thrown . . . and the ripples were spreading out'. The writer William Sansom, based in Westminster, described seeing a premature V-2 explosion in even more poetic terms:

When this occurred in daylight, there appeared suddenly and silently – as once in a clear-blue afternoon sky – a white expanding blossom of smoke like a puff of anti-aircraft fire, only larger; and only some seconds afterwards echoing down to earth its resonant, distant thunderclap of sound. At night a rocket-burst occurring far up, without warning, would paint an abrupt orange moon in the high black sky; again silently, suddenly, arriving and expanding and quickly fading, as though up in the night an evil orange eye had winked at man's frailty.

One of the first rockets to break up in the air disintegrated above the village of Tillingham, near the coast between Bradwell-on-Sea and Burnham-on-Crouch, one hot September afternoon. In the village school, suddenly 'shaken by a tremendous explosion', was one ten-year-old boy who, like his classmates, was excited rather than alarmed:

The window above my head shattered and we all rushed out into the playground. High above the village it looked as though a giant handful of silver paper had been thrown into the air as the broken casing of the rocket floated down in the afternoon sun. . . . On arriving home I found that the V-2's rocket engine had landed in the field opposite our bungalow. Only two or three feet of the six-foot, one-ton engine was visible above the ground. Some weeks later, my cousin with his team of four Suffolk Punches helped to drag the engine to the side of the field where it was later collected by the army.

To be in the middle of an airburst was even more impressive: One night-fighter pilot, travelling in an unarmed transport, an Airspeed Oxford, nearby achieved the unique feat of being shot down by a V-2:

We were flying over Hertfordshire, just north of London, at about 2000 feet. The naked fields rolled peacefully by, and from an almost cloudless sky the comforting sun smiled down on the frost-cracked earth. . . . I was feeling very moved by the promise of spring. . . .

And then, like a sudden blotch in the blue sky, there appeared a small, reddish cloud about half a mile ahead and high above us. . . . At one moment there was nothing and then, in a flash, it was there, complete, ugly and menacing. As we flew on, gazing in atonishment at this phenomenon, smoky tendrils spread outwards and downwards from its billowing heart. . . . This was no cloud; it was a V-2 rocket, exploding prematurely. . . . In a moment it was nearly overhead. Then something big and black smacked down heavily into a ploughed field just ahead of us. The soil spurted up as it went in and all over the field little puffs of earth begun to spring up as smaller fragments of the rocket rained down. . . . The air all around us was filled with assorted ironmongery . . . pieces of casing, cylinders, gear wheels, nuts, bolts and straggling lengths of wire went whizzing past. . . .

At last the air cleared. . . . We . . . turned and circled over the field. Some farm workers were running out to gather souvenirs and one of them made for the most tempting prize, the big casing that we had seen crashing to the earth. He had taken a good grip on the casing, but then he instantly let go of it and started hopping around sucking his fingers.

Welcome though they were, the airbursts deprived the British authorities of the opportunity to acquire a complete V-2, which was essential if the bomb-disposal section of the Royal Engineers were to learn how to deal with any rockets that failed to explode. An almost undamaged V-1 had fallen into British hands during the first ten days of the flying-bomb campaign, but the V-2s proved less accommodating. As one leading expert, Major Hartley, explained, 'with the outer casings made red hot by atmospheric pressure, any actual or other technical weakness was more likely to result in a premature burst than failure to detonate on arrival'. It was not until the night of Sunday, 11 March 1945, after six months of rocket bombardment, that the first unexploded V-2 was reported, and 'at first light on the morning of the twelfth,' Major Hartley recorded, the officer responsible for bomb disposal in the area – the missile had landed in a field at Paglesham in Essex – 'started to make his reconnaissance'.

The entry hole made by the rocket was impressive, a shaft five and a half feet wide and apparently some eighteen deep. [Major] Gerhold had himself lowered down it and soon discovered minute traces of grey paint adhering to the sides while in the loose soil at the bottom were small fragments of fibre glass and plywood. . . . There could be no reasonable doubt but that an unexploded V-2 warhead had passed that way. . . . From the nature of the entry hole it was evident that a large sized excavation was going to be necessary and . . . no very speedy recovery of the remains of the rocket could be anticipated. From the point of view of the Civil Defence authorities the incident in a field on a remote farm was of no particular urgency. . . . However, as a specimen it was obviously of great interest. A strong excavation party was soon at work.

The sweating soldiers were still digging when the following Sunday, 18 March, news arrived of a second unexploded rocket, at Hutton near Brentwood, also in Major Gerhold's area, and he immediately set off for it 'armed with authority to disregard speed restrictions'. Once again, however, it seemed that recovery was likely to be a long job – but this time there was another complication, sightseers:

The second unexploded V-2, like the first, had fallen in a field, but this time it had not penetrated deeply. The warhead was clearly visible and accessible from the surface. This naturally made the site a subject of considerable interest, and shortly after his arrival Gerhold found that representatives of the General Staff, the RAF, the Ministry of Home Security and various other bodies – in his words, 'all interested parties bar King Farouk' – had got wind of the affair and were turning up in force. . . . Gerhold did little to enhance his popularity with High Authority by insisting that safety precautions must be observed and the vicinity of the site cleared but . . . as dark fell police and military guards were posted and the area cordoned off.

As mentioned earlier, and as British intelligence had already learned, the rocket was set off by a radio fuse supposed to operate 10 feet from the ground, and the current to operate this and the detonation mechanism it set in train came via 'a complex electrical component known as the *Sterg* unit, situated immediately behind the warhead and connected with the assembly in the nose by leads that passed through the main filling'. It was this unit, fortunately fairly accessible, on which Major Gerhold and another officer now got to work:

Together they cleared away the earth from the crushed and tangled mass of wires, scraps of plywood and other debris. It was work that

237

demanded extreme care and concentration. Each wire had to be traced and scrupulously kept clear of its fellows in case a bared metal surface should cause a short circuit and subsequent detonation. At last the whole broken unit was identified and uncovered and all electrical leads connected with it severed. No current could now pass to the firing mechanism.

It was the Germans' genial practice to include secondary fuses and 'anti-handling' devices in many of their bombs, in the hope the bomb disposers would set them off where the original fuse had failed. X-ray photographs were often taken, therefore, of unfamiliar missiles to locate objects that seemed to have no good reason to be present. This was, very sensibly, done at Hutton:

After the short delays necessary to allow the rays from the radio-active source to penetrate the steel and explosive, the resultant film . . . showed nothing to excite suspicion, so the detonating mechanisms were removed by remote control and later the cast main filling of amatol steamed out. This last operation was a little tricky since the sensitive penthrite filling of the exploder-tube was still in position. However, it was safely completed and it was then found possible to extract the booster-charges by unscrewing a collar at the rear of the warhead and letting them slide harmlessly out of the tube.

The VIP sightseers, if they had not by now gone home, were now free to stare as much as they wished. Not so the unfortunate Major Gerhold, for just as he was finishing work at Hutton news arrived of yet another unexploded V-2, also in his area, so that 'he began to have intimations of persecution'. From a bomb-disposal point of view this was less of a problem, since 'impact had split open the warhead so that the shattered amatol filling could be removed by hand' and 'the *Sterg* was still more or less intact and having been disconnected was taken away for research' – revealing, incidentally, that it still 'retained a charge' so that it it could have set off the rocket even on the ground. This third rocket, however, in a built-up area – it actually enjoyed a precise address, 45 Northumberland Avenue, Hornchurch – was far more troublesome to the civilian departments than either of its predecessors. 'To enable the bomb-disposal personnel to deal with the unexploded section,' remembers one man then employed by the London

Electricity Supply Company to disconnect damaged or vacated houses, 'meant evacuation of some hundreds of properties . . . and then arranging for supplies to be switched off from the electrical sub-stations' – a necessary precaution to reduce the risk of fires if the V-2 exploded, or of cables being left bare and 'live' to endanger future visitors to the damaged property. He can still remember 'the tension of the wait . . . with all the various units and public utility companies at a safe distance'.

The first unexploded V-2 to land was the last to be dealt with. It was not till 7 April that the Paglesham rocket was at last dug out and the warhead recovered from a depth of 37 feet. By then any secrets it had to reveal about the rocket had become of academic interest only.

19

ORDEAL IN ESSEX

What the county endured was never widely known.

Essex resident, 1945, recalling the V-2 attacks

Most of the flying-bombs which had not got through to London landed in Kent. For the rockets, with the attack coming not from France but from Holland, Essex fulfilled the same role. But there was an important difference, psychological if not pragmatic: the V-2s were not shot down on to Essex by the British defences but plunged to earth at the end of their flight.

The county, the tenth largest in England, covering nearly a million acres, and the fourth largest in population, with 1,750,000 inhabitants, presented a large target, but the most closely built-up part of it, on the eastern borders of the capital, lay within the London Civil Defence Region. It was not only this which suffered, however. The rockets were spread over the whole county and very evenly distributed in time as well as space, including several exceptionally bad ones, so that four of the five 'outstanding incidents' occurring outside London – the exception was the Commer works V-2 at Luton, already described – took place in Essex, which was first hit by a rocket as early as the fourth day of the bombardment, at Magdalen Laver near Harlow, followed within ten days by four more. This pre-eminent place in the table of rockets within its boundaries, London only excepted, Essex never lost. 'Perhaps you would like me to start with the score,' wrote a Home Office official breezily, to the senior regional officer at Eastern Region HQ in Cambridge, on 6 December 1944, 'which is, at present, in extra-metropolitan Essex', i.e. outside the London Civil Defence Region, '91, in metropolitan Essex, 52, total 143.' However, as he explained, there was always an element of

uncertainty about such statistics, owing to the rocket's
annoying habit of paying no attention to local-government
boundaries:

> The initial explosion which throws off the propulsion unit of the
> rocket has led to these parts being scattered, in some cases, over a
> mile or so of country; quite recently we had one which scattered
> pieces from Labourne End, on the borders of Hertfordshire, right
> into Group 7. The second incident of this sort, at North Fambridge,
> where the explosion was rather high, left recognizable and substantial
> parts over so wide an area that to cover the whole layout gave us
> exercise comparable with a morning with the beagles!

Surprising as it seems, considering the rocket's size and
effect, establishing precisely where each missile had fallen
created in rural areas like much of Essex a perpetual problem:

> V-2 arrives a bolt from the blue, completely unheralded. . . . 'A pillar
> of cloud by day and a pillar of fire by night' may possibly give
> indication of the site of the incident . . . but . . . a good deal of
> luck will be required if accuracy is to be obtained. . . . The extreme
> difficulty of locating the position of the fall of a rocket . . . has
> produced what at times has appeared to be a competition between
> the [Civil Defence] services of neighbouring areas for the privilege
> of 'working' the incident. . . . I can quote a recent incident at Nazeing
> [four miles south-west of Harlow] where parties from Hertfordshire,
> from Waltham Holy Cross in the London Civil Defence Region of
> Essex, as well as the Western Area parties all arrived. On that day
> an Essex incident was handled by a Hertfordshire incident officer,
> and use was made of London facilities. . . . The effect . . . was to
> impress the inhabitants of this rural district considerably.

The Germans never deliberately aimed at the county town
of Essex, unlike Norfolk and Suffolk, but to its inhabitants it
must have seemed that they were doing so. On 15 October a
V-2 landed only six miles away, at Rettendon, forty yards
from the village pub, the Bell, which escaped with shattered
windows, though two people were slightly hurt. Another
followed at Little Waltham, only four miles to the north, in
November, landing in a sugar-beet field 200 yards from the
village school. Then, just before Christmas, it was the turn of
Chelmsford itself, in a particularly tragic incident, at a local
war factory, Hoffman's, at 1.30 in the morning of Tuesday, 19

December 1944, in the middle of the night shift. A local historian described the scene:

Only a quarter of an hour before the V-bomb fell, men, women and girls in the works had been singing Christmas carols to the accompaniment of the local Salvation Army band. There was a festive spirit in the air. The band left and the workers returned to their benches. Then the bomb fell. For a moment all was chaos. Even girders were twisted into fantastic shapes. Fire broke out. The streams of trapped workers were agonizing. . . . To add to the disaster some large barrels of oil caught fire. By the aid of an army searchlight the rescue work went on for many hours, well into the next day.

One of the girls who escaped later gave her account of the disaster:

We were singing when the place was filled with flames. Debris was falling everywhere and all the lights went out. It was terrible. . . . I had been singing 'You make me happy'. In the confusion I also remembered where I had left my torch. It was still there, although the lathes and all the workshop fittings had been blown all over the place. I grabbed two friends who were working beside me and somehow we scrambled through a gap in the wall.

Many people died in their beds when their houses in Henry Road, adjoining Hoffman's, were destroyed, and other property was damaged in Rectory Road, Marconi Road and Bishop Road. Apart from the rescue services, 'several motor food kitchens were on the spot within ten minutes', one local man noted, and the whole Civil Defence system stood up well to this sudden test. The final death roll was 39, with another 33 seriously injured. The valedictory address given by the Bishop of Chelmsford over the communal grave in the municipal cemetery was long remembered. 'They died for their country. They died at their post of duty. We honour their memory.'

Chelmsford was to suffer another, but lesser, industrial incident in February, when a rocket landed, on a Friday afternoon when the streets were crowded with shoppers, in a field by a timber merchant's in Roxwell Road. Some of the workmen were injured, one very badly, but the general feeling was that the town had got off lightly.

By now V-2s were a familiar part of Essex life, having, even before Christmas, come down at places as far apart at

242

Heybridge, Southminster, Danbury, Writtle and Roxwell, though only one, apart from that at Hoffman's in Chelmsford, had been classed as 'outstanding' – at Collier Row, Romford, on the morning of 16 November, when 12 people had been killed and 32 injured, illustrating once again the direct relationship between density of population and casualty figures.

Colchester, the only other large inland town in Essex apart from Chelmsford (if Romford, on the fringes of London, was excluded), escaped the V-2s altogether, though they were audible all around. 'As the explosion of the projectiles on a still night could be heard for a distance of ten miles', commented a local historian, 'the town heard and felt most of them.' Many of these were airbursts, for Essex was a constant victim of defective missiles. One of the most spectacular exploded over the centre of Brightlingsea, about six miles down the River Colne from Colchester; another blew up close to Clacton, on the coast twelve miles away, and a third, between Fingringhoe and Rowhedge, barely three miles from Colchester, left 'the countryside . . . peppered with fragments'. Many V-2s landed along the coast, having just 'made it' to the enemy shore. One badly damaged two of Clacton's leading hotels, the Grand and the Towers, on the sea front, only just above high-water mark.

Because nothing but sea lay between the east coast and the launching sites, people living there could often see a rocket being fired. 'You could see the rocket trails coming up from the other side,' remembers one keen aircraft spotter who often stood on the front at Clacton looking up into the clear, early-morning sky. 'Five minutes later you heard the explosion and saw the black column of smoke.' To one man working on a farm at Beaumont, near Little Clacton, the missiles soaring skyward seemed 'like a star going straight up into the sky', while to a journalist living on Mersea Island, at the mouth of the Blackwater Estuary, 'on a clear day, their vapour trails, twisty as a corkscrew, could be seen tracing a parabolic curve towards England'.

Not all the V-2s apparently heading for London reached it. Many must have plummeted down unrecorded into the sea or ploughed up the mud of the foreshore, harming only the eel grass and disturbing only the Brent geese that made the area their home. Two rockets are known to have fallen in or close to Thirslot Creek, an inlet of the Blackwater, and a third's remains are believed to lie in Southey Creek. These and other 'shorts' must have provided an additional hazard for the soldiers hoisted, no doubt with little enthusiasm, in an observation balloon into the chill east-coast breeze to try to provide advance warning that a V-2 was on its way – an attempt, as mentioned earlier, doomed to failure.

The best-known place in Essex was Southend and here the Germans scored what, if it had been intended, would have qualified as a remarkable bull's-eye, plunging a rocket straight through the roof of the Pier Pavilion. The police were told 'that every smallest piece of the rocket had to be carefully collected,' a then civilian driver with the Southend Constabulary remembers, and eventually these fragments filled to overflowing a 30-foot-long shed behind the Central Police Station 'known as the "Bomb Mortuary".'

Westcliff-on-Sea was Southend's smaller and quieter neighbour, and its experiences of the rocket are recorded in the regular letters which a couple living there sent to their soldier son, only mentioning it, like good citizens, once it was no longer a secret:

12 November 1944. You have heard about the rockets now. Several have landed about here – only one did damage in the town.

26 November 1944. We get quite a lot of rockets about here. They make a noise that can be heard for miles. . . . One fell at Wakering on Wednesday and one in the mud off Westcliff.

19 March 1945. One fell at Dawes Heath Road, Rayleigh, last week, but they still miss the Southend area pretty well.

No part of Essex escaped entirely; indeed, as a map makes clear, it was positively peppered with V-2s. The experiences of the rector of Purleigh (a village eight miles east of Chelmsford) who, as its warden, was responsible for his flock's temporal as well as spiritual welfare, were typical. On 15 December he noted in his log-book; 'Rocket. Somewhere near; unable to get information by telephone', but later added: 'Aerodrome', a former airfield now used for point-to-points, close to which some council houses received 'a severe shaking'. A second V-2 followed soon afterwards. 'We got enough of the blast at the rectory to bring down a bit of ceiling and various bits of glass,' he recorded. 'The only injury was to a horse, but the crater would have held a good half-dozen double-decker buses and its contents lay about in a horrible mess over a wide area of meadow.'

A little later the same clergyman had to endure the interruption of that most innocent of activities, the vicarage tea-party:

A study circle of clergy to which I belong holds monthly meetings in the houses of its members in turn, on the second Tuesday of the month. On Tuesday, 13 February, thirteen of us met at Great Braxted, where our host was the rector, the Rev. H. Douglas Neison. We had studied our Greek Testament in the morning and heard and discussed a paper in the afternoon and were standing round the dining-room table for our stirrup cup of tea before returning to our various homes when a very sharp bang resounded overhead. Nobody said anything, but we looked at each other, and the language of all eyes said plainly enough, 'Well, that's a near one. But we've heard the noise, so the thing must be miles away by now.'

The studious clerics had reckoned, however, without that common Essex phenomenon, the air-break, which left the warhead of a disintegrating missile intact:

After a short pause, there came the other noise, familiar enough to all of us, of the express train rushing through the tunnel. . . . Then, with another bang and a quake the thing arrived fifty yards away; the windows, glass, sashes and all, melted on to the floor and covered it. . . . Slates sprinkled the ground outside in fragments. We found ourselves looking out through unglazed apertures that had been windows and on to the floor and furniture which the windows now covered . . . and at our host and his sister, whose ruin this was, and at each other, wondering why we were still there. . . . I seized the telephone, perhaps by force of habit, to get through to Report Centre and found it out of order, so, as the house was isolated . . . I judged that it would be more useful to drive straight for Maldon and make sure that the Mobile Unit knew where to go. However Great Braxted wardens had managed to get through. . . . Mr Neison afterwards told me that only three windows had survived and that the cost of his War Damage was £750. The cost to him and his sister of the inconvenience and of cleaning up and straightening out was incalculable. He had been bombed out of his parish in Birmingham to come to this quiet country living.

The following day, also rudely interrupting teatime, another

V-2 landed at Mountnessing, around 5 o'clock on Wednesday, 14 February, plunging to earth only ten yards from the main Chelmsford-to-London road, so that its effects were widely seen and felt, as a local writer recalled:

The rocket made its crater close to New Cottage, a modern detached house, the residence of Mrs Florence Breedon. Mrs Breedon and her daughter were having tea when the back and one side of the house collapsed beside them. They were blown from their chairs up against the dining-room wall, rooms upstairs just disintegrated and every bit of glass was blown out. Not a plate dish or glass in the house remained unbroken.

A rescue squad, hastily mustered, rushed into the ruined house, expecting the worse, but the two occupants had no more than a few cuts and bruises. . . .

Across the road, Mountnessing's 'shopping centre' presented a sorry sight. From the post-office down to the Congregational chapel, every window had gone, every ceiling was down and furniture inside was all at sixes and sevens. The front of the chapel had completely caved in and what was left of the wind organ had been carried outside the building. . . .

Only three minutes before . . . a loaded Chelmsford-bound bus had passed the spot, while a bus going to Brentwood was almost due. . . . There were a few people standing outside the post-office waiting for it at the time. One of them was Miss Harris, the schoolmistress. They were almost blown off their feet by the force of the explosion. Miss Harris had a few minutes before locked up the school, the damage to which necessitated its being closed for five weeks. . . . Within a radius of 200 yards not a ceiling remained intact. But there was not a single serious casualty.

The following Sunday, 18 February, a man doing the early-morning milking on a farm at Woodham Ferrers, six miles from Chelmsford, had an even more frightening demonstration of the rocket's malevolence:

At 7 a.m. I left the cowshed to take two pails of milk to the dairy and then went over to the pond hole to relieve myself. As I crouched down I saw a flash in the sky. I do not remember anything else until I heard Duke E., the other cowman, calling. . . . I remember I was fighting for my breath but I have no idea how I had come out of the pond hole, which by now was filled with big lumps of clay, and I was now on top of the dungle, which was near the remains of a brick wall a few yards away. All the farm buildings had fallen.

246

Ordeal in Essex

I got up and a pig ran through my legs with its guts hanging out. It ran up on to the dungle and died. Twenty-one cows were killed and all that was left of one of them was a bit of hide. Two horses were buried in the debris, but were not hurt.

My C. [my employer] was in bed in the farmhouse when all this happened and he was showered with glass. The telephone was out of order and it took the ambulance about an hour and a half to come. Duke had been trapped under a beam and his leg was like jelly. We were both taken to hospital in Chelmsford but Duke died on the way. I was treated for shock . . . [and] kept in for a week.

That evening the rector of Purleigh, after his narrow escape the previous Tuesday, was settling down for a peaceful evening by the fire at 8.15 p.m., no doubt glad to be indoors again after evensong:

It was a thick night after rain. On hearing the explosion I tried to get in touch with Warden Lee of Cock Clarks but found the telephone was not functioning, so I got into the car with Mrs Walwyn and her first aid kit, and my daughter who was home on leave and drove. As we came into Cock Clarks we found the roads a thick mess of glass, mud and telephone wires. The Head Warden was already in the windowless post office telphoning to Sub-Control (probably via Corporation Farm). All Cock Clarks was there, though it was too dark to see who anyone was.

So many people had turned out to recue one local resident that it soon appeared that within the official 'incident' another of a different kind had developed:

Contrary to all regulations, Mrs Stuart-Jekyll had been extricated from her bed and debris by neighbours in advance of the rescue party, concerning which words appear to have passed . . . but as the neighbours, being men of their hands, had done the job safely and effectively . . . their words were fiercer, or at least more conclusive than the words of the men of the rescue party. When we arrived Mrs Stuart-Jekyll was seated in dignity and comfort in the back of a car which she directed to the house of an acquaintance near Danbury. Mr and Mrs Jordan, in their cottage a few yards beyond Mrs Stuart-Jekyll's, had been sitting on either side of the fire when . . . without any warning or noise of explosion the house just began to collapse about them. The chimney is the pillar of these wooden houses and with some of the uprights it stood firm and saved them from being crushed. . . . Neighbours took them in until they were able soon after to find another cottage. . . . Three houses . . . were wrecked beyond

247

repair. A number of others suffered more or less severely. It seemed a miracle that one was able to include in the Final Report: 'Casualties: Nil'.

This was one rural warden's rocket war, or most of it: Purleigh had yet another rocket two days later, only three-quarters of a mile away, the noisiest yet, since it wrecked some greenhouses as well as a private house. Other residents of rural Essex had further explosions to endure, like the elderly couple living in a thatched cottage, a fact which was to save their lives, along with the absence of a warning, for the shelter, to which they always adjourned when the siren sounded, was at the very edge of the 'crater in which', as a local historian described, 'a couple of Stoke Cottages could easily have been placed side by side'. Stoke Cottage was on the road midway between Writtle and Roxwell and was destroyed at 3.30 in the morning of Wednesday, 7 March 1945, as its sixty-eight-year-old occupant, peacefully asleep alongside his wife, explained:

As I came to my senses my first fleeting impression was that there had been an earthquake. . . . Everything around us and both of us seemed to be suspended in mid-air. There was a terrific crack, as though all the thunder I had ever heard in my life had been rolled into an awful roar. Then everything around us collapsed.

But as the cottage was thatched and not slated the whole heap of thatch a couple of feet thick, fell upon us, and instead of killing us protected us from bricks and timber. When my wife and I realized that we were still alive and apparently uninjured, we found we were on the ground floor, having fallen through the bedroom floor, with part of the thatched roof still forming a sort of triangle over us. We started crawling through bits of smashed furniture. We hadn't the faintest idea where the front or the back of the cottage was. Then, groping, half stunned, through a hole, we found ourselves out in the open at the back of where the cottage had been. The earth seemed to be still quivering from the effects of the explosion.

It was dark, but we could dimly see some of the fine old trees in the garden snapped and torn as though they had been matchsticks. Then the ambulance came and took us away. . . . The ARP workers quite expected to find us badly hurt but . . . we had no more than a few scratches between us.

Most of the more heavily developed part of Essex lay within the London Civil Defence Region, but the non-metropolitan parts of the county included the great industrial belt on the Thames, which formed its southern border, and, towards its south-west corner, the town of Romford, whose 36,000 inhabitants made it larger than Chelmsford though a little smaller than Colchester. Romford's situation made it uncomfortably rocket-prone. No fewer than 22 fell within the borough's boundaries, including an airburst over Ferguson Avenue, and, as a local resident wrote, 'Many more were close enough to give that momentary mental shock which, after some months, began to try even the strongest nerves. . . . It was difficult not to dwell on the possibility of one being even at that moment speeding on its way down towards us, like a giant dart with ourselves as the "bull".'

The local Civil Defence report centre, having labelled the V-1 'fly', logically but unofficially, recorded rockets as 'wasps'. The first wasp sting came on 16 September and by the end of the year there had been seven more, which included two on New Year's Eve itself, and one 'outstanding incident', 'near the junction of Rosedale Road and Collier Row Lane' – described in the ministry records as 'Colliers Row, Essex' – at 7.40 a.m. on 16 November, when 13 people were killed, 32 more admitted to hospital, with 34 houses demolished and 800 more damaged. Romford was hit by two more rockets in January 1945, four in February and, as if Kammler were firing off his stocks in a final burst of defiance, seven in March, one of which landed close to the County High School for Girls, as one of its not over-enthusiastic scholars, then aged fourteen and living in Upminster, still remembers:

There was a loud bang just as I was leaving for school . . . and I jokingly said to my mother . . . 'I bet that's hit my school.' I walked the short distance to the town centre and caught one of the local buses . . . got off and started to walk down a long road. . . . At the end of the road was a park which I had to cross . . . and as I reached the gateway I had to pick my way through clods of earth and other debris which littered the pavement. There were some workmen there clearing up the mess and one said to me, 'There'll be no school for you today, love'. . . .

As I entered the park I could see the crater, not a very big one, in the far corner, just behind the school's tennis courts, which were on the boundary of the school grounds and the park. . . . I couldn't

249

see how badly the school was damaged until I was past the tennis courts. Then I could see that the prefabricated science laboratory, which stood about a hundred yards from the main building, was in a state of collapse like a house of cards. Once inside the main building I could see whole window frames in the corridors leaning inwards, but most of the glass was still in them, as it had been shatter-proofed. After a while, a roll-call was taken and we were allowed briefly into the classrooms to collect our books and possessions. . . . We were dismissed for the Easter holidays two weeks early, which pleased us all. However, our joy was short-lived when we learned we would be returning a week sooner than originally scheduled, so the V-2 only got us one extra week's holiday.

Romford continued to attract rockets till the very end of the campaign. It suffered a second 'outstanding incident' at Harold Wood in mid-February, when 12 people were killed and 34 injured, and its last two V-2s did not arrive till Monday, 26 March 1945. The first destroyed 16 hourses in the Forest Road area, killing two people; the last, with unintended irony, demolished the so-called Victory Hut, in Noak Hill, but harmed no one.

Next door to Romford was Hornchurch, where two rows of houses were almost levelled to the ground in mid-December 1944 and it took eight hours to extract the last trapped person from the ruins, but there were no fatal casualties. In another incident, remembered by a woman, then a bright-eyed six-year-old, attending the Ardleigh Green infants' school, the town was less fortunate:

I was sitting at my desk . . . when suddenly there was a big bang and the ceiling in our classroom started to collapse. We all scrambled under our desk and crouched there terrified wondering what had happened. Evidently a V-2 had landed on a small factory (Lacrinoid's) situated behind our school and killed several of the workers.

I don't remember anybody in my class being hurt but, as the explosion had burst the water pipes and hot water was streaming down the corridors, we were all hurriedly sent home. It was bitterly cold at the time and I can remember people complaining when they were clearing up the mess from the shattered windows that they couldn't tell the difference between lumps of glass and lumps of ice. I went rushing home from school worried that my mother might have been hurt, but when I got home, although every window in the household had been blasted away, my mum was standing in the

250

kitchen with her hat and coat on, doing the washing-up as if nothing had happened.

Churches and clergy enjoyed no special protection, as many elsewere in Essex could have testified, but the rector of Laindon-cum-Basildon was particularly unlucky, suffering, his brother (whose own experiences in East Ham will be described later) remembers, twice in successive days. The first explosion wrecked his car in its garage in the rectory grounds, while 'The following day another rocket completely demolished the rectory and . . . my brother and his wife and children had to move to Billericay.'

Rainham was the site of another of Essex's 'outstanding incidents', shortly before midnight on Monday, 15 January 1945, when 14 people were killed and 4 seriously injured. Another, happily less lethal, rocket made her wedding day doubly memorably for a GI bride who was kneeling beside her future husband at the altar rail of a local church when its walls were struck by pieces of a V-2 which had come down 200 yards away and also blew the windows in. The groom reacted, all agreed, with a composure that could have been British, and, though the people and their guests instinctively ducked, the service went on. As the guests left fire engines and ambulances went roaring past, prompting an apt comment from the new husband: 'Waal, I wanted a war wedding and I guess I've got one!'

Purfleet, a little lower down the river than Rainham, was the scene of one of the lucky escapes which could be set against the all too frequent disasters. A rocket scored a direct hit on the Thames Board Mills, producing all kinds of packaging material for munitions, but though 'It wrecked the Pump House and the water supply lines' and 'did extensive damage to the neighbouring property', as the firm's war history recorded, it failed to start a major fire.

For shopkeepers the rockets added one more burden to a life already governed by regulations and coupons. One wartime WAAF, whose parents owned a children's outfitting and wool shop in Grays, between Purfleet and Tilbury, remembers how, during a visit home, a 'tremendous explosion' sent her sister cycling into town to see what had happened to the family business:

She managed to ring through to tell us to come quickly. . . . We tore to the shop and found the roof off, plate-glass windows blown indoors and windows hanging on hinges, stock turn to shreds in the windows, splinters of glass and chaos everywhere. . . . My father had to spend the night on the premises as it was completely open and customers came in the next day for wool which had been reserved for them. The bomb had fallen at the rear of the old public library, demolishing many houses in Cromwell Road and killing a few people. . . . Tarpaulins were in great demand. My father nearly had a fight to get one for the shop roof, as children's clothing and wool was in short supply and rationed to us by suppliers.

Essex was eventually to be hit by around a third of all the rockets that reached the British Isles, including those which burst in the air above it or fell along its shores. If the 'London' part of Essex, stretching from Waltham Holy Cross and Chingford to Barking and Dagenham, was included the total rose to more than 50 per cent. The local journalist who complained in 1945 that 'what the county endured was never widely known' was speaking no more than the truth, and many would have echoed the comment of a local NFS commander, prompted by the use of the blanket term 'southern England' in published reports: 'Essex took a devil of a lot of southern England.' Like Kent in the flying-bomb era, Essex undoubtedly felt that other places had no idea of what, if inadvertently in this case, it was suffering to save London, and, again like Kent, parts of the county for a time did not qualify for Morrison shelters. The lack of warning for anyone removed one old grievance, however, that there were few sirens outside the towns and where they existed, *Essex County Standard* reporters were regularly told, 'some districts could hear' them 'only when the wind was favourable'. Now everyone was equally badly off.

Essex's 378 incidents left 148 people dead and another 431 seriously injured, far ahead of any other county's toll. Next came Kent, with 64 V-2s, excluding the area within the London Region, which killed 45 people and seriously injured 109, though the county authorities put the total of V-2 incidents higher, at 67. Unlike the flying-bombs, the rockets were concentrated in the north-west corner of the county, but affected people over a much wider area, as one of them, then a sixteen-year-old motor-trade apprentice, who lived in Ashford and worked for the Canterbury Motor Company, discovered:

I travelled by train, the 7.36 a.m., stopping at Wye, Chilham and Chartham. . . . Trains became increasingly unreliable, one hour late, perhaps two. We stood on the platform, nobody said when the train was coming; sometimes a rumour, 'Rocket on the line at St Mary Cray.'. . . Sometimes we heard a V-2 from Canterbury or Ashford; the massive explosion followed by the awful rumble of the rocket's approach. . . . We never knew its terrible destructive power, we only knew it as a cause for endless delays and cold hours on unlit platforms. The war had lost its glamour!

A few places were more seriously affected, notably Gravesend, just across the river from the rocket-prone industrial belt of Essex. One place to suffer was the Fort House, once occupied by the future General Gordon of Khartoum fame. A man then teaching at Gordon School, 200 yards from the river and opposite Fort Tilbury, remembers it:

I was washing up after supper at about 11.00. . . . There was a bang and the window flew wide open. . . . I saw a huge cloud of smoke in the air so I took an axe and went out to see if I could help. When I got to Milton Place the fire brigade was already there. Half of a terrace of the big houses had gone and there was a hole in the road. Later I learned that the V-2 had landed almost in the middle of the road and blown down the old Fort House. . . . Some half-dozen houses were in ruins and I remember seeing high on the wall a fireplace with the fire still burning in the grate.

A few doors further a fireman and I were stopped by an agitated teenage girl who said her parents were at the top of the house, four storeys up, so the firemen and I climbed over the broken front steps and went up the stairs. The scene was almost comic, as her elderly father was searching in a drawer as if nothing had happened, though his wife was sitting on the bed. 'It's all right,' he growled, 'I'll get us down.'. . . . One boy from my own class had gone to bed and woke up in the garden. His mother, sister, her fiance, and brother were all dead. His father had been on night work and he and the boy only were alive.

Most of Kent's rockets came down in totally rural surroundings, like the grounds of a nursing home at High Brooms, where an elderly woman was killed by shock. The village of Farningham where, according to a local author, life in the 1940s 'flowed on much the same . . . as it was done for 1,000 years', added a proud new entry to its list of battle honours – 'H.E. 143, Incendiary attacks 12, flying bombs 6' – 'Long Range Rockets 1', which 'fell into the fields above Sparepenny Lane in February 1945, damaging houses many hundreds of yards away'. Nor was Westerham, where Churchill's country house, Chartwell, was located, spared, as one farmworker, then aged fifteen recalls:

I was unloading cabbages from a horse-drawn cart when, without any warning, there was an explosion. The old mare just shook. Having experienced the Battle of Britain, the blitz and the V-1s, she was quite a veteran in her own right. Then, after a brief pause, there came a strange noise . . . increasing in intensity for a few seconds. . . . This was too much for the horse, who took off through an open gate into a small paddock. As she did so, I lost my balance on the cart and fell off backwards. After a trot round the paddock she gave up and stood still.

No other county had to endure anything like the trials of Essex and Kent. Hertfordshire, with 34 rockets, Norfolk with 29, Suffolk with 13, Surrey with 8 and Sussex with 4 had not a single resident killed, though Bedfordshire, with only 3 V-2s, suffered 19 dead, from the incident at Luton already described. Buckinghamshire was hit by 2 V-2s which seriously injured 3 people, and Cambridgeshire by 1, which caused no casualties. Berkshire's solitary rocket was the longest 'overshoot' of the campaign, for it landed in a small but prosperous Thames-side village 35 miles beyond London and 230 from The Hague, with results recorded in the county archives:

19 March 1945. *Cockpole Green, Wargrave*. At 1007 hours the warhead of a Long-Range Rocket (which exploded in the air over Pinkney's Green) fell and exploded at Cockpole Green causing 2 serious and 10 slight casualties and blast damage to the *Four Horseshoes* and *Old Thatched Gate* public houses, Goulders Farm and five cottages. Portions . . . fell in various parts of Pinkney's Green, including field near Compton Elms and Littlehole Winter Hill Road. No casualty or damage.

20

THE BATTLEFIELDS OF ILFORD

The shopping centre resembled a battlefield.

Ilford Guardian reporter, recalling 8 February 1945

Ilford in 1944 was a place of which, thanks to the photographic suppliers Ilford Ltd, many people had heard – but few had visited. It was a prosperous suburb, largely residential but containing a good deal of light industry. Its population, esti mated at 130,000 in 1939, had grown rapidly, and Ilford was now to earn the unwelcome distinction of being hit by more rockets than any other borough in the country. Rockets from The Hague which fell considerably short of their aiming point came down in rural Essex; those which almost 'made it' to their target fell in Ilford. Ilford's 35 rockets placed it just ahead of Woolwich, equidistant from Holland on the other side of the Thames, but well ahead of West Ham, with 27. Its death roll was, however, lower and not one of its 35 featured in the Home Office 'top 50' of 'outstanding incidents'. Its casualties were the result of a steady drizzle of rockets descending on it throughout the whole V-2 period, each killing or injuring its handful of people and damaging its few hundred houses, not of any single spectacular disaster. They were scattered over the whole borough, but some districts suffered more than others, bearing witness to the remarkable degree of grouping that Kammler's crews were achieving; the extraordinary total of 11 rockets, for example, landed within half a mile of the first incident, in Courtlands Avenue, on 26 October 1945, when 8 people were killed, 15 seriously injured and about 20 more suffered cuts and bruises – very typical of the incidents that were to follow.

Some of Ilford's 35 burst on or over open spaces – the local golf course on 4 November, the Peel Institute Sports Ground in January, the grounds of Claybury Hospital in February, allotments in Loxford Lane in March – but most landed in residential areas, and a list of their locations reads like a local street directory, often with the same names recurring. Two rockets came down close to Tunstall Avenue, near the boundary with Dagenham, four around Eastern Avenue, which ran through the very centre of Ilford, and six were distributed along, and very close to, the railway line, including one in the goods yard itself and others close to Ilford, Seven Kings and Goodmayes stations. A council Civil Defence official later suggested, in his unpublished memoirs, an explanation:

These weapons were directed against the London area in lanes of approximately two miles wide and . . . the rocket was aimed for the centre of the lane, but was liable to go wide . . . up to a distance of one mile either side. . . . Each . . . danger lane . . . was separated from its neighbour by another . . . safe area . . . of some half a mile wide . . . which was almost unscarred by the V-2.

Ilford as a whole, one man then working for the Borough Council Electricity Supply Department remembers, became known as 'rocket country', but, he confirms, within its area some places were more dangerous than others:

The area around The Drive soon had the nickname of 'Rocket Alley'. . . . By the end of the attacks 7 had fallen in 'Rocket Alley', 3 of them within eighty yards of each other. . . . Working in The Drive area was soon regarded as unhealthy and a rota system was organized so that everyone had their fair share. . . . As I crossed from The Drive into Cranbrook Road away from Rocket Alley, I breathed that much deeper and almost sighed with relief.

The devastation of Ilford, once begun, continued week in week out without respite. October's solitary V-2 was followed by 5 in November, a lull – with a notable exception to be mentioned in a moment – in December, 5 more in January and 14 during the peak month, February. On the 24th of that month Ilford's member of parliament, Major Geoffrey Hutchinson, a barrister, wrote to the Secretary of State for Air to seek a meeting, no doubt to press for further measures to protect his embattled constituents, but with little result: in March alone, Ilford was struck by another 7 V-2s, the very last, like the

first, coming down in a totally residential area, the junction of
Atherton Road and Clayhall Avenue, just inside the boundary
with Woodford. The damage done to house property was enormous, as in many Ilford incidents, which often affected recently
built 'semis', cheap, practical and convenient, but not designed
to stand up to high explosive. In Ley Street, where there were
two incidents in ten days in that worst of months, February,
with the winter winds and rain seeking out every gap around
a door frame or missing tile, 2100 houses required repair; in
Kent View Gardens, on 19 February, another 2000; in
Breamore Road, on 4 March, 2300; in St Albans Road, two
days later, 2565 – a record, or near-record, even for a V-2. At
one time, noted the *Ilford Guardian*, just before the end of
the war, 4000 tarpaulins were in use simultaneously, and the
sight of them draped, flapping in the breeze, over tileless roofs
wherever one looked bore silent witness to Ilford's ordeal.

And yet life went on. 'One heard the explosions, some close
enough to shake the building,' remembers one Ilford man,
then aged eleven, who had just started to attend Wanstead
High School, 'but unless one was personally involved they
passed off as talking points. . . . One was more involved with
V-1s by the mere act of taking shelter from them.' It was
impossible none the less not to be aware that Ilford was under
siege. This man remembers a schoolmate being summoned to
the secretary's office after the boys had stared with interest at
'a great pall of smoke' visible from the classroom window,
who returned to report that 'he would have to return to his
grandparents' home after school since his own . . . no longer
existed'. Another boy was killed and it was announced that his
name would appear on the school roll of honour along with
others killed in action. Finally, at 8 o'clock in the evening of
Saturday, 30 December 1944, it was this informant's turn to
become 'personally involved' by a V-2:

My brother and I had spread our [Christmas] presents all over the
top of the Morrison shelter. . . . All of us were seated around the
fire in the front room. . . . I remember the dog, Paddy, was suddenly
scratching at the door as if trying to get out. . . . Soot started to fall
down the chimney into the hearth and there was a blinding flash in
front of my face. . . . I heard no explosion. The next thing I
remember is lying under the Morrison shelter on my own and seeing

blood on the pillow. . . . I got up and went out into the kitchen where my mother was sitting on a stool having some cuts on her shoulder attended to by my brother . . . obviously in . . . pain. They both asked me if I was all right. I felt as though I'd received a blow on the head, but I had not realized until they told me that it was my own blood I had seen. . . .

Having ascertained that we were all alive and kicking my father [a local post warden] dashed out to the site of the explosion. . . . Plaster from the ceilings lay all over the place in large lumps, small lumps and fine dust. . . . The three of us then got on with the task of clearing up the mess. . . . It took an hour or two. . . . When it was done it was noticeable . . . that the pile outside my own home was considerably larger than elsewhere in Gants Hill Crescent. . . . The full repairs on the house had only been completed for a couple of weeks [after a V-1 in August] and it all seemed a little unfair.

The 'unfair' rocket had in fact landed 'in Collingwood Gardens, just two roads away, almost opposite the site of the V-1 incident', killing 7 people and seriously injuring another 23, but, as it had demonstrated in other places, the rocket's effects in Ilford were often capricious. Around midday, always a time favoured by Kammler's crews, on Friday, 24 November 1944, as a local Civil Defence official learned, 'the park-keeper . . . was standing at the back of his lodge', in South Park, when 'to his amazement, and without hearing anything whatsoever, his house just disappeared from his view'. He was unhurt, but 'a soldier who had just returned home on leave' and happened to be crossing the park, was killed. So, too – as another local man, on the scene shortly after the explosion, learned – was a well-known local figure, 'Mr R., a part-time chimney sweep [who] delivered green veg. from a handcart', who vanished without trace, 'although pieces of his cart were found almost a hundred yards away'. His wife, standing by her front door when the rocket exploded, 'was badly injured . . . losing a leg, but survived'. The tale of escapes was completed by that of 'a baby playing in the front room underneath a grand piano' in a house in South Park Road. 'Splintered glass was scattered everywhere, walls cracked and ceilings caved in,' but the infant crawled out of this unusual shelter unharmed.

Because of its situation, this incident was talked about more than others even more serious, and another V-2 widely remem-

bered was the 'Early-Morning Special', arriving before breakfast during rocket-afflicted February. This damaged an
important factory, Plessey Ltd, a day nursery, a public house
and many homes, while, the *Ilford Guardian* reported later, 'a
diversion . . . was caused by a pony which, its stable completely
shattered, fled down Ley Street neighing furiously until it was
caught and re-harnessed.' Another public house destroyed,
earlier in the bombardment, was the Dick Turpin, the licensee,
who was killed, being famous locally for sending a gift each
month to 'regulars' now in the forces. Others died far from the
point of impact, most conspicuously on the worst day of the
whole attack, 21 February. 'A young lady . . . in the street
when the rocket fell . . . was later lifted from the crater uninjured,' the Civil Defence official quoted earlier wrote, while a
woman a full half-mile away, and in a downstairs room, was
killed when 'a large paving stone, thrown by the blast, crashed
through the roof-top'. The same day that brought these events
around Cranley Drive saw a second V-2 near Belgrave Road.
An off-duty postman who went out to look for the milkman
died, the rocket's only victim, though 50 others were injured.
The milkman himself, thanks to being delayed on his round,
escaped.

A rocket landing on a packed theatre or cinema could have
caused a disaster of Deptford proportions. This never
happened, and the entertainment industry, much affected by
the flying bomb, tacitly ignored the V-2s, with in Ilford some
extremely narrow escapes in consequence. On Friday, 12
January 1945, *Robinson Crusoe*, the traditional post-Christmas
pantomime, was playing to a packed house of 1500 at the
Hippodrome when a V-2 landed on a row of cottages just
behind the building. The female lead, Renee Houston, on stage
alone, was badly shaken and her co-star, Donald Stewart, was
pinned to the ground by beams which had fallen from the roof
backstage. At the same moment the water tank burst, deluging
the whole cast. The whole scene had overtones of the loss of
the *Titanic*, with water pouring over the footlights into the
auditorium as the audience left, while the orchestra played
them out. Outside the 'chorus girls, attired only in their flimsy
stage costumes, their greasepaint smeared and blotchy on their
faces', shivered in the cold of a January night, with 'all their

clothes destroyed in their dressing room', until decorum was restored by the WVS and ambulance drivers wrapping them in blankets. In St Mary's Cottages and the nearby public houses 17 people died, and 60 others were injured. In the theatre itself no one was killed and when, two days later, the roof and 'circle' collapsed, it was empty; the workmen on the site had all left for their dinner.

Soon afterwards a lunchtime rocket, at 12.45 p.m. on Thursday, 8 February, wrecked the Super Cinema, which was showing *Summer Storm*, supported by *Pass to Romance*, but luckily before the performance had started. Most of the seventeen people who had bought tickets escaped injury, but two of the four usherettes already in the auditorium were killed outright and the others seriously injured. With other victims in the street, the adjoining houses and a garage, the final casualty toll was 13 dead, 64 seriously injured, plus another 86 requiring first-aid treatment. Six of the dead, and many of the injured, were women working at the Ilford Manufacturing Company, just across the road from the Super, which was now turning out shirts instead of ball gowns. All these casualties had stayed behind to eat their dinner in supposed safety in the firm's shelters; 48 more, who had left the premises, escaped.

Actually passing the cinema was a workmate of the council electrician previously quoted: an ex-sailor, wounded at Dunkirk, he was not easily shaken, but he now 'visibly trembled' as he described what had happened after the two men had split up for the dinner break:

After leaving the Cranbrook Road office he was turning into Ley Street, right outside the front of the Super, when he was hurled from his bike into the foyer. . . . Sitting on the floor amid a pile of debris he gradually became aware of women screaming and made his way into the main body of the building. . . . A cloud of dust and dirt hung in the air but daylight was filtering through the cloud from the now open cinema roof. He soon found a woman crouched against the main wall crying hysterically for help and suffering from face and head wounds. Half dragging, he helped her to the foyer and sat her down. In between sobs she said there were two other cleaners inside. Returning inside he soon found the other two. . . . One lay still on the floor, but the other lay dazed and whimpering and with most of her clothes blown away. Half dragging, half carrying this woman outside, he had pulled down a door curtain to cover her when help arrived, in the shape of two firemen. . . . The third woman was brought out very shortly, alive but injured. . . . Percy, after about five or ten minutes, decided to leave, and going outside, found his cycle with paintwork missing, but otherwise undamaged, and cycled off.

A member of the staff of the *Ilford Guardian* happened by pure chance to be on the spot:

I was walking along the High Road when suddenly the air became filled with flying glass and dust. Masonry fell from the tops of the shops and two people a few yards in front of me were hit and fell moaning to the ground. The shopping centre resembled a battlefield, for people were stretched on the pavements and a number of shop assistants came running out with their faces streaming with blood. . . . I raced round to the Super Cinema and found a tragic scene of destruction. The NFS workshop had been demolished, cars were burning outside a garage, a trolley bus standing near the theatre had its windows smashed, the road was littered with rubble and the roof of the cinema had caved in. . . . The manager, who had been blown full length across the vestibule, had blood trickling down his face. He seemed totally unconscious of his own injuries and was only concerned with the fate of two of the usherettes who were buried in the main hall. They were found dead in their uniforms.

Twelve days later, on Tuesday, 20 February 1945, again at lunchtime, came what was remembered as the 'Ilford Ltd rocket', for it fell behind the factory, smashing the boiler house, so that, as the *Ilford Guardian* later reported, 'steam hissed across the road for some minutes, while debris from the houses' – over twenty were wrecked – 'piled up to add to the confusion'. Unusually, owing to some misunderstanding, 'the call for assistance was sent in a little late', and one Civil Defence member, whose office happened to be near by, was very conscious of what followed:

Several army ambulances were quickly on the spot and rendered some very valuable assistance, but there was not enough accommodation for the many casualties who required immediate removal to hospital. A Post Office van driver offered assistance and I used his van to send to hospital a small child, who was bleeding profusely from head and face wounds. I asked the mother to hold the child tightly to her breast in order that any vibration of the moving child would not unnecessarily aggravate the injuries. . . .

Women suffering from ghastly and bloody wounds were sitting or lying about the pavements and in front gardens, some receiving treatment and others waiting. It seemed ages waiting for our own services to arrive. . . . The rescue squad and ambulances did in fact arrive in about 25 minutes, but a delay . . . on these occasions appears to be unending.

As often happened in 'industrial' incidents, there were some unforeseen consequences. One woman living nearby, whose father was 'blown across the room . . . severely shocked and . . . died six weeks later', learned how at the same instant an Ilford Ltd employee had been crippled, for he was 'crossing the laboratory with a large bottle of ammonia' and 'had his fingers blown off as the bottle exploded'. He was one of 94 people injured in the incident; another 7 were killed.

By now even the dead could not rest in peace, for the occasion was marked by a gruesome accident, as the explosion damaged a house from which a funeral was taking place. According to current rumour, the coffin was blown into the road but the proceedings went ahead, although the mourners not merely suffered 'a terrible shake-up', as one man on the spot commented, but 'afterwards had to return to a badly damaged house'.

This third explosion in the vicinity of Ilford Broadway finally completed the destruction of the battered Hippodrome, inside which the electrician quoted earlier had been at work, helping to connect up a cable serving a crane employed on demolition work. It also brought him his own narrowest escape:

Suddenly a bright bluish light illuminated the sky. Before I could duck or crouch, I was thrown backwards against the doors and was surrounded by a rushing, roaring sound. The doors checked my fall and I was still on my feet . . . facing an ironmonger's . . . outside of which was a three-foot-high pile of galvanized buckets and a couple of dustbins. The buckets took off and went sailing in the air in all directions and the dustbins flew across the road among the passing traffic and the plate-glass window of the shop disintegrated into fragments. Several of the boarded-up theatre doors crashed inwards behind me. . . . The sky to my left had darkened and . . . the whole sky was blackened by a sheet of flame, blending into a huge black cloud of smoke and debris in which I could plainly see great chunks of wood and pipes twisting around. . . . I now threw myself . . . into the protection of the entrance corner wall . . . as lumps of debris rained onto the road and the sound gradually subsided.

His next step was to search for his workmate, whom he found in rubble-strewn darkness, hesitating to feel his way to safety along the wall for fear of brushing against 'live' terminals. But, with the help of a cigarette lighter and a policeman sent to look for them, both men eventually got out unscathed and another dinner hour in Ilford resumed its now all too familiar course:

We cleared our pushbikes of odd debris, said 'Cheerio!' and went outside to great activity as Civil Defence personnel and vehicles hurried by and policeman redirected traffic and pedestrians away from the roped-off area. We then went home to lunch and returned to work at two o'clock glad to be alive.

By the time Ilford's last rocket had landed, on Tuesday, 27 March, the town had reported 465 serious casualties, a total second only to Deptford's; of these 117 were dead, 349 badly injured. Undoubtedly the constant bombardment was too much for some people. 'Morale', believed the Civil Defence official quoted earlier, 'was at a very low ebb and many people, temporarily, completely lost their nerves' when the second V-2 within twenty-four hours landed in the same district, Uphall Road. But, fearful though they might be, the public carried on with their daily round, and there seems no reason to doubt the verdict of the *Ilford Guardian*, when it could at last tell the grimmest story in the borough's history, just before the end of the war:

Looking back one wonders how Ilfordians managed to carry on so splendidly, knowing that any moment might be their last. Certainly the shopping centre round Ilford Broadway did become slightly less crowded than usual, but on the whole housewives and workers alike made no break in their usual routine throughout the five months of constant tension.

21

WINTER IN WALTHAMSTOW

It can be stated that Walthamstow had more than its share of V-2s.

Civil Defence controller for Walthamstow, 1945

'The air was crystal clear, electric . . . and we hunched our shoulders and tensed our muscles in anticipation of the next rocket.' That is how a then fifteen-year-old schoolboy, living in Dagenham, remembers one moment in the long winter of 1944–45, while he stood on Becontree Station after three or four V-2s had landed within earshot within a few minutes. For if Ilford was like an exposed salient during the rocket offensive the area around and behind it also formed a distinctly unhealthy sector. The eleven boroughs which belonged to Group 7 of the London Civil Defence Region and made up the north-east corner of London and its immediate suburbs were hit by 199 V-2s all told, far more than any other group, and their casualty figures – 645 dead, 1441 seriously injured – were thirty times as high as the least-affected group in the region. Ilford's 35 rockets put it well ahead of other places in terms of incidents, but in the number of dead West Ham did even worse, for its 27 V-2s killed 215 people, though its total of seriously injured, 205, was smaller than Ilford's. Third in the group, with 21 rockets, came Barking, which lost 23 citizens dead and had 172 other serious casualties, and it was followed by Dagenham, which was also very close to the 'one death per rocket' formula, with its 19 V-2s, 18 fatal and 127 other serious casualties. Eighteen rockets hit Walthamstow (of which more will be said later) and 15 Waltham Holy Cross, whose low death rate – 7 dead, with 21 badly hurt – reflected the low density of population in this outer suburb. The socially and geographically 'mixed' area of Wanstead and Woodford, with

14 rockets, lost 51 dead and 77 hurt; East Ham, with 14 V-2s, had a somewhat similar toll to report: 50 dead and 124 other major casualties. Chigwell, with 13 V-2s, was lucky to escape with 1 person dead and 9 badly injured. Leyton, with 12 V-2s, did far worse: 67 killed and 162 injured. Chingford, with only one fewer rocket, 11, suffered far fewer casualties: 10 dead and 46 others.

Nowhere in north-east London that winter was out of earshot of a rocket for long, and to the schoolboy living in Dagenham previously quoted the rocket's ubiquitous character appeared almost to violate a law of nature:

The V-2s seemed to be more random in distribution, to scatter over a much wider area than the V-1s. Ilford seemed to get particularly clobbered for some reason. This seemed to conflict with the vaguely apprehended World War II convention that indiscriminate destruction should mainly be confined to the shabby areas like Plaistow or Canning Town or the docks. A better class of person generally lived in Ilford or Epping. Even Pitsea in Essex, where my father's sister lived in a bungalow, was hit. My aunt had a favoured neighbour . . . who was definitely middle class with a nice bungalow with accoutrements which I recognized as belonging to somebody a bit classier than us. Her manners showed breeding too. One night her bungalow received a direct hit from a V-2 and she was killed. Just a big hole where all this order and decency had formerly lived.

Clearly cursed with an overactive imagination, this boy found the presence of danger frightening rather than stimulating:

I tried to imagine what it would be like to be hit directly by several tons of rocket travelling above the speed of sound, but I gave up. It all seemed a bit esoteric when set against the humble background of life in Dagenham. . . . Life went on as usual. There was no point in taking shelter. . . . Everything was so normal. One's scruffy back garden, lessons on the top floor of the South-East Essex Tech., morning assembly, trips on one's bicycle, National dried egg, scrambled, or fried tomatoes for breakfast. The only difference was you knew that at any minute without warning *you* might explode . . . all over your familiar mantelshelf, or the classroom or the street you were walking to work.

The ending of the black-out added to the unreality of the whole experience:

265

An eerie feature of the last phase of the attacks in 1945 was that street lights were once again on in London. I remember walking along a street in East Ham on a visit to my future stepmother's house, seeing these lamps on for the first time since 1939 with all their suggestion of peace and the war coming to an end and being more than ever conscious of the fact that at any moment I could still get bumped off by a rocket. It's a bit poignant to have survived through all sorts of . . . lethal high drama and then get pipped on the post.

This boy was also troubled by a V-2 which landed on a church in a neighbouring borough, St George's, Barking, in mid-service:

I speculated on the theological significance of this event. Were the congregation perhaps less in touch with God than I had been at moments of crisis? It seemed a pretty abrupt sort of answer to public prayer, anyway.

Dagenham, a long, roughly axe-shaped borough, with its narrow shaft running alongside Ilford and its blade on that great sounding-board, the Thames, heard many more V-2s than landed within its borders. The roof spotters on the great riverside Ford factory which dominated the borough 'heard and recorded 579 rockets', according to its wartime history, though Ford's itself, as during the flying-bombs, continued to lead a charmed life:

Although seven crashed in the neighbourhood of the factory none . . . actually hit it, the nearest falling in the river some thirty yards south of the jetty on 15 March 1945. Though muffled by the water, the force of the explosion broke most of the windows in the General Office building. . . . On three occasions the blast from the explosion of . . . rockets which had narrowly missed the factory covered the boiler-room with a blanket of coal dust, so that the operators at work scanning the charts appeared like performers in an old-fashioned nigger minstrel band.

To the west of Barking, merging with the 'East End' proper, lay East Ham and West Ham, in both of which the V-2s constantly intruded into daily life. The Chief Superintendent for 'K' Division of the Metropolitan Police, which embraced these and some adjoining boroughs, speedily discovered that Kammler was no respecter of 'the Met.' Within a single week, around the end of January, one constable was killed while on duty at Upton Park, Plaistow, in West Ham, 80 bachelor police officers were bombed out of their section house behind East Ham police station, and West Ham police station was damaged – as his own house in Ilford had been – while almost every day he found himself visiting new incidents, many of them industrial, as will be described later.

Another guardian of public decency, of a different kind, the vicar of St George and St Ethelbert, East Ham, also found his activities constantly disrupted, as his wife has recalled:

One night a V-2 fell in Lonsdale Avenue. My husband immediately went into the house [from the Anderson where they were sleeping] for his overcoat so that he could go to the scene of the disaster, only to find our doors jammed and he had to climb over fences and walls to reach the road. Arriving on the scene, he found only an elderly lady whom he helped to rescue. Another time a V-2 fell in Haldane Road, which was near his church. . . . When daylight came, we saw a magnolia tree in bloom . . . still standing amid the devastation. . . . The next day, Sunday, my husband had to officiate at a wedding. . . . The west window of the church was smashed; the choirboys had cleared some of the broken glass, but the bride had to pick her way up the aisle among the splinters. . . . On the following Friday . . . the rocket burst on the roof of our house.* . . . We had all the windows blown out and no windows for many months. . . . The snow lay deep on the ground. The chairs were also damaged by shrapnel. Part of the rocket was hanging over the bed where our daughter was asleep. I remember pulling [it] away with a sense of trepidation. . . . The day following, we were holding a party for children and we tripped over pieces of the rocket that had fallen the previous night.

To the north of West Ham was Leyton, which suffered from two 'outstanding' incidents, one just before midnight on 16 February 1945 when 25 people were killed and 10 badly injured in Crownfield Road, and a month later, at 6.38 in the morning of 16 March, when 23 more Leytonians lost their lives in Albert Road, and 18 were badly hurt. The V-2s had a dismal effect upon morale, here as elsewhere, as one woman travelling each day from Woodford Green to work as a ledger clerk at a bank in Leyton High Road while her husband was serving in France,

---

*This airburst, at 4 a.m. on Friday, 26 January 1945, caused widespread damage in Cotswold Gardens.

observed. 'We public were mostly feeling rather depressed and thinking how much longer were we going to live in the tension and fear.' Still plagued by V-1s as well as rockets, the staff took what precautions they could. 'Some days we worked in the safe, but were afraid it would jam, so mostly worked at desks. I had frosted glass facing me but had to sit there.' As an ex-nurse, however, she did take the precaution of providing a first-aid box at her own expense, a prudent precaution as it turned out, for at the end of October the bank *was* damaged by a rocket in Leyspring Road, about 400 yards away, which killed 6 people and seriously injured another 30, among them the manager of the branch, while the lesser casualties, numbering 118, included herself,* the glass surrounding them proving as dangerous as she had feared.

A then thirteen-year-old girl attending Chingford County High School, previoiusly quoted, who lived in Waltham Abbey, remembers what happened after their house was badly damaged on 15 January 1945, luckily while she and her sister were sleeping downstairs:

I was blown partly out of bed and hit my head on the door, but not badly. Molly and I got up and went to the Morrison and soon we were asked to look after neighbours' children; some had been shocked by being trapped in bedrooms when doors jammed with the blast. About eight children joined us, reading comics, sipping soup, drinking tea, all in our Morrison; the following night they all wanted to come back.

No one in the area needed to be told the reason when suddenly called home. One steam-train fireman, 'working' the route between Liverpool Street and Chingford, 'guessed what that meant' when a relief fireman was waiting to take over from him in mid-shift, at Wood Street Station, Walthamstow. 'When I arrived home [in Gordon Road, Wanstead] . . . all that was left of my house was the front wall.'

Nowhere in this part of London were the rockets more resented than in Walthamstow, a largely working-class borough which perhaps felt that it had done its fair share of 'taking it', if not rather more. Its population of 131,000 was almost exactly

---

*See Chapter 27, p. 341.

the same as Ilford's, but packed into a much smaller area, and
its comparatively heavy casualty list was due to the steady drain
of average-sized incidents rather than to any major catastrophe. Walthamstow's disagreement with the original 'no
publicity' policy has already been mentioned, but the existence
of the V-2s was difficult to keep dark and people protected
themselves as best they could. The borough's mortuary at the
Queen's Road Cemetery proved adequate for all the demands
made upon it; the reserve premises, in the car park of
Walthamstow Stadium, never had to be opened.

Every one of Walthamstow's ten ARP districts, however,
had to cope with at least one rocket and, like Ilford's,
Walthamstow's rockets were spread out in time as well as
space. After the first, on 14 September in Farnan Avenue,
already mentioned, they arrived at frequent intervals, so that
life never felt really secure. In November a rocket landed on
a Sunday beside allotments, but luckily most of those 'digging
for victory' had gone home for lunch. Later that month,
another V-2 hit a road on the edge of Waltham Forest, causing
some casualties but missed, as the ARP controller recorded,
'the schoolchildren and others returning home to dinner'. At
times the missiles seemed to show a malign intelligence in
seeking out their victims. One 'fell in one of the few parts of
the Marshes where it could cause damage . . . at the foot of the
bank of the Warwick Reservoir . . . and managed to demolish a
boathouse' occupied by a watchman, who was fatally injured.
And so it went on, a few missiles landing harmlessly in the
adjoining Forest or River Lea Marshes, but most taking their
toll of three or four dead and another twenty or so badly
injured. To the ARP controller, Alderman Ross Wyld, the
'type of case in which casual travellers were killed always
seemed particularly hard luck', such as one where, 'in an area
surrounded by Forest . . . the driver of a lorry from Yarmouth
and . . . a soldier from Birmingham who was driving an army
lorry' were among the victims. To local residents the deaths of
servicemen while on leave also seemed exceptionally hard to
hear, like this one recorded by Alderman Wyld:

At teatime on a Tuesday in March . . . 'E' District received its
first rocket, which fell at the junction of College Road and Grove

Road. . . . The crater completely blocked the road and . . . 17 houses were wiped out. Included in the killed was a soldier who had called round to one of the houses to say goodbye to some friends before returning to his unit. . . . An RAF man returning home on leave . . . knew nothing of the death of his wife until he actually arrived at the incident where we were still searching for the body.

Among the memories of one man then aged eleven is the sight of 'thousands of blue salt packets' scattered around the junction of Woodford Road and Forest Road after a V-2 had caught a Smith's Crisps delivery lorry, the 'salt in the bag' being then almost the company's trademark. An outstanding recollection of the Civil Defence workers involved was that of a dog which dashed in excitement out of a wrecked house and promptly fell into the crater. 'He was found alive and unhurt at the bottom . . . out of which he was unable to climb owing to the steepness of the sides' and was 'duly retrieved by NFS ladder'.

The area witnessed a number of airbursts. A then sixteen-year-old, working on bomb-damage repair, witnessed one as he and his workmates were idling away their dinner hour listening to a local evangelist:

'Holy Joe', as we unkindly called him, was preaching the Gospel as usual at Child's Corner, when somebody said 'Look, leaflets!', and high in the sky was a vapour trail and hundreds of small shining objects followed by a dull bang. We stood watching these objects getting bigger and bigger and everybody started running. Suddenly we were showered with pieces of metal, the largest about the size of a dustbin. . . . A V-2 had exploded in the air and the warhead had gone on to fall in Walthamstow.

This may have been the rocket that caused some speculation at Civil Defence headquarters as to where it really belonged, as Alderman Wyld recalled:

As we had neither damage nor casualties we were unable to account for this being finally allotted to Walthamstow. We accepted this allocation with a certain amount of philosophy as some two weeks previously we had received large amounts of materials from a mid-air burst . . . allocated to Barking, although we had most of the stuff.

Between the end of the blitz, in May 1941, and the end of the war, in May 1945, Walthamstow suffered damage to 72,000 houses and shops, of which the rockets, although the exact total was censored for security reasons, must have accounted for a high proportion. The borough was credited, however, with only one 'outstanding incident', at Blackhorse Lane, at 2.20 p.m. on Monday, 19 February 1945, when the Germans hit a 'military objective', Bawn's factory, with results which Alderman Wyld described:

The whole of their office was demolished and all except one of the office staff were killed outright, including two of the directors. . . . The factory was completely put out of action and 12 houses were also wrecked. Over 500 other houses were reported as damaged. The difficulties of tracing missing persons . . . were considerable and it was not until the early hours of the next morning that we were able to satisfy ourselves that all . . . had been accounted for.

The difficulties of identification were brought home to one man whose business was ruined, a local shopkeeper who had taken up shoe-repairing when cripped by polio:

I arrived just as the area was being roped off at the nearby turnings . . . but when I told the policeman who I was, he let me through. . . . I got to where the shop had been and everything, including heavy machinery, the customers' boots and shoes, and stock, was no more. As I looked on the wardens and Civil Defence workers were busy among the rubble of the house next door and one looked up, saw me and said, 'I thought we had just taken you out of here', and pointed to a small van [used to remove the dead] but it turned out to be the man in the house. Up to this point I was managing to hold my own, but when he said this my inside was violently upset. . . .

My book recording the shoes in the shop was found 300 yards away unsoiled. . . . For a week or two I was at the site of my shop for the sole purpose of giving to customers a chit signed by me, signifying that the customer had lost a pair of shoes in the premises. Then if they took it to the town hall they were given seven coupons and thirty shillings cash [£1.50] for replacement.

This was to remain Walthamstow's worst incident, with a final death roll of 18, plus 53 seriously injured and another 150 slightly hurt. When the bombardment finally ended, with two rockets in March, few residents would have disagreed with its Civil Defence controller's verdict: 'Walthamstow had more than its share of V-2s.'

22

NOTHING LEFT OF LONDON

In another month there will be nothing left of London.

Statement on German radio attributed to Allied prisoner of war, February 1945

It had been the effect of the anticipated 'giant rockets' on central London which had most alarmed the government, but, in the event, even Kammler's more modest missiles left the West End and the 'establishment' quarter of Westminster and Whitehall almost unscathed. The area's escape was in fact almost uncanny. A rocket in November plunging down towards Victoria, within easy blast distance of Parliament and Downing Street, had burst in the air. The Duke Street V-2, in December, was just inside St Marylebone, though doing some damage in Westminster. And when a rocket did finally land within the confines of the borough – though only just – at 9.30 on the morning of Sunday, 18 March, it arrived at a time when there were few people about and in a relatively 'rural' part of it, Speaker's Corner on the edge of Hyde Park. The explosion smashed windows all round Marble Arch, stripped the trees of their leaves and broke a water main, but killed only two people inside the borough boundaries, a newspaper seller and a child he had tried to protect. A third person died in the incident and nine were seriously hurt, most of these casualties being in the adjoining boroughs of Paddington and St Marylebone, for which Marble Arch formed a 'frontier post'. This rocket, as Westminster's wartime historian, the writer William Sansom, commented, could have produced 'a catastrophe of appalling dimensions', for that afternoon 'thousands of people would have been there watching a march past by the National Fire Service'. The government's 'no publicity' policy meant that Speaker's Corner, the great symbol of free speech, was offici-

Rauchen verboten.

Ready for action. Completed A4s. in operational camouflage, stock-piled as Peenemünde in 1944 awaiting shipment to the launching units

Ignition!
Left: Technicians making final adjustments to the control gear before launching
Right: An A4 directly after lift-off

Impact   Staveley Road, Chiswick, after the arrival of the very first V-2 on 8 September 1944

'**A minor incident.**'   A casualty being removed from the wrecked road – Tewksbury Terrace, Southgate – on 16 September

Rescue by night
Most trapped casualties were buried and the ending of the black-out made the use of searchlights possible to help the Civil Defence teams. This picture was taken at Fairfax Road, Hornsey, on 11 December 1944

Rescue by day
Some injured people were marooned in upper storeys like this woman at Waltham Holy Cross on 7 March 1945. The fireman in the front is clearing mud from a hose intake draining water from a broken main, a frequent feature of V-2 explosions

Top: **'The Mayfair rocket.'**　Very few V-2s landed in the West End. This one, in Duke Street, near Marble Arch, in the late evening of Wednesday 6 December, damaged Selfridges, and caused eighteen deaths. *Above:* **'A shopping incident.'** The gap where Woolworths stood in New Cross, Depford, until a rocket landed during the Saturday morning shopping rush on 25 November 1944, killing 160 people

The London battlefield The devastation, complete with crater, recalls the Western Front in the First World War. This was Chingford Road, Walthamstow on 8 February 1945. *Bottom:* The most-bombed borough. Ilford was hit by 35 V-2s, including this one, at the junction of Wanstead Park Road and Endsleigh Gardens, in March 1945. By April, when this photograph was taken, several roofs had been protected by tarpaulins

Death at the market *Top:* A general view of Smithfield Market, Farringdon Road, site of one of the worst V-2 incidents, on 8 March 1945. This picture was taken the following day. *Above:* A tracker dog locating a buried casualty at Smithfield. The use of dogs, only occasional before, was now officially recommended

The finish *Top:* Hughes Mansions, Stepney, where 134 people were killed in the last major incident of the war, at 7 a.m. on 27 March 1945. *Bottom:* Kynaston Road, Orpington, after the final V-2, at teatime on 27 March. One man was killed, the Germans' last British civilian victim ally described as 'a piece of waste ground . . . in southern England', although the newspapers admitted that the explosion there had 'blown out the windows of an hotel and a cinema'. Londoners soon learned the true facts. 'Behind this description', noted Vere Hodgson in her diary only a week or two later, 'lies one of the most famous spots in London. . . . The hotel was the Cumberland. The cinema – the Regal.'

The Germans, having already claimed to have levelled most of London flat with the V-1s, now had to destroy it in their propaganda reports all over again. In early December, on the evidence allegedly supplied by captured British sailors, German radio stated that the public were afraid to go to work or stayed at home because their factories were smashed. By the end of the month the German Telegraph Service was asserting that three bridges over the Thames had been destroyed, that the Tower of London had been damaged, and that a high-speed evacuation of the capital was in progress. The truth was the British government's problem, thanks to its policy of playing down the rocket menace, was that of people returning to London, not of a panic exodus. But Goebbels persevered. 'The Houses of Parliament have been damaged extensively,' it was stated in December. 'There is not a building standing within 500 metres of Leicester Square. Piccadilly Circus has also been devastated.' In February an anonymous sailor was credited with the opinion that 'in another month there will be nothing left of London', a ludicrous statement designed, perhaps, to offer consolation to the inhabitants of ruined Berlin.

One famous building the Germans did succeed in hitting, the Royal Hospital, Chelsea, home of the red-coated Chelsea Pensioners who still provided a rare splash of colour in the drab wartime streets. This, Chelsea's solitary V-2, landed at 8.50 a.m. on Wednesday, 3 January 1945, on the north-east wing in Light Horse Court, killing two members of the staff and three residents, who had been standing peacefully in the chapel; 19 others were injured. By odd chance the V-2 landed on the same spot as a German bomb dropped in February 1918 and one of the rocket's victims, the Captain of Invalids, had escaped death on that earlier occasion. The white-haired, fragile residents helped in the rescue work, veterans of far-off

273

campaigns under fire again. 'Now', wrote its historian of the famous institution, 'it had its own honourable scars to set beside those of its In-Pensioners; Wren [the Hospital's architect] would have been greatly saddened; but he would also have been very proud.'

The Royal Hospital rocket, having also damaged a number of large houses in the elegant adjoining squares and streets, was much talked about, though only one of thirty-three buildings in London classed as 'hospitals' affected by a V-2. James Lees-Milne, who lived not far away, noted the after-effects in his diary:

In the afternoon I walked down St Leonard's Terrace and asked after L. He was in bed, but he and his servants were unhurt. All his windows on both sides of the house were smashed, doors wrenched off, both outer and inner; and partitions and ceilings down. Much of his furniture was destroyed. Yesterday rockets fell like autumn leaves and between dinner and midnight there were six near our house. Miss P. and I were terrified. I put every china ornament away in cupboards.

The impression of people in Chelsea that they were in particular danger was due to its geographical situation. Like Croydon and Hampstead it was shaken, thanks to its location, even by distant explosions, and James Lees-Milne's riverside home in Cheyne Walk was ideally placed to hear the sounds of battle from the working-class boroughs across the river. Mr Lees-Milne himself noted the same illusion on Saturday, 27 January:

While I was at Charing Cross there was a terrific V-2 explosion. It sounded right in my ear. I learned afterwards that many people in widely scattered parts of London thought the same thing.

Any lingering illusion that somehow with the New Year the bombardment of London would ease up was speedily dispelled. In the week ending 3 January 1945 34 rockets reached the United Kingdom, half as many again as in the preceding three weeks, and between 3 and 10 January the total soared to 62, much the largest number so far, followed by 45 from 10 to 17 January, 46 from 17 to 24 January and 48 from 24 to 31 January, a remarkably steady rate of fire which showed that the firing crews had now settled down into a comfortable routine. In the first week of February the same rate of fire was maintained, with 47 V-2s, and in the second week, from the 7th to the 14th, it rose significantly to 66, nearly ten a day, producing the highest total of serious casualties so far, 1888, of whom a tenth, 188, were killed or missing.

Once again, as in the blitz and the flying-bomb period, the most privileged parts of London got off lightest. The most prestigious of Civil Defence areas was Group 1, the wartime equivalent of postal district W1, though the latter covered a much smaller section of central London around Mayfair, while Group 1 took in, beside Westminster and Chelsea, the mixed but mainly wealthy 'royal borough' of Kensington, and two largely proletarian districts, Fulham and Hammersmith. Between them these accounted for only 5 rockets, including the Victoria airburst, and an extraordinarily small casualty list: 39 killed, 112 seriously injured. Fulham had no V-2s or casualties at all, Chelsea only 5 dead and 20 badly injured from its solitary rocket, at the Royal Hospital. Kensington's V-2, at the less wealthy, northern end of the borough, killed 2 people and seriously injured 42, among them a woman living close to the point of impact, in Grenfell Road, W11, who that December evening had gone to bed just before 11 p.m:

I went up to bed and, I don't know why I did this, I took my baby from his cot and put him in the bed with me. Not long after there was a terrible crash and the whole house seemed to crumble around us. . . . Everything went black, all the lights went out, there was water everywhere and gas, also glass. We did not know a lot about it. It took quite a time to get us out as the stairs and front of the house were gone. I was told some time later that there was a large part of the rocket at the front of the house. The gas stove was blown out of the kitchen and landed at the front door. There was one bit of wall left of the kitchen and on that wall was a mirror, not broken, not even cracked. . . . All the houses in the street were a write-off. We had nothing, no clothes and . . . were covered with the black powder from the bomb. . . . One of my neighbours, a woman I had been in the same ward with when our babies was born, was killed. . . . We had no clothes and were given blankets to wrap around ourselves and taken to St Charles Hospital. A young nurse said, 'In future, I am going to bed with *all* my clothes on.'

Most of the Group 1 casualties were caused in Hammersmith, in a similar incident to the one in Kensington, occurring

275

at 10 o'clock in the evening of Wednesday, 14 February 1945, in Wormholt Road, a heavily built-up area about a mile west of Shepherds Bush. Most of the 29 people killed and 41 wounded were in the block of council flats which the rocket demolished. A woman then working as a rating clerk at Hammersmith Town Hall remembers the silent evidence of the disaster which crossed her desk – money collected from the tenants in the wrecked flats being handed in covered with bloodstains.

The Hammersmith V-2 ushered in the worst 'rocket week' so far: in the next seven days 71 V-2s arrived, although the following week, 21–28 February, brought a welcome decline back to the previous average, 45. March, in rocket terms, came in like a lion: 58 in the first week, of which well over half, 36, reached the London Region. The following week, 7–14 March, showed a falling off in aim, but an unwelcome increase in the total numbers landing, to 62, which dropped, in 14–21 March, to 52, and between 21 and 28 March to 46, though these produced, as will be described, some of the worst incidents of the whole campaign.

Those that reached London continued to be very unevenly distributed. Civil Defence Group 2, north of Westminster, consisted of four boroughs, Paddington, St Marylebone, St Pancras and Hampstead. They were hit by 6 V-2s between them, causing 52 deaths and 171 cases of serious injury, although one vulnerable, densely populated borough, Paddington, escaped altogether. St Marylebone's 10 dead and 7 wounded resulted mainly from the Duke Street incident; some further casualties were caused by the Speaker's Corner explosion, which 'belonged' to Westminster. St Pancras's 2 V-2s both, however, had disastrous consequences, though only the former, at 4.08 p.m. on Friday, 8 February 1945, at Tavistock Place, in the heart of the capital's 'medical quarter' was classified as 'outstanding'. In this 31 people were killed, and there were 54 other major casualties, while the Central London Opthalmic Hospital and the Medical School of the Royal Free Hospital were both very badly damaged. St Pancras's second incident, only a few hundred yards away, just inside the borough boundary with St Marylebone in Whitfield Street, in the late afternoon on Sunday, 25 March, badly damaged one of the great shrines of the Methodist movement, the Whitfield Memorial Chapel in Tottenham Court Road, and left 9 dead and 46 badly hurt. The area, on the edge of Soho, was a mixed one of commercial property, including many small restaurants, residential housing and some small workshops. One woman close to the scene was working in a small factory in Whitfield Street itself; her father was nearby, post warden in charge of the ARP post in the basement of a local cafe.

Everyone screamed and we ran out of the door to see what had happened. When we looked down Whitfield Street we could see smoke and dust and nothing else. I knew my father was down there . . . so I flew up the road. When I got near there were bodies lying about and one was standing facing a wall as though it was stuck there. Someone on the ground had a piece of newspaper stuck on the back of his head that looked as if it had been slapped on to raw meat. I did not think about them and just jumped over things that were in the way. . . . I could not find where the post was and everyone seemed dazed. I saw someone coming up some steps out of the debris and I grabbed them and shook them asking, 'Where's my Dad?' They just said, 'Don't know.'. . . Then another one came out. I was screaming by then and I started shaking and then he clasped me tight and we both cried. It was my Dad.

No place outside their own 'village' had a stronger claim on the affections of Londoners than ' 'appy 'ampstead', so-named from its traditional Bank Holiday fairs, on the edge of the Heath, the constant resort of walkers and courting couples. Its large amount of open space did not prevent its 3 rockets all landing in more populous parts of the borough, though they killed only 2 people between them – three according to the borough records – and badly injured 74. Hampstead's first, and worst, rocket landed, like so many others, at teatime, 4.30 p.m., on a winter afternoon, pitching down, the local Civil Defence records agreed, at 'the junction of LMS and Met. Railway lines, back of 114 Iverson Road between West End Lane and Kilburn High Road', on Monday 8 January 1945. Kilburn High Road was one of the busiest shopping streets in north London, and one woman, then working in a shoe shop opposite the State cinema, a local landmark, recalls that moment:

There was this ear-splitting noise and we actually saw the small emerg-

277

ency shop windows of our large corner shop disintegrate before our eyes. A large elderly lady standing in our shop doorway waiting for a bus almost collapsed with shock as the glass fell round her feet.

The effects of the Iverson Road rocket were probably magnified by its landing high up, on a railway embankment and, apart from 14 houses destroyed, 152 were badly damaged and another 1600 needed some repair. Besides the 2 people killed and 64 detailed in hospital, 57 people required minor treatment.

The bitterly cold weather added to the misery this rocket produced in Hampstead, for 400 people had to be temporarily accommodated in rest centres, and eventually 110 families needed rehousing. Those able to stay under their own battered and leaking roofs were miserably cold and 'At the emergency coal dumps', a local historian reported, 'members of the Civil Defence services, under the leadership of the controller, worked at filling prams, tin baths, bags and sacks with coal, which the people took back as best they could to their homes.'

Hampstead suffered again at 2.30 a.m. on Friday, 16 March, when 200 houses were damaged by a rocket which also hit a railway embankment, this time in the neighbouring borough of Willesden, but its own second rocket followed close behind, when, in the words of the borough's wartime history, 'a little before 6 a.m. the following morning,' Saturday, 17 March, 'the swish of a V-2 rocket' was followed by 'the now familiar shattering roar in the rear garden of 212 Finchley Road, at the side of the Borough Central Library'. Thanks to the time of day, casualties were few, but nearly 1000 houses were damaged, along with the library, 'the Council's Works Depot, the Hampstead Telephone Exchange, the Lighting Station, Warden's Post No. 16 and the WVS offices'. Five days later, at a more dangerous time, mid-morning, in fact 11.40 on Wednesday, 21 March 1945, another V-2 landed on the second most famous open space in the area, Primrose Hill, just across the boundary in St Pancras, but 'credited to' Hampstead. Even on this green hillside some 'military' damage was done: a reservoir required repair, and four soldiers had to be taken to hospital. Once again the heights of Hampstead spread the noise far and wide. One woman, engaged that morning in the curiously

278

rural occupation of mushroom-rearing in Camden Town, recalls it as 'simply stunning and the vibration caused the door fastening to jam'. The crater on Primrose Hill briefly became one of the sights of North London, and prompted the author of *Hampstead at War* to an uncharacteristic flight of fancy:

Somehow, gazing into the hole made by the explosion, where this metal monster from the sky lay with its body torn open, powerless and futile, one seemed to sense with the acrid smell of cordite invading the nostrils, that this was the end. And so it proved to be.

The area of outer London beyond Hampstead, and stretching out to the edges of the region at Barnet and Cheshunt, was so large that it was subdivided into three sub-groups for Civil Defence purposes, which together formed Group 6, containing no fewer than 31 boroughs. Immediately adjoining Hampstead was sub-group 6C, with 10 local authorities whose territory was hit all told by 17 V-2s, which caused 23 deaths and 84 serious injuries. Two places, Bushey and Uxbridge, escaped altogether, Barnet Urban District had only one V-2, which hurt no one, Wembley had one rocket, which inflicted a single death and no serious injuries, and Finchley one which killed 4 people and badly injured 10. Elstree, famous for its film studios, had only one bad injury, and no deaths, from its two rockets, and Ruislip and Northwood, also with two incidents, had no casualties at all. Hendon, also with two rockets, had one fatal casualty, and 18 cases of injury. One of its incidents, on a 'bitterly cold Sunday morning in January 1945', is remembered by a man then working in a chemist's shop in Golders Green Road, Edgware:

I was making a drink of coffee on the gas ring in the dispensary . . . when a customer entered. As I passed into the shop to serve him I just turned off the gas and . . . crash!, a V-2 dropped just opposite the shop at the back of the Prince Albert public house, just after opening time. The customer and myself were thrown to the ground and broken glass and stock covered the floor. We both had a miraculous escape from serious injury, only suffering from shock and some nasty cuts to our hands and face; our heads were pitted with minute particles of glass. . . . We were taken to the casualty station at the Hendon Cottage Hospital, where there were already similar cases. . . . I shall always remember the man who, when asked where he was when the incident happened, replied, 'In the Prince Albert,

279

just got my drink and was waiting for my change, but that was the last I saw of the note or the change and I certainly didn't have my drink!' The wry look of disappointment on his face was pathetic.

Willesden, with four rockets, came off comparatively badly for the area, with 5 deaths and 41 people injured, but worst of all was Harrow, also hit by four V-2s, which caused 12 deaths and 14 serious injuries. Over most of the area, however, rockets remained so unfamiliar, that when, in March, one fell in Uppingham Avenue, Stanmore – 'the worst incident in the area . . . during the war', one local resident remembers – 'the police had to put barriers across the road to keep away sightseers'. His own house, 150 yards from the explosion, lost most of its roof, one of many badly damaged:

Some people, and especially my children, were dumbfounded that such a thing had happened to them and right on the doorstep . . . and being so young (seven and nine years old) really could not understand why this happened. The fact they lost some of their playmates doubtless made a greater impression on them. However, there was a silver lining . . . in the form of a mobile canteen. . . . Here they were able to get tea and buns and, what is more, nothing to pay!

Beyond, and to the east, of sub-group 6C lay sub-group A – there seems to have been no sub-group B – containing ten boroughs or urban districts, which attracted 41 rockets, producing a far heavier toll than its neighbour's 17 missiles: 162 dead and 572 injured. Edmonton had 9 V-2s, with 5 dead and 59 other casualties. Enfield also had 9 incidents, with a total death roll of 21 dead and 151 injured. Cheshunt, with 7 V-2s, had 10 dead and 56 seriously injured, Hornsey and Southgate 4 each – causing 25 dead and 66 other casualties in Hornsey, 30 dead and 53 injured in Southgate – Tottenham 3, with 25 dead and 59 other casualties, and Wood Green 2, producing 15 killed and 40 people admitted to hospital. East Barnet (12 dead, 59 injured), Friern Barnet (3 injured) and Potters Bar (21 dead, 26 injured) suffered one rocket each, illustrating once again how varied the consequences of individual incidents could be.

Many of the casualties in this part of London occurred on a single disastrous day, Saturday, 20 January, when there were three 'outstanding incidents'. The first came at 11 a.m. at

Potters Bar, accounting for all its 21 dead; the second followed two hours later, with all East Barnet's 12 fatal casualties; and at 8 o'clock that evening one of Tottenham's three V-2s accounted for 23 of its 25 dead. The East Barnet incident, at Calton Road, occurred at 1315 hours, just as one RASC sergeant was leaving his billet in the area on a weekend pass. The sergeant-major in charge promptly assembled all the troops left in camp and led them to the scene:

Many of the houses were just rubble, dust and smoke was choking, the gas pipes were alight. So we were put into sections of about eight persons, a sergeant in charge of each and the job in hand was to reach anyone trapped or injured. . . . My section was given an easy house and we soon made it to the kitchen because of the concrete floor. There was a pram on its side, all buckled, and, looking inside, well, I will not mention the terrible sight I saw but the mother escaped unhurt. We worked more or less non-stop for approximately nine hours, stopping for a cup of tea supplied by the Salvation Army . . . there with their canteen within half an hour. . . . I did have my weekend pass and when I got home a reaction set in and I had a good cry.

A woman then working as a Lyon's waitress, and living in Wood Green, remembers the rockets whenever Shrove Tuesday comes round, as do many other people, for this was a day in 1945 when Kammler's men were particularly busy.* Just as she and her sister were sitting down to their teatime pancakes on 13 February, 'there was a sensation and sound as though of an enormous wind. . . . The window blew in; plaster fell from the ceiling; the front door was blown off and what seemed like tons of soot came down the chimney'. For a man in Hornsey the trigger that touches off his memory is the sight of a horse-drawn cart:

A children's tea-party was in progress and the milkman with his horse and cart was making deliveries. The rocket landed, the party house and three others disappeared and so did the milkman and his cart. His horse was blown over the roof-tops and landed in Frobisher Road, where it lay disfigured and bleeding. The police came and the animal had to be shot there and then to put it out of its misery. The exhaust engine from the rocket was also blown over the roof-tops

---

*For another Shrove Tuesday incident, see Chapter 23, p. 294.

and landed . . . in Green Lanes, Harringay. . . . I remember seeing this wedged between two houses and it remained there for some time, being a curio and sightseeing piece for the neighbourhood.

Enfield, as mentioned earlier, had more incidents than any of its immediate neighbours and they included one 'outstanding' one, at 11 p.m. on 25 March, in Broadfield Square, earning its place in the list less because of the number of dead, 7, than because of the 100 seriously injured. Enfield's other eight rockets fell in an extraordinary variety of places, including a stud farm and the Garden of Remembrance at the crematorium, while a flour mill and a plywood factory were damaged by the blast from a 'border' incident in Chingford. But the main sufferers were private houses and private citizens, including one of Kammler's youngest victims, a baby only three weeks old.

The final part of 'Group 6' – 'sub-group 6D' in ministry records – covered eleven western boroughs, including Brentford and Chiswick, whose famous first rocket also proved to be its last. Acton, Feltham and Southall also had no V-2s, Ealing, Sunbury and Yiewsley one each, but causing no casualties, and Twickenham one which produced two cases of serious injury; Staines, also with one incident, did rather worse: 3 dead, 6 injured. Hayes and Harlington (a single borough) had two rockets, with 21 serious injuries, and Heston and Isleworth the same number of rockets, but with much worse consequences, almost all due to its second incident, which will be described later. Its first, on Thursday, 22 February, when a V-2 exploded in a field between the Bath Road and the Great West Road, both heavily developed with factories and houses, showed how often extensive damage went hand in hand with a light casualty list. One person was seriously injured, 27 were slightly hurt, but 1000 properties were damaged. All told, however, the eleven boroughs escaped lightly, with a death roll of 38 and a seriously injured total of 133, caused by ten V-2s.

The blitz had seen the reappearance on the bombed sites of the unassuming flower Rosebay Willowherb, popularly called 'fireweed'. It seemed for a time that the city's final ordeal might be commemorated by London Rocket (*Sisymbrium irio*), an 18-inch-high plant with a pale yellow flower, which had grown in profusion amid the wood ash of the ruined streets after the Great Fire of 1666. But reports that it had been seen again in 1945 proved false, being dismissed by the Director of the Royal Botanic Gardens at Kew as a 'pleasant legend'.

23

DOWN LAMBETH WAY

When you crossed Lambeth Bridge you realized at once that you were on a battlefield.

Writer in *National Geographic Magazine*, 1945

A gulf far wider than the River Thames separated the postal districts of W1 and SW1, which covered Mayfair and Westminster, from SE1, on the other side of the river, which stretched from the edge of Bermondsey through Southwark into Lambeth. In the central reaches of the capital, during the rocket months, it almost divided two nations. An American visitor described soon afterwards for the *National Geographic Magazine* the contrast one experienced leaving 'one of the well-known West End hotels' in 'one of those quaint turn-around-on-a-dime taxis' and travelling southwards through the almost unscarred West End. 'When you crossed Lambeth Bridge you realized at once that you were on a battlefield. Here it seemed that almost every other row of houses was either smashed or its windows were knocked out.'

Thanks to the popular songwriters, everyone had heard of the Old Kent Road (largely in Southwark), Camberwell and Lambeth Walk, but to the Ministry of Home Security the three boroughs concerned, plus Battersea and Wandsworth, were known less romantically as Group 5. It·was hit by 23 rockets, and – being heavily built-up, mainly with small, insubstantial houses and none-too-solid tenement blocks – these caused a far higher than average number of deaths, 245, and serious injuries, 487. Camberwell did worst, with 9 V-2s, 92 dead and 116 other bad casualties; Wandsworth, with 6 incidents, had 46 dead and 127 injured; Lambeth's 3 rockets caused 44 deaths and 41 cases of injury, Southwark's 3 also killed 44 people, but injured 145, while Battersea was least affected: 2 rockets, 19 dead, 58 seriously injured. No fewer than 8 rockets caused 'outstanding' incidents, 3 in Camberwell, 2 in Southwark and one each in the other three boroughs.

The worst incident in the area, already mentioned as having caused alarm across the river in Chelsea, occurred on 4 January, when a block of flats, the Surrey Lodge dwellings in the Westminster Bridge Road, was destroyed, with the loss of 41 lives; 26 other occupants ended up in hospital. The public baths near Surrey Lodge which Lambeth provided for its bathless citizens had been put out of action by an earlier V-2, but it proved 'possible to utilize the superintendent's office and the committee room for use as the incident officer's post and incident inquiry point respectively', and 'tea for casualties and CD personnel was brewed in the ticket office'.

Camberwell's worst incidents were at Friern Road, on 1 November, with 24 deaths; Varcoe Road, on 6 December, with 20 more dead; and Trafalgar Avenue, on 14 February, with 18 lives lost. In Southwark, 14 people were killed in Great Dover Street at teatime on 14 December and another 30 at around the same time in the Borough High Street, on 22 January. The effects of Battersea's most troublesome rocket, which landed in Usk Road at 4 o'clock on a Saturday afternoon, 27 January 1945, are described later.* Wandsworth's sharpest ordeal occurred at 8.31 on a Sunday morning, 19 November, in Hazelhurst Road, Tooting, where the ruins of the eighteen two-storey houses demolished outright were hurled into the exceptionally large crater, 20 feet deep, and searching this, with Heavy Rescue Parties brought in from Southwark and Battersea, went on all night, the final casualty roll being 33 killed. According to local legend, among those presumed dead was a milkman who vanished, along with his horse and van.

Another major, though not officially 'outstanding', incident, occurred at Poynders Road, Clapham, at 10.45 a.m. on Friday, 26 January. No one was killed, though there were 67 casualties, 25 of them serious, largely handled by the South London Hospital, and the sister in charge, when the chief casualty officer visited her later, was 'very appreciative of the expedition

---

*See Chapter 26, p. 333.

285

with which the casualties arrived and with the first-aid treatment administered'. The rescue men had also rapidly retrieved four trapped casualties:

Two of the women were extricated fairly quickly. . . . The third woman . . . was pinned down by collapsed woodwork across the lower part of one leg. She was in no pain and was concerned more by the fate of her little dog than by her own condition. She was freed by about 1300 hours. The man . . . though not so deep down, was worse off, for he was lying on his face partly covered with live debris and pinned by the legs. However, he was able to breathe without much difficulty and was quite talkative. . . . He was in some pain and Dr L. administered a small dose of morphia which worked wonders. He was finally freed at about 13.45 hours.

Wandsworth's next bad incident, in Nutwell Street, a small road off Tooting High Street, not far from Tooting Broadway and the site of the earlier incident at Hazelhurst Road, was officially described as 'a most distressing one both from the point of view of casualties and damage to property'. There were in fact 8 dead, 41 cases of serious injury and 138 minor casualties, with about 60 hourses wrecked beyond repair, including – the first time, it is believed, this had happened – four of the prefab 'Portal' houses recently put up to cope with the anticipated housing shortage. The rocket scored a direct hit on these houses and 'blew them to fragments'; the Germans clearly agreed with Churchill that post-war reconstruction, which to the public mind the Portal plans typified, was premature. A feature of the incident was the flood of VIPs, not merely the regional 'outdoor' commissioner, Admiral Evans, but his bureaucratic colleague, Sir Ernest Gowers, famous as the author of *Plain Words*, and the Soviet Ambassador, who was perhaps surprised at the casual and goodnatured British way of doing things. With ambulances scarce at first, the injured were ferried to hospital on fire brigade appliances, while when 'a large number of civilians and members of the armed forces "invaded" the scene of the incident . . . the rescue leader . . . successfully persuaded these would-be helpers to leave the job of rescue work to the CD and the NFS'.

South of Lambeth and its equally working-class neighbours

were the leafy, middle-class suburbs of Group 9, which covered a far larger area but escaped with only 12 V-2s. Nine of its 16 boroughs – Wimbledon, Sutton and Cheam, Surbiton, Mitcham, Merton and Morden, Malden and Coombe, Epsom and Ewell, Carshalton, Beddington – had no incidents at all. Barnes had one, which caused no casualties, Esher one, producing 3 serious injuries, Coulsdon one, causing 1 death and 4 serious injuries, Kingston one, with 4 deaths and 39 other casualties. Richmond, scene of the Chrysler factory incident in September, did distinctly worse, with 2 V-2s, causing 10 deaths and 7 cases of major injury; Banstead's 2 incidents, by contrast, caused 3 deaths and 24 patients hospitalized. Croydon, the worst-hit place in the country during the flying-bomb attack, was struck by 4 V-2s, causing 9 deaths, and, like Hampstead, its geographical location made other people's rockets particularly audible there, the high ground behind seeming to act as a reflector. The borough librarian, who later wrote its wartime history, was well aware of what he called its 'disconcerting' situation:

The sound of bombs which fell on adjoining districts could be heard up to a distance of twenty miles. Some passed right over the town: the effect being an instantaneous lightning-like flash of white light. . . . Its explosion on contact was tremendous in open spaces and in enclosed ones was an immense whip-like crash and after this there followed a sound like the rumbling of a heavy train. The sound of the explosion thrown from hill to hill had an enveloping and stunning effect.

Croydon's first, and worst, rocket, descended on a night of rain and darkness – Friday, 20 October 1944 – into a most inappropriately named road, Sunnybank. It proved hard to find the crater, from which rescue work normally proceeded outwards, and, with the telephone wires cut, it was some time before it was fully under way, while the weather made matters worse so that 'Dr S. and his [mobile casualty] unit . . . attended the injured under a ground sheet held over him and his patients to keep out the rain'.

When the whole search was completed it was learned that six people had been killed. . . . 14 seriously injured were taken to hospital and the First Aid Posts gave treatment to 31 with minor hurts. . . . 59

people had to go to the Rest Centre in Suffolk Road. The WVS had immediately set up an enquiry point and a mobile canteen arrived to serve food and drinks. Mobile baths had also done good service.

To those involved matters appeared rather different from what this tidy narrative suggested. Among them was a man living at 70 Sunnybank, who had just got home from the joinery works in West Norwood where he helped to build pontoon bridges, and was sitting quietly with his older daughters, Freda, aged nineteen, and Daphne, fifteen, while upstairs his wife bathed four-year-old Edna:

The wife placed a rice pudding on the table for 'afters'. I sat back in my armchair waiting for the pudding to cool down, listening to the radio and talking to my children and a young friend of Freda's, a lad of about eighteen known as Fred, a neighbour of ours. . . . Without any warning or sound I blacked out. When I partly gathered myself up I found the coal fire was spread all over the floor. . . . I was down on my knees picking up live coal and throwing it back in the fireplace. I felt no pain and still heard nothing. My eldest girl Freda and her friend had gone. It seemed a long time, then I heard the young man next door put his head in the opening where the window was and ask if we were all right. I remember scrambling through brick rubble and woodwork in the dark and finding my other girl, Daphne, who was also dazed and cut about the head. . . . After looking at the damage across the road, still not knowing what had happened, I began to realize this was serious. At this point I came across a Mr S. wandering about. He lived close by and had just said goodnight to a young woman who was at the front door of one of the Victorian houses, which had completely gone.

Then I began to hear. The first thing I heard was Mr S. saying 'Where's my bloody hat?' I had never heard him swear before. . . . Then we heard screaming. In the confusion I managed to hear my wife who was upstairs in the bathroom with the baby, Edna. Everything was thrown up the stairs, banisters, smashed front door and brick rubble. I scrambled up to the wife who was now in a pretty bad state. . . . Her nerves were completely shattered. . . . To get my wife downstairs was like mountain climbing. There was nothing to hold on to, the stairs were covered in bricks and rubbish. We made our way, climbing over heaps of debris, to Mr W.'s house, that was about 200 yards past the damage

At such a moment it was hard to take in what had happened,

but, as soon as one had done so, there always seemed urgent
tasks to be done:

After getting my wife and baby and Daphne settled with a 'cuppa' I
had to go back to find her false teeth. On the way back I met a young
lad, Brian, who worked with me. . . . We went through my house
and started to look for a needle in a haystack – that was Brian's
description. But, going outside of the back door, which was now
missing [we found] the teeth had fallen straight down by the side of
the wall, as if they had been put there. I went up and down the road
several times, to get insurance papers, ration books and the wife's
handbag.

By now the place was lit up with floodlights and swarmed with
police and other helpers. I discovered what we thought was some old
bedding was a young lady and Ken's sister had been standing by,
until someone came to the rescue. I was still unable to think clearly
but managed to keep on my feet. Then a warden told me to get going
and get cleaned up. . . . We were taken from Mr W.'s home to
Portland Road School. By the time we got to the school everybody
that was mobile was nicely cleaned up. This was about 10.30. . . .
The glass was taken out of my head and my hand bandaged. We were
taken to South Norwood Church at South Norwood Hill for the night.

Meanwhile this informant's eldest daughter, Freda, had
become separated from her father, in the confusing way that
often happened when a rocket had fallen:

There was suddenly without warning a tremendous thud, when we
were plunged into darkness and things began flying through the air
and vibrating. . . . When we came to our senses I remember getting
through the door of the sitting room, out into the hall, where we
were stepping over pieces of wood from the stair rails and doors and
bits of window frame. I can recall putting my head on the stair
banister that remained and having a good howl; and an air-raid
warden who appeared on the scene and comforted me. Fred and I
then picked our way through the rubble in the street, which was quite
deep, and made our way round to his home. . . . His folk were OK
but someone spotted that our hands were bleeding and we were
advised to go to the first-aid post at Portland Road School. . . . We
were seen by doctors and nurses, who cut away our hair and picked
out pieces of glass from our wounds, treated them and then bandaged
us, Fred having, I believe, five stitches in his head. . . . I then
rejoined [the rest of the family] and we spent the night at the rest
centre off Norwood High Street, which wasn't very comfortable,

owing to shock, and clothes being full of grit, plus [my] head, which had just been washed at the time of the rocket and was now full of plaster. I remember leaving the rest centre at first light and making our way back to the shattered home, which was minus tiles, windows and doors. We arrived back at Sunnybank about 5 a.m. to find faithful old Fred, bandaged head and all, standing guard outside what remained of our home.

Much was made in all the official reports of how efficiently the post-raid services operated. Whether they always functioned so smoothly may be doubted, if the experience of one woman's husband, summoned back, as mentioned earlier*, from his army unit, are any guide:

I arrived at South Norwood about 11 a.m. . . . . The road was blocked and guarded by police and troops and at first they barred my way but I soon explained that I lived there. . . . My house was totally demolished. I was dazed and saw no one I knew to find out anything as to what had happened. There was . . . a senior 'brass hat' with a red band standing in the road near my place, and there was I saluting him, with all this on my mind. Shortly afterwards I espied a little girl, about five years old, who had lived next door and she informed me that my wife and child had survived and had been taken to a place of shelter at a local church, although she did not know which one. I later found this was a church in Suffolk Road, South Norwood, and so I hurried there . . . but I could not see my family. A steward told me they had been taken to Croydon Hospital, probably the Mayday Hospital, so I hurried there, but they had no knowledge of my wife or child. They suggested I try the Croydon General, so I went there and, to my relief, found my wife and son . . . bandaged round his head. My wife had a bad cut down her leg and a cut on the head. We were brought out by ambulance and proceeded to my wife's parents at Penge, pending making arrangements where to go.

By Croydon's next V-2, on 29 December, the public were at least allowed to know how their homes were being devastated. This, in the words of the local historian quoted earlier, 'demolished a 'pretty, small house . . . in an enclave in the chalk cliffs on the north side of Croham Valley Road', a 'secluded and apparently protected spot', but all the occupants were killed. Croydon's third V-2, on the night of 5 January

---

*See Chapter 15, p. 195.

1945, infuriated local golfers, introducing a new and unwelcome hazard to Addington Golf Course, as a Civil Defence worker on duty that night remembers:

The secretary of the golf club rang to say that some sheep were running loose across some of his grass and added, almost as an afterthought, that his windows were broken too. There had been some people out on the course and we went looking for them. . . . The shepherd was lost and so far we hadn't found the crater. When we did, it was forty feet across and very deep. Happily no one was seriously hurst, although the shepherd had been taken to hospital with a suspected broken arm.

Croydon's last rocket, on 26 January 1945, fell harmlessly on open ground in a park. It was only its fourth but they had seemed far, far more numerous; indeed, a then seventeen-year-old schoolboy, who kept a detailed diary of all the explosions he heard, recorded 204 between 12 September 1944 and 27 March 1945.

East during the V-2 period meant increased danger, and the south-eastern suburbs of Group 8, which lay between Croydon and the Thames, had to endure 76 rockets, more than six times as many as the neighbouring group, as were the total of dead, 152, and seriously injured, 558. Worst hit in terms of incidents, though not of deaths, were Erith and the borough of Chislehurst and Sidcup, with 17 V-2s each, which left 36 dead and 137 other serious casualties in Erith, 30 dead and 103 others in Chislehurst. Orpington, with 14 incidents, escaped with 9 dead but had 116 injured, Bexley, with 12 rockets, had the worst death toll, 39, with 78 injured, not, however, so different from that of Bromley (6 V-2s, 31 dead and 109 injured), though in Beckenham 5 rockets killed only 6 people and injured only 11, and in Crayford another 5 claimed only 1 fatal casualty and 4 others. Penge, hard-hit by the flying-bombs, this time escaped altogether.

In spite of the more or less continuous bombardment, the area reported only one 'outstanding' incident, in Southborough Lane, Bromley at 9.15 on a Sunday evening when the Crooked Billet public house (later rebuilt as The Beckets) was destroyed as already described.* It was not the only 'pub' to suffer: the

*See Chapter 15, p. 204.

George, Hayes, in the same borough, and the White Horse Inn at Chislehurst were both damaged within four hours on 9 February 1945, and the Bickley Arms, Chislehurst, joined the melancholy list on 26 March, the last pub in England to receive the Germans' attentions. Churchgoers suffered with drinkers. Kammler's men also struck the Baptist Chapel in Chislehurst; Christ Church, Chislehurst; and St John's, Eden Park, Beckenham, the vicar of which was injured for the second time, though his daughter, asleep in a pram by the badly cracked kitchen wall, never even woke up.

Many other public buildings were also affected. Besides thousands of houses and shops of every kind, a fire station (in Orpington) also suffered, as did railways stations (at St Mary Cray, near Orpington, and Chislehurst), a cinema (the Commodore, Orpington), a hospital (Queen Mary, Sidcup), a working-men's club (Chislehurst), a golf club house (Sundridge Park, Bromley), and several schools, most notably Bickley Hall, Chislehurst, damaged by the penultimate rocket in the area, at 3.20 p.m. on Monday 26 March. Here a major disaster was narrowly avoided, for the boys were 'lining up . . . before proceeding to the gymnasium to watch a boxing match', and one was 'carried away to be given treatment for a gash in the head. . . . The boxing match was cancelled', but the boys instead hurried on to the playing field to hunt for rocket fragments.

Like much of outer London, 'metropolitan' Kent contained a great deal of open space. In January, for example, the Midland Bank sportsground in Beckenham harmlessly absorbed one rocket, while a week later another, on a nearby cricket field, killed no one. But any explosion could have tragic consequences, and the owner of a horticultural nursery which bore the brunt of one V-2's impact, and his son, were both killed.

Here, too, as in comparable areas to the north of London, there were a surprising number of small factories and other 'military objectives'. One of the last V-2s to land caused what could fairly be called an 'industrial incident', as this account by the area's wartime historian makes clear:

On 20 March, at breakfast time, the junction of Rectory Lane, Sidcup

292

Hill and Craybrooke Road was busy with workers arriving at local factories. Like a thunderbolt hurled by an angry god a rocket landed at this moment outside a printing works, killing seven people at the intersection and two others in Sidcup High Street. 80 others were reported injured. A dozen fires broke out in the ruins of houses, a dairy and T. Knight's builders' yard, while blast damage spread to printing works, municipal offices and shop and houses in the High Street, Old Forge Way, Sidcup Hill, etc.

There were lighter moments. One local Civil Defence worker who heard a strange voice in damaged premises he was searching in Mottingham village, eventually uncovered a grey parrot, safe in its cage, repeating angrily a single, most appropriate, line, 'This is a hell of a storm, mate!' The same man, based in Chislehurst, failed, however, to persuade an old lady to give up the bottle of whisky she was clutching and it was still with her when she reached the rest centre in the church hall. 'Later that night the vicar rang me up and said the lady would not go to bed unless I was there to tuck her up. I went with the greatest of pleasure and kissed her goodnight.'

As mentioned earlier, Bexley suffered more fatal casualties than any of its neighbours, and Welling, on its London side, seemed one of those small districts destined to attract rockets. A woman then serving as an ARP telephonist in the area remembers the arrival of the very first, while they were still a secret:

My job was to fill in a form, taking the details from the warden in whose area the bomb had dropped. . . . When I answered the telephone I knew immediately something was very different this time. The warden appeared to be suffering from shock. When we came to the question, 'How large do you estimate the bomb?' he said, 'The biggest yet, no idea how large.' To the question, 'How many houses destroyed or badly damaged?' his answer was 'Thirty!' I thought I had not heard correctly and he became very abusive at my doubts.

By February the V-2 was no longer a mystery, as the same woman, who had joined the ATS and was stationed in rocket-free Edinburgh, discovered:

My father wrote to me in the most alarming manner about the rockets. He reported that Welling and Bexleyheath hardly existed any-more. They had no food, as deliveries had been disrupted. He couldn't stand it any longer; he was obviously on the verge of a nervous breakdown. . . . I was very worried. I spoke to the Catholic padre. He very kindly arranged for a couple of nuns to visit my parents to find out what was wrong. That did the trick. The sight of the two Catholic nuns on our established low church doorstep was sufficient for both my parents to completely forget the war and V-2s. I then received a letter of fury and anxiety from them that I was perhaps embracing the Roman faith. To this day [1976] they remember the nuns' visit and have entirely forgotten the V-2s.

Also in Welling, was a girl then aged twelve, one of the occupants of what was 'known locally by us children as the "half-sandwich house" because the semidetached built on to ours had to be pulled down by the demolition squad'. Now the V-2s were to take a final bite at the sandwich on that rocket-plagued day, Shrove Tuesday, 13 February 1945:

We had saved up our rations and were looking forward to a rare meal of pancakes, but . . . on open land about a hundred yards from our houses an unoccupied air-raid shelter received a direct hit from a rocket at about 7.30 p.m. We had absolutely no warning of its arrival. . . . My sister was blown from one side of the room to the other but received very small injuries, as did the rest of the family. . . . Damage from the blast was colossal. I distinctly remember our back door being a mass of tiny wood splinters. The rescue squad was amazed to get us out alive. . . . There was no panic. The fireman were quickly on the scene to put out the blaze. People were once again handing out blankets and cups of tea. Our warden was amusing the frightened children by taking off his tin helmet, lifting it up to the skies and reassuring us he would 'catch the next one'. . . . The rocket did not seem to worry people for long and I remember the lady who used to come around collecting pennies for our Victory Party joking about the 'doodlebug delights' and 'rocket cakes' we would all be consuming once the war was over.

24

AT THE ARSENAL

Once again it was my shift that was elected.
Craftsman recalling V-2 at Woolwich Arsenal, 1944

The Germans' avowed intention in using the V-2 was to harm morale; any military damage they did was a bonus. But the London area contained so many factories and docks, warehouses and railway lines that some, under a continuous, indiscriminate bombardment, were almost bound to be hit. When the Ministry of Aircraft Production had made plans to move particularly important plants away from London it had seemed to other departments to be displaying excessive caution, but events soon endorsed its foresight. 'During the critical period of the use by the enemy of V-1 missiles and V-2 rockets', wrote the director of the ministry's Emergency Services Organization, 'as many as 50 factories were put out of action in one day in the London area.' Of about 30,000 factories engaged on essential work of some kind no fewer than 919 were affected by rockets, several often being blasted in the same explosion. War production in Greater London was never seriously threatened for the V-2s caused nothing like the interruption of the V-1s, which had constantly driven workers to take shelter. None the less as the winter wore on the number of V-2 incidents affecting output reached serious proportions. In September there were 8; in October 22; in November and December together 209; in January and February 436; in March 224.

Just how successful even an imprecisely aimed rocket could be was made clear by the experience of the most famous centre of ordnance manufacture in the country, Woolwich Arsenal, spread along the south bank of the Thames near the Germans' suspected aiming point on its north side. The borough of Woolwich was hit by 33 rockets, the second highest total in the country, and the number of V-2s landing there left one craftsman, a skilled fitter in the Heavy Gun Shop, convinced that 'it could only be a matter of time before the Arsenal suffered, for many rockets were dead in line, but a trifle short'. On the evening of Monday 27 November 1944 his forebodings proved justified:

Once again it was my shift that was elected [as by the flying-bombs]. The shifts had just changed over, days to nights, and this Monday started out as any normal shift at the time. I was working on the breech end of a 15-in in the lapping machine in 2 Bay. Tom M. was measuring the bore sizes at the muzzle. . . . Arthur R. had pulled strings to stay on nights for a while, and so was with us this shift, everything as normal. At our cocoa break – we had run out of tea until the next ration was due – Don S. and I were pulling each other's legs, bench versus the [gun] bore gang. As one of our [i.e. the gun gang's] manifold advantages I mentioned that if anything happened I would have a shelter handy, while he would find his bench no cover at all. I have regretted that joke ever since, for in half an hour, at 10.30, that is just about what did happen. . . .

I did not see or hear the actual impact, all I know is that the lights went out and I was blown over, guessed what had happened and rolled underneath the gun and watched a large section of roof or wall plating float past the window. Being in a natural shelter with the gun over me and alongside a heavy borer to take the blast I was not even deafened completely, while Ted M. at the muzzle was. . . . It was not possible to see in the shop until the dust and debris had settled but I went out through the door space to see where it had dropped. . . . Outside was a shambles with the tender shop partly demolished . . . the book-keeper's office blasted and the South Mill seeming to end at 4 Bay, with fires burning where 7 Bay ought to be. . . .

In spite of my twenty years' service in the shop I could not place myself, everything being covered by a mass of debris some three feet thick. . . . I heard a cry for help and making my way to it found that old Charlie the night-shift storeman was trapped between his counter and the drawing rack which was blazing and as I started to lift him clear Wally K. . . . from the press in 6 Bay came round and together we got him out. . . .

Charles . . . was the only survivor from 7 and 8 Bays. Don was dead under his bench, which was blazing matchwood, the unfortunate youngster [who worked with him] dead at his slab and [an inspector] under the gantry, or where it had been. . . . The blast had given him a clown's face, jet black except for a vivid red pulped nose. In a very short time mobile searchlight from the army and proper rescue teams turned up and a search seemed to indicate that all the casualties had been cleared, but a roll call was ordered. . . . There was a trifle of difficulty over this owing to the scattering of staff on various tasks . . . and . . . one gentleman . . . failed to answer his name at the roll call and we searched around in the wreck for some time before he was found standing by the searchlight watching us. . . . We were not the best pleased with him when we found that there was now no transport home and we would have to stay with the wreck till morning. Some bedded down in the first-aid posts, but I invited Pat C. and Harry N. to be my guests at my Home Guard armoury, where we spent what was left of the night. Passing through the [gun] carriage [area] we noticed the rocket on the scoreboard [marking the location of local incidents] as '10.30. Too bloody close', which was our sentiment exactly.

In spite of the damage done, this man recorded, 'we only had 6 killed and 17 or so injured out of a shift of about 90' with 'no machine . . . rendered incapable of repair', and it was not long before its effects had been overcome:

All hands turned to salvaging and clearing up and the women were sent to grease and oil equipment as it was brought to them. . . . Regardless of minor irritations the shop worked with a will to get . . . in production again as quickly as possible, partly as a matter of pride and partly to stop any transfer of the shop [elsewhere]. We did start production going in two and a half days after the blow-up. Mind you, the fact that we were all on flat rate until the work would start flowing again and could go back into piecework helped.

Industrial incidents, like domestic ones, left a legacy of losses to be made good, and not everyone was too scrupulous in valuing their property:

Some of the fitters whose tool kit was reputed to have consisted of a five-eighths Whitworth spanner put in claims for replacement kits that ran into hundreds of pounds. . . . [One man] claimed all salvaged private tools that were not marked as his private property and this was . . . difficult to disprove as some of the owners were dead and one tool from the same maker looks very like another. . . . Much the same thing happened in the women's changing rooms which . . . seemed to have contained everything from the bottom drawer to ball gowns.

Woolwich Arsenal was to be hit by two more V-2s, one 'on the extreme end of the Iron Pier from which the heavy guns were loaded', the next 'on the Heavy Gun gantry . . . an example of how limited damage could cause a great deal of delay', for it made it impossible to bring some 16-inch guns 'into the shop for their fitting' until one of the gantry supports had been replaced. These three rockets, with another which 'fell just short in St Nicholas's churchyard', this observer considered 'a very creditable group', but it was their incidental, rather than their direct, effect which damaged morale and output most, for a windowless tarpaulin-roofed workshop was just as uncomfortable as a damaged house:

After the excitement and high hopes of the autumn, the bogging down of the armies in Holland was depressing and . . . when the really cold weather set in . . . we were in trouble. With no doors, windows, [no] heating and not very much wall it was a case of do what you could do for yourself. This took the shape of running up shacks and lean-tos in the shop from packing cases . . . sometimes for single persons but more often for small groups. I shared one . . . that we built beside the big rifler [i.e. rifling machine for gun barrels] under the shadow of the gantry. Quite a substantial erection from a lease-lend packing case it gave us three sides, a roof and a floor and we used to say that it was the most useful thing that we had received from America.

The struggle to keep warm added to the rivalry between different groups and to the often pointed gossip which was a feature of life at the Arsenal:

When the cold snowy weather set in with a vengeance there was a rush for braziers, buckets or anything that would hold a fire and these were at a premium, and so was fuel. A supply of coke was dumped outside at intervals to be scrambled for and the borers again lost popularity by having their mates on the lookout for the lorry and cornering far more than they were entitled to. One was found to have five dustbins of coke hoarded for his private fire when there was not a bucketful of fuel in the rest of the shop. Equally unpopular was the office staff in 2 Bay, who were fitted out with a round cast-iron stove and kept a temperature of 70° in there when the rest of the shop was well below freezing. . . . At the worst period there was a rum ration issued, but reputedly it was so generous that one foreman drank the lot without realizing that it should have been shared out between a hundred men.

At the Arsenal

The Germans were clearly never aware that they had hit Woolwich Arsenal, and also never discovered that they had, by a remarkable piece of luck, scored a direct hit on what was classed officially as 'A Very Important Key Point', the 'bascule bridge', a swing bridge operated by a weight at one end of it, at Silvertown, North Woolwich, just across the river. A woman from Leytonstone, working in the offices of the shipbuilding firm Harland and Wolff close by that Saturday morning – it was 11.15 a.m. on 10 February 1945 – witnessed the incident, the outstanding 'military' success of the whole bombardment:

A blinding flash, and then all the windows, which were enormous and almost covered the walls, came in. Fortunately I was sitting with the windows on my left-hand side, one floor up, so glass missed me but those people who were facing the windows were badly cut. The other side of the building seemed to catch more of the blast. One of my friends had a fractured skull where the window frame came in as well as the glass. . . . We all filed out into the space between the offices and works, where those that were injured were taken to the Seamen's Hospital, at Custom House. . . . We, the uninjured, went back to our offices and tried to clear up, but were sent home.

Rapidly on the scene was the chief superintendent of police for 'K' Division, quoted earlier, whose diary recorded what followed:

The bridge carried the road between East Ham and North Woolwich . . . forming the lock gate linking the Royal group of docks with the River Thames. The bridge and lock were completely destroyed, barring exit from docks to river. . . . The Royal docks were being extensively used for shipping supplies of all kinds to the British forces moving towards the Rhine. A large number of vessels . . . were imprisoned. Action was swift and drastic. The Royal Engineers took charge. The shattered bridge and lock were cut away and, within a few days, temporary structures replaced the damage and the docks were reopened to traffic.

Power supplies were also a legitimate target and in the same area the V-2s scored a number of hits that threatened, and sometimes interrupted, supplies. A little ironically, in view of the earlier 'cover story' about exploding gas mains, several gasworks were hit in this riverside area, including, as mentioned earlier, the one at Beckton covering 400 acres and

299

said to be the largest in Europe. Other strikes occurred on the docks themselves, and the Ministry of Home Security drew attention in its report for 21–28 February 1945 to further serious damage to warehouses in Silvertown, the area of West Ham just up-river from North Woolwich, which had now been hit by seven rockets. Electric power stations were also affected. Another rocket, a member of the local electricity supply company remembers, 'scored a hit on the pulverised-fuel-fired boiler house' at Barking which 'seriously affected the use of steam raising plant for many months', though the public supply of current was not impaired. The diary of the chief superintendent for 'K' Division chronicled those events that concerned his area. It was an alarming list:

29 October	One V-2 at Beckton Gas Works.
30 October	Out, noon, to V-2s at Royal Victoria Dock and Earlham Grove, West Ham.
31 October	Afternoon, to V-2 incident at Royal Victoria Dock, north side.
12 November	One V-2, evening, at Bromley Gas Works, West Ham.
19 January	At 11 p.m. one V-2 at Town Quay, Barking.
7 February	One V-2 at railway sidings, Barking Marshes.
10 February	At 11.15 a.m. a V-2 scored a direct hit on the Bascule Bridge, Woolwich.
11 February	Three V-2s. One on Glyco Works, West Ham.
26 February	Two V-2 rockets at night. One at West Ham, direct hit on Northern Outfall Sewer.
27 February	One V-2, morning, at Royal Albert Dock.
17 March	One V-2 10.30 p.m. at Rippleway sidings, Barking.

The enemy's transport system could also, under the rules of war, fairly be attacked, and in one respect the rockets were more troublesome even than their predecessors, for the craters they produced tore up the tramways on which a large part of the poorer areas of east and south-east London still largely relied. As early as November 1944, the board's historian recorded, 'a track was cut by a crater measuring 40 ft by 20 ft', and similar incidents followed in Lambeth, Wood Green and Southwark, where 'sewer damage held up repair work for several weeks'. West Ham was the only tram 'garage' hit, but the trolley buses, still a novelty, and the famous red petrol-driven buses, suffered far more, mainly while being serviced. Forest Gate depot in Hendon was badly damaged twice in twenty-four hours, the first explosion, just after midnight, 'shattering the roof glasses, damaging 32 buses and depriving the garage of water, gas, electricity and the telephone'. Next morning, however, every bus left on time 'although some ran without windows'. Another V-2 the following day damaged the roof again and blew the windows out of three more buses.

Some parts of the transport network seemed marked out for misfortune. Athol Street, close to the docks in Poplar, was already notorious among those based there as London Transport's 'most-bombed garage', a reputation the V-2s helped to maintain, for one blew out the windows of twenty-five buses, at 6 a.m. on a Saturday, though the long-suffering staff got them all away on time. Next day, frustratingly, an airburst destroyed all the repairs so far carried out and still further damaged the roof, while two days later four pieces of yet another rocket plunged into it. Other garages, as far apart as Plumstead, in Woolwich, Swanley, in Kent, and Epping, in Essex, also had to replace damaged roofs and shattered doors and windows. Incidents affecting buses while on the road were rare, though there was one very serious one, at West Ham on 13 January, when two trolley buses were wrecked and 15 people killed, with another 35 injured. All told, 440 trams, buses or trolley buses needed minor repair, 56 being 'hospitalized' to the board's works at Chiswick for 'major surgery'.

Since there was no warning to make possible the closing of the flood gates protecting the underground network, the tubes suffered much less interruption than they had done from the flying-bombs, although the above-ground section was affected on several occasions and four stations were damaged, at Aldersgate (now Barbican in the City), Hounslow West, West Hampstead, and Whitechapel, though there was no serious interruption to the services.

On the main-line railways travelling conditions actually improved during the winter of 1944. In October previous cuts in services were restored, improved lighting was introduced on both trains and stations and nameplates identifying stations were brought back, and, though all told no fewer than 358 V-2s affected the railways to some extent, only 28 scored direct hits on railway property. The Southern Railway came off worst, with 16 rockets on or near its lines or premises. On 1 November two trains were damaged en route to London Bridge and on the following night a rocket demolished the embankment at Hampton Court, interrupting normal service for two days. On 5 November, the Southern's historian recorded, 'the bridge carrying the up main local and South London lines over Southwark Park Road, Bermondsey, was hit and collapsed in the roadway', and it took ten days to get the trains running to time again. The Deptford rocket later that month also damaged the station and signal boxes, and the dead included two women carriage-cleaners who had gone to Woolworths for their lunch. At Folkestone Gardens, Deptford, in March, another Southern railwayman was killed and three more died later that day in an incident near Charlton Junction. All told, the Southern's V-1s and V-2s – the casualties from both were bracketed together – killed 63 people on railway property, including some passengers; another 767 were injured.

The LMS – London, Midland and Scottish Railway – reported only six V-2 incidents, though two caused precisely the type of cumulative trouble the Allies had tried to inflict on the French railway system before D-Day. One rocket damaged 155 coaches and freight wagons at Tilbury, while another soon afterwards knocked out, though only temporarily, the wagon and locomotive workshops at Bow, where they should have been repaired. The Great Western Railway, serving the 'safe' side of London, was barely troubled by the V-2s, but they gave to the London and North-Eastern Railway, always notorious for unpunctuality, a topical excuse for its poor timekeeping. With its lines running through the eastern suburbs and East Anglia, the LNER was perpetually plagued by rockets, from November 1944, when one landed in Hornsey goods yard, to late March, when there was a major disaster, to be described later, near Farringdon Street Station. As the company's historian wryly remarked, 'the symbol V-2 had long been familiar to the LNER as denoting a certain type of locomotive. From September 1944 until March 1945 it became far too familiar in another sense.'

How varied the repercussions of a single explosion could be was well illustrated by the rocket which hit the 'High Meads paint shop, next to the loop line from Victoria Park', in Bethnal Green. As 'the paint shop was demolished and . . . telephone wires, signal wires and point rodding went to blazes', the nearest signalman, very rightly, 'at once threw all his signals to danger', halting traffic over a wide area:

He next telephoned Control [at Stratford] and then went out to inspect the damage. At times he found himself wading through water up to his knees, for water mains and drains had been shattered and heavy rain had recently fallen.

Within a short space of time the engineers came to put things straight. The track was relaid, the point rodding was repaired and new telephone and signal wires were run. No unnecessary time was wasted in clearing up the mess. In one place a carriage had been thrown right over so that it lay upside down, but it was found to be clear of the line. It was left where it was and the new signal wires were run in at one window, through the compartment and out at the other window. Within two hours trains were running once more over the line.

Dedicated railwaymen could almost forgive the Germans for the harm done by the V-2s, for one unforeseen consequence of their campaign – the reopening of the stretch of line known affectionately as 'the Khyber Pass', a deep cutting just north of Wood Green, on the local line to Enfield, which had for a time been sealed off after being blocked by a large bomb during the blitz. Now this obscure mile or so of track was to achieve railway immortality, after a V-2 had blocked the main line to the north, just south of Wood Green, at 3.30 a.m., on Friday, 12 January 1945. The assistant yard master from King's Cross, having nobly set out into the 'cold wind and drizzle' of that bleak winter night to investigate, returned with the gloomy news that only one line of the usual eight could be used. The answer came in a flash of inspiration: reopen the long-abandoned line around Enfield. 'The Flying Scotsman', recorded the LNER's historian reverently, 'was the first down train to honour the Khyber Pass by its presence', and by 7.10 p.m. that day the 'control sheet' at Kings Cross was able to record a major triumph:

7.10 p.m.   Normal working resumed with 5.35 p.m. Kings Cross
             to Baldock

The last V-2 to inflict major industrial damage landed not on the hard-pressed eastern side of London but ten miles due west of Whitehall on the Great West Road, a major highway between large modern factories and rows of archetypal 'thirties' houses only recently completed. It landed at 9.39 a.m. on Wednesday, 21 March 1945, scoring a direct hit on the great Packard factory, 'where', the local chief warden later wrote, '100 men were assembling marine engines. The building was completely wrecked and damage was caused to several other buildings nearby, including Pyrene's'. In fact no fewer than 13 factories were affected, of which 11 were classed as 'key points', 'probably the largest number', commented the official compiling that week's Home Office report on the rocket attacks, 'during the war'.

In Hounslow, two miles away, the impact rattled the windows of a junior school: class enjoying a games lesson in the playground, one of them (then a boy aged ten) remembers, displayed a duly Drake-like spirit:

Everyone suddenly stood still and all was quiet for about five seconds. In the distance we could see the smoke rising and the teacher said that it looked like another rocket, then we carried on with our game.

A sixteen-year-old draughtsman in the offices of the London Aeroplane Company which also fronted the Great West Road, was similarly brought up short:

We were about to have a mid-morning cup of tea when there was a tremendous explosion; the ground shook, windows shattered, dust flew, even tracing paper was wrenched from beneath the pins holding it to our drawing boards.

The Chief Warden for the area later described what followed:

The first report was soon received at the report and control centre and rescue parties and ambulances, mobile first-aid units and wardens [were] ordered to the scene. . . . Six wardens were on duty at. . . . St Mary's Crescent, Osterley, in charge of Post Warden Bert M. They were soon on the spot and Post Warden M. started to organize a reconnaissance and set up a control organization. Fire broke out almost at once and the NFS were there in less than no time. The mobile control vehicle kept at the Bridge Road depot was ordered to the scene and District Warden J.W.H., who . . . had had much experience, was instructed to take charge of operations. He set up his control HQ in the control vehicle on the spot and telephone communications were established.

Within two hours hundreds of people were at work in the ruins of the Packard and Pyrene factories, some of them from neighbouring firms like Firestone Tyres or Sperry's, the instrument manufacturers, some, like the WVS, who arrived in a mobile caravan-style inquiry point, from adjoining boroughs like Brentford. Within two hours 40 ARP vehicles were in attendance and 25 NFS fire engines and tenders, with so many ambulances and cars available that 'many slightly injured who could have been attended to on the spot' were 'rushed off to West Middlesex Hospital', now facing its largest influx of emergencies since the very first V-2. No one concerned could have known that this would be the last major incident in West London, but it was by any test an impressive display, a model of incident management. The Great West Road, briefly blocked, was rapidly cleared for single-lane traffic, a 'director of Gillette's', less badly affected than some other firms, 'came over and invited the ARP workers to go across to their canteen for refreshments' and the homeless and bereaved gained what comfort they could from a visit by Herbert Morrison's deputy, Ellen Wilkinson, and – a sure sign of a major incident – from the King and Queen.

21 March was the first day of spring, and felt like it. The sun shone, all the more welcome after such a wretched winter, and there seemed at long last, the smell of final victory in the air. This made the Great West Road massacre seem all the harder to bear, as one Pyrene office worker tried to convey in a pamphlet sold in aid of the firm's distress fund:

Outside, above us, the skies are so bright and peaceful. . . . [It] is just one of the many of the 2,000 days that have elapsed since . . . Germany invaded Poland. . . . The hour is approaching 10 a.m. . . . In our department we are thinking the tea girl must be on her way. . . .
The earth is opening upon us, a blinding flash accompanied by a terrifying explosion. . . . 'Get down!' Stunned, staggered, but still semi-conscious, we fall to our knees, a bloody mess. . . . A girl's scream echoes through the office above the falling debris. . . . We rise from our knees, stricken and dazed, bloody and bleeding, wondered what has happened. . . . Stunned, we endeavour to tread

over the wreckage that was once the Planning Department. . . . I look at young Margie B . . . her face is covered in rich red blood. It must be a horrible dream. . . . As we go further and out into the passage I see a bloody trail and realize this tale is now a terrible reality. We make our way to the First Aid Station and come face to face, unrecognizable . . . with many more more casualties.

All told, 32 people were killed outright or died later and 500 others were injured, 100 of them badly; 662 houses were damaged, as well as the 13 factories already mentioned. The Pyrene factory was out of action for a week, the longest period of lost production of any of the affected companies, though it was Packard's, where a major fire broke out, whose employees suffered most. Among the victims was one man who had consoled his wife, when they heard V-2s exploding in the distance, 'If one comes here you won't know anything about it. . .''. That', she now reflects, 'is what happened to him.' When his body was at last found, two days later, it was burnt beyond recognition, but having contracted frostbite thirty years before when serving in the Dardanelles he still wore 'a pad of cotton wool in his socks', and this homely precaution now enabled him to be identified. But the censorship deprived her, like the relations of other rocket vitims, of seeing a fitting account of his death in the local press. 'They didn't', his wife remembers, 'say where, just that he died of enemy action.'

25

WHAT CAN'T BE CURED

What can't be cured must be endured.

The Prime Minister to the Ministry of Home Security,
1 March 1945

During the winter of 1944–45, the British government's counter-measures did have some effect, for in November at least two consignments of missiles had to be returned to Nordhausen after being damaged in transit by 'machine-gun fire'. Dornberger's main difficulties, however, came from the Russians. Having earlier been driven out of Blizna by the Red Army, by the end of the year the development team's fall-back position at Heidekraut had also become endangered by the Russian advance, as Dornberger observed:

At the end of December I was paying the last of many visits to *Heidekraut*. I had discussed evacuation with the officer commanding the Training and Experimental Unit. . . . He was to go first to the woods south of Wolgast. His target area would then be selected somewhere in the broad, uninhabited region of the Tuchel moors. . . . It was then afternoon and the last rocket was to be launched after dark. The sky had cleared. Stars shone brightly as the chilly winter dusk came on. It was nearly eleven before the glow of the ignition flame reddened the sky. The rocket began its journey. The gas jet, which alone was visible, described its dazzling arc. I watched from the running-board of a carriage of our special train at the little station of Lindenbusch, deep in the great Tuchel forest. The 'all-burnt' came at the appointed time. Through my binoculars I could see clearly against the dark sky the small, bright point of light of the white-hot graphite vanes. . . . I could still see the dim point of light after two minutes, three minutes, four minutes. . . . Not until 4 minutes and 32 seconds had passed did it disappear into the haze of the earth's atmosphere. . . . We [had] learned from reports in neutral

307

newspapers that in England the rocket had been seen at the end of its flight, as a red-hot sphere. . . . I had found the explanation.

This proved to be the very last A-4 fired for research or practice purposes:

In the middle of January 1945 *Heidekraut* had to be evacuated. In deep snow the long-range rocket Training and Experimental Unit, with all its vehicles and equipment, moved to the Wolgast woods, which they left in the middle of February without having managed to launch a single rocket. Their last move was to the neighbourhood of Rethen on the Weser, where their aim ran north along the coast of Schleswig-Holstein. But even here no more rockets were launched. Practice shots by the troops with the A-4 were finally abolished.

Although Dornberger continued to resent Kammler's insistence on giving priority to the operational formations at the expense of the research echelon, the proportion of failures was remarkably small. In December 12.3 per cent of rockets were rejected on final inspection and a further 7 per cent, which had been passed, misfired. In January, with the pressure on to fire every possible projectile, Group North, with London as its target, had 16.5 per cent of A-4s rejected and 12.2 per cent misfired; in February the figures were 5 per cent and 10.4 per cent, still within the acceptable limits, and 85 per cent of rockets produced were being launched at London.

The British government, at the receiving end of both the bombardment and public discontent, were encountering far worse technical problems. Hopes of being able to provide even a brief public warning were fast fading. A report on 25 September 1944, based on the data gathered by the radar and sound and visual observation teams, had confirmed that on three occasions in the past five days no warning would have been given at all, while only one warning in sixteen from these areas would have been followed by an incident in London and only one in six elsewhere, the rest being false alarms. Nor, it was clear, was it going to be possible to disrupt the rocket's guidance system. The Crossbow Committee's seventeenth report on 22 November 1944, covering the period from 1 September to 20 November – i.e. the opening of the attack and the first 210 V-2s – had a melancholy tale to tell:

The projectile . . . cannot . . . be intercepted by any existing methods of air defence. . . . All efforts to interfere with its radio control mechanism have so far proved fruitless. . . . Nor is the rocket vulnerable in the production stage. The plans for its manufacture have clearly been devised with an eye to security against bombing. The production of the component parts has been widely dispersed over German-occupied Europe, whilst the final assembly is carried out in a few carefully protected factories. The only assembly plant about which we have conclusive information is situated underground at Nordhausen in Thuringia. . . . The depth and design of the underground tunnels are such as to make a successful attack most difficult.

As for the future, the outlook was even bleaker:

Given time, there can be little doubt that the effectiveness of the existing A-4 rocket could be appreciably increased. Moreover, it is possible that larger rockets with longer-range or heavier warheads are already in course of development by the Germans.

By the end of the year about 350 rockets had arrived and on 11 January 1945 R. V. Jones submitted a detailed analysis of their accuracy to the Chiefs of Staff. The fall of shot showed, he explained, 'a lopsided dispersion' with a 'long tail stretching through Essex to he North Sea', due, he believed, to a small 'error in velocity' of 'about 0.8 per cent' and a rather larger 'error in elevation' of 'about 8°'. In other words, the rocket was not going quite as fast as the Germans had calculated and was not being fired at precisely the right angle to reach its supposed aiming point, which Dr Jones believed to be Wapping, on the north bank of the Thames just down-river from Tower Bridge. There was also, thought Dr Jones, a 'probable error in bearing', i.e. the direction in which the rocket was fired, of 1.5 per cent, sufficient, at this distance, to explain the dispersal of shots, combined with the rocket's tendency to fall slightly short, over the area between – though Dr Jones did not name those unfortunate places – Ilford and Deptford. The Germans, he suggested, had chosen their aiming point knowing that many missiles would fall around rather than on it, and even a small increase in accuracy would have serious consequences for central London.

If . . . elevation errors . . . were reduced to 3° . . . the bombardment would become much more central, while the intensity in, say, Westminster would be increased more than twofold for the same

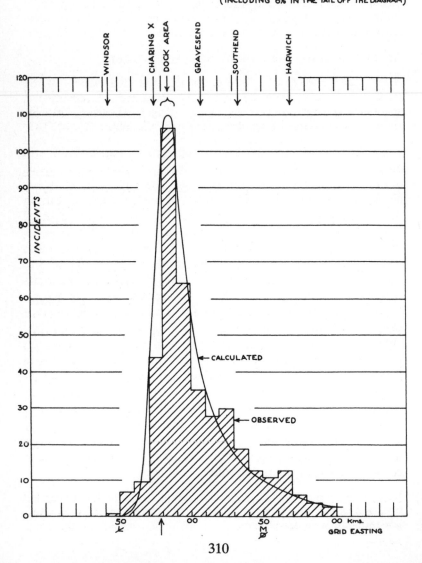

HISTOGRAM OF EAST-WEST DISTRIBUTION OF ROCKETS IN SOUTHERN ENGLAND

DATA UP TO 3·1 45 INCL   TOTAL 394   WITH THEORETICAL CURVE

ASSUMING

PROBABLE ERROR IN ELEVATION   8·1°

PROBABLE ERROR IN VELOCITY   0·83%

AIMING POINT   L7900

TOTAL NUMBER OF SHOTS   420

(INCLUDING 6% IN THE TAIL OFF THE DIAGRAM)

WINDSOR · CHARING X · DOCK AREA · GRAVESEND · SOUTHEND · HARWICH

INCIDENTS

← CALCULATED

← OBSERVED

50   k   00   50   M   00 Kms.

GRID EASTING

number of rocket firings. If in addition Westminster were made the aiming point instead of Wapping, the intensity here would be increased by a further factor of two.

And, like the Crossbow Committee's report of six weeks before, Dr Jones had nothing to offer for the government's comfort:

It is possible that the Germans have now found the trouble, for during the first few days of January the tail appears to have been proportionally smaller.*

The total impotence of the defence forces against the rocket was by now evident. The Air Defence of Great Britain had always been a misnomer so far as the V-2 was concerned, but Fighter Command, which replaced it in mid-October 1944, had no more success. The services which worked with it were equally ineffectual. 'One form of enemy raid', later admitted the historian of the Royal Observer Corps, 'the ROC could do little about: the V-2 rocket . . . was not susceptible to the fighters, radar or the ROC.' All the observer posts could do was 'give a bearing and angle on rocket trails which could be seen rising from the continent and also to inform centre of the approximate position of impact'. The very first V-2, at Chiswick, proved symbolic, for it gave the crew of Post 17/D.2, in the adjoining borough of Acton, as they reported 'The biggest shaking we ever had'. As the bombardment went on, the Observer Corps continued to enjoy a grandstand, if distant, view of it. 'Sightings from the Midlands', confirmed the Corps's historian, 'were frequent, but . . . on the night of December 29, 1944 . . . half a dozen posts south-east of Manchester reported a V-2 which hit London 200-odd miles away.'

For the Commander-in-Chief of Ack-Ack Command, General Sir Frederick Pile, whose batteries had finally justified their existence during the flying bomb offensive, the realization that they could once again do nothing but watch proved particularly disagreeable. Pile was determined to find some way of countering the V-2, though under no illusions about the scale of the task:

---

*The actual diagram prepared by Dr Jones to illustrate the rocket's aiming point is reproduced opposite.

Here we had a target that was travelling at over 3,500 miles an hour, or about five times the speed of sound. It was no use puncturing it if we did not detonate the warhead . . . and the warhead was not only protected by a casing of quarter-inch steel, but was also . . . a fraction of the whole rocket. . . . The majority of people – even the more enlightened ones – thought that it was an impossible problem for us to solve . . . Fighter Command, when we put the matter up to them, were not exactly encouraging in their attitude. But . . . it was some measure of the seriousness of the situation that Fighter Command agreed that if I could produce scientific data to support an outside chance of 100–1 against hitting any rocket my proposals might go forward to higher authority.

The technical problems were enormous. Radar sets 'designed to detect aircraft flying at heights up to 30,000 feet and at ranges of up to 30,000 yards' had to be modified to 'detect rockets . . . at heights of more than 300,000 feet and at ranges of up to 140,000 yards', while 'we had only two seconds in which to make our prediction, for the guns had to be fired when the rocket was still more than 30 miles from London'. The hope was that a horizontal curtain of shells could be put close enough to a descending rocket for it to set off their proximity fuses, but even General Pile estimated the maximum likely rate of kills at only from 3 to 10 per cent of the rockets actually engaged, and most of the experts put the chances of success much lower. Sir Robert Watson Watt, the leading authority on radar, assessed them at 1000 to 1; the Army Council's scientific adviser, Professor Ellis, at 100 to 1; a panel of scientists, asked for an independent opinion, at 30 to 1 at best, assuming that 400 rounds could be put in the path of a particular target.

In the event, by the time operational trials were beginning to seem promising, the rockets had ceased to arrive, and the 'textbook' answer to the offensive proved to be the only one ever tried, a counter-offensive against the launching sites and the production and supply system which served them. Because, presumably, of the difficulty of mounting standing patrols over the suspect areas, no sustained attempt seems to have been made to try to catch the rockets while still moving slowly enough to be intercepted, just after lift-off, though at least one astonished pilot found himself, as he later reflected, 'in a perfect position' to do so, while flying a Mosquito on intruder operations:

As we cross in just north of The Hague we see a white flame pulsing at ground level and, because nobody has told us that V-2s don't take off with a rush like a child's firework rocket, we don't realize what we are looking at. A pity, because . . . it would have been nice to be able to say that we had shot down a V-2.

One Spitfire pilot also caught a V-2 just as it left the launching pad and pursued it with cannon fire, but missed, and the only known claim to have destroyed a rocket in flight – duly recorded in a symbol painted on the fuselage of his aircraft – was made, it would not have surprised members of the RAF to learn, by 'a Yank'. The left-waist gunner in a B-24, his aircraft, on a routine mission over Holland, was flying at 10,000 feet when, according to a fellow crew member, 'a telephone pole with fire squirting from its tail' passed smack through the middle of the group, until, so the gunner claimed, a burst from his 0.5-calibre machine gun sent it crashing back to earth.

Destroying the rockets at source proved as hard as intercepting them in flight. The location of the Central Works was known by mid-October 1944, and 'tallboy' bombs for bringing down the roof became available from November – previously they had been husbanded for use against the *Tirpitz*, which Bomber Command had now sunk – but Nordhausen remained extraordinarily difficult to attack. The bombs aimed at it fell mainly on the adjacent labour camps, adding their inmates to the long list of the rocket's victims, and were far less effective than the general attack on transport in the area.

The launching sites were attacked not because anyone hoped to achieve very much from the attempt but because there was no better alternative. Here, too, the Allies were operating under difficulties. No sooner had Dutch agents signalled the location of one of Kammler's batteries than it moved elsewhere, while saturation bombing of the surrounding area was ruled out by the presence of Dutch civilians. All that could be done was to plaster with bombs and gunfire any suspect clearing or roadway – with no guarantee of hitting any useful target – and to send constant missions over Holland to let fly at anything military-looking that was spotted. Everything, including the weather, which often made the ground, let alone individual sites or vehicles, invisible from the air, aided the Germans and helped once again to demonstrate the limitations of supposedly invincible air power.

The V-2 absorbed a vast amount of effort which might otherwise have been directed against the enemy armies. In the opening phase of the campaign alone, between 15 October and 25 November 1944, nearly 10,000 sorties were flown by the Second Tactical Air Force, based on the continent, against the district between The Hague and Leiden, and around the Hook of Holland. Fighter Command flew 600 more from British airfields, much of the burden being borne by the Spitfire, employed as a fighter-bomber. During November and December 1944, 12 Group dispatched machines laden with two 250 lb bombs whenever the weather permitted against suspected storage areas at Wassenaar, Voorde and Hus te Verve, and repeatedly strafed with bombs and cannon fire the Haagsche Bosch, the 'Hyde Park' of The Hague, an attack also being delivered on the Hotel Promenade, believed to contain Kammler's headquarters. If they achieved little, these attacks at least made possible such morale-boosting reports as that which appeared on the front page of the *Daily Mirror* on Tuesday, 5 December:

Power-diving 5000 feet though a rapidly closing gap in thick cloud, RAF Spitfires raced against deteriorating weather to pin-point a V-2 storage depot and vehicle park in Holland yesterday. More Spitfire bombers made pinpoint attacks under equally bad weather conditions on V-2 erection and launching sites.

On Christmas Eve 33 Mark XIV Spitfires, from 229 and 602 Squadrons RAF and 455 Squadron, Royal Australian Air Force, managed, by refuelling in Belgium, to increase their load to one 500 lb and two 250 lb bombs each, and aimed them against a block of flats thought to house rocket troops near the Haagsche Bosch. It was badly damaged and had to be evacuated, but requisitioning new accommodation presented no problems for the Germans. Attacks were also made on Leiden station, rightly suspected of being a rocket collection point – they were taken from there to the De Wittenburg area of The Hague to have their warheads fitted – and on the Langehorst estate and Duindigt racecourse, which were favourite launching sites betweeen November 1944 and January 1945. But as the RAF's own historians admit, these efforts were 'largely ineffective', being kept up because they were 'the only riposte the Royal Air Force, or indeed the armed forces of the crown in general, could make'.

For years the 'bomber barons' had maintained that they held the real key to victory, but they too proved impotent against the rocket. On 22 December 1944 Herbert Morrison urged, in a paper addressed to the Chiefs of Staff, that the heavy-bomber force should be used against the launching sites in The Hague, which could, he argued, be annihilated. The following day General Ismay tendered their professional advice firmly rejecting the suggestion. To do the job thoroughly, they believed, would require a force of 150 Lancasters to make ten sorties each, resulting, if normal accuracy was achieved, in complete devastation within a radius of 600 yards of the aiming point, and some damage for twice that distance. The loss of life of friendly civilians was, the Chiefs of Staff advised, unacceptable, especially as the Germans would simply recommence operations elsewhere. Herbert Morrison persisted in his campaign until the matter reached the Cabinet, where on 18 January 1945 the Chiefs of Staff firmly squashed it.

We . . . strongly recommend that heavy bombers should not be employed to attack rocket installations in Holland, but that present efforts to destroy them by precision bombing with individual aircraft should be intensified, and we understand that this recommendation [when made in December] was accepted.

That a heavy-bomber attack would have been either ineffectual or, for the Dutch, catastrophic, there seems little doubt, but in any case the weather kept the Allied air forces grounded day after day. In the first two weeks of January nearly one-third of the 300 sorties mounted against The Hague had to be abandoned, and in the second two weeks only nine attacks were launched. Seven armed reconnaissances, in search of targets of opportunity, were attempted, but only two completed, and the only real success of this period came on 22 January 1945, when four squadrons of bomb-carrying Spitfires knocked out a liquid oxygen factory at Alblasserdam. Another such factory, at

Loosduinen, was attacked five times between 3 and 9 February, the pilots, in the official historian's words, 'trickling their bombs towards the target' from the one open side; on three others it was surrounded by civilian houses. About a third landed in the target area and it was believed that the factory had been put out of action. Mostly the Allies' response to the steady rain of rockets on London was, however, merely to 'strafe' suspect wooded areas, and 'the general results', the RAF's historian admitted, 'must be described as meagre'.

No one liked acknowledging that the Germans, on the verge of defeat, had outwitted and out-generalled the Allies. On 26 January 1945 the Cabinet Defence Committee urged that precision bombing should be intensified, with assistance from the medium bombers of the Second Tactical Air Force, that SOE should be asked to extend their operations against rocket-orientated activity – it does, in retrospect, seem remarkable that British agents and saboteurs achieved so little – and that the Central Works should be bombed. Variations in the number of rockets arriving did suggest that RAF activity over Holland helped to keep down the number of daytime launchings, and Fighter Command now redoubled its efforts, especially against the Haagsche Bosch. Reconnaissance on 24 February showed that, if there had been *Meillerwagen* there, they had gone, and the Duindigt racecourse now became the main object of attack, along with a transport park located north-west of Rotterdam.

That week rocket arrivals reached a new peak, of more than ten a day, intensifying the discontent already widespread in the affected areas, and even some of those which had so far escaped lightly. On 24 January Herbert Morrison had obtained Cabinet consent to respond favourably to a request from Alfred Barnes, Labour MP for part of East Ham, that he should discuss the rocket situation with all the MPs for London constituencies, and this seems to have cleared the air for a time. On 20 February, however, William P. Sidney, the recently returned Conservative MP for Chelsea, now serving in the army in a position that made him, as he explained, aware of 'the main facts of the situation', wrote a private letter to the Prime Minister:

What Can't Be Cured

As a London Member, I am deeply concerned about the possibilities of an intensification of the long-range rocket attack. . . . The average number of incidents per 24 hours remained very steady at 7 for nearly four weeks and has lately risen to 10. It seems quite probable that this figure may rise still further to 17 to 20. If such a rise were accompanied by a shifting of the mean point of impact 3 or 4 miles to the west, the results would be very serious indeed. . . . I know . . . that it is the policy to inflict the minimum of injury and damage to Dutch life and property. Nevertheless I cannot refrain from asking whether by a comparatively small increase in the strength of the air forces devoted to attacking the launching sites, effective delays and interruptions could not be imposed on the enemy's supply system and greater embarrassment caused him during the launching operations. . . . A fairly small diversion of effort now might save a great many casualties later both in this country and in Holland.

This letter was referred to General Ismay, who reported that two more Fighter Command squadrons, as well as the Second Tactical Air Force, were now being diverted to attack rocket targets, and William Sidney was invited to hear this explanation for himself, at Downing Street. He remained dissatisfied, repeating, a note of 1 March by the Prime Minister's staff revealed, that in his view heavier bombing was needed to improve the situation. Meanwhile other MPs were also becoming alarmed – and none with more reason than the Conservative Member for Ilford, Major Geoffrey Hutchinson, who as mentioned earlier, on 24 February, four days after William Sidney's letter to Churchill, had written to the Secretary of State for Air to ask for a meeting. Some of what was said on this occasion can be deduced from a letter Sir Archibald Sinclair wrote to the clearly discontented MP on 2 March, which set out the familiar arguments about the danger to Dutch civilians, but also dealt with an entirely different issue.

The idea that we are influenced in any degree whatsoever by the situation of the palace of the Queen of Holland is utterly fantastic. The queen is not in residence there, and the situation of her palace has never entered into our calculations.

By now dissatisfaction about the V-2s was widespread, as the Prime Minister's private secretary, J. H. (later Sir John) Peck, formally warned him, in a note on 26 February:

317

I think you should know that the daily post contains a growing number of letters about rocket attacks from your constituency [Epping] and from Ilford and the most seriously attacked areas in East London and Essex. Unlike the letters when the flying-bombs were at their worst, they are for the most part not anonymous or couched in abusive terms. They do, however, make three points:

1. There is an underground feeling that if the main weight of attack had been falling not on the East End but on the Whitehall area and Buckingham Palace, far more vigorous attempts would have been made to counter the attack.

2. If the rocket sites are being spared heavy bombing attacks in order to save Dutch life and property, they would much prefer if there have to be victims that they should be Dutch rather than English.

3. They ask for some public announcement which would show the discontented members of the population that the government took some interest in them and would inform them whether any serious attempt is being made to put an end to rocket attack.

I understand that Sir James Hawkey [a leading local Conservative and former mayor of Woodford] is becoming rather anxious abut the attitude of the constituency. The Secretary of State for Air is considering whether he can include in his 'Estimates' speech next week some references which will reassure the districts most affected by rockets that they have not been forgotten or neglected.

General Ismay wrote on the same day to the Prime Minister repeating the Chiefs of Staff's opinion that the only real way to stop the rockets was to liberate Holland. Churchill was clearly not impressed. On 28 February he sent a note to his private office which he presumably intended should reach the ears of their opposite numbers in the Air Ministry and the latter's military 'masters':

I am not at all convinced that they are exerting themselves as they should, or as they would be forced to do if the bombs were falling in the Whitehall area. I am not at all satisfied with the efforts the Air Ministry are making in this matter.

The following day Ismay tried again, repeating the Chiefs of Staff's arguments and pointing out that they had been accepted by the Defence Committee on 26 January and again on 26 February. That same 1 March, however, another note arrived, from Herbert Morrison:

Nearly every 24 hours bring further loss of life and homes and sleep to the war-weary inhabitants of the areas experiencing their fifth year of bombardment. Members of Parliament are receiving complaints and there is a growing murmur that 'It's time the government did something about it', with a suggestion that the government is indifferent to the loss of life and suffering. People cannot help contrasting the spectacular advance now being made into Germany against the seemingly static position of our troops in the north of Holland. To the layman it seems that our line in the north need advance only slightly to overrun or cut off the firing points. Instead of this comforting prospect, we are having to consider some reopening of evacuation arrangements, a measure which, when it becomes known to the troops in the front line, is bound to cause them additional anxiety about the safety of their wives and children at home.

Churchill, practising his own 'Action this day' philosophy, replied immediately:

I would be glad if you would go yourself and discuss the matter with the Chiefs of Staff. I have put pressure upon them and I am satisfied that they will do all that is possible. I will also discuss the matter with Field Marshal Montgomery and General Eisenhower when I see them tomorrow and the next day. No one feels it more than I do, with my poor constituents bearing the brunt, but 'What can't be cured, must be endured'.

What Churchill said at his meeting with the Allied commanders is not on record, but from the Chiefs of Staff on 7 March Herbert Morrison received little consolation. Field Marshal Sir Alan Brooke assured him that a land attack in the Arnhem area and a seaborne assault on the Dutch coast had both been considered but turned down, while Air Chief Marshal Portal said that as soon as the RAF cut one railway route serving The Hague the Germans opened another and that the Central Works, because of its site, would be almost impossible to knock out by bombing. Morrison could only repeat that both the police and the Regional Commissioner for London shared his concern abut morale, which, he argued, could only be adversely affected by the growing emphasis on night launchings, since 'perhaps the chief cause of anxiety was the feeling that no night was free from the danger of domestic disaster, if not serious personal injury'.

Meanwhile, under pressure from all sides to do *something*,

Sir Archibald Sinclair had made the public case for the RAF's inability to stop the nuisance in the middle of a far-ranging speech on the Air Estimates on 6 March 1945:

The government are deeply conscious of the strain to which these attacks are subjecting many thousands of our fellow countrymen. The loss of life and homes, the injuries and the human suffering which they inflict are grievous. . . . No practical means of abating these attacks has been neglected by the Royal Air Force, but the launching site of a V-2 is small and hard to identify. Any space of ground – hard or artifically hardened – 23 feet by 23 feet, will serve as a launching site for the rocket. . . . We may know that certain areas near or in a particular town or village in Holland are being used for launching. To send some squadrons of Bomber Command to obliterate that town or village would destroy the lives and homes of hundreds, or even thousands, of our Dutch allies, who are already suffering terribly; but the men who operate the rockets would emerge from their deep shelters when the bombardment was over, and either carry on their nefarious work elsewhere, or perhaps clear a space, and continue to operate from the same devastated town. By attacks on storage sites, on supply routes, motor transport parks and lines of communication, we are reducing the scale of attack far below what the Germans hoped to achieve; but . . . the only way to silence this form of long-range artillery is the physical occupation of the sites from which these weapons are fired.

Sinclair did not say, as he did not yet know, that events had just strikingly vindicated the Air Ministry's reluctance to intensify attacks on The Hague. On Saturday, 3 March 1945, 57 Mitchells and Bostons of the Second Tactical Air Force, which Supreme Headquarters had been loath to see diverted from their normal ground-support role, had been sent to make the heaviest attack yet on the Haagsche Bosch. The result, it was learned in London on 8 March, the day after Sinclair's speech, had been a disaster and later further details emerged. The nearest bombs to the wooded area believed to be housing the rocket units had, it appeared, landed 500 yards away, while the surrounding streets of Bezuidenhout occupied by Dutch civilians, had been plastered with 69 tons of bombs, some of which had caused major fires. These had been left to rage unchecked, leaving many people to burn to death; the Germans had refused to let the fire brigade enter the area, declaring that 'the stupid Dutch have to learn what it is like'. What it had been like, it now emerged, was Hamburg or Dresden on a smaller scale, and on 14 March 1945 the Foreign Minister of the Netherlands' government in exile, which had hitherto loyally supported the British government's policy of bombing The Hague, went to dictate, more in sorrow than in anger, a formal protest. An earlier attack by Typhoons on the same area in the second half of February, he pointed out, had been totally unsuccessful, with no damage done to the V-2s stored there, since the bombs had fallen wide. Meanwhile worthwhile targets, in the shape of the railway lines leading to The Hague carrying the Germans' supplies of liquid oxygen and alcohol, had been left untouched. But this lesson had not been learned and the result, on the fatal Saturday of 3 March, had been a disaster, with 800 Dutch civilians killed by their allies, and 100,000 homes,* ruined by bombs or fire, having to be evacuated. 'The temper of the civilian population', summed up this senior Dutch minister, 'has become violently anti-ally as a result of this bombardment.'

Even if the scale of the disaster *had* been exaggerated it had clearly been far worse than any V-2 incident in London, and the affected area remained for years afterwards an open space on which no one ventured to build. As soon as the basic facts were realized, a major inquest was launched in London, although the true reasons for the fiasco were never finally established. The Dutch charitably attributed it to the stiff north-west breeze which had pushed the bombers, or their cargo, off course, but the rumour was current in the Allied air forces that a bombardier in a leading aircraft had held his map upside down and that those behind, bombing when he did, had aimed at the very area they had been briefed to avoid. That the map-reading had been inept and the bombing altitude too high seemed indisputable, and the resulting criticism came at a bad time for the RAF, already under a cloud since the devastation of Dresden three weeks earlier. On 18 March the Prime Minister sent to General Ismay, for the Chiefs of Staff,

---

*This figure appears in the document attributed to a Dutch citizen who had reached Brussels. It was almost certainly too high.

with a copy to Sir Archibald Sinclair, one of his sharpest memos of the war:

This complaint reflects upon the Air Ministry and Royal Air Force in two ways. First, it shows how feeble have been our efforts to interfere with the rockets, and, secondly, the extraordinary bad aiming which has led to this slaughter of Dutchmen. The matter requires a thorough explanation. . . . I will bring the matter before the Cabinet.

The embattled Secretary of State for Air did his best. In his reply to Churchill on 26 March Sir Archibald Sinclair admitted that the mission had been a disaster. An internal investigation had been launched on 8 March, but, he pointed out, 'The Germans are deliberately placing their launching and storage sites in and near built-up areas in occupied Holland. A railway interdiction plan would not necessarily avoid losses in Dutch civilian life.' The Chiefs of Staff, replying on 28 March, also mingled apology with self-justification. There had, they acknowledged, been a fault in the way the crews concerned had been briefed, but many earlier operations, such as Spitfires dive-bombing the launching sites, had been a success. They, the Chiefs of Staff, had always advised against the use of heavy bombers and the decision to use medium bombers – which had actually caused the trouble – had been taken by the Defence Committee, not themselves.

The danger to Dutch civilians has always been inherent in the use of aircraft against the rocket area of The Hague. . . . If the risk of damage [*sic*] to Dutch civilians is unacceptable for political reasons, we can only suggest that our air attacks should be confined to harassing the railways at a safe distance from centres of Dutch population and that the consequent increase in the rocket attacks on the United Kingdom (which may at most be only slight and may at best be prevented by the course of land operations) should be accepted.

The subject clearly rankled with the Prime Minister and when, in opening a large-scale RAF exhibition at Dorland Hall, Lower Regent Street, Sir Archibald Sinclair claimed credit for 'the frustrating attacks by the RAF on V weapons', this was too much for Churchill. The text of the speech appeared in *The Times* on the same day, 28 March, that the Chiefs of Staff's memo arrived, and Churchill's response was immediate. 'You have no grounds to claim that the RAF frustrated the attacks by the V weapons,' it began, and went on to say that, so far as the flying-bombs were concerned, 'the RAF took their part, but in my opinion their efforts rank definitely below that of the AA artillery and still further below the achievements of the army'. The real sting lay in the tail:

As to V-2, nothing has been done or can be done by the RAF. I thought it a pity to mar the glories of the Battle of Britain by trying to claim overweening credit in this business of the V weapons. It only leads to scoffing comments by very large bodies of people.

26

A ROUTINE JOB

At 1900 hrs the incident had settled down into a routine job.

Report of incident officer on incident at Usk Road, Battersea,
1600 hours, 27 January 1945

'The public continue to praise the Services, in which they
have complete faith.' With this sentence one Ministry of Home
Security official ended the draft of his report on 'Lessons from
Recent Raids – Long-Range Rockets' in December 1944, and
it was a verdict which almost all of those who had suffered
personally from the rocket would have endorsed. The picture
he painted was indeed reassuring in almost every respect.
Although, owing to the lack of warning, fewer people now
used shelters, 'Anderson and Morrison shelters have again
stood up well,' the same report concluded. 'Several Anderson
shelters within a few feet of craters, and even on their very
lips, have remained practically undamaged, though their earth
coverings have usually been blasted away.' There were similar
cases of people brought out unharmed from Morrisons after
the shelter had been totally submerged in the ruins of their
home. The picture for surface shelters, always less popular,
was not so satisfactory:

Reinforced brick communal shelters have also stood up satisfactorily
as far as their main structure is concerned, but there has been damage
to internal fittings. Bunks have been wrenched away from the walls,
smashed and twisted. . . . Where any of the few remaining unre-
inforced brick shelters have been involved, there have been cases of
collapse on their sites from earth tremor.

Overall, however, even a surface shelter increased one's
chance of survival, and especially of escaping injury from flying
missiles and falling masonry; it also gave protection against a

324

new, specifically V-2, danger. 'There have', mentioned the report quoted earlier, 'been several cases of injury from burns and these have been ascribed to liquid oxygen, or hydrogen peroxide, containers of which are found in the missile.'

The report made much of the problem of locating the precise spot where a rocket had fallen, especially in rural areas, but even in towns finding the precise point of impact was not always easy. Westminster, its historian recorded, made wardens' posts 'responsible for sending in Vicinity Reports based on the sound of clattering glass', a somewhat rough-and-ready guide, as windows might be broken a mile and half from the explosion. 'Border' incidents were a constant trial, both in town and country, a classic example occurring after the ministry's interim report just quoted, at one in the morning of Thursday, 15 March 1945, when a V-2, with no regard for local authority boundaries, landed on a group of houses in Crystal Palace Park Road 'just foot inside Beckenham's borders', but causing casualties and damage in Lewisham and Penge. The result, a local historian admitted, could have been tragic:

No message was sent to Beckenham Control for ambulances or resuce parties while the search went on to establish whether the incident was in the borough. Fortunately Lewisham showed greater initiative and despatched eight ambulances and a heavy rescue squad to the scene without worrying too much about boundary lines. . . . Until 3.30 a.m. Lewisham controlled operations when responsibility was transferred to Beckenham.

Untrained and often over-enthusiastic helpers had always been a source of vexation to the professionals, and it had not lessened with experience:

Everybody in the vicinity, as soon as the dazedness has been shaken off, is immediately anxious to help, and generally succeeds in adding to the chaos. Much harm may be done until order is restored; and the later an incident officer arrives on the scene, the harder is his job of undoing what has been done before his arrival.

The incident officers were the élite of the Civil Defence service, usually senior wardens of long experience who had been on a special training course. In Ilford, the local newspaper reported, the incident officer 'became known simply as "the man with the blue hat" and to him everyone turned in trouble'. In theory at least the black and white chequered flag which flew over his command post marked out a calm, still centre in the middle of storm and chaos, where frayed nerves were soothed, raised tempers lowered, and decisions on which lives might depend were taken promptly but carefully. One of his lesser jobs was that of a superior traffic warden, a profession not yet invented. The ministry report quoted an example:

At one incident in a main road, which was blocked during the early stages, there were 11 rescue parties, 21 ambulances, 5 cranes with their debris lorries, and two mortuary vans, as well as the NFS pumps and towing vehicles, mobile canteens and cars. Here the incident officer at once arranged for the clearance of roads round the incident so as to let vehicles circulate and get away without backing.

The incident officer now often had at his disposal a facility unknown earlier in the war, an incident-control van, 'providing', according to the official intention, 'a mobile office which contains everything the incident officer wants, and which can be sited at the best spot regardless of damage'. Control vans were often linked by field telephone to the nearest warden's post or private home with a line still intact, and another innovation, in response to the huge V-2 crater, was the use of two incident officers, one on either side of the obstruction. The technique was tried out at the Woolworths incident in New Cross and in Walthamstow where, as the local controller recorded, 'the crater completely filled the road and the water main continued to spout for a long period, with the result that the whole of the roadway was flooded'. In Walthamstow this division of responsibility became a regular practice, but elsewhere the ministry knew of one occasion where a crater formed 'two *culs-de-sac*', leaving 'the Medical Officer with serious casualties on one side awaiting ambulances which . . . were waiting on the other'.

Everyone's ambition was to 'close' an incident rapidly, with casualties removed, roads cleared and – above all – everyone who might have been involved accounted for. The record in Ilford was half an hour but this was exceptional and major incidents were often kept 'open' for days, or reopened when someone was discovered to be missing. The V-2s added enormously to the difficulty of listing actual and putative casualties, since people were so often caught in the street, and local records were out of date.

Many evacuated persons have returned and some have left without informing the wardens. People seem to be less willing to notify the wardens of their movements now that a number of wardens' posts are closed. They will not trouble to go to a more distant post.

The sheer scale of the area affected by every V-2 also vastly increased the wardens' problems:

The difficulties of tracing and identifying persons who might, or might not, have been on the scene . . . are increased because the numbers are greater. This particularly applies to passers-by and passengers in public-service vehicles which have been involved. Casualties have occurred amongst passengers in railway trains when identification and recording have been difficult. . . . At one incident, which occurred at about 5 p.m. on a Sunday, in a residential area, many of the houses involved contained one or more visitors. This complicated the reconnaissance problem enormously. . . . At another, after 40 hours of work the incident was closed, but on the third day additional human remains were found and it had to be reopened. . . . Despite all the difficulties, the time taken to account for everybody who might be concerned has generally been most creditably short.

The work of the rescue services was assisted by the introduction during the V-2 period of a number of new pieces of equipment or techniques, some costing nothing. A useful innovation was the practice of chalking a large 'S' on the door of every wrecked or abandoned house to indicate that it had been searched. Methods of locating buried casualties were also improved. The *Gravesend Reporter* described how at the Milton Place incident in November 'Microphones were placed around the rubble . . . to listen for buried victims', who were instructed over 'powerful loudspeakers from the control van . . . to tap the rubble so that their general position could be ascertained.' About the value of the most newsworthy arrival on the Civil Defence scene, however, the Ministry of Home Security were cautious:

Trained dogs belonging to the Ministry of Aircraft Production have been tried at these incidents. They were not trained specifically for this purpose but have been very useful in indicating the presence of casualties, dead or alive, under the debris. Their usefulness increases with experience, and others are being trained.

It is essential that they work under their trainers, who understand them thoroughly. Each dog has its individual way of working and of indicating the presence of casualties. The best results have been obtained when dogs have worked in pairs. The trail of one can then confirm that of the other, or they may scent the same casualty from different angles. . . .

There have been several incidents when information of the whereabouts of trapped casualties has been vague or faulty, in which the dogs have saved hours of labour and delay by pointing to the casualties, sometimes under four or five feet of debris. They can also get through comparatively small spaces into voids. . . .

But they must be regarded as an aid to reconnaissance and not a substitute for it. A positive indication, if followed up, may save life, but a negative one should never be taken as conclusive.

This carefully balanced conclusion, so typical of the Civil Service mind, those who used dogs would have endorsed. In Walthamstow, the local controller found, 'dogs . . . from time to time proved very helpful in indicating casualties hidden below debris . . . although they were not by any means infallible'. They proved useful, however, when given a trial run at Blackhorse Road in December, when 10 dead bodies and 100 other casualties had to be recovered from 2000 damaged houses. At Iverson Road, Hampstead, in January the dogs found nothing when a missing woman was searched for and it was eventually human, not canine, ears which located her eight hours after she had been trapped. The presence of a dog certainly added a new element to a familiar scene, as in South Norwood, for Croydon's 'Sunnybank' incident:

In the glare of floodlights, silence was called for as the dog, in the hush, nosed his way over and into the ruins now dripping in the rain, becoming intensely excited when near a live casualty. It was an eerie experience.

At the Lewisham/Beckenham 'border' incident in March, mentioned earlier, the debris of a row of four-storey Victorian houses proved 'too tightly packed' for the dogs to push their way in, and one warden present 'confided that the dogs in Lewisham had never proved any good'. At Hazelhurst Road, Wandsworth, a dog 'was successful in locating one trapped dead casualty' but not the other thirty people still missing nine hours after the explosion. Dogs were also easily diverted by the presence of animal casualties, as the district rescue officer for Wandsworth in February discovered:

The rescue dogs were employed in Usk Road, but owing to the amount of livestock (cats, dogs, rabbits, chickens and horses) kept on the premises the value of the dogs was destroyed. Wherever they indicated bodies, cats, dogs, rabbits, chickens and horses were found.

Of all the changes in coping with incidents that occurred during the V-2 period the most valuable was that of abundant light, made possible by the ending of the black-out. The ministry recommended making the fullest use of this new facility:

One borough owns a battery of searchlights, with its own power unit, presented by the US Navy, and this has often been lent to neighbouring authorities. AA and RAF searchlights have been used and have greatly helped work. The best results have been obtained by projecting the beam against a blank wall and working by the reflected light. This avoids deep shadows.

Army searchlight crews – the only part of Ack-Ack Command actually employed against the V-2s – welcomed this break in their normally boring routine. One wartime ATS member recalls how her unit in mid-January 1945 found themselves in Beckenham, responsible, like the other six sites in their troop (which was itself one of four in 432 Battery), for providing an incident light within a two-mile radius of their base.

There was always a great demand to go on the incident team. We had . . . a large 150 searchlight projector and . . . the incident light, which was a small 90 searchlight projector, mounted on a lorry. . . . The team consisted of a man to drive the lorry . . . a No 5 who looked after the carbons on the searchlight, a No 9 who looked after the running of the generator . . . and a No 1 who was NCO in charge of the team and saw to packing the lorry with haversack rations, waterproofs, first-aid kit, etc., so we were quite self-sufficient. . . . We prepared for action every evening one hour before nightfall. We would get word over the RT set of the location and had to report to the incident officer on arrival. . . . All we had to do was turn on the motor, switch on the searchlight and put it out of focus, so it gave a greater area of light, then illuminate the debris.

Cranes, because nearly every V-2 incident caused great

damage, had also become a familiar sight, but the ministry had reservations about them:

Cranes have proved very valuable but . . . should be used with discretion. . . . There is a danger that their presence may distract rescue parties from what should be a technical rescue job, following careful reconnaissance, into filling skips and clearing debris. Cranes, by speeding the removal of debris from the site, should be regarded as an aid to scientific rescue work, and not a substitute for it; in any case, the risk of unsuspected persons, such as passers-by, having been trapped, makes careful handling of debris essential. There is still a tendency for too many people – some of them visiting officials – to stand about on debris.

About the treatment of casualties the ministry was also reassuring. 'There is', its report concluded, 'no doubt that casualty handling has much improved with experience and training and the number of deaths from shock have declined. . . . First-aid treatment of casualties and their removal from the site has generally been expeditious.' There was, it suggested, only one 'important lesson' to be learned, namely 'the necessity for summoning a sufficient number of ambulances in the early stages of a big incident', when 'the greatest number of free and lightly trapped casualties are found'. Still unsolved was that old problem of inadequate or duplicated records, as a result of 'injured persons' being 'taken by friends or unofficial helpers to hospitals or surgeries' or Form MPC 44, on which all statistics ultimately rested, being completed both 'at a mobile unit and subsequently at a first-aid post'.

Few V-2s caused serious fires, but the red appliances and grey-helmeted men of the NFS were often the first on the scene when a rocket fell 'because of their observation posts and their special training in getting away quickly'. With little fire-fighting to do, they had, the ministry acknowledged, 'rendered most valuable service, particularly in quickly cordoning the site, in clearing roadways, dumping debris and furniture salvage', and when help in rescue operations was required the firemen readily provided it:

In one incident this . . . resulted in the rescue of two people alive after four hours in a semi-basement under burning debris. The NFS kept the fire under control, avoiding flooding of the basement, and kept much of the heat and smoke from the trapped persons.

The rescue service had always had a distinct character of its own. Its work, the Ministry of Home Security reported, 'has again been consistently excellent'. The service's forthright, independent outlook is well conveyed by the report written by the Bermondsey officer in charge at the start of the major incident at Folkestone Gardens on 7 March, previously mentioned:*

At 0320 hours an explosion was heard and Supervisor gave orders for Express Party to go out. . . . We . . . went towards Old Kent Road, but were stopped in Rotherhithe New Road by Mobile Police, who asked where incident was. On being told we were looking for it, they gave us information that it came from the Dock direction. We turned round and belted towards Red Lion and Plough Way, but at Crystal Bridge, Rotherhithe New Road, we were stopped again by the Police, who pointed the incident out by a fire. It was Deptford, so not wasting anytime we went up Bush Road, Trundleys Road, up Knackers Bridge and when we reached the top the incident was in front of us.

The Fire Brigade was there. The Supervisor asked a warden if the Incident Officer was there, but he replied 'No' and that he had lost his wife and three children in [the] flats. Supervisor got squad to work, not on the flats but the houses opposite, as there were trapped casualties. Going further along, acting as Incident Officer, called on firemen to give assistance, which they did. There were also police. Supervisor then ran back over bridge to Wardens Post, C.2., in school and phoned Control where incident was. After phoning, supervisor hurried back to incident where he saw a Heavy Rescue lorry coming onto incident and this had a searchlight on the cabin which was switched on . . . this was a good thing. . . .

Supervisor told the Incident Officer that the Bermondsey Squad were already at work, and on being requested to remove blue cap so that no confusion would take place [i.e. with the incident officer, in his blue steel helmet] supervisor said he would go and help the squad he had working. On finding squad, supervisor was told to listen and a child was heard whimpering underneath a collapsed house. Tools, gloves and household shovels were sent for and the man was told to hurry. Supervisor gave instructions not to pull any long timbers out,

---

*See Chapter 16, p. 214. The report given here is reproduced exactly as written, with the original punctuation, etc., and only a few small cuts.

no-one to get on top of debris, digging with hands and throwing debris out into the open. The baby kept quiet for a while, supervisor requested the little bugger to cry so as to get at him. While moving bricks, small debris, a voice said 'Mind my face' from the debris, this turned out to be the baby's father. On being asked where he was, he spoke again. As there was no room where supervisor was working for more men to work, instructed another man to edge through broken door and scrape away debris into passage and be bloody quick about it, seeing as both casualties were right under a collapsed house. Supervisor spoke to the unseen man again, who said he couldn't move at all. [Rescue] Party member was now in a crevice scraping away with his hands. After a time, by the light of hand torches, the man moved his head in an effort to shake dirt from his face. Party member was told to wipe the man's face and cover same with triangular bandage to keep dirt off, as supervisor was still trying to get to the baby while giving instructions. While all this is going on, another man tries to get into passage to where other Party member was, in doing so he started to shake broken and hanging debris, this was promptly stopped by supervisor, saying to the chap 'Come out, you bloody fool, do you want the rest of it down', no arguing, out he came. Supervisor had now got to cane cot, the baby was quiet and also moving. Supervisor had been working in an awkward position, with an obstruction pressing into his abdomen (belly) and when reaching out to get the baby from the cot, supervisor suddenly retched or tried to vomit, immediately stepping to one side, gave instructions for the next man to take baby from the cot which was done by Party member C. M., Bermondsey Light Rescue. . . .

Officer of Deptford Light Rescue Party came to scene and said the crane would lift the top of debris, this was on the [adult] casualty, so Supervisor said 'Take the bloody crane over to the flats' as he was doing the job. Now the baby was out. Supervisor asked for pruning saw and cut away a joist which was not supporting anything to be able to get inside the debris.

The cutting was done, Supervisor then got through opening and down, and with lamp was able to see the man lying parallel with window, brick, rubble and masonry was still on top with a bed and bedding from top floor. This proved to be a good thing. After a while we got the bedclothes of the top floor bed, getting a man either end, and each man got hold of one side of the quilt, they were told to pull opposite ways, thus taking the weight from the mattress. Supervisor pulled these out and then the bed itself. The man was complaining of pressure. Supervisor had another look at what position the man was in, turning on his side, he told about six men, some of Deptford men and police to put their shoulders under the timbers that were sticking out through the bay window. This was also smashed down. Supervisor gave orders to lift carefully. As this was being done, supervisor observed another man standing on a joist, he was told quickly what a bloody fool he was and also that the joint he was standing on was the one that was pinning the man down underneath. The joist was lifted in continuance with the other timbers and the man was got out. Covered with blankets and put on stretcher he was sent to ambulance to be taken to hospital. He was asked for information about anyone else in the house, this was taken and as there were a lot of Civil Defence Services there, another squad of Deptford men was put on the house. Supervisor, after nearly two hours (and Party had attended 12 casualties), returned to Depot, after reporting to Incident Officer at 05.15 hours.

An equally vivid picture is provided by the diary kept of the sequence of events after a rocket had landed one Saturday teatime, 27 January 1945, in Battersea. Although the incident officer's van arrived only twelve minutes after the explosion, several ambulances, NFS pumps and rescue parties were already on the site and within the next three hours he logged twenty-five further arrivals. They included more ambulances and rescue teams, a mobile crane, a searchlight, a gas-repair party, a window-repair lorry, 'dogs and trainers', a Metropolitan Water Board turncock, an incident inquiry point team, two mobile canteens and – always a sinister sign – the mortuary van. The detailed 'Final Report' which the incident officer later submitted set out, succinctly but comprehensively, how the afflicted had been aided and order restored to this embattled corner of Battersea.

The I.O. post was established in Usk Road at the junction of York Road. I contacted P.W. [Post Warden] L., who had before our arrival made the entrance of the Savoy Cinema, York Road, a F.A.P. [first-aid post] and loading ground and . . . it was arranged that he should continue there. Loading grounds were later established nearer the incident in Usk Road and Petergate. . . .

The information now gathered was that the centre of the incident was approximately 50 yards in the rear of York Road between Usk Road and Petergate, slightly closer to Usk Road. Between 15 and 20 houses had been rendered uninhabitable and 120 to 130 badly damaged. . . .

At approximately 16.30 hrs Wandsworth C.D. informed me that

they had been instructed to consider the incident as a Battersea one, but were keeping a sub I.O. post in Petergate, this being a part of the borough boundary. . . .

At 16.30 hrs Column Officer J., NFS, reported with two pumps and two salvage tenders. He was requested, owing to the absence of large fires, to use his personnel in rescue and reconnaissance duties. . . .

At approximately 16.55 hrs I was contacted by the Town Clerk, who offered me additional services, but as the approaches to the incident were somewhat congested with vehicles of H.R. and L.R. parties, who were doing a most excellent job, I declined more of these but accepted the offer of a mobile crane. At about this time it was decided that there were probably five points where trapped casualties might be and the rescue dogs and sound location apparatus were sent for and arrived quickly.

The situation was now easing up somewhat; most of the casualties had been removed for medical attention. The police were efficiently controlling crowds and traffic and parking of vehicles had been organized, Ambulances, repair lorries and other vehicles which were not immediately required were parked in Wynter Street and York Road. At 16.55 hrs two Incident Enquiry Points were established by the WVS of the respective boroughs, one in the York public house at the corner of Usk Road and York Road, and the other in Petergate. The local Wardens Posts census cards were up to date and proved of great assistance. . . .

At dusk refreshment vans were in attendance and rescue parties continued work at the incident floodlit with army searchlights. . . .

At 19.00 hrs the incident had settled into a routine job, with three persons unaccounted for – Mr O. of 8 Usk Road and two boys who were known to have been in a wood shed in the rear of York Road shortly before the explosion, and the search for them continued. At 07.40 hrs Sunday . . . the remains of the two boys were found. . . . At 13.45 hours on Monday . . . Mr O.'s body was found. . . . The incident was then closed. . . . There were 17 fatal casualties and in addition 44 people were detained in hospital, 63 treated in the Out Patients Depts., and 7 treated at F.A.P. . . .

Everyone concerned carried out their duties in an efficient manner. . . . Once the initial chaos had been sorted out the incident ran smoothly.

The police were a feature of every incident and tended to take on the miscellaneous duties which every violent disruption of other people's lives left behind. An RAF electrician, stationed in Nottingham, was much struck by the contrast between the indifference of his own superiors, who only grudgingly allowed him a single day's leave when his house in Clapham was damaged, and the reaction of the special constable he met on the scene:

The constable had an incident chart and my house was in the 'severely damaged zone'. He was most helpful. To my relief he said that if I gave him my name, service number, RAF station, he would telephone the station sergeant [near my base] who could contact my unit. . . . In the short time it took me to walk to the police station after I had left the constable . . . the police had found my RAF station telephone number way out in the wilds of Nottinghamshire and convinced the duty officer I needed extended leave.

'As always, the WVS have given most valuable service of every sort and have done much towards keeping up the spirits of the public.' This was the official ministry opinion of the contribution of the Women's Voluntary Services for Civil Defence (to give them their full title), and it was one which thousands of bombed-out or shaken householders would have echoed. The mobile canteens which dispensed tea and sandwiches within an hour or so of a rocket's landing were the most visible sign of the WVS presence, but there were others, less obvious, like the 'visiting teams' which in some areas systematically called at every house to see if they had any undisclosed problems. 'These visits', considered the male ministry report-writer, 'accomplish most when made in pairs, one single and one married woman', the latter presumably being there to receive confidences unfit for spinster ears.

The centre of WVS effort, apart from the canteen, tended to be the incident inquiry point, which had made itself indispensable during the flying-bomb period. Some were on a large scale. One, kept open all night, required a staff of seven, while outside 'a queue had to be formed,' the ministry report commented, 'attended by a mobile canteen. The IIPs were now given official guidelines:

They should be near the incident post but outside the cordon erected to keep the public away from the incident. A modicum of comfort for staff and enquirers is essential. The point should be under cover, with seating for enquirers. If possible there should be arrangements for providing tea for those who are waiting.

How effectively an incident inquiry point could become a little oasis of calm and compassion in a desert of death and destruction was observed by an American writer, who visited one in Bermondsey, set up in a shop opposite 'a row of what had been pleasant cottages':

I shall never forget that sight of chaos and ruin where so short a time before there had been the peaceful, orderly routine of a neighbourhood breakfasting and starting off to shop and school. Nor shall I soon forget the quiet, earnest way the women of the WVS went to work to help broken families find their way back to something like a normal life again. . . . You were suddenly aware of the threads of human life that trailed off in all directions. 'My husband is coming home on leave in a day or two. . . .' 'The boy is in school and he must be told.'. . . A child's pet dog could not be found. Patiently, and with quiet understanding, the women of the WVS worked to put to rights the lives of these victims of the battle of London.

27
HORRIBLE AND SUDDEN DEATH

*During the period . . . to seven o'clock this morning there was
enemy air activity against southern England. Damage and
casualties have been reported.*

Evening Standard, 14 February 1945

The German promise, back in November 1944, that the V-2
would bring 'horrible and sudden death' to the people of
southern England* was amply fulfilled. By the end of the
campaign, 2754 civilians had lost their lives and another 6523
had been seriously injured, plus an unrecorded number of
servicemen and women. The numbers requiring first-aid treatment are uncertain, but if the experience of Wandsworth is
typical, where 271 people became 'minor' casualties against
123 'serious' cases, the total of lesser casualties for the whole
country must have been about 14,400, making the total casualty
list, including killed and all categories of injured, just under
24,000. This was substantially less than the numbers who
suffered from the blitz or flying bombs, since the attack was
shorter and on a smaller scale, but in terms of killed or seriously
injured the rocket was the most 'cost-effective' of the three.
Each ton of supposedly aimed bombs caused on average 0.82
fatal casualties and 0.98 serious injuries, each flying bomb 1.06
and 3.08 respectively, while each V-2 killed 2.61 people and
badly hurt another 6.18 – demonstrating, incidentally, that this
type of indiscriminate bombardment, which posed no risk to
the aggressor, was more efficient in undermining morale, if this
were related to casualties caused, than conventional bombing.
The figures confirmed, too, that risk depended overwhelmingly
on location. Just under 50 per cent of the V-2s reached the

---

*See Chapter 15, p. 203.

London Civil Defence Region but they caused 90 per cent of the casualties.

Who died because of the rockets? The case of a Bermondsey family, who moved back there after returning from Northampton, to which they had evacuated themselves when bombed out in 1941, was typical. The daughter of the house, married and then living in Wembley, recalls the circumstances:

When my father's employer heard of the suggested move he almost went on his knees to him, not to bring the family back to London. . . . My mother was terrified about coming back, but was more terrified of my father so in February [1944] they moved back again. . . . In June the V-1s started to come over and . . . when I visited her she said how frightened she was when one or the other was away from home and if they had to die hoped it would be all together. . . . I did not visit again until November and learned that my Marine brothers were safe back in England after . . . the D-Day landing and there was a chance of Christmas leave, so we decided to pool our rations and make a cake and pudding in case we could have a family Christmas. In the afternoon my sister Louie arrived with her two small sons and told us she would have to leave her father-in-law's house as she had trouble with him while her husband was away [in the navy]. It was decided she would share a large room with my mother until other arrangements could be made and she moved in with them on 2 December. At 2.30 a.m. on Wednesday, 6 December, a V-2 hit the house and my mother got her wish; they all died together: Mum, aged 48, Dad, 49, [my sisters] Louie, 25, Florrie, 17, Joyce, 16, Doris, 7, [my brothers] James, 14, and Bernard, 12, and Louie's two sons, Frankie, 3, and David, two months. We buried ten coffins in Camberwell New Cemetery, 13 December, and till the day I die I will not forget the armless, legless, headless bodies that once were my family.

The regular refrain in the exceedingly uncommunicative communiqués issued by the Ministry of Information, which reported that 'casualties were caused', gave little hint of the long wake of tragedy that every such incident left behind it. One woman then teaching at Higham's Park, Hackney, remembers a typical case, that of a pupil who, on going home for dinner, learned 'that his home was destroyed and a parent killed. The next day that little lad sat for "the scholarship" ' to decide his whole academic future. A Walthamstow man recalls another of von Braun and Kammler's achievements. The sole survivor of one family, lying blinded in hospital, learned that her 'sister' and 'parents' were dead – and for the first time that she had been adopted: 'a very deep double shock'.

Blindness, though the papers never mentioned it, was a common consequence of being close to an exploding V-2. A woman dug out alive, as described earlier, from the Holborn V-2 incident in November 1944, encountered another case:

In the bed next to mine was a young mother who had been blinded by a bomb and her two-month-old baby, with a broken arm. Her husband was also in the hospital, but her biggest grief was that she was unable to go to the funeral of her four-year-old son who had been killed. Also in my ward was a 23-year-old girl who had lost both hands. . . . She could not wash herself, nor comb her hair, go to the toilet alone or even wipe her nose, or wipe away the occasional tear which she understandably shed. Her mother had died from the shock of her injuries.

Frequently those injured had no recollection of the actual moment of the explosion, like a Hounslow woman who had been enjoying her morning tea-break in the Pyrene factory in March 1945:

I was knocked unconscious but came to as the rescue squad got me out. My right arm was badly damaged. I remember saying to someone, 'It isn't fair'. As I was able to walk, I was put into a private car and sent to West Middlesex Hospital, Isleworth. . . . I remember sitting outside the hospital for a time and an air-raid warden came and popped a tablet in my mouth. We were put into bed – clean sheets with all our dirt. Now and again I lost consciousness and when at last the sister came to give me my injections it was 4 p.m. I had lain there all that time, so you can tell the number of casualties there must have been. I was very ill with shock and injuries to my right arm and stayed in hospital about three and a half weeks.

'For a few moments there was a deadly quiet, a solemn hush, as though the world had come to an end. Then, when I realized I was still alive, I pulled myself out of the debris.' That is the outstanding memory of one woman who became one of those seriously injured by the V-2 which, as described later,* landed in the early afternoon of Friday, 10 November 1944, on Goulston Street, Stepney.

---

*See Chapter 29, p. 360.

Hitler's Rockets

It was two days before my son's sixth birthday. We had carefully hidden his presents ready for Sunday. My son was at school, my father at work and my mother resting in bed . . . when suddenly, without any warning, the street door, the scullery door, the mirror that was above the fireplace, were all lying on top of me. . . . I could hear people screaming. . . . I called to my mother, who at that moment couldn't speak. She had lost her voice with shock. I then managed to get to the bedroom to her and we were able to reach the street, although, even to this day, I don't know how. Then we saw people dead and injured being brought out, horses from Brooke Bond tea warehouse lying dead. . . . I stood talking to a neighbour who had been split wide open from her left shoulder to right breast. How she was able to stand I will never understand, although she died on reaching hospital. I had a few small wounds but rather a big hole in my right leg, which was so deep that the doctors were unable to stitch it together, so put a plaster cast on to help pull it closer. The lady who sold tickets at Goulston Street baths was blinded, the baths damaged and I was told some American servicemen were killed. My father was working for the Americans in a goods station near Aldgate. On hearing the bomb and finding out where it had landed, he dashed home. . . . He reached us just as I was being helped into the ambulance. . . . My father went to school to see how my son was. The windows at the school had been blown out so the teacher let my parents bring him to the London Hospital, where I was sitting in a wheelchair waiting for the doctor. For a moment he didn't seem to recognize me. What with the blood and soot I was smothered in I must have looked like a being from another world.

The test of 'serious injury' was being kept in hospital overnight, but many V-2 casualties faced months of treatment and convalescence. The Holborn V-2 victim quoted earlier, taken first to the adjacent Great Ormond Street Hospital for Sick Children, was, on the following Tuesday – she had been hurt on Saturday morning – moved with her airman husband who had 'both legs in plaster, both arms in splints and his head and neck . . . swathed in bandages' to 'Bart's evacuation hospital in Hill End, St Albans'. This she found a former 'mental hospital and . . . a rather dreary place, very crowded with ordinary patients and bomb casualties', and though she was allowed to leave within a few weeks her husband faced a twelve-month stay in hospital.

Being 'slightly injured' did not always seem like that at the

time, as a woman making woollen garments for the forces in
a factory at Leyton could testify. Her particular rocket landed
ten minutes before knocking-off time:

I remember saying to a girl on the next machine, 'I hope my date
turns up tonight. He's a GI and I could do with a pair of nylons or
a bar of candy.' All of a sudden there was an almighty explosion and
I felt a terrible pain in my back. There was silence for a time, then
I could hear girls screaming. The next thing I remember was one of
the men picking me up and carrying me through the glass and debris.
We had caught the full blast. It had fallen on a row of houses opposite.
I remember a lorry taking us injured girls to the Connaught Hospital,
where it was full of injured people, mostly women and children, from
the houses. When I came out of my daze, I realized I had a big hole
in my left calf which was pouring with blood and a nurse put a bowl
under my foot to catch the blood. I heard someone say, 'She's got
glass in her back', and the next thing I knew I was lying on a table.
There was a doctor there and nurses and other injured people and
then to my horror someone was just ripping all my clothes off, which
were soaked with blood. To me at nineteen years of age that seemed
almost as bad as the injury. I had to lie down on my front while the
doctor stitched me up. My back was gashed by glass. . . . I have
never felt so much pain in my life. They had to do it without freezing
it or anything. A nurse gave me her hand to grip, but the tears just
rolled out of my eyes. I said to the doctor, 'I'm sorry, I don't mean
to cry, but I can't help it.' He said, 'Don't worry. . . . You're being
a brave girl. . . . Now we'll do your leg, but that won't hurt quite so
much because that's not quite as bad as your back.' That over, I had
an injection and was put in a wheelchair and taken to a rest centre
next to the hospital, where the bombed-out people were, until
someone collected me to take me home. They gave me an old pair
of shoes and a blanket and there I stayed until my uncle came and
got me about two o'clock in the morning. I was off work for about
a month, and although I still have my scars to remind me, I consider
myself very lucky to be alive.

Some of the injured did not appear in the official statistics
at all, like an ex-nurse, mentioned earlier, who was working
in a bank in High Road, Leytonstone, on the morning of 27
October 1944.*

A Friday about 10 a.m. we were all getting on with the day's work.

*See Chapter 21, p. 268, for details of this incident.

Quite a few customers in the bank also. There was a terrific 'crack' and the thud of explosion, falling glass and breaking outside and inside. I was working, sitting at my ledger under the window. The next thing I recall was sitting on a heap of rubble, with dirt on my head and face, crying. The only thing in my mind was, 'Was my face disfigured?' . . . The young man [the junior member of the staff, aged eighteen] came and pulled me up and said 'You're quite all right. It is red ink on your hands and face and on the ledger. We've real trouble! The manager is badly hurt.'

Blood spouting on the front of my nice mauve dress. . . . I got the first-aid box and sat 'sir' in his office, stopped the haemorrhage by pressure on the artery, then packed the glass and wound with wads of cotton wool and bandaged in position. Nobody else was hurt but the whole place was a shambles. I then took the manager outside and found a private car doing hospital journeys with mobile victims. . . . We went to Whipps Cross Hospital and found the Casualty Room. Casualties were being wheeled in on stretchers and we just sat with many others about an hour . . . when I found my boss getting weaker. So I went into a ward and spoke to a doctor attending a victim and begged him to see my boss, saying, 'I'm a nurse and it's urgent. He'll be dead if not [seen].'. . . . We sat patiently and smoked, we may have had a cup of tea, I can't really recall, [being] just horrified at the number of casualties still being brought in. Eventually I went in again and saw the doctor, pleaded for him to see the boss . . . and he did. Then I found a bus and went back to the bank.

The inspectors from head office were there and men from the local builders repairing front door, etc. An ex-policeman customer asked if I'd had my head looked at. It was full of glass powdered and had cut and bled. . . . I gave Mrs S. [a colleague] a laugh. She thought I was delirious as I went to the lavatory and told her, 'I had to take my knickers off because I felt glass sticking in me where I'd sat'. She and I both heard a shower of glass on the rubble in there as I shook them out. Then they sent me home for the weekend to get over the shock. . . . My neighbour next door was surprised to see me home about 3 o'clock and I made her literally clean my head up. [She was] terrified of blood, but there was nobody else to do it. Then I had a hot bath and found powdered glass stuck to my skin and lodged in my bra. . . . I got to bed and had an attack of ague. The bed rocked and shook. I was so cold and felt so ill. After about three weeks my voice went to a husky whisper – very tiring, as I needed to be heard as ledger-keeper. I saw the doctor and he gave me two weeks' leave. The voice was better but 'gin-husky' like Tallulah Bankhead, the actress. It has never returned.

Some people who had been exposed to similar, or worse, experiences became 'shell-shocked', like a man remembered by a Leytonstone woman who 'asked for an interview' at her office several months after the 'bascule bridge' incident at Silvertown:*

He had been standing by the King George Vth Bridge when the rocket fell. I have never forgotten the state he was in. He could walk, but mentally and physically he was in a bad state. His speech was badly affected.

Civil Defence workers became accustomed to gruesome sights, but they could still be nauseated by some especially grim experience. One man, then aged eleven, remembers his father, a veteran incident officer in Ilford, being physically sick on returning home after having 'come across an arm and part of the stomach' of the only victim of one local rocket. A then seven-year-old girl has never forgotten hearing her fireman father describe, after the 'Echo Square' V-2 in Gravesend, finding 'a woman still sitting in her fireside chair in a wrecked bungalow . . . almost a skeleton, with the flesh blown off her bones'.

Only occasionally did the newspapers give a real indication of the ordeal through which the London area was passing. The usual communiqué resembled the one which appeared in the London *Evening Standard* on Wednesday, 14 February 1945:

During the period from dawn yesterday to seven o'clock this morning there was enemy air activity against southern England. Damage and casualties have been reported.

A brief reference to three 'recent' incidents was included, though whether they involved a flying bomb or rocket was not revealed. More disturbing was a short item on an inside page:

She Vanished When V-Bomb Fell
When an application was made at a Southern England coroner's court today to presume the death by enemy action of Miss Mary Grenoff (18) of Harvey-road, Hornsey, it was stated that she had not been seen or heard of since a V-bomb dropped near a station she was passing early in November. A witness described her as having been 'the happiest girl living'.

---

*See Chapter 24, p. 299.

Such events, distressing to all concerned, were far from rare. After the Woolworths incident in New Cross there were said to have been no fewer than eleven people finally unaccounted for, a source of unhappiness to their families and of trouble and concern to the Registrar of Deaths, the probate courts and the insurance companies. For wholly understandable reasons, little publicity and no honours were given to the unsung heroes of the mortuary service who tried to piece bodies together for identification. The oustanding work in this field was done by a borough which rarely made the headlines, Hackney, and the innocuous title of the paper which it submitted to the Ministry of Home Security in the spring of 1945, 'The Work of the Incident Inquiry Team', gave little indication of the horrors it contained. They make distressing reading, so that some readers may prefer to pass over the remainder of the present chapter.

The Hackney paper began by stating that it 'should explode the bogey of the oft-heard expression "There are too many white hats" ' – i.e. officials from borough control – 'at incidents', and went on to describe the three-stage technique the borough had perfected. Stage 1, completing a case card for every suspected occupant of a damaged building, was straightforward enough, but Stage 2, establishing what had happened to any of these potential casualties not accounted for, set the aptly named assistant inquiry officers a formidable task:

Special attention must be given to snatches of conversation by persons who profess to have witnessed the occurrence at close range since this is invariably the earliest source of information of the presence in the vicinity of passers-by . . . and is of vital importance because, in the absence of such information, the unidentifiable remains of an unsuspected passer-by might be credited as the remains of a person who is, in fact, still trapped under the debris.

But it was Stage 3, establishing identification where the normal routines had failed, which would, the author of the Hackney scheme acknowledged, require 'laborious and unrelenting effort':

It involves the inquiry officers in work both morbid and gruesome and entails the responsibility of pursuing inquiries with relatives under conditions of pathos and mental strain. Such inquiries must be pursued sympathetically and tactfully but with unswerving purpose if the incident is to be brought to a successful conclusion. . . . One single case of mistaken identity will upset the whole balance of an incident and can result in hours of unnecessary labour. . . . Surprising as it may seem, there have been numerous occasions where parents have failed to identify the bodies of sons and daughters, even where the mutilation is not great, and also occasions where parents have claimed to identify the body of a son or daughter which has subsequently been established to be that of a totally different person.

Cases where 'badly mutilated and dismembered remains' were 'recovered without particles of clothing by which the relatives can establish identification' were likely to prove particularly upsetting. Hackney advised against showing 'gruesome remains' in such circumstances, since 'it is doubtful whether any useful purpose could be served'. Occasionally, however, it was 'possible . . . to set up portions of the remains suitable for viewing by relatives who have been suitably primed as to the nature of the unpleasant task to be performed'.

The Hackney Report gave a detailed account of the follow-up work after one typical incident, involving the destruction of four flats and four three-storey houses, at 6.55 p.m. one Sunday in February, only the names being altered. By the following morning, apart from others already identified, the mortuary contained 'three male bodies, none in a fit state for identification, also various remains which it said were female'. A detailed search on site 'yielded only small pieces of clothing', making it clear 'that at least one person had been literally blown to pieces'. Meanwhile 'inquiries were being made for four lads, but no inquiry was outstanding for any female'.

This was the starting-point for a classic investigation which, like so many detective stories, began with a false trail. One missing woman, a Mrs Gridling, was said by a warden to have been taken to hospital, but a friend failed to find her there and it turned out that the patient was 'not the person in question, but another of the same name from a different address'. Where, then, was the other Mrs Gridling?

Further enquiries revealed that Mrs A. Gridling was in the habit of taking her dog for a walk on the Green during the evening and, being a woman of fixed habits, should have been crossing the road to her house at the time of the occurrence. It was learned that a dog had been seen wandering aimlessly about and was now being taken care of by a person who knew the dog belonging to Mrs A. Gridling. The dog was examined and found to have its coat and ears impregnated with powdered plaster and since it had been established that the dog was always on a lead when out walking and no lead was on it when found it was obvious that the dog had escaped from beneath the debris. The search for its owner was therefore diverted to the debris of her house and the body was subsequently recovered from it.

Already, therefore, the team had discovered a previously unsuspected body, but this created a new mystery. Whose supposedly female body was it that lay unclaimed in the mortuary? Meanwhile the mortuary seemed to be missing another body, for the case cards recorded 'two young babies (5 months old) having been recovered dead and subsequently identified by relatives', while the mortuary only contained one. The woman who had identified it had to be called in again and stated that the body she had seen at the incident site was not the one now shown to her. Once again the incident was reopened, and the body of little Collin Smith, lying where he had died, was 'recovered within ten minutes of these details being passed on to the rescue officer'.

Everyone now concentrated their efforts on finding out what had happened to the 'four missing lads . . . all between 12 and 15 years of age', two of them brothers. The prospects seemed umpromising. One of the 'sets of remains' in the mortuary was headless, another was thought to be female, and the other two consisted of such remains as 'a shoulder and neck with one ear and some back hair attached', although the neck was 'encircled by the remains of a collar and tie'. Even the 'clothing recovered was in such small fragments that it was difficult to tell what it had originally been', while there was a disagreement between the bereaved families and between the parents of the two missing brothers about the ownership of a leather belt. A further complication was that one father was 'a former rescue worker' who 'had, on account of his experience, had a nervous breakdown' and was an unreliable witness. In a macabre scene all three fathers were brought together at the mortuary to try to decide which mutilated teenager was which, and, though the results were inconclusive, tentative identifications of three of the boys were agreed. There remained the supposed female body, whose sex had been assumed 'because of the shape of the hands and because a piece of scalp had long hair', but the parents of the boy still unaccounted for now 'said that he had very long hair – in fact other boys used to laugh at him for it'. They were unable, however, to identify the only surviving scraps of clothing, and 'it was obviously impossible to ask the parents to see what was in the mortuary'.

Members of the team undertook the gruesome job of trying to find some conclusive means of identifying the lad.*. . . [One] member [of the inquiry team] took a piece of scalp and thoroughly cleaned it in spirit, which, incidentally, made it quite a different colour from what it had been when covered with dirt and scorchmarks. One portion of neck and shoulder had a piece of shirt, collar and tie on it and these were taken and washed. A finger on which the nail was unusual was found and a sketch made of it showing the malformation of the nail.

The parents were then again visited . . . but they would not commit themselves and it became evident that . . . the parents . . . dreaded having to identify their son, as that would put his death beyond all doubt. They were shown the pieces of shirt, collar and tie, but they were sure these were nothing like those their son was wearing. . . . To the inquiry team, however, it seemed too strange a coincidence that a lad should be missing [and] that these remains should belong to someone about whom no enquiries had been made. . . . Accordingly one of them went round to have another friendly chat with the parents and he elicited the fact that the shirt and the tie that the boy had been wearing had been purchased only on the previous Saturday. . . . He therefore took them in a car to the shop from which the shirt and tie had been purchased and here the shop assistant definitely identified the pieces produced as being of the shirt and tie which he had sold to the woman on the previous Saturday. . . . Mrs Kraft was still not satisfied and a further visit to the mortuary was arranged so that she could view the actual remains. . . . Accordingly the shoulders and neck were set up to resemble a body lying face downwards with only the neck and shoulder exposed and the head swathed in bandages and sunk in a pillow. . . . Mrs Kraft . . . immediately gave signs of recognition by collapsing with the cry 'My Georgie!' and so brought to a conclusion the work of the incident inquiry team on this particular incident.

The Ministry of Home Security showed little appreciation of

---

*At this point I have omitted some of the more upsetting details but I hope sufficient remains to show the dedicated work of the people concerned.

Hackney's pioneering work and the paper was now passed around the ministry, collecting observations as it went in the traditional Whitehall fashion. 'I think there is every possibility of this set-up becoming a little "inhuman",' wrote one official. 'Efforts on the part of a determined team might well cause quite unnecessary grief and added horror to bereaved people.' 'I can't agree that Hackney's attempts . . . are in the least inhuman,' riposted another. 'The subject is a gruesome one and that can't be helped.' Everyone agreed – as Hackney had itself generously proposed – that it would be desirable 'to leave out the name of the borough as other LA [local authorities] are sometimes jealous of any particular borough being apparently singled out', and it was finally decided only to 'issue the first 2½ pages, slightly amended' – a feeble, foolish decision which robbed the document of its whole value by omitting the detailed examples, which showed the system in action, so that Hackney's enterprising work in this delicate field has hitherto gone unrecorded.

28

DAMAGE WAS CAUSED

Attacks on this country with long-range rockets have continued throughout the past week, causing further damage in various parts of southern England.

Ministry of Home Security Operations Bulletin No. 242,
21 February 1945

'My immediate thought was that we were having an earthquake.' That is the dominant recollection of one woman, then aged nineteen, of what she still remembers as 'the night of the rocket', in October 1944, when her home at South Norwood fell about her ears. Precisely how many houses were destroyed or damaged by the V-2s is almost impossible to determine, since until November 1944 their very existence was a secret and after that date the damage caused by the two secret weapons was bracketed together. The Minister of Reconstruction, Lord Woolton, publicly stated on 22 September 1944 that since June 130,000 houses in London alone had been destroyed and another 720,000 had needed repair, but nearly all these totals must have been due to the V-1s. By March 1945 an additional 600,000 houses had been destroyed or damaged, and as only 80 flying-bombs reached London in this period almost all of these properties must have suffered from the V-2s, the number totally destroyed or having to be pulled down being at least 20,000. Many houses were affected several times and some families became expert in coping with the consequences of nearby explosions. One Sidcup woman had become proficient, she remembers, at putting back the Essex boarding forming the ceiling after every distant flying-bomb impact, but the V-2 nearer at hand proved too much for her new skill. And one could be too clever, as a Silvertown man discovered:

Window frames persistently jumped out at the slightest blast until I eventually plugged the walls and fixed ours solidly with long screws. . . . One day, just as I was congratulating myself about our window frames 'staying put', a rocket dropped at the back. Everybody's frames jumped inwards as usual but . . . ours pulled the whole back wall down with a crash. The consequence was that our house received more damage from blast than other houses much nearer to the exploding rocket.

Almost worse than being on the spot was to return to find one's house in ruins or knocked about. One woman remembers how her apprehension grew as she travelled home from her job in central London after hearing that familiar double bang:

I was not reassured when I saw numerous wives had come to meet their husbands at East Finchley tube station. However, I was thankful on turning into our road to see that our house was still standing. . . . Most of the boarded-up windows were out again, three or four tiles had dropped from the kitchen wall, things had been dislodged and there was plenty of dust around. We found out the next day, which was a pouring wet one, that our roof had been affected too and we were kept busy mopping up and standing pails and basins at strategic points.

A telephone was still a comparative rarity in 1944, but people possessing one now put it to a new use: telephoning their empty house after hearing a rocket explosion to see if the bell rang. A dead silence indicating 'line out of order' made one fear the worst. But even the ringing tone was no guarantee of having escaped. A woman who received it on telephoning her home in Forest Hill from her office recalls her disillusionment on getting back to it:

I was thankful to see the house standing but every window had gone and the water tank in the loft was leaking water down the stairs. All the tiles were off the roof and our poor black spaniel, Scamp, was sitting on the stairs looking terrified. The houses opposite looked untouched but actually they were like a film set, because the back rooms and walls had disappeared. . . . Our roof was covered with tarpaulins before dark, with tiles tied to the corners to keep them on but, during the night, a gale blew and it poured with rain. Hour after hour we heard the rattle of the tiles tied to the tarpaulin being pulled along the roof.

In addition to the 'military' damage, already described, which the rockets did to factories, docks and other transport facilities, they earned a rich dividend for the Germans in the diversion of the building industry's efforts to non-productive areas. During 1944, 20 per cent of all building work, excluding the large number of small firms consisting solely of working partners, involved demolishing ruined property, clearing debris and repairing damaged homes – more than was devoted to military construction and twice as much as was going into building or extending factories or warehouses. In 1945, most of which was in peacetime, damage repair became by a long way the largest single item, accounting for nearly 40 per cent of the building industry's output. Including V-1 damage, at least one family in every four or five in London suffered some physical inconvenience from secret-weapon damage, often having to endure a leaking roof, constant draughts and the perpetual irritant of flapping, opaque glass-substitute fabric in the window frames through one of the worst winters of the century. Even in this generally miserable time there were lighter moments. In a small house in Bethnal Green there was great hilarity when the lodger, in a room covered with dirt and debris, politely asked his landlady where he could put his cigarette ash. In Ilford one woman remembers eyeing the small sandbags used to anchor the tarpaulin over their tileless roof. 'How tempting it was to look out of your open window and see a sandbag dangling there. How I would dearly love to have snipped the bag and let the sand slither out!' The same respectable suburban street, now tarpaulin-bedecked, blossomed at ground level with hitherto hidden, almost unmentionable, appliances:

The day after the rocket dropped all our houses were inspected for emergency repairs and most of us had to have new wash-basins and WC pans as the blast had cracked them. What a funny sight it was to see rows of WC pans on both sides of the road and all the surrounding roads.

Nothing could compensate for losing one's home, and many people still mourn the loss of some especially treasured possession. A scientist then working on armament research at Woolwich recalls his wife's fury when a rocket smashed 'some pieces of our dinner service, which we had used without any breakages since our marriage in 1940'. A Sidcup woman still has a Bible given her by a niece, the sole subject worth recovering after her home was destroyed. And wartime shortages meant that securing a replacement for some ruined article was a triumph, as a woman bombed out in Harrow remembers. She and her husband had been rapidly rehoused in Pinner in a property formerly occupied by Italian prisoners of war:

At first I could not see how we could live in it, but we managed to get some dark brown paint and covered the dirt over with this. What was left of our home was dumped in the house. It was all wet and filled with glass and rubble and took days to sort out. We had no floor covering or bedroom furniture so had to manage with hooks round the wall which the soldiers had left. . . . One day we decided to go up to Maple's to see if they had a stair carpet. . . . They had just found some up in a store which they did not know was there. It had been there since before the war.

The outstanding memory most people whose homes were damaged by V-2s have of the immediate aftermath is the dirt – from plaster, pulverized brick, dust hidden in corners and crevices which had gone undetected in years of spring cleaning and, above all, soot, which was sometimes sucked out of a chimney by the vacuum which followed the first blast wave, with small black columns rising above the chimneys of all the houses in a road like so many exclamation marks. More commonly, however, the soot billowed out in clouds from every fireplace, as the wife of a licensee in south-west London recalls:

We got the carpet out in the front and were shaking the soot off with the help of our friends and one woman came past made up to the nines and thought it was just disgusting to shake the soot in the street where people had to walk. We were just in the mood for anything, so up went the carpet and the soot all over her.

With V-2 incidents occurring singly and over a wide area, all a borough's resources could be concentrated on each one, and most were impressed by the speed with which initial help arrived. 'They were marvellous' is the verdict of a Sidcup woman of the 'ARP and firemen' who came to her aid and were soon 'fixing all the doors and windows and putting back the ceilings'. A Romford woman feels an equally soft spot for the Boy Scouts: 'They were so helpful with their trek cart. They piled on our salvaged bedding to take to the rest centre.'

352

Subsequently, the family were 'given a blanket and a beauti-fully made quilt sent by the American Red Cross, some money and extra coupons. The money paid my fare to Leicester, where I stayed with my parents. Oh, the peace and quiet!'

Taking charge of what were officially known as domestic chattels from uninhabitable houses provided a useful occu-pation for those Civil Defence staff now underemployed, like the assistant fire-guard training officer for Ilford, who now became 'liaison officer responsible for the handling of orders for removals'. The work tended to be given a low priority by those in charge on the spot – wrongly, in his view – and he became adept at doing his best for his clients, virtually hijacking a van which had 'reported in error' to him, to such effect that the driver 'in the space of a few hours . . . dealt with five removals, which were taking several days to be handled under the existing arrangements'. Equally essential, but little publicized, work was done by the men from the public utility services. There was, it was realized, a real risk of fire when the current was restored to a block of vacated houses, for a cooker or heater might well have been 'on' when the power was cut off, and one man then working for the north-east area of the London Electricity Supply Company, covering the Dagenham area, found he had his hands full persuading people whose own houses had been undamaged 'to switch off the house circuit at the mains' when a whole road was being disconnected, and checking that everything was safe before the supply was restored. The effort involved was considerable. In a typical incident, in November 1944, of 400 properties damaged 'over 90 had to have their . . . supply disconnected'.

Efficient though the post-incident services were, it could take months to convert 'first-aid' repairs into permanent ones, and even longer to restore a house to its normal condition. Grum-bling about the slow speed of house repairs provided a means of protesting indirectly that the government had not stopped the rockets arriving and it was hard for people whose homes were at last being made good to see the men concerned suddenly removed, to carry out emergency repairs elsewhere. Lord Wool-ton had, at his press conference on 22 September, announced a drive to bring housing in London back to at least its condition when the first V-1 arrived in June, but he had reckoned without the rockets, and to those in charge it must have seemed at times that they were trying to bale out a boat in which as each leak was stopped half a dozen new ones sprang open.

Although his Ministry of Reconstruction was officially responsible for post-war housing policy, it was the larger but less glamorous Ministry of Works which directly supervised the building industry, and had the job of coping with V-2 damage. A military-style staff was set up by that ministry, with an intelligence section manned twenty-four hours a day to keep track of the changing situation, as new incidents were reported. A central planning group, the 'Drake House Organization', was set up in Drake House, Dolphin Square, and, for the capital, a London Repairs Executive, presided over from November 1944 by Duncan Sandys, promoted to Minister of Works from his previous rank of Parliamentary Secretary at Supply. Several other ministries were represented on these bodies, which, laying aside the leisurely traditions of peacetime, met for a period every day, including Sunday. A flow of updated instructions, known as 'Serial Notes', were sent to local authorities, and an equally unexcitingly titled newsletter, the *London Repairs Bulletin*, was issued to contractors, clerks of works and senior chargehands.

The speed with which a small army of workmen now descended on a street within hours of a rocket falling did much to restore public confidence in the government. In Ilford a large Welsh contingent, already busy on V-1 repairs, was at hand when the V-2s started, to such effect that a force of 1500 men, including those from local builders, might be at work, under the direction of the borough surveyor, within an hour of an explosion. The *Ilford Guardian* described, just before the end of the war, the high level of efficiency achieved:

When rockets fell at night arrangements were made for inspectors to visit and categorize the damage at dawn, and within an hour or two of daylight men were working on the spot. At the height of the attack . . . the men worked at night by the light of searchlights and electric lamps from the chimneys, on several occasions carrying on until 2 a.m. On at least one incident the men worked until 6 a.m. and then, after a wash and something to eat, returned again two hours later to put in a normal day's work. . . . They had to contend with icy roofs and gales, in fact during high winds several of them were swept off the roofs they were attempting to cover with tarpaulins. The problem of materials became acute. . . . The Borough Engineer's Dept had to scour Essex and London for various materials, sometimes having to send lorries far afield to get enough to keep the work going.

When the V-1 attacks began in June, about 21,000 men were already at work on war-damage repair work in the London Region; by December the total had multiplied sixfold, to 129,000, 96,000 of them employed by local authorities, direct or via contractors, and the rest provided by the Ministry of Works as a mobile reserve, or – in the case of 5000 – lent by the forces or the National Fire Service. Another 3000 civil-engineering workers were kept busy demolishing unsafe buildings. At first there was little movement of labour between boroughs, but eventually building workers on repair contracts found themselves liable to be moved to other districts and having to sleep in lodgings, hostels or even requisitioned schools or halls. Not all went willingly. 'The grievances of the men', the official history discreetly records, 'were sometimes exploited for political ends,' but 'the inconveniences of regrouping were on the whole cheerfully endured by management and workers alike.'

The need to secure the maximum cooperation of the building trade meant a notable step forward in joint consultation between management and men. The official historian believed that 'the local progress committees' now set up, consisting of representatives nominated by the Building Employers' Federation and the building trades unions, 'played a notable part both in keeping up the pace of the repair work and in sustaining the morale of the public and the workers'.

In spite of general criticism of the bomb damage repair in the press and elsewhere, the people of Greater London were on the whole greatly cheered by the energy and success with which large-scale first-aid repairs were carried out, and they were gratified to see their local representatives joining with those of both sides of the industry in the control of the work.

By January 1945 about 25,000 of the 130,000 building force were living in hostels and camps and many more were in other accommodation away from home. There existed, it was offici-ally acknowledged, a need for 'hot drinks on the site' – i.e. the cherished tea-break – and for 'lavatory, washing and drying facilities', but even feeding an influx of carpenters, bricklayers and plumbers could provide a problem. Occasionally such men were given priority in local cafés during the dinner hour or taken by lorry to British Restaurants, the cheap publicly-run cafeterias opened earlier in the war, which were now sometimes kept open on Sundays for their benefit. Mobile canteens, operating on at least a hundred sites, also helped, and the Ministry of Labour thought the feeding arrangements satisfactory in 83 per cent of the places inspected. A fair index of morale was unjustifiable absenteeism, and at the end of November this was put at under 3 per cent, most of this occurring on Sundays.

Sensibly enough, men away from home sought what recreation they could, and one man then employed on repair work in West Ham remembers seeing an Irish gang one Sunday afternoon playing toss-halfpenny:

There was quite a large ring of men with pound notes at their feet. One man was tossing the halfpennies, I was standing watching, when suddenly a hot wind started screaming around us, lifting the money into a whirlpool. I threw myself down just as the houses around started falling. Then came the explosion. . . . On looking up, the first thing I saw was pound notes flying about and the Irishmen trying to catch them with no worry about falling debris.

To conserve scarce materials as well as labour, maximum (rather than, as was customary, minimum) standards of repair were laid down by the government, which ruled that, during first- and second-stage work, only essential rooms in daily use should be dealt with, and that walls and woodwork should only be painted to make them weatherproof, not for decoration. Non-standard doors and window frames which could not easily be repaired could be replaced by others, however ill fitting and unsightly: half the roof could be covered with slates below standard size, or with concrete tiles; and half the windows given opaque glass. To increase the total number of dwellings available, preference might be given to larger houses, to be occupied by several families, at the expense of smaller ones providing shelter for only one or two people.

The normal limit on repairs was a value of £500, sufficient

before the war to buy a comfortable semidetached house in most places. It was realized that often it would take fewer man-hours to build a brand-new house than to reconstruct an existing one, but this solution, owing to shortage of materials, was not possible. House building had, for practical purposes, ceased in 1940 and in the whole of 1944–45 only 5500 permanent homes were built by local authorities and another 1800 by private firms, mainly for the police and armed forces. A few – a very few – 'Portal' houses had been built, and some (as mentioned earlier) had already been destroyed by a V-2, but by the end of the war only about 2000 were finished and occupied. The V-2s, in other words, did a great deal to create the housing shortage that was to be the dominant social problem of the immediate post-war years, and before the war finished their effects were visible all around in the oddly unfinished and usually shabby look of houses where the repairers had been at work and in the makeshift, temporary appearance of such property inside.

It was to be a long time before those bombed out were able to forget the experience and resume a normal life. These were the experiences of a South Norwood woman, a soldier's wife, whose home, as described earlier, had been destroyed in late October 1944:*

The only clothes we had were those we stood in. . . . We were sent to various centres, such as the WVS, etc., but were finally fixed up handsomely at the American Red Cross, who gave us some really good clothes, also some toys for my son. . . . The remains of our home were carted off to a large empty house in Auckland Road and when the council eventually found us a requisitioned place at Addington, Surrey, we went to collect our stuff from this house. The sight was most pathetic. It looked completely useless, covered in dirt and dust, a piano half smashed, tables with legs missing, broken chairs. One of the clocks, however, still survived in working order, also a utility wireless set. . . . We obtained some compensation under the War Chattels scheme, plus a full quota of furniture and clothing vouchers, but this did not help a lot, as things could not be obtained. . . . In fact we did not obtain a bed to sleep on for about another twelve months, having to sleep either on the floor or on some camp beds provided by the council.

---

*See Chapter 23, p. 290.

357

29

SPRING IN STEPNEY

My final report on this incident is that it was one of the most difficult ones that have had to be dealt with.

Civil Defence official on Hughes Mansions, Stepney,
27 March 1945

The V-2 attack had begun gradually. It ended suddenly, at the peak of its ferocity. The last week was, in terms of casualties, one of the worst of the whole campaign. As spring approached there seemed no good reason why the rockets should not continue to fall in undiminished, or even greater, numbers till the end of the war. At least, however, the weather had improved, as a strangely complacent Ministry of Information handout later recalled: 'In March clear blue skies made it possible for people to see rockets bursting in the air.'

On 1 March 1945 Dr Jones, better aware than anyone of the country's danger from the rockets, updated the analysis he had prepared in January of where the rockets were landing. The diagram he prepared showing the distribution of the first 420 rockets – about half of the total – confirmed his earlier impression of a 'comet-like' distribution stretching back to the east coast, with its foremost edge on the north bank of the Thames, and an apparent aiming-point at Wapping, one of the poorest parts of that distinctly poor borough, Stepney.

Stepney was in turn one of ten boroughs within Group 3 of the London Civil Defence Region, which, including V-2s still to come, came fourth in the table of rocket-affected areas, with 45. Where Stepney and its neighbours were exceptionally unfortunate, however, was in the number of 'outstanding incidents' which occurred there: 12 of the whole country's total of 50. The group's casualty figures, 602 dead and 1141 seriously injured, were the second largest. This was, of course, due to the relatively small area, 20½ square miles, the group covered, much of it, like Wapping itself, a place of large warehouses and mean streets of small terraced houses, heavily built up. Within the ten boroughs the rockets were very unevenly distributed, roughly in inverse relation to the wealth of those who lived or owned property there. Thus the famous 'square mile' of the City of London had no V-2s at all within its privileged precincts, though 146 people were seriously injured there by missiles falling outside its boundaries, and twenty landed near premises owned by the City Corporation in other parts of London, a reminder of how widespread the rocket nuisance was. Holborn had one V-2 incident, already described,* Stoke Newington, Shoreditch and Bethnal Green each had two. Stoke Newington's two incidents, in Green Lanes on 8 and 10 January 1945, apparently – if the Ministry of Home Security list is correct – caused no casualties. Shoreditch's two rockets killed 18 people and injured 197, Bethnal Green's 26 and 80 respectively, all but one of the fatal casualties, and more than half of the rest, occurring in Totty Street and the neighbouring Lesada Street, at 7.40 p.m. on the evening of 22 November. 'I have never heard such a bang in my life', wrote a woman, previously quoted, who helped to run a local evening institute, to her soldier husband from her home in Earls Court next day. 'It was louder than the landmine that went off on top of us in the Dover Road, Blackheath, and . . . seemed to jar one's whole body as if one had fallen downstairs.' Its effect on the East-Enders, who had already endured so much, was traumatic, as her subsequent letter, on 28 November, makes clear:

Three of our members, of the regular stalwart variety, have been killed, and dozens have lost their homes. . . . These wretched little houses collapse at the breath of a blast. We had about thirty kids in last night instead of the usual 120 and even these were quiet and dismal to the most astonishing degree. T. and his wife [the school caretakers] are very much the worse for wear, shivering with cold, tired, headachy and exhibiting all the characteristic symptoms of shock.

The New Year brought no respite to Bethnal Green. Early in February another V-2 landed in Parminter Street, in the

---

*See Chapter 15, p. 205.

centre of the borough, close to the town hall, as the same correspondent reported to her husband.

6 February 1945. You will be sorry to learn that poor Mrs X [who ran the institute canteen and lived nearby] was severely blasted by a rocket on Sunday evening [4 February]. You may remember that she had her home totally destroyed in 1940. This time it was merely windows, doors and badly damaged furniture. Mr T., who was visiting, had a bash on the head and glass cuts in his scalp, which are, I think, much more serious than he pretends. He seemed only half conscious yesterday.

Stepney's first, but by no means its last, 'outstanding incident' occurred in Goulston Street, very close to the site of the famous Sunday morning 'Petticoat Lane' market in adjoining Middlesex Street. Fortunately this rocket landed on a weekday, at 2.20 in the afternoon of Friday, 10 November, but the results were bad enough: 19 dead and 97 other major casualties.* A fireman stationed in Whitechapel was 'in attendance'.

We had finished our lunch and were on 'stand-easy', which was normal after a complete scrubbing of the station floors. All appliances cleaned up and everything freshened up and ready for . . . another week of routines and incidents. I was talking to one of my mates on the first floor when there was a terrific double bang, near enough to shake the whole building. In no time I was down the pole and on the pump, the bells were still ringing as we left the station, their ringing to be taken up by the deeper clanging of our fire bells as we sped towards the dense cloud of reddish brown dust, so thick it was hard to see through it. We stopped a few yards down Middlesex Street, the glass and bricks thick underfoot. . . .

We jumped from the pump and it was a case of each member of the crew of five working on his own, locating and rescuing trapped victims. Shovels could not be used, debris had to be moved piece by piece, brick by brick. My first job came within a few yards of where we stopped our pump. A red Brooke Bond van lay on its side; the horse had gone but the driver was trapped under the van. By this time quite a number of men were around, and shouting to them to lift the van, I crawled under and dragged him free. He was injured and with willing hands was laid near the van. He was worried about his wallet with the day's taking in it, which was in his overcoat under

---

*See Chapter 27, p. 339 for an account of this incident by one of those affected by it.

the van seat. I went back and got his coat and wallet, placing his wallet in his hand and making a pillow of his coat. A doctor came along and said 'OK, fireman, I'll look after him.'. . . .

Moving on, I met a number of people and some of our crew. They said they were looking for a girl, missing from a shop or office demolished by the rocket. I believe by that time all others had been accounted for. What had been blocks of flats and shops and offices were now a smoking heap of rubble.

Pieces of timber and large pieces of concrete were passed hand to hand and placed in a space already searched. Occasionally we came to a spot where we could scrape bricks and dust away fairly easily. It was on one of these occasions that I thought I could feel a cushion through a hole I had made, but soon realized that it was human hair I was holding. Calling for help, I was relieved when the other members of our crew came and soon enlarged the hole enough to show the girl's head. A doctor and stretcher were called for and both were there within a minute. The doctor asked me to hold her head back whilst he looked at her eyes and examined her head, which was severely gashed. He shook his head and we finished getting her body free and on to the stretcher. We spent the rest of the time on this incident putting out a few minor fires that were still smouldering among the debris. I remember looking up at what had been the inside wall of a third-floor flat and seeing not only the fire grate still intact but the ashes of a fire still glowing red and smoking.

An officer of the LCC heavy rescue service has equally vivid memories of what became known as 'the Petticoat Lane incident'. First came the strange sight of 'men and women . . . running out into the street minus their clothes' because 'the public baths had been partly demolished'. Then, as darkness fell and a fog descended, the searchlight unit was called in, producing another incongruous spectacle:

During the evening it had been snowing heavily. . . . The fierce glare of the searchlight lit up every corner of the snow-covered debris and thousands of twittering starlings, no doubt thinking it was sunlight, were circling amid the falling snowflakes around and around overhead, their wings silver in the rays of the light.

Stepney averaged during the V-2 campaign roughly one missile a month, so that one could never feel free of danger. The fireman whose experiences at Goulston Street have just been quoted became, one spring-like morning in 1945, a casualty himself:

I came off duty one fine sunny morning at 0900 hours. . . . Having a whole day to myself I decided to walk along Commercial Road towards Stepney Station to buy myself a sponge roll and a few things to take on duty next morning. . . . A few hundred yards along on my return journey to Whitechapel, I was passing a bombed-out shop, the windows of which had been barricaded with corrugated-iron sheets. The sun was shining and people were going about their normal daily routines. . . . A double-decker bus was discharging passengers about fifty yards ahead of me . . . when I suddenly found myself on the ground, buried by the corrugated-iron sheets from the shop front. All was dark and dusty. . . . I managed to get to my feet. My fireman's cap was still on my head, the swiss roll still in my hand and, like the rest of me, was as black as the ace of spades with dust and soot from the damaged shop.

I realized that a V-2 had fallen, yet I had not heard a thing, and, to my surprise, had not even been scratched. Looking along the road I saw the bus on its side, with people being assisted from it. Somebody in the pub shouted something about his mate bleeding. . . . My ears were gaining their normal sense of hearing and the bells I thought were ringing in my head were actually those of the pump from my own station arriving to help in the rescue work. . . .

Next morning I was back on duty at 0900 hours and at tea-break, about 10.45, agreed to have a quick game of darts, but when I tried adding up my score I found that I could not count properly. . . . The 'old man' [in charge of the station] . . . sent me to my doctor who said I was suffering a severe nerve shake-up and promptly put me on the sick list for one week. Actually I was fit again within a few days, but the extra days off gave me a good chance to catch up on some much-needed rest.

Hackney, in the north-eastern part of Group 3, was hit by 10 V-2s, which killed 51 people and seriously injured 58, largely in two 'outstanding incidents', in Canley Road in the early hours of Thursday, 7 December, and in Woodland Street exactly four weeks later, around teatime on 4 January. Islington, with 8 rockets, suffered far more casualties, 161 dead and 133 badly hurt, thanks to four 'outstanding incidents'. The first was at Grovedale Road, on 5 November; the rest were concentrated in a three-week period about Christmas, which included the 'pub bombing' at Mackenzie Road already described,* a serious residential incident at Stroud Green

*See Chapter 17, p. 221.

Road, just before midnight on New Year's Eve, and another at Salterton Road at 6 a.m. on 13 January. Poplar had 9 V-2s, leaving 51 dead and 51 seriously injured, with an 'outstanding incident' early on in the campaign, at 8.30 p.m. on 24 November in McCullum Road, already mentioned and another near its end, around midday on 7 March in Ide Street, in each of which nearly half the total casualty list occurred.

Throughout this period the steady drain of 'minor' incidents, in which perhaps a dozen people were killed or injured, continued, contributing to the perpetual cloud of grim anticipation which hung over the whole East End and of more prosperous suburbs further out. The evening-institute teacher previously quoted, travelling daily between rocket-free Earls Court and rocket-plagued Bethnal Green, was deeply conscious of how localized the nuisance was, as she made clear to her husband in a letter in early February:

I am surprised at your ignorance of the present rocket situation. . . . They are still coming over but in a very restricted area. Almost everyone I know in the eastern suburbs, Ilford and Epping Forest way, has been blasted two or three times in the past month. One Sunday the district was positively plastered, and they all came to work looking like ghosts. The papers are so quiet about it that no one seems to be particularly concerned. . . . How incredible it is that this business should be still going on, with the Russians almost at the gates of Berlin!

Nor, at last, was it only the Russians who were advancing. On 16 January 1945 the British and American armies containing von Rundstedt's pre-Christmas thrust into the Ardennes joined hands; the German counter-offensive had finally failed. On 5 March the Western Allies reached the Rhine, crossing it in strength on the 23rd. The Germans in Holland still held grimly on, firing off V-2s in undiminished numbers in what the woman just quoted considered 'the last display of spite before the surrender'. In the week ending at noon on 7 March 1945, 58 V-2s arrived, 36 of which reached London. From 7 to 14 March, and again from 14 to 21 March, 62 reached the United Kingdom; in the following week, the 29th of the offensive and the 249th in the Ministry of Home Security's wartime records, there were 46.

These final shots included some of the most deadly of the whole campaign, producing no fewer than eight 'outstanding' incidents, two of which, at Folkestone Gardens, Deptford, on 7 March, and the Great West Road at Heston, on 21 March, have already been described.* Four of the others, at West Ham, Poplar, Leyton and Enfield, attracted little attention outside their immediate localities. Two more of Kammler's closing salvoes were to demonstrate that, whatever might be happening to the German armies elsewhere, Abteilung 485 was still very much in action.

Neither of the borough of Finsbury's two earlier rockets had prepared it for its third and worst, which dived down out of a bright, clear sky at 11.10 a.m. on the morning of Thursday, 8 March 1945, into Smithfield Market in the Farringdon Road, close to the City and to the newspaper precinct of Fleet Street. It provided a climax to the Germans' campaign against the daily commercial life of London, just as its disastrous successor in Stepney, to be described in a moment, provided a classic example of how to kill people in their beds.

The shock of the Smithfield rocket echoed over London, reminding everyone in earshot that the war was far from over yet. A woman living in West Hampstead remarked to the locksmith busy in her house that 'it was probably south London', a tactless observation, for it turned out he lived in Catford. Much nearer to the scene was a man who had been entrusted with the collection of one and a quarter million pounds in banknotes from the Bank of England for his own bank at Poultry in the City:

Driving along Farringdon Street . . . we heard a terrific explosion. I immediately stopped the vehicle and, at that moment, the petrol tank exploded and the van was a mass of flames. I was badly burnt on the face and the hands. My colleague, fortunately, escaped from the other side with a scratch. I managed to stagger across a short pavement, but fell into a space about thirty feet down. I then realized I had a serious injury to my right foot. After a short time I was found and taken to Bart's Hospital. After some hours, a temporary wooden splint was fixed to my leg but by the next day I was in a ward with my leg in heavy plaster. The doctors on duty in the ward informed me that I

---

*See Chapter 16, p. 214 and Chapter 24, p. 304.

had a third-degree Potts' fracture and called me 'the man with the million'.

This man had had a miraculous escape, for, as the Midland Bank's own wartime history recorded, his van was 'only twenty-five yards from the point of impact'. No fewer than three of its branches were affected by the explosion, and first-aiders from its head office were called in to 'assist the medical staff at St Bartholomew's Hospital', overwhelmed by the flow of casualties. In the last major 'shopping' incident, at Deptford, saucepans had drawn a crowd. This time, an LCC heavy rescue officer learned on his arrival, 'as luck would have it, a consignment of rabbits had come on sale and the information had spread around the neighbourhood like wildfire', so 'the market was . . . thronged with women shoppers, many of them accompanied by their children'.

For a long time, so many people were buried, the situation was obscure. Admiral Evans, on the scene within an hour, was told it was impossible even to guess at the number of casualties. When he came back at 6 p.m. with his senior colleague, Sir Ernest Gowers, and the ARP controller and Medical Officer of Health for the City, with the Lord Mayor of London – for many of the casualties and much of the damage had occurred within the City – the figures were still unknown. It was several days before the final toll was assessed, at 110 dead, 123 seriously injured and 243 with lesser injuries.

Two hours after the incident, 'Barts', with 300 patients choking its casualty department, had to ask for further cases to be sent elsewhere – the Royal Free, Great Ormond Street, the Homeopathic Hospital and University College all received some – but many of those requiring treatment were soon afterwards allowed to go home. Four surgical teams at Bart's had worked at full stretch, with only short breaks, until noon on 9 March, more than twenty-four hours after the first victims were wheeled in, the cases giving most anxiety, it was found, being penetrating wounds of the abdomen and major compound fractures of the longer bones. The Royal Free, meanwhile, was keeping a special watch on patients who had been buried, to see if they revealed symptoms of 'crush syndrome', to forestall which bicarbonate of soda was, where possible, administered while they were still trapped.

It was not for some time that the reason for the enormously high casualty figures – apart from the obvious factors of time of day and the large number of people about – was established. The V-2 had, the official report explained, 'penetrated two-storey shop and fishmarket buildings at NE junction of Charterhouse and Farringdon Road and detonated at a lower level than the roadway of Farringdon Road', and thus brought down 'the concrete and iron vaulted floor, also the lattice-framed roof of the single-storey fishmarket'. In other words, a huge and exceptionally heavy mass of rubble had poured down from ground level on to the floor below, and then into the goods yards of the railway running beneath it. The result was a volcano-like cauldron of brick, stone, steel and timber, and the rescue teams had to begin work by adding to the destruction, pulling down the still-standing remains of the eleven shops on the Farringdon and Charterhouse Roads frontage 'to allow skips of the mobile crane being operated over the cleared spaces into the railway siding area', where railway trucks were used to take away the debris. The rescue work brought its own dangers, for, as the twisted steel girders were cut by oxyacetylene equipment to give access to the rubble below, they were liable to 'skid' and start a new landslide in a hitherto stable part of the ruins. Another problem was unique to this incident. 'The smell of decomposing fish, etc., was very bad,' it was reported the morning after the incident, 'and . . . as it would increase during the day and would interfere with the working of the personnel, Mr Upton was asked to get the Medical Officer of Health of Finsbury to take action to spray the debris.'

As usual at 'shopping' incidents, determining who was missing was a major undertaking in itself. 'A very much over-worked WVS inquiry point operated in a local public house,' the casualty services officer reported, 'until the Holborn Heavy Mobile Unit vacated Pearces' Restaurant, which was then taken over by the WVS. It was still here at full pressure on the 10th instant.'

Surely, everyone at the Ministry of Home Security must have thought, with victory clearly only weeks away there could be no worse incident than Smithfield. In fact one of the Germans' very last rockets was now to cause the second-largest number of deaths, 134, of the whole campaign, though the number of seriously injured, 49, was substantially smaller than at Smithfield. The site this time was an estate of five-storey flats, known as Hughes Mansions, in Vallance Road, Stepney, the time 7.21 in the morning of Tuesday, 27 March 1945. The missile scored a direct hit, on the very centre of the three block estate, forming a crater 30 feet by 10 feet and totally demolishing the adjoining central block. The one immediately to the east was almost destroyed, the one to the west very badly damaged. This was essentially a 'domestic' incident, but on a huge scale, presenting its own perils, to victims and rescuers alike, as the regional casualty services officer noted in his report three days later:

Much of the work, especially in the eastern block, was being carried out under conditions of considerable danger where overhanging walls and copings were likely to fall at any time. . . . Several of the personnel were attended to at the mobile unit for minor injuries, including two or three who had evidently got into a pocket of coal gas.

As often happened when old apartment blocks collapsed, small pockets of space remained in which the former occupants were buried and as late as 5.15 that afternoon 'trapped persons', a visitor from regionl headquarters reported, 'were still being recovered alive from voids in the debris', the last not being retrieved until 10 p.m. Thereafter attention turned to 'the removal of compact debris' in which there was no hope of finding anyone still breathing.

Hughes Mansions provided the London Civil Defence Service with its last great test, and it emerged with its battle honours undimmed. By midday that Tuesday five cranes were on the spot, and others on their way, and 16 heavy rescue parties, 11 light rescue parties and 75 NFS men at work amid the rubble. Among the hundreds of veteran helpers was the Whitechapel fireman quoted earlier, and his recollections provide the last eye witness account of a major incident during the Second World War.

We at Whitechapel Fire Station had almost finished breakfast when we heard the usual double report, the lights momentarily dimmed and we realized that a V-2 had dropped somewhere near. Still eating, we rushed to our machines and were getting our gear on when the bells went down and we heard the address of the incident, Hughes Mansions, Vallance Road. As we stopped near what had been a large block of flats we were met by many people, some trying to find relatives or friends, others demented and just running around wildly. I remember one chap covered in blood running down the road carrying what had once been a whole, live baby, calling his wife, and some people grabbing him and leading him away.

The V-2 had dropped in the middle of the block and the inside walls . . . had been sheered away by the blast. Beds, people and furniture had all dropped into a large mound at the base of the standing walls.

The usual procedure had to be followed, tearing at the rubble to free trapped victims, lending first aid to the injured, lowering from floors where stairs had gone. Nearly all persons had been accounted for and I was edging along a mound of rubble when I heard a voice calling 'Fireman'. I looked but could see nobody. Suddenly I heard the voice again, 'Can you see me, fireman, I'm down here near your feet. . . .'

Bending down, I noticed a slit between the bricks and I could just see someone trapped behind the wall. There appeared no way of reaching whoever it was from my position, so answering, 'I can see you, I am coming round the other side', I made my way around the wall until I could hear the call again. Getting between broken walls and timbers I eventually saw a bed standing on its end, trapped by a fallen staircase and squashed against a wall, The occupant was an old lady, still tucked in, but unable to move.

I managed to pull her, in her blankets, clear of the bed but could not manage to get her over the debris. By this time help arrived in the form of one of our crew. Fireman Z., whose hobby was weight-lifting. Saying 'Let me have her!', he picked her up by the shoulders and with myself at the feet we got her out on to the rubble where a stretcher was waiting. She would not be shifted until she had taken my hand and said 'Thank you, son, God bless you!'

Operations at Vallance Road, described by the regional official reporting on them after his fifth and final visit as 'one of the most difficult that have had to be dealt with', were still in progress when Rocket No. 1115, Kammler's final throw, landed thirteen miles south-east of Stepney, in a residential area of Orpington, not wholly unlike Staveley Road, Chiswick, in character, at 4.37 p.m. on 27 March. Numbers 61 and 63 Kynaston Road, built in the 1930s, were destroyed, and another fifteen properties, there and in the adjoining Court Road, badly damaged. About seventy people were injured, but many had lucky escapes. A then fourteen-year-old girl, so close – at 51 Kynaston Road – that she did not hear the explosion, suffered nothing worse than having a door blown down on top of her, and in Court Road one resident got away with a severe, impressively bandaged, bump on the head, from a similar cause. One of his daughters, entertaining a WAAF friend to tea in the same house, had a severed artery and lost a lot of blood; the WAAF beside her was almost unhurt.

For the very last time, people over a wide area faced the agonizing uncertainty of wondering if it was their road, and their home, which had been hit. Another daughter of the family just mentioned was sitting with a friend at the Embassy Cinema, Petts Wood, 'weeping our way through the *Constant Nymph*', when a message on the cinema screen summoned her from her seat and she was given instructions to meet her father at Orpington Station. Their house was uninhabitable and he wanted to prepare her for the shock. Having just missed a train, the two women ran along the track to Orpington 'completing the journey in only fifteen minutes', a notable achievement, and, having heard the news, 'went to the scene and saw it by moonlight . . . damaged furniture, glass shattered, all the fish in the garden pond dead, and a neighbour's pyjama trousers flying from a chimney'. She was, though she could not know it, the last person to undertake such a vigil by her ruined home, which three months later had been repaired. For another family in Court Road, however, their former life could never be regained. One of the occupants of number 86 was killed, the only fatal victim of this final rocket, dying, as so many had feared, from 'the last bullet' on the eve of victory.

30

THEY HAVE CEASED

No further attacks have been made on this country with long-range rockets.

Home Security Operations Bulletin No. 248, for the week ending Wednesday 4 April 1945

On Wednesday, 28 March 1945, while the last bodies were still being dug out of the ruins of Hughes Mansions in Stepney, not a single V-2 arrived. That day Mrs Gwladys Cox returned to her flat in West Hampstead from a holiday in the Lake District to find that it had suffered from the last rocket in the area, in the Finchley Road on 17 March.* 'The porter had boarded up the shattered window,' she noted, 'but having been obliged to leave all the others open a few inches, to ease possible blast, the whole place was covered in a layer of black dust.' On Thursday the 29th, although no one yet knew this, the last flying bomb landed in Kent, and on Good Friday, 30 March, a 'fine and mild' day, Mrs Cox began the Easter weekend with a modest outing:

After tea, we took a walk along the Finchley Road and saw the bomb damage to the public library. The building had been cut clean in half, and there is a huge crater, like that of a small volcano, in the adjoining gardens. There was a notice posted up in the library gate as to the latest V Bomb casualties [for the whole of London]. On the 28th inst. . . . no less than 119 people were killed.

It was the most peaceful weekend since September, and to add to the feeling of returning normality spring seemed to have arrived along with the last rocket. On 9 April Vere Hodgson in Notting Hill confided almost incredulously to her diary: 'No more bombs for more than a week. No one knows what it

---

*See Chapter 22, p. 278.

means to us to go to bed in peace and not . . . wonder if we shall wake up in pieces, or with the roof collapsing on our heads, unless they have lived with it.' 'As you have probably heard, there has continued to be complete quiet over London,' wrote the East End evening-institute lecturer previously quoted, to her husband on 10 April. Next day it was the same story. 'No bombs!' recorded Vere Hodgson joyously. 'The trees are fresh and green. We are fanning [out] over Holland, but the Germans are still fighting.' Soon, she thought, 'they will declare the end of the war. But it came for us here when the last bomb dropped.'

The siege of the capital had been lifted by the advance of the Allied armies. In late February, thanks to the Russians, Peenemünde was evacuated and 4000 technical staff and their equipment moved to Bleicheröde, 12 miles from Nordhausen, where it was planned to set up a new experimental establishment underground. Kammler, with his usual ferocious energy, planned to build another ten miles of galleries under the mountains, plus a large liquid oxygen plant, and static testing rigs were built into a quarry. This was in its way Kammler's finest hour, as Dornberger recognized, with something approaching admiration:

He dashed to and fro between the Dutch and Rhineland fronts and Thuringia and Berlin. He was on the move day and night. Conferences were called for one o'clock in the morning somewhere in the Harz mountains, or we would meet at midnight somewhere on the autobahn and then, after a brief exchange of views, drive back to work again. We were prey to terrific nervous tension. Irritable and over-worked as we were, we didn't mince words. Kammler, if he got impatient and wanted to drive on, would wake the slumbering officers of his suite with a burst from his tommy-gun. 'No need for *them* to sleep! I can't either!' . . . Kammler still believed that he alone, with his Army Corps and the weapons over which he had absolute authority, could prevent the imminent collapse, postpone a decision and even turn the scales. The transporters still moved without respite to the operational area. Convoys of motor vehicles bridged the gaps in the railways. Kammler's supply columns, equipped with infra-red devices that enabled them to see in the dark, rumbled along the Dutch highways. When the only railway supply line to The Hague V-2 launching base had been blown up by Dutch resistance groups and the local commander was short of men to protect it, Kammler took over with reserve and training units brought overnight from Germany, together with improvised contingents of the launching troops. He managed to hold the line clear.

Almost to the end the Central Works were still turning out more rockets. In January 1945 690 rolled off the production line, in February 617, in March 362. Kammler was ordered to abandon the battle with ample stocks still in hand, being instructed on 27 March, when in danger of being outflanked and captured, to withdraw his men to Germany. On 3 April Kammler ordered that the training and experimental unit be disbanded and converted into an ordinary infantry battalion to strengthen his 5th Army Corps, which on 5 April was formally entrusted with the defence of the Nordhausen area, now the sole surviving enclave for rocket production and testing, and here this 'frenzied warrior', as Dornberger described him, hoped to prevent the American and Russian armies joining forces. Events proved too much, however, even for his iron will. He was not, as he wished, given the opportunity to fight to the last man, and the rocket units, having killed so many civilians themselves, survived to go home and boast of their achievements to their compatriots.

Fighting to the last man, at least if he were cast for that role, made no appeal to von Braun. He was already planning to surrender to the Americans and hoping to buy privileged treatment for himself by betraying his country's secrets to them. According to a sycophantic American biographer, who wrote an admiring life of her hero for American schoolchildren, 'Werner's heart pounded in admiration and love' for his pretty young cousin who 'looked like a Dresden doll', but he cheerfully abandoned her to the Russians to make good his own escape, having established his parents in a comfortable spot where 'there had been no bombings and food was plentiful'. Ever a man to get his priorities right, von Braun now appropriated the surviving stocks of rocket fuel, in the absence of petrol, and fled in style in a chauffeur-driven, alcohol-powered car, until his exhausted driver fell asleep at the wheel.* The

---

*A post-war song by the American satirist Tom Lehrer aptly referred to von Braun starting to learn Chinese, so strong was his instinct for self-preservation.

same malign providence that a year earlier had saved Hitler from death now protected his devoted servant: von Braun awoke in hospital with an injured arm and shoulder, but suffered no permanent harm, though his already imposing figure became even more conspicuous than ever with his left arm stiffly extended in a plaster cast. While the soldiers who had fired the rocket were left to face the advancing enemy, von Braun and Dornberger, accompanied by '450 old Peenemunde executives', left Bleicherode on 6 April for Oberjoch, near Oberammergau in the Lower Alps, escorted by Security Service men who, they feared, were keeping them safe for use 'as hostages in armistice negotiations' or, even more alarmingly, had orders to prevent them 'from falling into enemy hands' On the journey, tons of films, drawings and documents were hidden for safety in an abandoned mine in the Harz mountains, and the entrance blasted shut, so that, if they proved to have backed the wrong horse they could return to resume work on the more advanced and destructive missiles von Braun was already designing. While in Deptford and Finsbury, Heston and Stepney, hundreds of families were still mourning their recent dead, and many more mutilated survivors were beginning to come to terms with a life of blindness or disablement, the scientists directly responsible settled cosily down in their rural retreat to await capture, as Dornberger described:

All development work had stopped. We lay on the terrace of our quarters and let the sun beat down on us. We gave ourselves up to our thoughts, argued about our more important projects and slowly achieved detachment from the march of events. Above us towered the snow-covered Allgäu Mountains, their peaks glittering in the sunlight under the clear blue sky. Far below us it was already spring. The hill pastures were a bright green. Even on our high mountain pass the first flowers were thrusting buds through the melting snow. It was so infinitely peaceful here!

The British press carried no report that the V-2s had ceased to arrive, though those with access to the weekly Ministry of Home Security Operations bulletins learned from No. 248, for the seven days ending on Wednesday, 4 April, that 'no further attacks have been made on this country with long-range rockets'. A week later, instead of Bulletin No. 249 there came

373

an even more encouraging message: 'It has been decided that, in existing circumstances, the Ministry of Home Security will not issue "Nil" Operations Bulletins.'

It had been two months after the first V-2 landed before the news was made public. It was a month after the last before the British people were allowed to learn that their final and most bitter ordeal was over; no one wanted to risk a repeat of the 'Battle of London' fiasco. At last, on 26 April, the day after the Russian and American forces had joined hands on the Elbe, the matter was raised in the House of Commons by the MP for Ilford, no doubt with prior government approval:

Mr Geoffrey Hutchinson asked the Prime Minister whether he is now able to make any statement with regard to the enemy rocket attacks.

The Prime Minister (Mr Churchill): Yes, sir. They have ceased.

Mr Hutchinson: While thanking my right honourable friend for his reply, may I ask him whether he can give an assurance to the House that there is no prospect that they are likely to be resumed?

The Prime Minister: It is my duty to record facts rather than indulge in prophecy, but I have recorded certain facts with a very considerable air of optimism, which I trust will not be brought into mockery by events.

Mr Rhorne [Labour MP for West Ham, Plaistow divison]: Should we not offer congratulations to the Royal Air Force for stopping these rocket attacks?

The Prime Minister: We must offer them to the Royal Air Force for what they did, we must offer them to the anti-aircraft gunners for what they did, but we must not forget it was the British Armies that took the sites.

The RAF's performance against the rockets was in fact, as indicated earlier, a sensitive subject, and Churchill's reply to his next questioner showed little desire to discuss the V-2s further:

Capt. Gammans [Conservative MP for Hornsey] asked the Prime Minister when he expects to be in a position to make a comprehensive statement on the V-2 activities against London and Southern England.

The Prime Minister: Later on an account of this ordeal so valiantly borne – of which the brunt fell on London in an almost overwhelming degree – should certainly be prepared.

Capt. Gammans: Can my right honourable friend say when he is likely to be in a position to make a fuller report on these rockets? *The Prime Minister*: I have got to make a fuller report on all sorts of things in the near future and I am not sure the rockets will stand in a very high priority.

During the next few days the advancing American armies occupied Nordhausen, liberated its slave labourers and seized its arsenal of finished and partly finished rockets – they filled 300 large railway wagons – for shipment to the United States. Enough parts were captured to make 75 V-2s, and the Americans wanted to remove everything before leaving the area to the Russians, as it was in their occupation zone.

The scientists and soldiers assembled at Oberjoch, where von Braun and Dornberger were comfortably billeted in a holiday hotel, followed on the radio the news of their country's deepening defeat and when, on Tuesday, 1 May, listeners were asked to stand by for an important announcement, they cheered, believing that the Führer was about to produce another 'miracle weapon' to turn the tide at the eleventh hour. Instead they learned of his death, causing even the most optimistic to recognize that the war was irretrievably lost, and Dornberger gathered his key colleagues round him and piously informed them that 'It is our obligation to place our rocket knowledge in the right hands.' What this meant was that they thought the Americans would be a softer touch than the Russians and von Braun's brother, Magnus, who had been brought along because he spoke good English, was sent out to try to find an American to whom they could surrender. Almost at once he encountered a Pfc (private first class) with an anti-tank company whom he tactfully addressed as 'Herr Officer!' and within hours the cream of Germany's scientists were safe in US hands, installed, as befitted their station, in rooms 'with views of mountain peaks' surrounded by 'lawns and flowers' at Garmisch-Partenkirchen. For them the war ended that day, 2 May, and von Braun realized that once again his instinct as one of nature's survivors had triumphed. While all over Europe families sought missing relatives, mourned their dead or struggled to rebuild their shattered lives, 'Werner', his admiring biographer later learned, 'was amazed at his first American breakfast of fried eggs, bacon, toast with real butter, and genuine coffee.' Already his rehabilitation was beginning. 'One soldier spoke his mind: "He looks too fat and jolly to have launched anything more deadly than a kite".'

But the scientists were not out of the wood yet. The Americans, having suffered nothing from the rockets, were indulgent; with their allies it was different. The British people, Dornberger heard, planned to give him 'a fair trial and hanging', but they were not consulted. Soon after the formal end of the war, on Tuesday 8 May 1945, the Americans, treating their prisoners not as mass murderers but as honoured guests, brought their wives and children to Landshut near Munich, where they were cared for even better than their husbands and fathers until the whole lot were shipped to the United States. While GI brides in England were publicly demonstrating to demand a passage to join their husbands, who had fought against Hitler, Hitler's dedicated scientists were found priority transport; by September 1945 von Braun was in Boston under contract to the US government, ready to start work in his old profession on the material brought from Germany. Along with him were a hundred other scientists identified by the Americans as key men. But the British were not quite shut out. En route von Braun was interrogated by Sir Alwyn Crow of the Ministry of Supply and other British scientists who had doubted the rocket's practicality.

By December most of the Germans who had helped to develop the V-2 were in the United States and in April 1946 the first V-2 was launched from America's Peenemünde, the White Sands testing ground in New Mexico. Von Braun jovially referred to himself and his colleagues as 'prisoners of peace', but all restrictions on them were rapidly lifted. He was even allowed to return to Germany to marry his cousin and to bring her and his parents back to the United States. In 1955 he became an American citizen, at Huntsville, Alabama. According to von Braun's biographer, 'The Huntsville mayor proclaimed that date "New Citizens' Day." The town turned out to honour them at the high school auditorium. Celebrities spoke; bands played. The world appeared happy.' That night von Braun appeared on television to refer to 'We Americans' and he remained a leading figure in rocket research, living long enough to see his dreams of firing rockets from underwater, and between continents, even his distant hope of space travel, become reality. He died of cancer in 1977, aged 65. His former chief, Dornberger, also settled in the United States, but his later years were relatively obscure. What happened to Hans Kammler is uncertain. At his last meeting with Dornberger, in April 1945, he still refused to admit the possibility that the Third Reich could be defeated and he is believed to have mounted the final defence of Czechoslovakia against the Russians, until, no doubt on his own orders, his adjutant shot him to prevent his capture.

The later history of those on the Allied side most involved with the V-2 is less dramatic. Duncan Sandys went on to hold a series of senior posts, including those of Minister of Aviation and Minister of Defence and now, as Lord Duncan-Sandys, is retired. R. V. Jones became Professor of Natural Philosophy [i.e. science] at Aberdeen University, and, though now also retired, has become well known as an authority on wartime intelligence. Lord Cherwell, who died of heart disease in 1957, aged seventy-one, served again as Churchill's scientific adviser in his first post-war government. He had remained sceptical of the rocket's value to the end of the war, long after its destructive potential had been demonstrated. This all too characteristic inability to change his mind, however overwhelming the evidence, had been witnessed by General Pile while lunching at Chequers in November 1944.

We discussed the V-2 rocket during the meal and Churchill got in several humorous digs at Lindemann, who kept on repeating that it was a stupid sort of weapon. The PM said it was becoming a very accurate weapon, and, obviously, he had not forgotten that Lindemann had said that it could not be produced as an effective weapon of war.

In a memo to Churchill a month later, on 5 December, Cherwell reaffirmed his sceptical view of the missile's future:

Although rockets may play a considerable tactical role as long-range barrage artillery behind the lines at twenty, thirty or even fifty miles, I am very doubtful of their strategic value. It seems likely that it will always be possible to deliver the same quantity of explosive much more economically and accurately from aircraft than from rockets and without anything like the same limitations of range.

To this view Cherwell clung with unshakeable peristence and on 6 April 1945, with the last V-2 already fired, he again wrote to the Prime Minister on the subject, this time comparing the V-2 unfavourably to the flying bomb:

V-2 has the merit against V-1 that it can be fired without any launching site other than a flat bit of road or hard surface a dozen yards square and that it cannot be shot down in flight. There is not much difference in accuracy between the two weapons and as the V-2 costs at least ten times as much as the V-1, it scarcely seems as economic proposition. The comparison with a bomber, of course, is still more unfavourable.

R. V. Jones showed greater prescience. In September 1944 he wrote for the United States Air Force – who were far quicker than the British government to grasp the V-2's long-term significance – an article attributed only to 'a British source':

There can be no doubt that with the A-4 the rocket has come to stay. . . . Reviewing . . . reasonable extrapolation from present prac-tice, a two-stage rocket of about 150 tons starting weight could deliver a one-ton warhead to nearly 3,000 miles range, with a probable error of 10 miles in range and three miles in line. This might be a feasible weapon for delivering a uranium bomb, should such a bomb become practicable. . . . At the moment such a rocket could not be inter-cepted, but by the time it becomes a serious possibility it may itself be a target for smaller defence rockets fitted with predictors and homing devices. . . . The long range rocket can be developed much further. In the light of this fact, we must watch.

The legacy of the rocket in the shape of bereavement and grief, serious wounds and minor scars has already been mentioned. Apart from them most evidence of the V-2's exist-ence has now vanished. All that are left are souvenirs, a source of interest rather than alarm. One wartime schoolboy still has in his garden shed in Tottenham the piece of rocket casing which nearly ended his life forty years ago, when it landed where he had been standing just before the milkman, whom he had been helping before school, pushed him under his cart – 'one of the last of the push type with two large wheels and a small one in front'. In Kent a wartime fireman still cherishes part of the very last V-2 to fall; at Bramerton, near Norwich, a portion of one of the very first now revolves harmlessly as a weather vane. The most enduring of such relics were the combustion chambers that formerly littered the fields of East Anglia, one of which was described by a Suffolk newspaper in February 1984. 'Rabbits had used it as a burrow and pheasants had nested in it', before a local farmer moved it to his home and 'planted flowers in it to brighten up his drive'; it is now in the local aviation museum, near Bungay. The V-2, so feared in its day, is now everywhere a museum piece. One can be seen in the Imperial War Museum and another, with its casing cut away to show the fantastically complicated network of pipes inside, in the Science Museum in South Kensington. Elsewhere it survives only in the memory of people now well on into middle age. In The Hague older residents may still point out open spaces which mark the spot where a misfired rocket plunged back to earth, while a few people in Hackney can even now identify the spot on the famous Marshes where a rocket landed, creating a crater that was, most fittingly, used as the site for a huge bonfire on VE night.

Information about the V-2s is surprisingly hard to come by. Churchill's hint in April 1945 that telling their story had a low priority proved amply justified. In his own war memoirs they are mentioned very cursorily, in the official war histories they receive far less space than the conventional raids or the flying-bombs, and in Air Chief Marshal Hill's official report on the secret-weapon campaign, published in October 1948, they are given only 10 paragraphs out of 247, although Hill himself admits that the rocket 'was in some ways a more disturbing menace than the flying-bomb'. Local authorities which wished to publish full details of V-2 incidents in their war histories, even after the war was over, were forbidden to do so, and many local libraries and record offices lack even the scantiest information about local incidents, while possessing a mass of documents on earlier events. It is as though the whole subject, where British scientists fell so far behind their German rivals, and British ministers and commanders proved totally unable to protect their citizens, was too painful and embarrassing to be properly documented. Only with the release of the files in the Public Record Office has it become possible to study the

V-2's effects comprehensively, and even here there are tantalizing gaps.

The Germans have felt no such inhibitions as their former enemies. A mass of records about the development of the V-2 have survived and been used by previous writers, and von Braun himself, in collaboration with an American writer, published a massive *History of Rocketry and Space Travel* in 1966, which, very typically, takes for granted that, having invented it, the Germans were right to try out the missile in action. There is no hint of guilt in the authors' comment that the missiles 'were responsible for more than 2,500 deaths and great property damage', and they make clear that the offensive was abandoned only when it appeared that the V-2 'clearly was going to neither influence the war's outcome nor delay its end'. Dornberger, in his time an honourable soldier, raises the moral implications of using such an innately indiscriminate weapon only to dismiss them:

The operational use of the A-4 at an imperfect state of development will . . . be called pointless, brutal and inhuman, but, if so, all long-range artillery and bombing must accept the same condemnation. The dispersion of the V-2 in relation to its range was always less than that of bombs and big guns.

His only regret was that he had not been able to make more, and better, rockets sooner and thereby enable Hitler to defeat and enslave his most persistent enemy:

We were well aware that operational employment of the A-4 in the autumn of 1944 could not of itself win the war. But what might have happened if from two years earlier, say summer 1942, for years on end, by day and night, more and more long-range rockets with ever-increasing range, accuracy and effect had fallen on England? . . . The use of the V-2 may be aptly summed up in the two words: 'too late'. Lack of foresight in high places and failure to understand the technical background were to blame.

But was the V-2 even in its relatively primitive stage of development so unsatisfactory a weapon? On this there seems to be a curious unanimity between those who have studied the subject in both countries. Lord Cherwell, for example, in his note of 6 April 1945 already quoted, made the point that 'a Mosquito, which is comparable in price with one or at most two V-2s, can drop about 250 tons of bombs in its life, with at least a hundred times greater accuracy, on any target within 600 miles'. David Irving, author of the standard (and excellent) account of the rocket's development, who is certainly no uncritical admirer of Cherwell – his book's very title, *The Mare's Nest*, immortalizes Cherwell's most notorious error of judgement – also thinks the argument of price decisive. 'No A-4 rocket', he comments, truthfully enough, 'could . . . have cost much less than £12,000 by the time it was delivered to the launching troops; this was certainly not the cheapest way of delivering 1,620 pounds of conventional explosive . . . to a maximum range of 200 miles.' Albert Speer, no mean authority on munitions manufacture, was equally sceptical, looking back twenty-five years later, of the rocket's economic viability:

From the end of July 1943 our tremendous industrial capacity was diverted to the huge missile later known as the V-2. . . . Hitler wanted to have nine hundred of these produced monthly. The whole notion was absurd. The fleets of enemy bombers in 1944 were dropping an average of three thousand tons of bombs a day over a span of several months. And Hitler wanted to retaliate with thirty rockets that would have carried twenty-four tons of explosives to England daily. That was equivalent to the bomb load of only twelve Flying Fortresses. I not only went along with this decision on Hitler's part but also supported it. That was probably one of my most serious mistakes.

The argument that the V-2 was unviable because of its cost had, however, been answered by R. V. Jones in his paper, already quoted, circulated in 1944, when only a few missiles had arrived:

The protagonists for the development of very long range rockets would probably have, in Britain at any rate, to meet the criticism that it would not be worth the effort expended. The A-4 has already shown us that our enemies are not restrained by such considerations and have thereby made themselves leaders in a technique which sooner or later will be regarded as one of the masterpieces of human endeavours.

The truth is that in war the normal rules of finance cease to apply. When it comes to weapons, nations can always afford what they want, as Germany, which so many experts had proclaimed bankrupt and unable to sustain a long war, had already amply demonstrated, and as the Allies had shown when shouldering the staggering cost of producing the first atomic bombs. Nor was the suggestion that the V-2 was less cost-effective than the German equivalent of a Mosquito or a Flying Fortress valid, for the reason Cherwell and Speer preferred to ignore: that the rocket always got through, while – as the British bombing offensive confirmed – the defence was more powerful than the offensive in the case of manned aircraft. A V-2 which landed in Stepney or Ilford was infinitely more useful than a bomber which ended, as any German manned bomber was likely to do by 1944, in the Channel. The history of the flying bomb underlined this truth. It had been unbelievably cheap, at £125, a fantastic military bargain, which cost not a single German life, until it became almost as vulnerable to the RAF as the Heinkels and Junkers of the Luftwaffe in its heyday. The rocket was – all moral considerations set aside, as they were by the Germans – a superb weapon, an immense leap forward in warfare, because it was totally unbeatable. As time, experience and further research increased its power and accuracy, it could have become a war-winning one.

What, then, did the rockets achieve, apart from providing the necessary first step into a new world of military technology? The official British historian, using enemy as well as domestic sources, put the total launched at 1403, of which 288 went astray or exploded en route, 61 landed offshore and 1054 exploded on the mainland, 517 of these in London, 537 in eleven other counties. As mentioned earlier, they killed 2754 people and seriously injured 6523, a total of 9277 major casualties; they did a great deal of militarily significant damage; and they caused a great deal more destruction to other property at a time when the building industry was already badly stretched. In attacking morale, that target which so many champions of air power had proclaimed as even more important than weakening the enemy's industrial potential, the rocket was incomparably the most effective weapon so far devised: the low ebb to which spirits in southern England sank during that last and, as it seemed, unnecessary winter of the war is evident again and again in the reminiscences of the time. And all this excludes what the V-2s achieved in Belgium, which suffered proportionately far more than England: 1214 V-2s fell in the Antwerp area alone, one of them killing 242 servicemen and 250 civilians in a single direct hit on a cinema, the largest death roll caused by any missile of the whole European war.

'If we had had this rocket in 1939, we would never have had this war,' Hitler told Dornberger in 1943, apologizing for his previous lack of faith in the V-2. He may well have been right; sufficient reason by itself – when the horrifying alternative, a Nazi-dominated world, is considered – for giving the rocket its belated due as not merely a masterpiece of scientific and engineering brilliance but as the most formidable and fearful weapon of its time.

Where the V-2s landed in London
The map on p. 384 shows the London Civil Defence Region as it was in September 1944. The map shows all the boroughs within the Region, identified by numbers, to which the key is given above. The number of V-2s which landed in each borough is given in bold type to the right of its name.

Where the V-2s landed outside London
The map on p. 385 shows all the counties in which V-2s landed, the county names and boundaries being those which existed in September 1944. The number of V-2s in each county, excluding any which landed in any part of it included in the London Civil Defence Region, is shown below its name.

0   5

miles

1 Bushey	25 Hornsey **4**	49 Hackney **10**	73 Bermondsey **7**
2 Elstree **2**	26 Wood Green **2**	50 Shoreditch **2**	74 Deptford **9**
3 Potters Bar **1**	27 Tottenham **3**	51 Finsbury **3**	75 Greenwich **22**
4 East Barnet **1**	28 Walthamstow **18**	52 Holborn **1**	76 Woolwich **33**
5 Enfield **9**	29 Wanstead **14**	53 The City of London	77 Erith **17**
6 Cheshunt **7**	30 Ilford **35**	54 Stepney **8**	78 Surbiton
7 Waltham Holy Cross **15**	31 Staines **1**	55 Bethnal Green **2**	79 Merton
8 Uxbridge	32 Sunbury **1**	56 Poplar **9**	80 Mitcham
9 Ruislip **2**	33 Feltham	57 Leyton **12**	81 Croydon **4**
10 Harrow **4**	34 Heston **2**	58 West Ham **27**	82 Penge
11 Hendon **2**	35 Twickenham **1**	59 East Ham **14**	83 Beckenham **5**
12 Barnet Urban District **1**	36 Brentford **1**	60 Barking **21**	84 Lewisham **12**
13 Southgate **4**	37 Acton	61 Dagenham **19**	85 Bromley **6**
14 Edmonton **9**	38 Hammersmith **1**	62 Esher **1**	86 Chislehurst **17**
15 Chingford **11**	39 Kensington **1**	63 Malden	87 Bexley **12**
16 Chigwell **13**	40 Fulham	64 Malden	88 Crayford **5**
17 Yiewsley **1**	41 Chelsea **1**	65 Richmond **2**	89 Epsom
18 Hayes **2**	42 Westminster **2**	66 Barnes **1**	90 Banstead **2**
19 Southall	43 Paddington	67 Wimbledon	91 Sutton
20 Ealing **1**	44 St Marylebone **1**	68 Wandsworth **6**	92 Carshalton
21 Wembley **1**	45 Hampstead **3**	69 Battersea **2**	93 Beddington
22 Willesden **4**	46 St Pancras **2**	70 Lambeth **3**	94 Coulsdon **1**
23 Finchley **1**	47 Islington **8**	71 Camberwell **9**	95 Orpington **14**
24 Friern Barnet **1**	48 Stoke Newington **2**	72 Southwark **3**	

384

SOURCES

This book is based upon material drawn from the following sources: published books and pamphlets, contemporary and subsequent newspaper and magazine articles and reports, a wide range of official documents in the Public Record Office and elsewhere (from statements prepared for publication to minutes and memoranda which were then highly secret), diaries and letters written at the time, and contributions specially written for me following a public appeal in the press for recollections of the V-1s and V-2s. The place of publication of books is London unless otherwise stated. Where the source of a quotation is obvious from the text (e.g. if a particular issue of a specific newspaper is named) this information is not repeated in the 'Detailed references' section below. In making use of official documents it should be noted that more than one copy may exist, under different file references. Where a single file (such as PREM 3/111, which proved particularly useful) contains a great many relevant documents I have given the written folio number, the later numbers being the more recent. I used two documents constantly. 'Report of Attacks on this Country by . . . Long-Range Rockets . . . to March 29th 1945' in File Air 20/3439 includes a list of casualties for each borough in London, and each affected county outside London, and, at Appendix 'B' a list of 'outstanding incidents'. File HO 202/10 contains a series of weekly reports numbered from 221 to 250, giving the total number of incidents with notes about items of special interest. Wherever no other source is indicated it can be assumed that the figures in the text came from these documents. File HO 191/198 contains lists of incidents, giving precise time and map reference, a summary of damage caused and other essential facts, for incidents 1–26, 91–123 and 124–160. These have provided additional information given in the text for the periods covered and are not separately identified below.

Books, pamphlets and articles

After the Battle, no. 6, 'The V Weapons', Battle of Britain Prints International, London E15, 1974

'Air Raids on Norfolk', in *Britannia*, no. 29, February 1947

Angell, Joseph Warner, 'Guided Missiles Could Have Won', in *Atlantic Monthly* (Boston, Mass., USA), vol. 189, January 1952

Arct, Bohdan, *Poles against the V-Weapons*, Interpress Publications, Warsaw, 1972

Ascoli, David, *A Village in Chelsea*, William Luscombe, 1974

Babington Smith, Constance, *Evidence in Camera. The Story of Photographic Intelligence in World War II*, Chatto & Windus, 1958

Baker, H. A., *The Memoirs of H. A. Baker, 46 years in the Royal Arsenal*, vol. 1 (typescript), Imperial War Museum

Baker, R. B., *The Year of the Buzz Bomb*, Exposition Press, New York, 1952

Banger, Joan, *Norwich at War*, Albion Books, Norwich, 1974

Bartholomew's Reference Atlas to London, Bartholomew & Son, Edinburgh, 1940 edition

BBC Monitoring Service Reports

Benham, H. *Essex at War*, Essex County Standard, Chelmsford, 1946

Berwick Sayers, W. C. (ed.), *Croydon and the Second World War*, Croydon Corporation, 1949

Birkenhead, Earl of, *The Prof. in Two Worlds: the Official Life of Professor F. A. Lindemann, Viscount Cherwell*, Collins, 1961

Blake, Lewis (pseud.), *Red Alert, South East London 1939–1945*, published by the author, 1982

Blake, Lewis (pseud.), *Bromley in the Front Line*, published by the author, revised edition, 1983

Braun, Wernher von, and Ordway, Frederick I., *The History of Rocketry and Space Travel*, Nelson, 1966

Brookes, A. J., *Photo-Reconnaissance*, Ian Allan, Shepperton, Middlesex, 1975

Bullock, Alan, *Hitler, A Study in Tyranny*, Odhams, 1952 (page references are to Pelican edition, 1962)

Carter, Ernest F., *Railways in Wartime*, Fred Miller, 1964

Childs, Marquis W., 'London Wins the Battle', in *National Geographic Magazine*, vol. LXXXVIII, no. 2., Washington, DC, USA, August 1945

Churchill, Winston S., *The Second World War*, vol. V, Cassell, 1952, and vol. VI, Cassell, 1954

Civilian Air Raid Casualties, 1939–April 1945 (typescript), Imperial War Museum, no. KH 9816

Clark, Ronald W., *The Rise of the Boffins*, Phoenix House, 1962

Collier, Basil, *The Defence of the United Kingdom*, HMSO, 1957

Collier, Basil, *The Battle of the V-Weapons, 1944–1945*, Hodder & Stoughton, 1964

Collier, Basil, *A Short History of the Second World War*, Collins, 1967

Cox, Gwladys, *London War Diary 1939–45* (manuscript), Imperial War Museum, 1950

Cross, Colin, *Adolf Hitler*, Hodder & Stoughton, 1973

Crump, Norman, *By Rail to Victory, The Story of the LNER in Wartime*, LNER, 1947

Crutwell, C. R. M. F., *A History of The Great War 1914–1918*, Clarendon Press, Oxford, 1934

Damaged by Rockets (typescript), Imperial War Museum, no. K 39102

Darwin, Bernard, *War on the Line. The Southern Railway in Wartime*, Southern Railway, 1946

Dean, C. G. T., *The Royal Hospital, Chelsea*, Hutchinson, 1974

Despriet, Philippe, *De V-1 en de V-2 in Frans-Vlaanderen*. Cartoeristiek, Roeselare, Belgium

Donoughue, Bernard, and Jones, W. G., *Herbert Morrison*, Weidenfeld & Nicolson, 1973

Dornberger, Major-General Walter, *V-2*, Hurst & Blackett, 1954

Drew, Bernard, 'Farningham against Hitler', Kentish District Times, 1946

Ellis, L. F., and Warhurst, A. E., *Victory in the West, The Defeat of Germany*, vol. II, HMSO, 1968

Foot, M. R. D., *Resistance*, Eyre Methuen, 1976

Freeman, Roger, *The Mighty Eighth, A History of the US 8th Army Air Force*, Macdonald, 1970

Freeman, Spencer, *Production Under Fire*, C. J. Fallon, Dublin, 1967

Garlinski, Jozef, *Poland, SOE and the Allies*, Allen & Unwin, 1969

Garlinski, Josef, *Hitler's Last Weapons*, Friedmann, 1978

Gilroy, James, *Furred and Feathered Heroes of World War II*, Trafalgar Publications, 1946

Graves, Charles, *London Transport Carried On*. London Passenger Transport Board, 1947

Gwynn, Sir C. S., and Hammerton, Sir J. A., *The Second Great War, A Standard History*, vols 6 and 7, Amalgamated Press, 1946

Sources

Hampstead at War, 1939–1945, Hampstead Borough Council, n.d., c. 1945

Harriss, C. F., *Hotchpot: A Domestic Journal of the War Years from the 1st September 1939 to the 10 May 1945*, vol. 3 (manuscript), Imperial War Museum

Harrod, Sir H. R. F., *The Prof. A Personal Memoir of Lord Cherwell*, Macmillan, 1959

Hartley, A. B., *Unexploded Bomb. A History of Bomb Disposal*, Cassell, 1958

Helfers, Lt.-Col. M. C., *The Employment of V-Weapons by the Germans During World War II* (duplicated), Department of the Army, Washington, DC, USA, n.d.

Helfers, Lt-Col. M. C., 'Chaotic Command', in *Army* (Washington, DC, USA), vol. 6, no. 9, April 1956

Henry, Mrs Robert, *London*, Dent, 1955

Hill, Air Chief Marshal Sir Roderic, *Air Operations by Air Defence of Great Britain and Fighter Command in Connection with the German Flying Bomb and Rocket Offensives, 1944–1945*, published as *Supplement to the London Gazette*, 19 October 1948, no. 38347

History of the Photographic Interpretation Unit (duplicated), September 1945, in File Air 34/80 in Public Record Office

Hodgson, Vere, *Few Eggs and No Oranges. A Diary Showing How Unimportant People in London and Birmingham Lived Through the War Years, 1940–1945*, Dennis Dobson, 1976

Hall, W. E., *Civil Defence Goes Through It. Paddington 1937–1945* (typescript), 1946

Howard-Williams, Jeremy, *Night Intruder. A Personal Account of the Radar War Between the Luftwaffe and the RAF Night Fighter Forces*, David & Charles, Newton Abbot, 1976

Irving, David, *The Mare's Nest*, William Kimber, 1964

John, Evan, *Timetable for Victory*, British Railways, 1947

Johnson, David, *V for Vengeance, The Second Battle of London*, William Kimber, 1981

Johnson, D. E., *East Anglia at War*, Jarrold, Norwich, 1978

Jones, R. V., *Most Secret War, British Scientific Intelligence 1939–1945*, Hamish Hamilton, 1978

Jones, R. V., 'The Rocket's Red Glare', talk broadcast by BBC Radio 4, 1 August 1974

Jones, R. V., 'Lord Cherwell's Judgement in World War Two', in *Oxford Magazine*, new series, vol. 3, no. 18, 9 May 1963

Jones, R. V., 'The Future of the Rocket' in *US Air Force intelligence journal*, c. 1944

Keesings Contemporary Archives, 1944–45

Kennedy, G., *Vengeance Weapon 2, The V-2 Guided Missile*, NASA, Smithsonian Institution Press, Washington, DC, USA, 1983

Kohan, C. M., *Works and Buildings*, HMSO, 1952

Lambeth Civil Defence (duplicated), Lambeth Civil Defence Association, 1948 (Imperial War Museum, no. K 15907)

'The LCC Hospitals in Wartime', in *The Medical Officer*, vol. LXXVI (new series), no. 8, 24 August 1946

Lees-Milne, James, *Prophesying Peace*, Chatto & Windus, 1977

List of Incidents of Fly Bombs and Long-Range Rockets Affecting Corporation Property in the City of London and Elsewhere (duplicated), Corporation of London, n.d., c. 1945

Longmate, Norman, *The Doodlebugs*, Hutchinson, 1981

Longmate, Norman, *The Bombers*, Hutchinson, 1983

Longmate, Norman (ed.), *The Home Front*, Chatto & Windus, 1981

Luton at War, The Luton News, Home Counties Newspapers, Luton, 1947

Macmillan, Norman, *The Royal Air Force in the World War*, vol. IV, Harrap, 1950

Middlebrook, Martin, *The Peenemünde Raid*, Allen Lane, 1982

Moody, G. T., *Southern Electric*, Ian Allan, Shepperton, Middlesex, 1957

Montgomery, Field Marshal Viscount, *The Memoirs of Field Marshal Montgomery*, Fontana Books, 1960

O'Brien, T. H., *Civil Defence*, HMSO, 1955

Ordway, Frederick, I., and Sharpe, Mitchell, B., *The Rocket Team*, Heinemann, 1979

Orwell, Sonia, and Angus, Ian (eds), *The Collected Essays, Journalism and Letters of George Orwell*, vol. III, Secker & Warburg, 1968

Panter-Downes, Mollie, *London War Notes 1939–45*, Longmans, 1972

Pearson, F. T., *Memoirs* (typescript), Imperial War Museum, no. P 398

Pile, General Sir Frederick, *Ack-Ack*, Harrap, 1949

Platts, W. L., *Kent, The County Administration in War, 1939–1945*, Maidstone, 1946

Pound, Reginald, *Evans of the 'Broke'*, Oxford University Press, 1963

Raczynski, Count Edward, *In Allied London*, Weidenfeld & Nicolson, 1962

Richards, Denis, and Saunders, Hilary St George, *Royal Air Force 1939–1945*, vol. III, HMSO, 1953

Richards, G., *Ordeal in Romford*, 1945

Sanson, William, *Westminster in War*, Faber, 1947

Sources

Saunders, Hilary St George, *Ford at War, 1939–1945*, privately published, 1946

Shepheard-Walwyn, Rev. B. W., *Purleigh in Wartime*, J. H. Clarke, Chelmsford, 1946

Smith, J. R., and Kay, Anthony, *German Aircraft of the Second World War*, Putnam, 1972

Snow, C. P., *Science and Government*, Oxford University Press, 1961

Speer, Albert, *Inside the Third Reich*, Weidenfeld & Nicolson, 1970, Sphere Books (to which page references refer), 1971

Staples, Les J., 'Somewhere in Southern England', Pyrene Social and Athletic Association, n.d., c. 1945

Statistical Digest of the War, HMSO and Longmans, 1951

Summary of Damage Caused by Enemy Action Against the United Kingdom (duplicated), Ministry of Information, September 1945, Imperial War Museum, K 12863

Swanwick, F. W., *ARP (Civil Defence) in the Borough of Heston and Isleworth 1938–1945* (duplicated), 1961

Thompson, George P., *Blue Pencil Admiral. The Inside Story of the Press Censorship*, Sampson Low, 1947

Thompson, R. J., *Battle over Essex*, Chelmsford, 1946

Turner, E. S., 'Ack-Ack', in *Soldier*, vol. 8, no. 8, October 1952

Vale, George F., *Bethnal Green's Ordeal*, Bethnal Green Borough Council, 1945

Wadsworth, John, *Counter Defensive, Being the Story of a Bank in Battle*, Hodder & Stoughton, 1946

Walters, Helen B., *Werner von Braun, Rocket Engineer*, Collier-Macmillan, 1964

Wanless, Alexander, *British People at War, Compiled from the Daily Express*, J. & G. Innes, Cupar, Fife, 1956

The War and Thames Board Mills, Thames Board Mills, Purfleet, Essex, n.d., c. 1945

War Damage to Buildings in Great Britain, Part II. Schedule of About 100 Bombed Buildings in London and the Provinces Chiefly Selected for their Historic or Architectural Interest (duplicated), Ministry of Information, June 1946

War Damage to Hospitals, Part I, London (typescript), Imperial War Museum, no. K 17728, 7 May and 22 May 1945

Webster, Sir Charles, and Frankland, Noble, *The Strategic Air Offensive Against Germany, 1939–45*, 4 vols, HMSO, 1961

Weymouth, Anthony (pseud.), *Journal of the War Years and One Year Later*, vol. II, Littlebury, Worcester, 1948

Whitaker's Almanack, 1944, Whitaker & Sons, 1943

Who's Who, 1942, A. & C. Black, 1942

391

Wilmot, Chester, *The Struggle for Europe*, Collins, 1952
Wood, Derek, *Attack Warning Red. The Royal Observer Corps and the Defence of Britain, 1925–1975*, Macdonald & Janes, 1976
Wright, Robert, and Rawnsley, C. F., *Night Fighter*, Collins, 1957
Wyld, Ross, *The War Over Walthamstow. The Story of Civil Defence, 1939–1945*, Walthamstow Borough Council, 1945

Other periodicals consulted

ARP and NFS Review
Daily Express
Daily Herald
Daily Mirror
Daily Telegraph
Eastern Daily Press
Essex County Standard
Gravesend Reporter
Ilford Guardian
Ilford Recorder
Ipswich Evening Star
Kentish Times
News Chronicle
Orpington Times
South London Press
The Times

Detailed references

1 The Beginning (pages 15–22)

On the early history of the rocket, see Jones, 'Future', p. 11, and von Braun, pp. 24–37. The 'red glare' verse is from Francis Scott Key, *The Bombardment of Fort McHenry* (1814). On the Paris Gun, see Cruttwell, p. 531, and Dornberger, p. 55. On early German researchers, see Dornberger, p. 32; on his own early life, see Irving, p. 16; on von Braun's, Dornberger, p. 39. On Dornberger's plans for the rocket motor, see p. 32; on Reidel, pp. 37–9; on Kummersdorf, p. 33; on the 1932 test, p. 35 and pp. 37–8. On German politics at this time, see Cross, pp. 208–209, and Bullock, pp. 322–4. Dornberger, p. 42, describes the 1934 test and 'early years of our activity', pp. 47–8 the 'secret experiments' correspondence, pp. 43–4

392

Sources

the dimensions of the A-1, pp. 44–5 the gyroscope problems and p. 46 contains the 'beginning' quotation. See also Smith and Kay, p. 646, on the research in general.

2 Towards Perfection (pages 23–37)

On German foreign policy, see Bullock, p. 333; on the search for a new research site, Dornberger, pp. 48–50; on the prevailing exchange rate, Whitaker's, p. 202; on the Paris Gun and the 'military requirements' for the rocket, Dornberger, p. 56, on Thiel, p. 60, on the 'young man' at Peenemünde (in fact Dr Steinhoff), p. 28, on the Greifswalder Oie test, pp. 51–63, on the A-5, p. 75, on Hitler, pp. 71–3, on the first Peenemünde test of the A-5, pp. 66–9; on Peenemünde in general, Smith and Kay, pp. 646–50; on von Brauchitsch's help, Dornberger, p. 74; on the A-4 test and the 'perfection' quotation, Dornberger, pp. 17–28.

3 Taking It Seriously (pages 38–47)

'The Hitler Waffe' report was supplied to me privately but is quoted by Jones, pp. 65–6, who describes his own career on p. 10 and p. 28 and refers to 'analphabet' agents on p. 21. On Oberth, see Irving, p. 33; on Lindemann's family feud and 'authentic passions', see Birkenhead, pp. 335–6; on his 'erroneous assumptions', Jones, p. 10; on his refusal to make peace with Tizard, Jones, p. 83; on his 'gleeful sneer', Snow, p. 13. Lord Boothby is the former minister quoted. On his own work for SIS see Jones, p. 167, on his memo to his superior and the resulting recruits, pp. 322–6, on his own assistant, pp. 37–8, 51 and 144. Irving, pp. 33–4, and Jones, p. 322, give slightly different accounts of the reports from Stockholm. I have followed the latter. On von Thoma, Irving, p. 35, and Jones, pp. 332–3, are agreed. The 'agents could be briefed' quotation is on p. 336. On War Office reaction and the two memoes quoted, see Irving, pp. 36–8.

4 A Decisive Weapon of War (pages 48–62)

Dornberger, pp. 75–6, describes his 'begging expeditions', and pp. 79–82 his reaction to Degenkolb and Saur, on whom see also Irving, p. 136. On the production programme, see Irving, p. 26, and Dornberger, pp. 83, 90–91, 98–9. The valuation of Peenemünde is on p. 85, Degenkolb's 'plot' on p. 100, Hitler's dream on pp. 93 and 196 and in Irving, pp. 26–7. On VIP visits and the soap in the washroom, see Irving, pp. 56–8; on rivalry with the V-1 my book *The*

Doodlebugs, pp. 26–8 and 41, and Dornberger, pp. 95–9. The Zoo conference is described by Dornberger, pp. 111–13, and its results by Irving, p. 29. On Himmler and the Gestapo, see Dornberger, pp. 172–9, 185–6 and 197, on the visit to Hitler, pp. 101–107 and Speer, pp. 496–7. On the interference with flying-bomb manufacture, see Irving, pp. 87–8 and 93–4, and Smith and Kay, p. 751. Dornberger, p. 110, describes Peenemünde from the air, p. 143 the heroic cameraman, p. 145 his office.

5 A Distinctly Unpleasant Prospect (pages 63–80)

On the War Office paper and Duncan Sandys's appointment, see Irving, pp. 37–44, and Jones, p. 335. Cherwell's memo of 20 April 1943 is in PREM 3/110, Brookes, pp. 193–4, mentions the 'outsize firework'; Constance Babington Smith, p. 203, the study of the resulting photographs; Jones, p. 328, his meeting with the PRU pilots; PERM 3/110 contains Sandys's first report, reference COS (43) 259 (0). On 'Captain C.', see Irving, pp. 46, 53 and 61, on the neglected British experts, pp. 55–6; on Cherwell's note of 11 June 1943 and Cripps's of 16 June, PREM 3/110. Jones, pp. 340–3, and the caption to Plate 19b in his book, Constance Babington Smith, p. 205, Brookes, p. 194, and Irving, p. 67, describe the discovery of the rocket. The paper of 27 June is COS (43) 342 (0) and Sandys's report of 28 June COS (43) 349 (0), both in PREM 3/110. On Findlater Stewart I consulted *Who's Who*. Jones, pp. 343–6, describes the meeting of 29 June 1943, and private information from him supplemented the official minutes which are in CAB 69/5 Defence Committee (Operations). Irving, pp. 79–82, quotes the reports from agents and Cherwell's memo of 29 July. Morrison's memos are folios 396 and 374 in PREM 3/110 and Sandys's fourth report is COS (43) 369 (0).

6 Poor Peenemünde (pages 81–91)

The 'rocket meeting' conclusion is on p. 41 (f) of CAB 69/5; on plans for Operation Hydra (as defined by *Chambers' Dictionary*, 1973 edition), see Irving, p. 80; on the petrol allocation clue, Jones, p. 348; on the raid itself, including the air-gunner's comment, my book *The Bombers*, pp. 276–7, Irving, pp. 99–119, Dornberger, pp. 151–64 (including 'Poor Peenemünde' on p. 163), Webster, vol. II, p. 159, PREM 3/110, folio 331 – the Air Ministry telegram – folio 346, COS (43) 481 (0), Sandys's tenth report, and Churchill, vol. V, p. 208. On Friedrichshafen, see Webster, vol. II, p. 188 and p. 293 (footnote),

Sources

and Jones, pp. 230 and 304. His 'two months' estimate is on p. 346. Irving, pp. 28–9 reports the saving of the blueprints, and p. 309 the raid on Wiener Neustadt.

7 Revenge Is Nigh (pages 92–112)

On Speer's report, see Irving, pp. 122 and 124–3. On Blizna, see Jones, p. 430, Irving, p. 141, Garlinski, p. 114, and Dornberger, pp. 203–204. Irving, p. 122, describes Himmler's involvement and pp. 135–6 the Bombardment Commission; Speer, p. 314, and Dornberger, pp. 199–200, the latter's appointment. On Nordhausen, see Irving, pp. 123, 143–5 and 166–7 and the caption to the picture facing p. 160; Garlinski, pp. 107–10, on the prisoners' initial conditions and duties; Speer, pp. 498–500, and Garlinski, pp. 111–12, on subsequent improvements. Speer, pp. 503–5, and Dornberger, pp. 187 and 199–200, describe Kammler, and Irving, pp. 122–3, his involvement in the A-4 programme. Dornberger's 'sheer momentum' quote is on p. 211, his 'troubles', including the disastrous test of 5 November, on pp. 203–205, his hopes for rockets 'that disintegrated' on p. 212. Irving, p. 204, sets out the transport arrangements and firing plans and p. 28 describes the Watten site, on which see also Collier, Battle, p. 20. On Medmenham's report, see Irving, p. 53; on MacAlpine's advice, pp. 123–4; on Cherwell's note, PREM 3/110; on the US raid, Roger Freeman, p. 72, and Dornberger, p. 169. On Dorsch's plans for Wizernes, see Irving, p. 137, and Dornberger, pp. 169–70, which also testifies to Hitler's 'ghastly pallor'. The Führer's private doubts are mentioned by Irving, p. 237. On Sottevast and Equeurdreville, see After the Battle, p. 28, Collier, Battle, p. 20, and Jones, p. 462. On the small sites, see Jones, pp. 432–3. The 'hour of revenge' quote is from Irving, p. 177; Collier, Battle, pp. 64–5, mentions HARKO; Dornberger, pp. 195–6, recalls his nightmare trip of March 1944 and p. 191 his later travels. Irving, pp. 146, 204 and 221, refers to 'major difficulties' and the first output from Nordhausen, pp. 237–8 to Cement and pp. 258–9 to Goebbels's enthusiasm. Dornberger describes his feud with Kammler on pp. 200–201, and Irving, p. 259, mention's Fromm's arrest.

8 No Immediate Danger (pages 113–127)

Sandys's report of 27 August is in PREM 3/110, reference COS(43) 493 (0). The meeting of 31 August is minuted in COS (43) 202 (0), and Brookes, p. 195, quotes MacAlpine's comment. The meeting of 14 September is in PREM 3/110, under reference DO (43), eighth meeting. Cherwell's 'loaded' questions are described by Irving, pp. 130–32, and Sandys's response is on pp. 152–3, while 'C's' report is in PREM 3/110 as COS (43) 592 (0). Irving, pp. 131, 149–155 and 163, describes the work and membership of the Scientific Committee and the Fuel Panel and p. 159 carries the famous 'mare's nest' remark. On the meeting as a whole, see CAB 69/5, DO (43), tenth meeting, and for Smuts's remark, PREM 3/110, folio 257. The German airmen's reports are mentioned by Irving, p. 162. Cherwell's 'proof' that the rocket was impossible is in PREM 3/110, DO (43), eleventh meeting; Cripps's findings in the same file, DO (43) 27; Cherwell's memo of 2 November is folio 196 of PREM 3/110 and of 4 November folio 184. The Cripps inquiry is described by Irving, pp. 172–3; the Peenemünde pictures by Constance Babington Smith, p. 214; the Lord Mayor's austerity lunch by Weymouth, vol. II, p. 359. The second Cripps report is COS (0) 715 (0) in PREM 3/110. On Cherwell's opinion of Cripps's diet, see Irving, p. 169, and on his own, Harrod, p. 33. The minutes of the Defence Committee of 18 November are DO (43), thirteenth meeting. The change of code-names is in paras 2, 14, and 21 of the *History of the PIU*. Dr Jones's memo is quoted by Irving, pp. 174–5. The minutes of the Civil Defence Committee are in CAB 73/7, reference CDC (43) 35, for 28 December 1943, and in CAB 73/8 (CDC (44) 1), for 18 January 1944. The Chiefs of Staff's discussion is recorded in CAB 79 (COS (44), 23rd meeting). On Crossbow bombing, see Collier, *Defence*, p. 522. The 'Big Ben' letter is in HO 186/2271, the meeting of 27 April 1944 in CDC (44) 5.

9 *We Have Been Caught Napping* (pages 128–136)

On the threat to the underground, see folio 624 in PREM 3/111; on the post-V-1 evacuation, *The Doodlebugs*, pp. 211–13; on Morrison's apprehensions, WP (44) 348 in CAB 66/51; on the Cabinet's reaction, WM (44) 82 in CAB 65/46; on Ian Jacob's note, folio 835 in PREM 3/111; on the lack of rocket tracks, Jones, pp. 430–31; on Ultra evidence, pp. 430 and 435; on the Poles' exploits, Garlinski, *Weapons*, pp. 115–16 and 154. The Kalmar rocket is described by Irving, pp. 263–7, by Macmillan, vol. IV, p. 195, by Jones, pp. 431–4, by Dornberger, p. 246, and in the contemporary News Digest (a summary of foreign press reports circulated to British government departments), nos 1476 and 1477, references D43, D78, D81 and D82. Jones, pp. 433–4, describes his concern for Cherwell and pp. 437–8 the 'caught napping' meeting, of which the (less illuminating) official minutes are CRC (44), seventh meeting, in PREM 3/111.

Sources

10 The Battle of London Is Over (pages 137–155)

Cherwell's self-justifying memo is folio 834 in PREM 3/111, Ian Jacob's note is folio 830, and Morrison's letter is folio 803. His paper of 26 July is in WP (44) 412 and the Cabinet's response in CAB 65/ 47 as 'Annexe to WM (44) 97'. On Double Summer Time, see PREM 3/111, folio 224, and RA (44) 24 of 5 September; on Findlater Stewart's proposals, WP (44) 413; on Eden's objections to them, WP (44) 435 in CAB 66/53. Graves, pp. 90–91, gives details of the evacuation routes, HO 186/1848, document no. 24, of the ministry map. Jones, pp. 443–5, and Garlinski, *Weapons*, pp. 160–65, describe the transport of the spoils from Poland; WP (44) 427 in CAB 66/55 warned of the 'Imminence of Attack'; Jones, pp. 446–9, describes the 'great white dummy' and his search for the rocket's fuel and true dimensions; PREM 3/111, folio 757, immortalizes Cherwell's view of Dornberger; and Dornberger gives the true facts about the rocket in an illustration facing p. 32 of his book. 'Pop Gun' is mentioned in documents 2 and 10 in HO 186/1848; and Jones, pp. 452–8, explains how he deduced the likely rate of fire and his subsequent report. Irving, p. 205, mentions the discovery of Nordhausen. On 'tallboys', see *The Bombers*, p. 163; on their effects on Wizernes, Dornberger, p. 171, and Irving, p. 247; on the ill-starred 'drones', Irving, p. 275; on the damage to A-4 factories, Collier, *Defence*, pp. 347 and 386–8; on US losses, Roger Freeman, p. 174. The Rocket Consequences Committee rejoiced prematurely in RA (44) 24, folios 221–5 in PREM 3/111; the Vice-Chiefs are quoted by Collier, *Defence*, p. 406; the Ministry of Information's plans for the worst are given by Thompson, p. 205; Morrison's statement is quoted by Holl, p. 158, and his advice to the Cabinet is in WM 118, which forms folio 204 of PREM 3/111. On the press conference, see folios 218, 206, 201 and 200 in that file. The transcript is in Air 20/6016. Jones, p. 458, mentions the cocktail party.

11 Ignition! (pages 156–161)

Irving, pp. 30, 59, 77, 137 and 225, sets out the successive launching target dates and pp. 19 and 142–3 the Germans' operational plans. Dornberger, pp. 224–5, comments on Kammler's appointment. The V-2 supply system is described by Collier, *Defence*, pp. 399–400, and shown on his map 30. See also his *Short History*, pp. 452–3. *After the Battle*, p. 30, Jones, p. 451, and David Johnson, illustrations on pp. 126–7, explain the launching procedure. 'Frozen lighting' appears in Dornberger, p. 165, and his praise of the *Meillerwagen* on p. 102. The position on 7 September is set out by David Johnson, p. 113,

Hitler's Rockets

Collier, *Battle*, pp. 109 and 113, and Irving, p. 284. The launchings against Paris are mentioned by Collier, *Defence*, p. 405, and Irving, pp. 286–7. *After the Battle*, p. 30, gives the aiming point.

12 Incident at Staveley Road (pages 162–169)

Gwladys Cox describes the weather on 8 September; Panter-Downes, pp. 340–41, the flying of the Dutch flag; Wanless, p. 426, and Vere Hodgson, p. 423, the atmosphere in London. Chiswick Library provided the details of the borough's war history and information about Staveley Road. The incident itself is described in the *News Chronicle* for 7 September 1945; in a report, dated 11 September 1944, in HO 186/2418; and by Irving, p. 286. R. V. Jones's comment is on p. 459 of his memoirs. Subsequent rumours can be read in R. B. Baker, p. 84, Vere Hodgson, p. 423, and Gwladys Cox, the West Hampstead 'diary-keeper' quoted. On Epping, see Collier, *Battle*, pp. 113 and 170; on the letter to Cherwell, Irving, p. 286.

13 A Plume of Black Smoke (pages 170–184)

The quote from Thompson is on p. 204 and on the application of censorship see *After the Battle*, p.33, and David Johnson, p. 130. The signal to Montgomery is folio 195 in PREM 3/111. Folio 191 contains the Vice-Chiefs' decision and the Cabinet's conclusions, given in full in WM (44) 122 of 11 September. The details of subsequent incidents are taken from Table I in the list of long-range rocket incidents in file HO 191/198, mentioned earlier. On Walthamstow, see Wyld, p. 21. The 'stocktaking' report was on 24 September, in HO 191/198. On the first 25 V-2s, see folio 189 (WM 123 of 18 September) in PREM 3/111. Thompson's meeting with Morrison is on pp. 204–206; the government's hopes of Arnhem in Irving, p. 287; the anti-rocket measures in Collier, *Defence*, p. 408; and the Chiefs of Staff's report of 25 September is WP (44) 534, folio 185 in PREM 3/111. R. B. Baker, pp. 84–6, attended Buck's club; the early casualty figures are in the list of incidents 1–26 in HO 191/198, cited above. The location of the batteries in The Hague is in *After the Battle*, pp. 30–31, and the move to Walcheren in Collier, *Defence*, p. 408. Jones, pp. 441–2, and Irving, p. 285, describe the mission to Blizna, though the former dates its end at 27 September, not 22 September.

14 A Splash in the Marshes (pages 185–194)

Irving, p. 289 (footnote), mentions other V-2 targets; Collier, *Defence*, pp. 410–11, how the Germans' plans were disrupted;

Sources

Dornberger, pp. 225–6, how he responded, p. 224 his agreement with Kammler and pp. 227–8 his supply and development problems. On the launching batteries' moves, see Collier, *Defence*, p. 409, and Collier, *Battle*, p. 110. On the Norfolk campaign, see the Air 20/3439 report, 'Air Raids on Norfolk', p. 60; Banger, p. 89, which places the Hoxne rocket at 6.10 p.m.; and document C/ARP/1/33 in the Norfolk Record Office, my principal source throughout the chapter, which lists every incident in the county. For a retrospective account, by Christopher Elliott, see the *Eastern Daily Press* for 2 January 1969, which mentions ice-laden fragments and vapour trails. The 'splash in the marshes' quote is from a private informant. Collier, *Defence*, pp. 409–10, sums up the military value of the campaign and p. 413 describes Hill's problems. Collier, *Battle*, p.172, *Defence*, p. 412, and Irving, p. 289, describe the end of the Norfolk interlude.

15 The Liar on the Thames (pages 195–206)

On the resumption of the bombardment of London, see David Johnson, p. 146, HO 202/10 and Air 40/1653. Berwick Sayers, p. 111, mentions the secrecy in Croydon. The 'official summary' mentioned is in HO 191/198. On Chelsea, see Lees-Milne, p. 127. On the Luton incident, see *Luton at War*, p. 99–100, and HO 191/198; on subsequent V-2s, Air 40/1653; on the study of the accuracy of long-range rockets to March 1945, SORS/1/92. The *New York Times* lapse is recorded on folio 182 of PREM 3/111. Thompson, p. 207, describes censorship arrangements and their unpopularity. The Cabinet minutes of 16 October are in WM 137 (44) 3, its meeting of 23 October is in WM 140 and the discussion about a public statement is on folios 155, 154 and 138 of PREM 3/111. The text of the German communiqué is in WM 148 of 8 November (folio 137 in PREM 3/111) and David Johnson, p. 154, states (without quoting any source) that it was issued at 6.15 p.m., but this is contradicted by the 'Daily Digest' report of the BBC Monitoring Service, Part I, IA (II) Home (v). Heinz Rieck's talk is in report IA (I) Home (ix). David Johnson, p. 156, incorrectly attributes Churchill's statement to 'the day after' the German communiqué. The 'liar on the Thames' extract and the German article are in 'German Press Reports' for 10–11 November in HO 199/374. Thompson, pp. 204–207, describes later censorship arrangements, Irving, pp. 291–2, and Jones, p. 452, the number of rockets arriving and the inability to jam the V-2's guidance system. Blake, p. 86, which puts the number of dead at the Crooked Billet at 'at least 21', records events in the Bromley area, and my anthology *The Home Front* carries an eyewitness account of the Holborn rocket on pp. 203–204.

Hitler's Rockets

16 Disaster in Deptford (pages 207–216)

Apart from private informants my main sources on the Woolworths incident were the reports in HO 186/2381, i.e.: E. G. Bax: 'Notes of a Visit to Deptford', 25 November, and 'Incident at New Cross Road. Report by Casualty Services Officer', 29 November, and the *South London Press* for 28 November. On Folkestone Gardens, see 'Notes of a Visit to Deptford . . . by Admiral Sir Edward Evans on 7th March 1945' in HO 186/2381 and 'Report for Mr Travers' by W. Padmore, the rescue officer referred to, in the same file.

17 Christmas in Islington (pages 217–224)

R. B. Baker, pp. 93 and 100, refers to gloom over the approach of winter. The *Daily Express*, 19 October, gave details of Woolton's 'Christmas box'. The *Tribune* article is reproduced in Orwell, vol. III, pp. 279–80. The survey of V-2s so far is in Air 40/1653 'Enemy Air Activity'. R. B. Baker (the 'OSS official'), pp. 110–11, David Johnson (who places the explosion at 10 p.m., not 11 and mentions Rainbow Corner and Broadcasting House), pp. 170–71, and Weymouth (the 'BBC producer' quoted), p. 365, describe the Duke Street incident, as does Gwladys Cox's diary for 9 December. Report 234 in HO 20/10 gives the number of casualties, but the *Daily Telegraph*, 27 April 1945, puts the number of US dead at 7, not 8. The optimistic official spokesman was quoted by the *Daily Express*, 18 December; David Johnson, p. 157, is the 'American historian' quoted. On Mackenzie Road I used mainly 'Notes of a Visit', at 0300 hours on 27 December, and 'Report by G. Walker', 1 January 1945, in HO 186/2400. I also consulted the *North London Press* for 29 December. The 'retired resident of Worthing' was Harriss, p. 31. On New Year's Eve, see Air 20/3439 and Report 237 in HO 202/10. Casualty figures appear in IWM doc. no. K H9816. The Polish diarist was Raczynski, p. 260. The Dutchman story is in David Johnson, p. 177.

18 Worse than the V-1s (pages 225–239)

The 'Chelsea resident' is Lees-Milne, p. 151. Orwell's article is in vol. III, p. 280. HO 191/198 records the break-up of the twentieth V-2. The ministry report was 'Lessons from Recent Raids' in HO 186/2299. Childs, p. 134, was the 'one American' quoted. Sansom's description of an airburst is on p. 199; and Wright and Rawnsley, pp. 361–2, passed through one. On unexploded V-2s, see Hartley, pp. 189–194.

Sources

19 Ordeal in Essex (pages 240–254)

The Home Office letter is from J. P. Jamieson, dated 6 December 1944, in HO 186/2271. On the Hoffman's incident, see R. J. Thompson, p. 65, and Benham, p. 77, which describes the food kitchens and Bishop's address. On the other Chelmsford incident, see Thompson, p. 66; on Colchester and other V-2s in the area, Benham, pp. 80–82. The 'journalist living on Mersea Island' was Quinton Winch, in the *Essex County Standard* for 10 January 1975. The clerical warden was Shepheard-Walwyn, who describes the first local V-2s on pp. 41–2, the tea-party rocket on pp. 44–5 and the Sunday evening one on pp. 42–3. The Mountnessing and Stoke Cottage incidents are recorded by R. J. Thompson, pp. 66–9, the Woodham Ferrers one by a private informant. On Romford, see G. Richards: the 'giant dart' quotation is on p. 19 and a list of incidents on p. 28, though the details do not always agree with those in Air 20/3439, which, for example, refers to 12 dead at Collier Row, while Richards mentions 13. R. J. Thompson, p. 71, describes Hornchurch and the 'wedding' incident at Rainham. On Rainham, see also *The War and Thames Board Mills*. 'What the county endured . . .' was written by Benham, p. 82, which also quotes the NFS commander. On Kent, see Platts, p. 38; on the figures for other counties, the list in Air 20/3439; on the Wargrave incident, a Civil Defence diary entry in the Berkshire County Record Office.

20 The Battlefields of Ilford (pages 255–263)

On Kammler's grouping, see the map in the *Ilford Recorder* for 4 October 1945. The 'Civil Defence official' quoted is Pearson, p. 54. On Hutchinson's letter, see folio 645 in PREM 3/111. The 4000 tarpaulins are mentioned in an *Ilford Guardian* article of 3 May 1945, a major source for the chapter. Pearson, pp. 55–6, describes the South Park casualties and those at Belgrave Road. On the Hippodrome, see Pearson, p. 55, and the *Ilford Guardian*, op. cit. Information on the Super Cinema's programme was provided by Redbridge Library. Pearson, pp. 55–6, was an eyewitness of the Ilford Ltd incident and also describes the temporary loss of nerve in Uphall Road.

21 Winter in Walthamstow (pages 264–271)

On Ford, see Saunders, p. 89. Wyld, p. 11, mentions the reserve mortuary in Walthamstow and the deaths of 'casual travellers', and on p. 22 the College Road incident, the dog in the crater, the airbursts and the Bawn's factory incident. Other accounts are from private informants.

22 *Nothing Left of London* (pages 272–283)

On incidents affecting Westminster, see the *Air-Raid Damage Reports* filed in the Archives Department, Victoria, of Westminster City libraries. On the Hyde Park V-2, see Henrey, p. 8, Sansom, p. 198, and Vere Hodgson, p. 461. The absurd German claims are in the weekly Home Office reports in HO 202/10, nos 233, 237 and 243, which includes the chapter epigraph. On the damage to the Royal Hospital, Chelsea, see Ascoli, p. 181, who mentions its 'honourable scars'; Dean, p. 295, the *Chelsea Society Annual Report*, p. 26, and *War Damage to Hospitals*. Lees-Milne, pp. 151 and p. 158, describes his reactions and the 27 January explosion. On the St Pancras V-2s I used *War Damage to Hospitals* and the *List of Incidents . . . in the City of London* (Doc. Misc. MSS 350.5). On the Hampstead incidents, see *Hampstead at War*, pp. 28–32 – where the 'this was the end' quotation appears – and the duplicated document *Civil Defence Corps, Hampstead Division, Copy of Incident Reports*. The other accounts are from private informants, and the list of incidents in the Group 6 boroughs is taken from Air 20/3439. The London Rocket plant is mentioned by Childs, p. 146.

23 *Down Lambeth Way* (pages 284–294)

The 'American visitor' is Childs, pp. 129 and 134. On Lambeth's V-2s I consulted *Lambeth Civil Defence*, pp. 36 and 42–4. Details of the Hazelhurst Road incident in Wandsworth came from the report dated 20 November 1944 in HO 186/2418; on the Poynders Road incident from the report of 29 January 1945 in HO 186/2428; and on the Nutwell Street incident the report by G. Morris, of 7 March, and E. Bax of the same date. Berwick Sayers, pp. 112–14, mentions the effects of Croydon's situation and describes the Sunnybank and later incidents. On Bromley, Chislehurst and Beckenham, see Blake, pp. 88–90, the 'wartime historian' quoted.

24 *At the Arsenal* (pages 295–306)

On the Emergency Services Organization, see Spencer Freeman, pp. 77–8, and a decriptive note on the book's dustjacket. On Woolwich Arsenal, see H. A. Baker. The Silvertown bascule bridge's importance is explained in Report 243 in HO 202/10, and Report 245 mentions Silvertown's seven rockets. The chief superintendent quoted was a private informant. Damage to London Transport is given in Graves, pp. 93–4, although the West Ham trolley bus incident is referred to in Report 239 of HO 202/10. Moody, p. 119, refers to improving travel conditions; Carter, p. 190, summarizes the number of railway incidents. On the Southern's trials and casualty figures, see John, pp. 258–9; on Southwark Park Road, Moody, p. 119; on Folkestone Gardens, Darwin, p. 93. On the LMS, see John, p. 259; on the LNER, Crump, pp. 177–82, the 'Khyber Pass' appearing on pp. 179–81. Swanwick, p. 61, and Report 249 in HO 202/10 give details of the Great West Road V-2; the quotation from the Pyrene pamphlet is from Staples, pp. 4–5.

25 *What Can't Be Cured* (pages 307–323)

Irving, p. 292, mentions the damaged missiles; Dornberger, pp. 229–30, the last test at, and evacuation of, Heidekraut; O'Brien, p. 666 (footnote), the report of 25 September on warnings; the Crossbow Committee 17th Report, folios 602–10 in PREM 3/111, the absence of possible counter-measures. Dr Jones's study of the rocket's accuracy of 11 January 1945 was supplied to me privately, as was some additional information on the subject. I also consulted the document 'Accuracy of Long-Range Rockets Fired at London during the Period September 1944 to March 1945, in file SORS/1/92, which breaks the attack down into six phases of varying effectiveness. On the ROC's rocket sightings, see Wood, p. 178. Pile, pp. 386–8, describes his difficulties and the attempt to overcome them. Turner mentions the limitations of existing radar sets; Collier, *Battle*, p. 136, the despondent view of most scientists; Turner the general difficulty of intercepting V-2s. Howard-Williams, p. 142, had the encounter with a V-2 north of The Hague; David Johnson, pp. 168–9, mentions those of a Spitfire and a B-24. Jones, p. 454, mentions British knowledge about Nordhausen; Richards and Saunders, p. 172, the effect of the *Tirpitz*'s sinking; Garlinski, p. 141, the fate of the unfortunate slave workers. On operations in 1944, see Richards and Saunders, pp. 172–3, and *After the Battle*, p. 31. Morrison's plea for heavy bombers to be used and the Chiefs of Staff's reply are in PREM 3/111, folios 299, 292, 291 and 284, and the Cabinet call for intensified bombing is folio 265. William Sidney's letter is folio 580 in PREM 3/111, General Ismay's comment is folio 238, the note of 1 March (by 'JRC') is folio 574, Sinclair's letter of 2 March folio 639, Peck's note of 26 February folios 252–3, Ismay's comments folio 247, Churchill's rejoinder folio 242, Morrisons's plea of 1 March folio 236, Churchill's reply 235, and the Chiefs of Staff's reaction folio 232. On the Haag-sche Bosch fiasco, see *After the Battle*, pp. 31–2, Richards and Saunders, p. 175, Johnson, p. 186 (which includes the 'stupid Dutch' quote), and folio 535 in PREM 3/111 for the Foreign Minister's protest. Churchill's sharp memo is folio 533, and Sinclair's and the Chiefs of Staff's respective replies are nos 529–32 and 525–8. Churchill's final comment is in no. 547.

26 A Routine Job (pages 324–336)

The most valuable account of the distinctive effects of the rocket is in a draft entitled 'Lessons from Recent Raids – Long-Range Rockets', undated but being circulated for comments around 6 December 1944, in file HO 186/2299. It was subsequently issued in a less detailed and explicit form as 'Lessons from Rocket Attacks', Home Security Circular No. 3/1945, which can be found in file HO 196/1848. Public confidence in the services is mentioned on p. 13 of the draft, the effects on shelters are described on p. 3 and injury from burns on p. 4. The dangers of untrained helpers and the need for two incident officers are on pp. 6–7. Field telephones are mentioned on p. 7, and searchlights on p. 9. Difficulties in tracing casualties and missing people are set out on pp. 9–10. On dogs, see p. 11 of the 'Lessons' draft, Wyld, p. 22, *Hampstead at War*, p. 28, Berwick Sayers, p. 111, the report on Hazelhurst Road dated 20 November in HO 186/2418, and on Usk Road, to the Battersea ARP controller, on 5 February 1945 in the Wandsworth Borough Archives. See also Blake, p. 89, for doubts about the dogs' value. The *Gravesend Reporter*, 12 November 1965, described the Milton Place incident. The use of cranes is discussed on pp. 8–9 of HO 186/2299, and the contribution of the NFS on pp. 10–11. The forthright rescue service officer at Folkestone Gardens was W. Padmore, whose report is preserved in HO 186/2381, n.d. but *c*. 7 March 1945. The diary and final report of the incident officer at Usk Road are filed as Incident Report no. 1060 in the Wandsworth Borough Archives. The argument over IIPs can be followed in marginal notes on the 'Lessons' draft. The American writer is Childs, p. 135.

27 Horrible and Sudden Death (pages 337–348)

The promise of 'horrible and sudden death' is in a German Telegraph Service article in English, for 11 November 1944, in file HO 199/374. On casualty figures, see Collier, *Defence*, p. 528, and O'Brien, p. 677. The eleven missing at New Cross are mentioned in an article in *The*

Sources

Standard (formerly the *Evening Standard*) of 3 May 1984. The Hackney paper is in HO 186/2418, with comments by J. W. Oatley, 26 March 1945, and Col. Whitworth Jones, 29 March.

28 Damage Was Caused (pages 349–357)

On damage statistics, see *Summary of Damage* and *War Damage to Buildings*. On experience in Ilford, see Pearson, p. 56, and the *Ilford Guardian* article of 3 May 1945. On Lord Woolton's press conference, Kohan, p. 223; on the Ministry of Works' efforts, Kohan, pp. 224–9 and 234.

29 Spring in Stepney (pages 358–369)

The MOI handout was *War Damage to Hospitals*. Dr Jones's Air Scientific Intelligence Report of 1 March 1945 was privately supplied to me. For the group casualty figures, see Appendix A in Air 20/3439. On the City, see the *List of Incidents . . . affecting Corporation Property*; on Stoke Newington, document SN/A in the Hackney Borough Archives; on Bethnal Green, Vale, p. 8; on the Midland Bank, Wadsworth, p. 94. (The driver sent me his account privately.) Details of the Smithfield incident are given in the 'Notes of a Visit by Admiral Evans' for each of his four visits on 8–9 March, and an account of the handling of casualties in the reports by G. Wallace entitled 'Incident at Charterhouse Street' on 8 and 12 March, all in file HO 186/2388. On Hughes Mansions, the comparable source is the notes of successive visits by E. G. Bax, 27–8 March, in HO 186/2420. On the last incident, I used the *Kentish Times* for 3 November 1983, the *Orpington Times* for 30 January and 30 July 1981 and Blake, p. 90.

30 They Have Ceased (pages 370–385)

The epigraph comes from a file of Ministry of Home Security Operations Bulletins in the Norfolk Record Office, reference C/APR/1/18. Sansom records relief in Westminster on p. 199; Irving, pp. 300–301, and David Johnson, p. 183, cover the evacuation of Peenemünde; Dornberger, pp. 250–51, describes Kammler's 'finest hour' and the disbandment of the training unit. V-2 output figures appear in Irving, p. 306 (footnote). Walters, p. 81, describes von Braun's escape and accident, pp. 86–8 the wait at Oberjoch and p. 91 his first American breakfast. Dornberger, p. 254, reports the scientists' fears and describes their living conditions. The 'They have ceased' exchanges are in Hansard, Commons Debates, vol. 410. On the scientists' surrender, see Irving, p. 301, and Walters pp. 86–8, while p. 91 describes von Braun's breakfast. On their later adventures, see Walters, pp. 94 and 133, and von Braun, pp. 122–3. Kammler's presumed death is mentioned by Kennedy, p. 44. On Cherwell's death, see Birkenhead, p. 335; on his views on the V-2, Pile, p. 366, Irving, p. 297, folio 600 in PREM 3/111 and his note of 6 April 1945 in the same file. Jones's article is reprinted in 'The Future of the Rocket' and quoted in Jones, pp. 459–61. The combustion chamber used by rabbits is mentioned in the *Ipswich Evening Star* for 17 February 1984; the open spaces in The Hague in *After the Battle*, p. 32; the ban on the publication of incident details in Wyld, p. 5; Hill's view of the rocket is in para. 238 of his *Air Operations* report. Von Braun, p. 108, mentions the casualty figures and damage; Dornberger, p. 255, his regret at the rocket's imperfect state of development; Irving, p. 514, questions its cost-effectiveness, as does Speer, pp. 492–3. The final quotation from Jones is in 'Future', p. 13. On the Antwerp incident, see Helfers, *Employment*, pp. 38–47, Helfers, 'Chaotic Command', p. 23, and Angell, p. 63, quotes Hitler's remark to Dornberger.

CONTRIBUTORS

Ronald G. Absalom, Southend-on-Sea, Essex; John Ames, Roberts-bridge, Sussex; Mrs Sybil C. Armstrong, North Harrow, Middlesex; C. Stuart Bailey, Purley, Surrey; J. B. Baird, London SE2; Mrs K. E. Bannister, Cheam, Surrey; Peter R. Barnard, Ashford, Middlesex; W/Cdr R. B. Beamont, CBE, DSO, DFS, FRAES, Sunbury-on-Thames, Middlesex; Ray Billings, Pinner, Middlesex; Mrs Joyce Blackburn, Doncaster, Yorkshire; J. D. Blayney, Romford, Essex; Mrs Rosetta Brazil, Basildon, Essex; James J. Breslin, Bromley, Kent; Roy S. Brooker, East Farleigh, Maidstone, Kent; John Brown, London W3; Dr E. T. Burtt, Newcastle upon Tyne; Mrs Elsie Butcher, Clacton-on-Sea, Essex; Mrs Irene Calvert, South Tankerton, Kent; Richard A. S. Carter, Aylesbury, Bucks; S. Clapham, Norwich; George B. Clarke, Great Yarmouth, Norfolk; F. A. Cluett, FRSA, Gravesend, Kent; A. G. Collins, Piltdown, Sussex; F. C. Coppard, East Croydon, Surrey; Albert Copping, High Wycombe, Bucks; Miss E. M. Corben, London SW17; Peter Cornish, London SE19; John W. A. Dann, Lowestoft, Suffolk; Mrs Margaret L. Day, Ashford, Middlesex; Mrs Doris Dayan, Boscombe, Dorset; Mrs W. Derham, North Lancing, Sussex; Mrs Elizabeth Dodds, Bedford; Mrs Jean M. Dovey, Windsor, Berks; George R. Downing, Horstead, Norwich; Mrs E. L. Eadon, Broadstairs, Kent; Mrs B. A. Elliott, Wickford, Essex; Mrs Hazel Escott, Rayleigh, Essex; Gordon R. Everson, Brentwood, Essex; Norman Ezard, London SE4; Mrs Sheila Faber, London NW11; Dr R. H. Farmer, Aylesbury, Bucks; Mrs Pauline E. Favell, Crowborough, Sussex; Mrs Margaret Fish, Norwich; John Fisher, Colchester, Essex; Mrs Iris N. Fitton, Lowestoft, Suffolk; S. N. Forster, London SE19; A. W. Gordon Franklin, Northwood, Middlesex; Miss G. M. French, London W4; Mrs H. Friend, Buck-hurst Hill, Essex; Terence Gallacher, Brentwood, Essex; Mrs Eliz-

407

abeth E. Gamhan, Diss, Norfolk; Peter Gardner, Horsham, Sussex; John Garlick, London E17; Mrs Doris Gash, Clifton, Manchester; Hector Gent, Thornton Heath, Surrey; Ken Gibbons, London SW19; Mrs Gym Glover, Margate, Kent; P. H. Godfrey, Norwich; Mrs Doris Goode, Iver Heath, Bucks; Mrs Florence Gorton, Ilford, Essex; Frederick G. Gould, Hookley, Herts; Mrs Doris Graham, Billericay, Essex; Dr Alfred E. Gray, BA, PhD, High Wycombe, Bucks; R. G. Gray, Trowse, Norwich; Andrew M. Green, FRSA, Robertsbridge, Sussex; G. W. Green, New Costessey, Norwich; A. E. Hammer, London SE26; Albert Hands, Ilford, Essex; C. J. C. Harris, London N8; Mr and Mrs H. W. Hart, Frinton-on-Sea, Essex; Mike Hasler, Aylesbury, Bucks; J. P. Hebb, Westerham, Kent; John Hemmings, Cirencester, Glos; Sidney Hendry, Melton Constable, Norfolk; Stan Hodgson, London N15; Miss Constance Holt, London WC1; Mrs C. A. Hudson, Herne Bay, Kent; Canon Anthony Hulme, Bedford; Arthur Impey, Wembley, Middlesex; Miss Connie Ives, FRGS, London W3; A. J. Jackson, Harrow Weald, Middlesex; A. James, Southall, Middlesex; W. M. Jarvis, Richmond, Surrey; Mrs Ruth Jenkinson, London SE14; Mrs E. G. Johnson, Gillingham, Kent; Noel Johnson, Twickenham, Middlesex; R. Johnson, Pinner, Middlesex; S. P. Johnson, Ramsgate, Kent; Mrs Eileen Johnstone, Redruth, Cornwall; Miss Thelma Kay, Brighton, Sussex; Mrs George Kevan (formerly of New Cross), Eastbourne, Sussex; A. Kewall, London E15; Mr and Mrs Kieser, Whitstable, Kent; Mrs G. Kynaston Nicholas, Epsom, Surrey; Ken Lake, London E17; D. G. Lane, Orpington, Kent; W. Langley, Dereham, Norfolk; Donald Law, Romford, Essex; Mrs Patricia Ledsham, Ewell, Epsom, Surrey; Miss D. Lee, Bexleyheath, Kent; Donald Lee, Lindfield, Sussex; L. R. Lincoln, London NW2; Harry Long, Sanderstead, Surrey; Mrs M. Selby Lowndes, Mundesley, Norfolk; Mrs E. McCarthy, Purley, Surrey; Mrs Doris McCartney, Sheringham, Norfolk; Miss Sarah McGough, Blaydon-on-Tyne, Tyne and Wear; Dr Hugh C. Maingay, Norwich; Mrs D. Maisey, Wallington, Surrey; Mrs Irene Mason, Farnham, Surrey: John E. Mason, Farnham, Surrey; Mrs Rose Mathews, Horsham, Sussex; P. A. W. Merriton, Rocheville, France; Roderick D. Miller, Rayleigh, Essex; Mrs Hilda Mirams, Aylesbury, Bucks; Mr and Mrs Molnar, Birmingham; Mrs Ethel Moore, Herne Bay, Kent; Frederick E. Moorc, Telscombe Cliffs, Sussex; H. Douglas Moss, Hove, Sussex; Alfred Moyse, London W14; Adrian Murray, New Malden, Surrey; E. E. Natali, Woodford Green, Essex; H. A. Neason, Folkestone, Kent; A. W. J. Neighbour, Basingstoke, Hants; D. F. Nichols, Basildon, Essex; C. W Norris, London E9; E. H. Norris, London W11; Don Nowers, Hythe, Kent; N. Nugent,

List of Contributors

Clacton-on-Sea, Essex; Arthur James Parker, Bromley, Kent; Norman Paulding, Chelmsford, Essex; Mr and Mrs Pearce, Canterbury, Kent; F. C. Pearse, Morden, Surrey; Miss Patricia Peasnell, London NW10; Clement Phillips, Warlingham, Surrey; Mrs Yvonne S. Pike, Rayleigh, Essex; F. G. Pont, London SE19; H. G. Pooley, Haslemere, Surrey; John Pope, Isleworth, Middlesex; W. H. Prentis, Mitcham, Surrey; Mrs Gladys Prisley, Bournemouth, Dorset; Mrs Enid G. Prole, High Wycombe, Bucks; Mrs Muriel Quigley, Bury St Edmunds, Suffolk; Miss Elizabeth Rathbone, Sevenoaks, Kent; Mrs Ruth Raybould, Thetford, Norfolk; M. Redshaw, Milton Regis, Kent; Mrs A. Reeves, Crowborough, Sussex; Rev. A. G. and Mrs Reynolds, Harwich, Essex; Mrs P. M. Reynolds, Winchester, Hants; Reginald Rham, Whitton, Middlesex; Mrs Marion Richards, Haywards Heath, Sussex; Walter G. Richards, London SW18; Alan W. Rolfe, London SW2; Mrs Lily Rose Rose, London E2; Edwin S. Rosenthal, Witnesham, Suffolk; L. V. Rowe, Frinton-on-Sea, Essex; Mrs Givenda Sanders, Haywards Heath, Sussex; Mr and Mrs H. J. Saunders, Worthing, Sussex; Mrs Iris Shepherd, King's Lynn, Norfolk; A. R. Simmonds, Brammerton, Norwich; Mrs B. A. Slade, Ramsgate, Kent; Mrs Alice Smith, Canvey Island, Essex; Chris Smith, Westerham, Kent; Mrs D. Smith, Sutton, Norwich; Donald Smith, Hounslow, Middlesex; E. L. Smith, Canvey Island, Essex; F. Smith, London W12; G. I. Smith, Pulborough, Sussex; Leslie Smith, Mitcham, Surrey; Cdr R. J. Smith, cvo, kpm, Eastbourne, Sussex; Dr W. E. Snell, Hambledon, Oxon; N. T. Stack, London SW20; Mrs E. F. Stanton, Heston, Middlesex; C. W. Stark, Gravesend, Kent; John Stone, Cranleigh, Surrey; I. T. Stratford, Colchester, Essex; Mrs M. Streeter, Eastbourne, Sussex; Alan Stuart, Reading, Berks; Mrs Jean Swindell, London SE7; Mrs Sybil Tarr, Pinner, Middlesex; Mrs D. Taylor, Romford, Essex; Mr William and Mrs Norah Taylor, Hadley Wood, Herts; Roger Thurgood, Pinner, Middlesex; W. Timms, Woking, Surrey; Miss Joyce D. Tobin, Hove, Sussex; Mrs Rhoda Tompkins, London SW13; Mrs Gwen M. Trash, Burgess Hill, Sussex; T. H. Troughton, Greenford, Middlesex; Miss L. R. Tuck, Englefield Green, Surrey; Derek Underwood, Horsham, Sussex; Philip Unwin, Haslemere, Surrey; Clarence Uren, Edgware, Middlesex; Mrs E. Walker, Glasgow, Scotland; Mrs Audrey Wall, Reading, Berks; Robert Wanden, Maidenhead, Berks; John Warburton, London SW11; Geoff Warne, Bexley, Kent; Mrs E. Watson, Newcastle on Tyne; Eric Wayman, Bexleyheath, Kent; F. R. Weaver, Cambridge; Harold Webster, Rocklands, Norfolk; Mrs Joyce White, London N1; Mike Willsmer, Chelmsford, Essex; R. W. Noble Woodward, Colchester, Essex; Victor Wright, Holt, Norfolk.

GENERAL INDEX

INDEX OF PLACE NAMES

Index of Place Names

421

Index of Place Names